· AMERICAN SAMURAI ·

· F. G. NOTEHELFER ·

AMERICAN SAMURAI

CAPTAIN L. L. JANES AND JAPAN

PRINCETON UNIVERSITY PRESS
PRINCETON, NEW JERSEY

Copyright © 1985 by Princeton University Press

Published by Princeton University Press, 41 William Street,
Princeton, New Jersey 08540
In the United Kingdom: Princeton University Press, Guildford, Surrey

All Rights Reserved

Library of Congress Cataloging in Publication Data will be
found on the last printed page of this book

ISBN 0-691-05443-6

Publication of this book has been aided by a grant from
the Louis A. Robb Fund of Princeton University Press

This book has been composed in Linotron Sabon

Clothbound editions of Princeton University Press books
are printed on acid-free paper, and binding materials are
chosen for strength and durability

Printed in the United States of America by Princeton University Press
Princeton, New Jersey

FRONTISPIECE: L. L. Janes as a West Point cadet, 1861

FOR MARIUS B. JANSEN
Scholar, Teacher, Friend

· CONTENTS ·

· ILLUSTRATIONS ·

(frontispiece) L. L. Janes as a West Point cadet, 1861

(Illustrations appear between pages 112 and 113.)

MY INTEREST in Leroy Lansing Janes was first aroused at Harvard College some twenty years ago. Writing a senior honors thesis on one of the members of the Kumamoto Band, I found myself intrigued by the American officer who had gone to Japan in 1871 to run the school for "Western Learning" through which the Kumamoto domain hoped to restore its lost position in the Meiji Restoration. While the Captain's achievements in Japan, his unusual success as a teacher, and more dramatically his accomplishments as a religious leader were duly recorded on the Japanese side, almost nothing was known about him in the United States. Moreover, the American information available suggested that his achievements in Japan were later clouded by controversy. What this controversy consisted of was never openly discussed. And yet, its seriousness was indicated by the fact that the documents of the American Board that touched on his years in Japan were restricted and not open to public scrutiny.

While a graduate student at Princeton University in the mid-1960s I had the good fortune of locating Janes' daughter, Iris, who shared my views of her father's significance and carefully preserved many of his late-life writings, including the manuscript covering his important Kumamoto years. Particularly close to her father, Iris recalled special injunctions regarding the disposition of his writings and hoped to prepare the Kumamoto manuscript for publication in the near future. Unfortunately, these hopes were never realized—although a small private edition of the Captain's *Kumamoto* was issued in Japan in 1970.

Other research occupied my attention in the interim, but a year spent in Kyoto in 1970–71 renewed earlier interests. Participating in the seminars of the Institute for the Study of Humanities and Social Sciences at Dōshisha University, and working closely with Professor Sugii Mutsurō, the leading Japanese authority on Janes and the Kumamoto Band, I was able to gain access to letters and materials that had surfaced in Japan and to review the missionary documents and correspondence dealing with Janes that were contained in the American Board materials available on microfilm in Dōshisha's Institute for the Study of Christianity and Social Problems. At Kyoto University I had the privilege of working with Professor Yoshida Mitsukuni in the Institute for Humanistic Studies. As a result of this research, two articles on Janes ensued that were published in Japan.

In 1977 Iris Janes presented her father's manuscripts to the Princeton University Library. With this long awaited gift, for which the gracious good work of Marius Jansen was largely responsible, a full-scale study of the Captain became a possibility. A two-decade search for documents now paid increasing dividends. Sifting through the Department of Army records in the National Archives, through court records in Maryland, and through the Archives of the Constitution Island Association at West Point, as well as countless local archives, I was provided with insights into what became a remarkable detective story. Long-closed materials were kindly opened for me. Mr. David M. Stowe, the executive vice president of the United Church Board for World Ministries, allowed me to use the restricted American Board file at Harvard. The Veterans Administration, after years of petitioning, finally allowed me access to the Captain's "Pension File," and I am particularly grateful to the kind help of Mr. Roland A. Martone for making this possible. Searching for legal documents in Maryland produced the official records of the *Janes vs. Janes* divorce proceedings.

Two years spent in Japan with the University of California's Education Abroad Program from 1979 to 1981 allowed me the opportunity to finish the Japanese side of the study. I particularly benefitted from the assistance in Kumamoto of several local scholars. These included Professor Tanaka Keisuke, with whom I have long corresponded regarding Janes and to whom I owe a grateful thanks for obtaining materials and information pertaining to the Captain's life. The same is true of Professors Hanatachi Saburō and Ushijima Morimitsu, both of whom assisted me with this project. I also wish to thank Mori Toshiko, whose hospitality during my stay in Kumamoto in 1980 will always remain my image of Japanese graciousness and generosity.

I particularly want to thank Marius Jansen, Sugii Mutsurō, Albert Craig, Akira Iriye, Gordon Berger, George Moore, George Bikle, Daniel Howe, Donald McCallum, and Harold Bolitho for reviewing the manuscript and making many helpful suggestions. Mabel Baker, in England, kindly shared information on the Warner sisters. And I owe a great debt to various archivists and librarians who generously provided their time and expertise to find materials or locate and order my interminable interlibrary loan requests. In this regard, special mention should be made of the Manuscripts Division of Princeton University Library, which assisted me in using the Janes Papers.

Financial help from various sources made this book possible. The Fulbright Commission, the Henry Luce Foundation, and the Academic Senate of the University of California generously provided grants that supported different aspects of the project, and this aid is greatly appreciated.

Many scholars, students, and friends provided the intellectual stimulation and moral support that sustained me while putting the Captain's life between hard covers. To each I would like to indicate my hearty appreciation. Special thanks go to Anita M. O'Brien of Princeton University Press for valuable assistance in copy editing the manuscript. I am also particularly grateful to Mrs. John S. Wright, who provided me with the physical comforts of her beautiful home in Princeton, as well as many stimulating conversations, while I was working on the Janes Papers at the Princeton University Library in 1978. And above all I would like to express my appreciation to my wife, Ann, whose love, dedication, and encouragement, not to mention her sound editorial advice and research help, made all this possible.

Photographs have been reproduced by courtesy and permission of the following, to whom I would like to express my thanks: Princeton University Library (Janes Papers); The Archives of the United States Military Academy at West Point; Dōshisha University's Institute for Humanistic Studies; and the Tomishige Photography Studio, Kumamoto.

Finally, a special debt must be acknowledged here to Iris Janes, whose decision to place her father's papers in the public domain made this biography possible. It is my hope that in the book that I have written, the respect for her father's accomplishments in Japan that both of us share has not been lost or distorted.

· AMERICAN SAMURAI ·

On January 30, 1876, forty young men climbed a hill on the outskirts of the southern Japanese city, Kumamoto. The day was a Sunday. The air was crisp and cool. As they made their way up the mountain they sang a song in English: "Jesus Loves Me This I Know," the great missionary hymn that Karl Barth once said symbolized the essence of Christian theology. The sound of their voices echoed through the trees. Reaching the summit the group stopped for prayer and scripture reading. Then, in a loud, clear voice, one of the boys read out Japan's first modern Christian Declaration. "Our eyes have been opened by the study of Christianity," he stated, "and along with the increasing admiration and gratitude for this teaching, we strongly desire that it be proclaimed over the whole empire in order to dispel the ignorance of the people." Explaining further that it was their "duty as patriots" to explain this teaching to their fellow countrymen, thirty-five of the assembled put their signatures to the declaration.

None of the young men took this step frivolously. From their vantage point it was difficult to avoid looking down on Kumamoto's imposing castle. Symbol of a bygone era, they were well aware, that it still rallied to its standard dissident elements—men who hated Christianity. In fact, a few years earlier Kumamoto's leading thinker had been cut down by assassins on charges that he had been a secret believer. As they knew only too well, it was less than three years since the signboards that proclaimed death as the proper punishment for any believer of this "evil religion" had been quietly removed.

Looking out over Kumamoto from the summit of the hill, they could just make out the buildings of their school and the home of their foreign teacher. Both were perched above one of the broad stone ramparts that led to the heart of the castle. Seen from afar the school looked tiny—the castle huge. And yet, as the students knew, the hopes of their territory rested on that tiny school and not on the castle. The future of their country, as well as that of their region, required the advanced knowledge of the West, and not the prejudices of the old order.

Gradually making its way down the mountain that Sunday afternoon was not only the dominant wing of the Meiji Protestant movement, the Kumamoto Band, as it was to be known in later years, but a set of brilliant minds that made Christianity a central theme in the intellectual development of modern Japan. Fearless in their commitment to individualism, fervently devoted to their country, and firm in the Christian reformist belief that serving God meant helping one's fellow men, these young men were to constitute a generation of university presidents, professors, and journalists who left a deep imprint on modern Japanese thought and education.

Of Meiji Japan's leading publicists and editors, three—Tokutomi Sohō, Kozaki Hiromichi, and Ukita Kazutami—were members of this group. Four of Meiji Japan's most important Protestant ministers, Ebina Danjō, Kozaki Hiromichi, Miyagawa Tsuneteru, and Yokoi Tokio, were on the mountain that day. The influence of these men was to be widespread, particularly for the younger generation. Ebina's Hongo Church, for example, became the center for a large number of Meiji Japan's writers and intellectuals for whom Christianity served as a carrier of Western civilization. Dōshisha University, of which Ebina, Kozaki, and Yokoi were all presidents, served as the dominant intellectual voice of the Church, and of Christian socialism in the Meiji Period, and later went on to become one of Japan's leading secular universities, a position it retains today.

On January 30, 1876, all this lay in the future. More at hand was the young men's desire to announce their public declaration to their teacher, the man who had introduced them to the secrets of Western wealth and power and who, in the course of doing so, had engineered not only a mental but a spiritual revolution.

Of course, there would have been no teacher, school, or Christian band if the feudal lord of Kumamoto, the local daimyo, and his advisers had not set out in the early 1870s in search of an "American samurai." With the help of this man, the daimyo saw himself and his territory making the leap from feudal backwardness to modernity. Under the tutelage of such an individual, the young men of his domain could master the skills of the superior Western powers and in the process not only defend their country against foreign domination but assure the prosperity and prominence of the domain.

Leroy Lansing Janes, the American samurai for whom the daimyo was searching, was himself an unusual individual. A West Point graduate, officer in the Civil War, and for a time teacher at the United States Military Academy, he resigned his commission in 1867. Arriving in Kumamoto in 1871, just three years after the Meiji Restoration, he was one of the few Westerners who received permission to reside in the interior, away from the comparative safety of the treaty ports. This was uncommon, and that he did so with a wife and two young children made it even more exceptional.

As teacher and headmaster of the Kumamoto School for Western Learning from 1871 to 1876, Captain Janes became the central figure in one of Meiji Japan's most interesting experiments in Western education. But more than an outstanding teacher who molded a generation of young men to play central roles in the development of modern Japan, he was to serve as a leading regional voice for the "civilization and enlightenment" movement that swept Japan in the early Meiji years. Combining a passionate dedication to education with strong convictions of Christian service to the community, he became not only an effective teacher, but the director of a local revolution in agriculture, hygiene, animal husbandry, and the general improvement of the economic well-being of the local citizenry. Destined to leave an indelible imprint on the minds of his young wards, he also did much to transform the environment in which they lived.

During his years in Kumamoto, Janes truly loomed larger than life. His accomplishments at the Kumamoto School for Western Learning were to earn him a place among the rare handful of Westerners who grace the pages of Japan's *Who's Who*. The students who studied with him saw him not merely as their Western mentor, but as a classical Japanese hero worthy of following with their lives. Even the rabidly anti-Western malcontents for whom Kumamoto was famous were so disarmed by his bravery that they paid him the ultimate compliment of refusing to permit his assassination. As one of the missionaries later observed, "he had the samurai spirit to the full . . . indeed, in absolute fearlessness and assumption of superiority, he out-samuraied the samurai."[1]

When Janes left Kumamoto in the autumn of 1876 he had become a legend in his own time. A Presbyterian layman who never saw himself as a missionary, he had in effect become the most successful missionary in Japan. As his students arrived in Kyoto to attend the American Board's training school the legend expanded. By the time he left Japan in 1877, the missionaries in Kyoto fully expected that he would return to head the newly emerging Dōshisha College. But the Captain's life is remarkable for its constantly changing images and the controversy that accompanied his achievements.

During the ten years after his departure from Japan, the hero was to plunge from the apex of veneration and sainthood to the nadir of ostracism and contempt. Missionaries who had praised him to the heavens and had tried their best to induce him to join their board no longer spoke of him at all. While in the United States on furlough they refused to visit him. In explaining the Kumamoto work they attributed its successes to his wife's prayers. Even his students, who continued to regard him as their second father, were troubled by veiled rumors that hinted at his moral fall.

Was Janes guilty of conjugal infidelity during his years in Kumamoto, as his wife and father-in-law insisted? Indeed, was he "insane," as some in the Army thought, and as the head of the American Board concluded? The study that follows attempts to explore these questions in detail. In doing so the issues of personality and personality development cannot be avoided. Janes' troubled childhood, the deep religious split in his home and upbringing, guilt feelings about a wasted youth, and the trauma of war that led to conversion all played a part in molding the personality he brought to Japan. In addition there were the "strange joys," to which he was subject and which he associated with a heightened sense of religious mission—usually following overwork, exhaustion, and physical illness. And yet, what is most intriguing is the way in which a personality that was destined to fail in the American setting could rise to greatness in Japan.

In essence Janes demonstrated what many members of the Allied occupation of Japan were to demonstrate nearly a hundred years later, that basically ordinary individuals were capable of playing crucial historical roles in Japan by being placed in the right circumstances at the right time. In his case it would be important to add, however, that an extraordinary personality was to do its share in heightening the overall effect.

Nor was his life without its mysteries. Subject to a constitutional inability to defend himself against false accusations or, as he saw it, "impose his cares on others," he often concealed his private relationships. Few of the students climbing the "Mount of Flowers" on that January Sunday in 1876 had any idea that the author of the song they were singing, Anna Warner and her sister Susan Warner were among the most widely read American novelists of the nineteenth century and close personal friends of the Captain. Until now, no one, not even those most familiar with the Warner writings, has known of the broken promises the Captain made to Anna years earlier. Nellie, the Captain's first wife, who played a central role in his conversion and died within two years of their marriage, is equally cloaked in silence.

While clearly a distinct individual, our American samurai was also a product of his times—a typical carrier of the nineteenth-century American ethos that stressed reform and was founded on the religious conviction that the millennium could be achieved in this world. Like other Americans of his generation, he was determined to do his part to spread this message to the farthest reaches of the globe.

But things do not always work out as planned. The feudal lord searching for his American samurai wanted a technological revolution. He got this and a revolution of a different order. The American samurai thought he could impose a transformation of values, only to discover in later years that values often change much more slowly than their external manifestations. And yet, despite their disappointments, both were thoroughly a part of the process of change that transformed Japanese society in the late nineteenth century. Moreover, in their relationship, particularly in the cross-cultural perception each had of the other, we are exposed to the dynamics for change that on the micro level permitted a rather ordinary individual to play an extraordinary historical role.

Here something further must be said about the setting in which all this took place. The emergence of Japan as a modern state in the latter half of the nineteenth century was an event of great importance not only for Asia, but also for the modern history of the Western world. Japan's transformation from an isolated feudal state into a major military power capable of defeating both China and Russia by the first decade of the twentieth century marked the first distinct break in the prevailing Western conception of Asia as backward, stagnant, and in need of enlightenment. Japan's successful modernization demonstrated all too clearly that industrialization was not to remain a monopoly of the Western nations, and that power based on industrial wealth, which had subjugated much of Asia, could also be used by Asians to defend themselves against foreign oppression.

The Japanese drive to establish the modern state, industrialize the country, and seek equality with the West has to be seen against the backdrop of Japan's mid-nineteenth century experiences. The arrival in 1853 of the Perry expedition, with its stated purpose of "opening Japan" to trade and foreign relations, dramatically underscored feudal Japan's fundamental weaknesses. Two hundred years of isolation, during which contacts with the Western world virtually ceased, did much to preserve internal stability and the Pax Tokugawa, but they also prevented Japan from participating in the scientific and industrial revolutions that vastly augmented Western military power. Commodore Perry's black ships with their superior guns revealed quite openly what many of Japan's more astute samurai intellectuals had come to concede privately, that Japan was technologically backward and could survive in a struggle with the rapacious West only if it initiated major reforms.

Well aware of the need to modernize, and at the same time shouldered with the impossible task of ridding Japan of the hated foreigners, the Tokugawa Shogunate found itself more and more on the horns of a dilemma. Incapable of throwing the West out, and at the same time compelled to make concessions to the Americans and Europeans, the Shogunate revealed itself a failure in controlling and subduing barbarians. Having shown itself weak in the face of the West, it was soon challenged domestically by a coalition of samurai whose xenophobic urges were matched by an intense patriotic loyalty to Japan's ultimate source of legitimacy, the Emperor, and ambition to supplant the Tokugawa.

The political history of Japan in the 1860s was therefore composed of a mounting confrontation between those who supported the Imperial House and called for the expulsion of foreigners, and the Tokugawa camp, which tried to combine minimal concessions to foreign demands with a concerted effort at self-strengthening using the technology of the West. But time was not on the Tokugawa side. By the late 1860s, pressured on the one hand by the West and on the other by dissident samurai who questioned its legitimacy, the Shogunate finally gave way to a new order.

The restoration of imperial rule in 1868 set Japan on a different course. Rallying to the standard of the boy-emperor, Meiji, the able and for the most part young samurai who had deftly wielded the club of antiforeignism to destroy the Tokugawa now went through a remarkable metamorphosis. Their new attitudes were clearly illustrated in the imperial government's first policy declaration, which stated that knowledge would now be sought from around the world in order to strengthen the foundations of imperial rule.

The decision to rely on the outside world as a means of transforming Japan in the 1870s and 1880s set the tone for the early Meiji years as an era that not only concentrated on the dismantling of Japan's formidable feudal structure, but simultaneously provided a massive influx of Western ideas, techniques, and institutions. To select the best models for Japanese development, hundreds of students were sent to the United States and Europe to master subjects ranging from the world of ideas to the manufacture of soap and matches. If the training of students represented an investment in the intermediate future, the bringing to Japan of a broad cross section of Western teachers and technicians sought to deal with the nation's more immediate needs.

Behind Meiji Japan's harbors, lighthouses, and bridges, behind its mines, railroads, spinning mills, and modern agriculture, behind its schools, hospitals, and prisons, and behind countless other aspects of its modern transformation, there stalked not only the Meiji modernizer in search of national wealth and power, but numerous, and now largely faceless, Europeans and Americans who taught, innovated, and helped to establish the infrastructure upon which modern Japan was built. Handsomely paid, elevated to the status of semi-deities, heeded as if their voices resonated with the wisdom of Mt. Olympus, ordinary men were often asked to perform unusual feats during their brief sojourns in Japan.

This book is about one of these men. By focusing on his complete life it attempts to explore not only the important Japan years but the years of preparation and the final years of reevaluation. As such it is a book about America as well as about Japan. It is a book about a unique chapter of American-Japanese cultural relations. For twentieth-century Americans, it reminds us of what our nineteenth-century forefathers tried to teach the rest of the world. For Japanese, this is the study of a heretofore "inscrutable occidental," an inner look at one of the men who despite his role as a foreigner and outsider was to leave a deep imprint on modern Japanese intellectual history. It is also an effort to come to grips with the particular charisma that allowed an American who knew no Japanese to become such a powerful leader in the Japanese setting.

Nor was Janes' influence confined to the Church. There were those who did not choose to accept his religious predilections, but who were moved by other aspects of his vision for modern Japan. Yokoi Tokiyoshi, Meiji Japan's leading agricultural scholar and later president of the agricultural branch of Tokyo University, followed Janes' love for farming and agriculture into a secular career. Tokutomi Sohō took another of Janes' ideas into the world of journalism and became immensely influential as a leader of the younger generation with his journal, *Kokumin no tomo*. But while neither chose to follow the Captain's Christian path, they never forgot his lessons, which constantly stressed that their ultimate goal should be to serve the people and to aid and assist in lifting up the common man by devoting their lives to public service. The name of Tokutomi's journal, "The People's Friend," and Yokoi's continuous effort to aid poor and downtrodden farmers indicate that Janes' teaching could bear secular as well as religious fruit. There were certainly no limits to the intellectual seeds that sprouted during those five years in Kumamoto. Influential professors such as Ukita Kazutami were to transmit the Captain's ideas of Christian liberalism and democracy to their students, which in Ukita's case included Yoshino Sakuzō, the leading spokesman for "Taishō Democracy." Others took Janes' ideas into the world of business, finance, and politics with as much zeal as the band took them into the Church.

Nor was the American samurai's influence limited to his students. Much of the drama of his five years in Kumamoto involved a direct effort to transform the Japanese environment. Whether this entailed construction projects, the importation of agricultural equipment, plants, and seeds, lessons in animal husbandry, or the simple efforts of his "civilizing dinners" designed to indicate the advantages of a Western diet of bread and beef, they were all part of those remarkable days of cultural exchange that went with the quest for "civilization and enlightenment" and guaranteed that everything the Captain suggested would be considered with the weight of a heavenly proclamation.

That such days could not last is hardly surprising. But here too Janes typifies the general phenomenon of those who were part of the early

Meiji experiment, men such as Lafcadio Hearn and Ernest Fenollosa, whose initial experiences became the highpoints of their lives. By the 1890s, when Janes returned to Kyoto, the glories that had been Kumamoto were clearly in the past. Japan had changed. Foreign teachers were no longer needed. Japanese were no longer prepared to embrace American ideas without criticism. In the end both societies had matured in their evaluation of each other.

But while this book is about Japan and America, and about one of a group of influential men, it is above all an effort to deal with an individual. As such it is a very personal story in which real-life incidents often blend with fiction, and in which the historian must function as much as a detective and an unraveller of mysteries as a recorder of facts. It is a tale, if we may use the Captain's fictionalized self-portrait, of the "plainest of plain people" who struggled against his own "ill nature" to "make a man out of very poor material." What follows is therefore a biography of one of the important Westerners in Meiji Japan. But it is also a very personal account that emphasizes the importance of an individual's inner self, as well as his public career.

CHAPTER I

BOYHOOD IN THE OHIO HILLS

IN 1837 the American brig *Morrison* sailed into Edo Bay carrying a missionary, a medical doctor, and an enterprising merchant. Ostensibly the ship's reason for violating Japanese seclusion was to return seven Japanese castaways. But the real purpose of those on board was to "open" Japan to trade and missionary activity. In this they were sorely disappointed. A few well-placed Japanese warning shots quickly convinced the Americans to withdraw. The first ship to bear the Stars and Stripes into the inner defenses of the land of the shoguns was summarily dismissed. Japan wanted neither trade nor the missionaries.[1]

On March 27 of the same year, in a land that was described by the crew of the *Morrison* as lying "two months journey to the East," Leroy Lansing Janes was born in the small Ohio town of New Philadelphia.

Despite his later reluctance to extoll the virtues of his ancestors, Janes' family was not without its pedigree. William Janes, the family's North American patriarch, had emigrated to the New World as a charter member of the New Haven Colony, arriving from Essex, England, in 1637. A schoolteacher like his eighth-generation offspring two and a half centuries later in Japan, he was most admired for "molding and training the minds of the young" and "educating the rising generation of colonists to the fullest extent of their faculties."[2]

Typical of the general movement that accompanied America's growth and expansion, the Janes family pushed westward from the Atlantic coast, across the Alleghenies, and into Pennsylvania and Ohio. Janes' father, Elisha Janes, was in step with the broader currents of the day. Born on an extensive farm near Canaan Center, New York, in 1802, he decided to seek his fortune in the West. In 1825 he moved to Akron, Ohio, where he worked on the construction of the Ohio Canal, and two years later he settled in New Philadelphia.[3]

The New Philadelphia to which the young canal contractor came in 1827 was little more than a frontier village of less than 300 inhabitants.[4] While it held promise as the county seat of a growing and expanding region, its promise still lay in the hopes and dreams of its founders, men such as John Knisely and Gabriel Cryder, who had hitched their wagons, if not to the proverbial star, to the future of the Tuscarawas River and the Ohio Canal.[5]

And yet, as Leroy Lansing Janes was to write later in one of his unpublished novels, "realization followed upon anticipation with such swift footed attendance" in the region "that it was rational and prudent to live much in expectation." In retrospect, the reasons for this seemed clear to the Captain: "A happy climate, a teeming fertility of soil, a central location across every path of north-western settlement, multiplying facilities for communication and intercourse with the East," not to mention a "population gathering moral purpose and physical stamina and accumulating opportunities with ceaseless accession of numbers." All these "favored and justified heroic endurance of present privation as a condition of certain and early fruition."[6]

To what extent Elisha Janes was willing to endure present privation for future prosperity is not entirely clear. What is clear is that his son, Leroy, identified the values of deferred gratification with the course of American development. It was men such as his father—farmers, merchants, and manufacturers—who were replacing, as he wrote, "the Indian fighter, trapper, and hunter as the builders of the new nation." Moreover, it was such men, he liked to point out, who had little time for the "diversions" and "luxury" of "home building" and "home adorning," tasks which Janes argued they had to defer to the "severer duties and responsibilities of organizing the physical foundations of empire."[7] While Janes' views of American development, and the role that men such as his father played in it, were to strike a sympathetic chord among Japanese who possessed their own preoccupation with the physical foundations of empire in the 1870s, they were, like many of his later views, somewhat idealized interpretations of the past.

If deferred gratification was important to Elisha Janes, it was important within clearly defined limits. Home building and home adorning, in the physical sense of the stately houses that would eventually grace New Philadelphia, might have to await the fulfillment of other priorities, but home building in its marriage sense was another matter. In 1830 Elisha Janes, now in his twenty-eighth year, married Elizabeth Cryder, the daughter of one of New Philadelphia's most prominent men.[8]

Gabriel Cryder was the personification of the local developer. A native of York County, Pennsylvania, he had emigrated to the valley of the Tuscarawas in 1808.[9] Always sensitive to new opportunities, Cryder had successfully turned several wagonloads of bartered goods—acquired in exchange for his Pennsylvania house—into New Philadelphia's first mercantile enterprise, a general store. County commissioner from 1811 to 1817, he resided briefly at Dover and subsequently on a large farm five miles south of the county seat. In 1823, after having been elected county treasurer, an office he was to hold until 1836, he returned permanently to New Philadelphia. Gabriel Cryder's achievements were considerable, but, as his grandson later remarked, there were also less commendable sides to his role as a developer.

Records of Tuscarawas County show that Cryder was responsible not only for the construction of the region's first grist mill, a $5,000 operation on the Tuscarawas River built in 1820, but also for the establishment of the district's first "still house," a contribution that, given its economic implications for the eastern part of Ohio, may have been of even greater significance.[10] It was, of course, the latter that elicited the Captain's subsequent disapproval. A committed supporter of the temperance movement in his later years, Janes was hardly enthusiastic about this legacy. At the same time he was quite prepared to discuss even this aspect of the family's history within the mild disguise of a fictional character named Daved Holland, who constituted a composite portrait of Gabriel Cryder and Elisha Janes.

Writing of the motivation that typified Gabriel Cryder, Elisha Janes, and others of the new generation, Janes noted:

> The leading difference between Mr. Holland and his predecessor is now easily pointed out. The former had been long employed in the construction and completion of adjacent sections of the great commercial artery, the Ohio Canal, which connects Lake Erie with the leading eastern tributary of the mighty Mississippi. His work had brought him into contact, however distant and by means of whatever of occult processes which mighty minds employ to communicate their thought and influence to far-off agencies, with the leading spirits of the age. He had been, all unconsciously, touched with the same ever unfolding purpose which sent forth Columbus and Degama and Magellan, and which has pushed the individual on and on until, in our day, its lines of electric intelligence, and of practical neighborhood, have "gone out into all the earth," and are seeking to make brethren and one family of every nation and tribe on the globe.[11]

But if the Cryders and Janes' had been swept forward by the tide of national growth and expansion, Janes was quick to add that his composite hero, Daved Holland, "responded in his own way to the touch, and with a slightly more intelligent faith in the grand design." If he felt the push, he also possessed the courage to "bend it to the service of his individual propensities."

"In the first days of his occupancy of the re-christened log structure up on the dividing ridge," Janes writes in lines that remind one of the blockhouse in which his mother's sister, Aunt Polly, subsequently lived, and of which he grew particularly fond as a child, Daved Holland "sometimes stopped in the doorway and traced the silver line of the canal, 'my canal,' he would musingly call it, as, in close companionship with the beautiful river, and flashing in the autumn sunlight, both skirted the broad sweep of the Calumet Plains."[12]

Janes' hero, Daved Holland, was, however, less moved by the aesthetic beauty of the silver ribbon that became so closely associated with the Captain's memories of his childhood home than with its economic implications. As the passage amplifies, "he easily calculated the inevitable bearing of that highway to foreign markets upon his own personal interests. It was only incumbent upon him to put his possessions in order, and keep them headed with the current to realize the purpose of his life— to become a proprietor of land, in baronial, ducal, or princely proportions."

Understanding the potential of the new canal and adjusting it to the limitations of local production were not necessarily as easy as Janes' fictional Daved Holland suggested. When Gabriel Cryder and Elisha Janes arrived in Tuscarawas County, agriculture was still the source of wealth and public standing, but cash crops were few. Tobacco, which showed considerable promise in the early decades of the century, had severely depleted the soil and by the 1830s had given way to corn and wheat. But corn and wheat retained limited marketing potential. Prices were generally low and unpredictable. In fact, Janes' narrative argues that the "good bavarian" (more likely German Moravian) who sold his land to Daved Holland sold out precisely because he had not been able to dispose of a two-year supply of grain that lay rotting in his ricks.[13]

To one accustomed to taking risks and self-reliant in meeting them, as was the case with Daved Holland and Gabriel Cryder, the local abundance of grains suggested new possibilities. As Janes records,

> the first of succeeding steps towards a distant purpose were quickly taken. . . . It was a triple stroke of industrial and business policy which in a few short weeks made of the late constructive engineer, a producer, a manufacturer, and a manipulator of freights by the double and simultaneous process of diminishing their bulk while enhancing their value. Almost within that fragment of time, the energetic man had purchased and brought to this grotto all the paraphernalia of a still for the reduction, by distillation, of his bulky and superabundant grain crop. Partly embracing the old spring-house, utilyzing the crystal elements of its fairy fountain in many ways and spoiling by a different set of odors its pastoral perfumes, the wonder inspiring manufacturing establishment was soon in full running order, actually engaged in the "production of grog for the

markets and navies of the distant sea-board!" as the intrusive little sheet of the county seat boastingly proclaimed.[14]

While the portrait of Janes' fictional hero combined the entrepreneurial talent of his grandfather, Gabriel Cryder, with the cool, rational planning of his father, Elisha Janes, and in the process served to illustrate the way in which American society in the 1820s and 1830s was engaged in the transition from agriculture to nascent industry, the rosy prospects of an industrial career seem to have flashed across the mind of the historical Elisha Janes with less light and force than his son's fiction indicated. If realization followed anticipation with such swift-footed attendance, as the Captain suggested, and if New Philadelphia was resplendent with new possibilities—including Gabriel Cryder's still house—both anticipation and possibilities seem to have held little initial attraction for the young and newly married canal engineer. Swift-footed attendance seems to have been bestowed only on his departure from New Philadelphia. Waiting just long enough to pack up his bride, Elizabeth, he removed himself to the little town of Trenton, where he kept hotel, built a warehouse, and engaged in the shipping of grain for the next seven years.[15]

For Elisha Janes, the years in Trenton were years of sacrifice and accumulation. Unlike Gabriel Cryder, who was quick to grasp the possibilities of the new age, and who readily moved from landed wealth to industrial enterprises, Janes' father seems to have been more concerned with the exploitation of new possibilities for traditional ends. "Land avarice," as the Captain was later to write, was still a leading passion not only of Daved Holland and many of his generation, but of Elisha Janes, who pursued his projects for its gratification with stubborn pertinacity. By 1837, the year in which his son Leroy was born, the elder Janes had acquired enough capital to purchase 122 prime acres in the New Philadelphia area.[16] With a later addition of 60 more acres, the farm on which Janes grew up was respectable by all the standards of the day.[17] While success had at last come to "Colonel Elisha Janes,"[18] as he now came to be known, Janes' father was a good enough Calvinist to recognize that the signs of election, which hard work and God's grace bestowed, also required reciprocation. Growing public trust was acknowledged by growing public involvement.

The official record shows this process quite clearly. From 1838 to 1842 Elisha Janes served as sheriff of Tuscarawas County.[19] In the latter year he helped found the First Presbyterian Church, a church in which he was to remain active as a member and elder for much of the remainder of his life.[20] By 1849 he was spearheading a new agricultural movement and serving as founding president of the Tuscarawas County Agricultural

Society.[21] And in 1851 city documents show him presiding over a citizens group that had raised $50,000 in an effort to bring the railroad to New Philadelphia.[22] The first two decades of Leroy Lansing Janes' life were therefore to transpire not only in the "best period of a wonderful century," as he liked to remember it, but in a home that was rapidly achieving the hopes and dreams of its founder. Landed wealth was being combined with public status. Indeed, by all external standards Elisha Janes was well on his way to the position that history was to record for him: that of one of New Philadelphia's "oldest and most esteemed citizens."[23]

While the official record provides the bone structure of Leroy Lansing Janes' family background, it does not offer extensive insight into the flesh and blood aspects of his childhood experiences and the effects that the inner life of the family had on his maturation. For one whose later years were to be filled with controversy, including allegations of mental instability, a more detailed exploration of these early years is in order.

In many ways Janes' childhood resembled that of other children living on the edge of what had recently been the frontier. It is obvious, from fragments of his projected autobiography, that the growing boy formed deep and lasting attachments to the physical environment of New Philadelphia and the family farm. The Janes home, lying halfway between the river and the hills on the eastern edge of the town, was ideally located. The sun, he recalled, rose over miles upon miles of wooded hills that flanked the farm's eastward approach, and it set beyond the river and canal to the west. The hills were a dense wilderness of oak, chestnut, maple, and beech, and in the lower sections walnut and hickory. In the westward valley there were splendid orchards of peaches, pears, grapes, and plums, and, to the delight of the child's heart, a superabundance of golden apples.[24]

Within such a setting a child given to wandering and a search for adventure had ample opportunity to roam and explore. Janes' autobiographical notes indicate many of the usual childhood fascinations.[25] An early interest in firearms was soon followed by hunting expeditions for squirrel, possum, and rabbits. Swimming and fishing ranked high on a list of childhood priorities, as did visits to Aunt Polly's blockhouse, playing indians, and breaking colts. Machines of all kinds appear to have been fascinating. "Taking apart father's watch" was followed in his notes by an entry that suggests a similar procedure for cases of clocks discovered in the family attic. There were, of course, also the usual chores: helping with the milking and butchering, harvesting fruits and nuts, and looking after the chickens.

While the surface reading of the autobiographical materials Janes preserved for posterity leaves the general impression of a cheerful, affirmative young boy, a closer examination of these materials also reveals hidden currents that run counter to such an interpretation. There is considerable evidence that the Janes home was less than fully harmonious. Even in later years he seems to have remained strangely preoccupied with tensions in the family, tensions which as an ardent believer in the power of heredity he felt he had inherited, and which may well have left deep imprints on his psychic development.

What the exact nature of the family difficulty was is not entirely clear. There are, however, indications that the problem involved the mother-father relationship and, more importantly, the relationship of each of the parents to the young boy. The situation appears to have been further complicated by the political and religious turmoil that swept America in the 1840s and 1850s and the individual personalities of Janes' mother and father.

Janes' efforts to come to grips with his family and childhood environment was no easy process. The transformation of direct childhood experiences, many of them of intense emotional impact, into a more concrete analytical framework required years of intensive searching and a sometimes desperate effort to come to grips with his rational and emotional heritage. In dealing with his images of his home and childhood environment we are consequently faced with two polarities. On the one hand we are confronted with a deep inner need to idealize the home and its occupants. On the other there was the countervailing tendency to see the world more directly and to portray its characters with a more realistic brush. As we shall see, the paradox between what was and what ought to be was to remain a troubling one for Janes throughout his life.

We have already discerned something of the positive Janes who saw his early years as transpiring during the best period of a wonderful century, a mood he was to underscore in his work in Japan, and such feelings were also extended to the human and environmental resources of the section of the country in which he was raised. "As to the people," he later recalled, "there was a certain high uniformity of intelligence and a measurable freedom from worn out prejudices of the East." And as to the region, "there was a pronounced exuberance of fertility and a universal abundance, which taken together were perfectly certain to produce in a generation or two a race of women and men of exceptional capacities, of lofty moral aims, of cheerful disposition, and of broad and active sympathies."[26] Within such a setting a boy could have a childhood of the healthiest sort, he observed, "animated by an intense love of liberty, devoted to books, longing for travel, delighting in adventure," and above all, "dominated by the usual lively imagination."[27]

In such a home, as he was later to tell his students in Japan, "there was a father of the noblest and courtliest Christian character, a man of military bearing and Washingtonian integrity, the very thought of whom was calculated to swell a wild and wandering son's heart with devotion and pride."[28] At the soul of such a home, he added, there was "a mother of matchless beauty of character and temperament, a woman of great intelligence, and of tireless devotion to the hope of human progress and the cause of an enlightened humanity."[29]

For the child of five or six, Janes later recalled, the mother was a "guardian angel and fountain of all the diviner effluences of heart, and feeling, and moral inspiration."[30] The father, now merging into the ripest stage of dignified manhood, was the fixed and exalted idol of the budding intelligence. To the young boy, he was a superior being who could do no wrong, and "whatever the logic of his mind had determined, and the lips of a man so noble had announced," he wrote, "let none dispute, it must be right and consequently truth and law."[31]

Here, through the tinted glasses of an idealized childhood, we get a glimpse of the perfect parents and the perfect home. On the one hand we have the portrait of a warm and affectionate mother, and on the other of a rational, dignified, and successful father. The mother's role is identified with the emotional realm and with the sustenance of the normal oedipal needs of the boy; that of the father is given due play as the intellectual and rational model that the budding intelligence might emulate. Given such clear role models, particularly at the crucial stage of the child's development in which he was to move from the home to the broader social environment of the school, one might have anticipated a well-integrated personality development for the young Leroy.

But there is ample evidence to suggest a different picture. It might even be argued that the preceding description of home and parents incorporated a heavy dose of wish fulfillment—an effort to rectify the past through a restructured history. In glossing over the contradictions of the home, the Captain later sought to transcend the polarities of his own personality, which often served as sources of grief as well as glory.

To understand the later Janes we must explore the home in greater detail. After their marriage in 1830, Janes' parents moved to Trenton, a few miles south of New Philadelphia. Here their first daughter, Ann Elizabeth, was born in 1832, but she survived only a few days. Two years later, in 1834, the family was more fortunate with the birth of a son, William Warner, who lived to maturity. There may also have been problems with William, however, for he is rarely mentioned in the family records, a curious silence that runs counter to the normal expectations for the eldest son in a property-conscious family. A year after William's birth, a second daughter, Delia Ann, was added to the family, but she lived only a year and a half. The birth of Leroy Lansing in 1837 therefore represented the fourth child, but only the second to survive. Although the shadow of infant mortality was partially lifted with the birth of Leroy's younger sister, Ellen Mariah, in 1838, it soon returned with the birth of Catharine Mary, who died in 1842, and a set of twins, Mary and Martha, born in 1845, the latter of whom died in 1854.[32]

The repeated loss of her children seems to have profoundly influenced Janes' mother. With each death the basic religious tensions in the home mounted. An elder in the Presbyterian Church, Elisha Janes adhered to a strict Calvinist view of life. As his son later remembered, "his father dealt with his own heart sternly and at the bidding of his faith, no matter what the complexities." "He sacrifices himself, dies to his convictions daily." "For such a man," Janes later observed coldly, "it is possible to immolate even a son."[33] If Janes' father was a product of the rational, though puritanical, tradition of American Presbyterianism, "a man whose mind worked best in the traces of the sternest of theological logic, provided it proved itself consistent," his mother, he noted, "preferred to reason from within against the strictly 'just' injustice of life's experiences."[34] A Methodist by upbringing, and consequently more emotionally in tune with the revivalism of the frontier, Janes' mother refused to accept the death of her children as God's will.

"What mother that has buried her first born and later two young children before they had even come to a consciousness of the possibilities she has cherished for them," Janes wrote, "ever yet accepted with a whole heart, or a non-protesting mind a scheme of fatalism born in the brain of a bachelor Apostle."[35] In a scene that obviously made a deep impression on the young boy, his mother's anti-Calvinistic feelings burst into the open. The occasion appears to have been a visit to the Janes home in 1842 of several Presbyterian clergymen, a common enough occurrence in a home known for its hospitality, and which often served as an inn for ministers and missionaries moving West. But this was also the year of the death of Elizabeth's fourth daughter, Catharine, and the fundamental issue seems to have been the question of "infant baptism." How the issue was raised is not entirely clear. What is clear is that Janes' mother refused to believe that her child, which had died unbaptized, was doomed to perdition. Angered at the injustice of such a theological view, Janes tells us that "in the presence of three of the Church's ordained sponsors," she "renounced forever a system which by any sort of theological implications could consign her buried infant to an eternity of misery."[36]

The effect of such a renunciation on the home of a Presbyterian elder is not difficult to imagine. And yet, his mother's stand on the Church represented a denunciation only of the coldly rational aspects of her husband's theological tradition. For a woman suffering the pains of repeated loss, religion continued to play an important role, but it was a different Christianity that provided her with sustenance and solace.

For Leroy the death of his sister was to prove particularly troubling. On the one hand, it now became obvious that he was to be caught between the diverging religious patterns of the home. On the other, there was the changing nature of the home itself. Janes was to refer to his sister's death as his "first grief," and he later wrote of the experience poignantly in a letter to his students in Japan:

> Only a little way from where I write, one day in June when I was a very small boy, the dead body of my little sister was carried out and rested a moment under the locusts, while friends covered it with flowers. Then it was borne away and hidden in the grave. That was my first grief, all the world was changed for me! The green of the leaves has never been the same green to me, nor the grass so soft. A shadow has been in the sunlight since, and it will not paint things in the colors they wore, when her hand was in mine, and the light was in her eyes. For seven long years I never named her name. I could not.[37]

As was often the case with emotionally disturbing experiences, Janes later discussed his sister's death through the eyes of one of his fictional characters. In an unpublished novel, "Out of Stony Lonesome," a work that retains strong autobiographical overtones, Janes deals with a young man brought up in a strict Calvinist home. "My early existence," he observes, "was one of pains and penalties as the law books say, for never was a household more rigidly subject to the least human and most divine of all codes, the Mosaic law modified by Paul, and recast in the stony matrix of John Calvin's gloomy temperament." "I had a sister," he tells us, "but she died . . . one day in June." "My father would not allow us to lay the flowers we brought in her little coffin, to be buried with her. Our neighbor's boy and I had no other way of expressing our inconsolable grief!"[38]

In Janes' fictional version the death of his sister is soon followed by that of his mother. "Worn out with incessant striving against the incubus of fatalism that haunted, and threatened to separate her forever from her child, my mother soon followed and was laid beside my little sister's grave." "With the light of my life all gone," Janes tells us through his hero, "you may well believe I needed the sunshine and free air of the neighboring hills to remold and support my own stunned and stagnant being. For long I wished and prayed to die. But they were my father's bones and sinews that framed in me my mother's nature. And that was not to be."[39]

While the memory of his sister's death confirms the deep emotional impact that this experience had on the young boy, the shadow that was thereafter to be in the sunlight was, in fact, a shadow that seems to have engulfed the entire house. "Air and sunlight were both rigidly excluded from the home that death had darkened," he wrote symbolically of the transformation, "from only one window were the shutters thrown open, and that lighted my school and bedroom."[40] Here again the ideal family was to contrast sharply with reality. The rejection of her husband's church appears to have ushered in a decided period of withdrawal on the part of Janes' mother—a withdrawal that her son later fictionalized as death. A home that had served as a caravansary for guests of every sort suddenly ceased to ring with conviviality. Guests became scarce. Janes speaks of illness on the part of his mother, and of a growing passivity.[41] "And yet," as he noted, "behind the passive attitude and through the *silent* lips of the little woman of the bright intelligence and boundless sympathies, the instincts of childhood could discern the force of a conclusive protest, feel the notes of denial, and hear the still small voice of remonstrance that kept *her* conscience clear."[42]

Although the interpretation of his mother's mood clearly retains the reason of hindsight, it is obvious that the boy was seriously influenced by the changing home environment and feelings of his mother. This was particularly true as the mother's silent protest came to be combined with a deep emotionalism that was disturbing for the child. Having rejected Presbyterianism, Janes' mother found solace in the emotional outbursts of revivalistic camp meetings. In the process, whether by intent or by accident, she exposed her son to emotional pressures he never forgot. As he recorded, one of his earliest memories was of such a meeting. "I shall not pause to say how I came there," he wrote, "but in my enforced reverie I saw myself again, a tow-head of five or six years only, mounted on a fence-post in the enjoyment of a free exhibition more exciting and far more mysterious than ever canvas covered for me in later years."[43]

New Philadelphia was in the midst of a revival "gravely conducted by men and women grown grey in the 'cause.' " Prompted by his inquisitive nature the young boy was determined to investigate: "The big wooden building was a scene of commotion even before my arrival," he wrote. "The light of numerous candles would have opened the whole interior to my gaze but for the noisome moisture of hot breath that very early dimmed the huge windows." Even years later his ears still rang with those strange sounds, "the trumpeting of the exorters, the groans and wailings of distressed mourners, the cries and screeches of hysterical creatures everywhere in the room, the thundrous 'amens' of pious clackers, the shouts of the emancipated, and a general deafening chorus of emotional vociferation. At times this discordant din would dissolve into a more methodical madness of prayer," he remembered, "as the champions and leaders wrestled with the reluctant spirit; but this was only to dam up the flood of emotion. Higher and higher the tension rose, until feeling found vent in piteous appeals and tears, or rushed forth in a torrent of tumultuous triumphant song. Out and in through the two doors poured a stream of restless humanity. Later on in the night the doors were closed and the thinned assembly settled down to the serious work of 'getting religion.' Through it all I kept my perch until near midnight," he noted, "when I heard my father's voice behind me."[44]

As one can detect from the vividness of his recollections, Janes' exposure to revivalistic protestantism led later to a strong, if peculiar, attraction to the emotionalism of revivalistic Christianity. This may account, in part, for the deeply emotional religious experiences to which he was subject on several occasions in his life.[45] While the anti-intellectual biases of revivalistic Methodism were part of the environment in which he matured, one must not lose sight of the fact that his education and training were predominantly centered in the pragmatic rationalism of the nineteenth-century American educational system and its growing belief in science, not faith, as a cure for man's ills. If the pressure of his own, and his mother's, sorrow over the death of his sister pulled him toward the former tradition, the staunch rationalism of his father continued to provide a counterbalance against capitulation to such a tendency.

To what degree Leroy comprehended the growing estrangement between his mother and father following his sister's death is not clear. As in other aspects of the family relationship there are mysteries that lie beyond historical resolution. In fact, there may have been greater consequences of that death than his mother's search for emotional release in revivalistic camp meetings. On one occasion, Janes recalled, his mother objected to Sunday school children being taught the miracle of the Feast of Cana, where Christ turned water into wine. She insisted that this was a spurious miracle that had been added to the New Testament by the Corinthian wine trust. The sanctions expressed by this miracle, she warned, were dangerous and contrary to the dictates of common prudence. "Wise little Mother!," Janes noted in one of his more cryptic remarks, "had her pure heart and discerning mind prescience of trials and tragedies to come, too numerous for record, too terrible for patient contemplation?"[46] While there is a hint of alcoholism here, possibly on the part of one of the family members, and while we know that Janes subsequently became an ardent supporter of the temperance movement, the details remain extremely sketchy. If Janes did respond to the shadow that hung over the family home, that response seems to have constituted an effort to move beyond the walls of the home into a broader public sphere. School, and school activities, gradually came to occupy much of his time.

Like other aspects of his childhood environment, the educational system to which the young Janes was introduced in 1848 was still largely in its formative years. An early Ohio effort to achieve the ideal of public education had ended in disappointment. Free schools, supported by a school taxation law, were soon regarded as "poor schools"—schools to which, as one local historian observed, "all the poor of the parish went" without a "real desire for education." Many of these students eventually dropped out, but enough remained to "vex and overwork the teachers with their lack of discipline and inability to learn."[47]

Janes' first educational experience seems to have taken place in such a school. The Market House School, he recalled, was disturbed not only by the din of hundreds of pattering feet—the meat market was next door—but also by incompetent teachers, some of whom fomented discord. Janes' father soon joined other members of the community who refused to vote extra funds for the public schools and chose instead to support private education. When the Market House School collapsed, these men "were not satisfied to have their children's mental culture end with that of the district school." Instead, they secured the services of old Mr. Everhard, "a most capable man for the duty, and opened a sort of special, or select, school in the basement of the Lutheran Church."[48]

Janes was much impressed with the portly, grey-haired Everhard, whose dignified demeanor, gentle and patient manner of instruction, and positive passion for the higher forms of English literature introduced him to a field of study he treasured throughout his life.[49] Exposure to the world of poetic beauty was a totally new experience for Leroy. Here was a world in which his own sense of loss found numerous echoing voices. Samuel Roger's "Ginevra," Nathaniel Parker Willis' "Rabbi's Return," and the biblical account of King David's lament over the death of his son Absalom may have been a long way from Milton, Wordsworth, and Burns, which his Japanese students remembered constituted his favorite reading at home, but they all shared a common theme of loss and provided a source of solace.[50]

To what degree Janes' recollections of these years involved a telescoping of later tragic deaths, including those of his sister Martha in 1854 and his mysterious first wife, Nellie, in the mid-1860s, is difficult to determine. The Ginevra theme of the beautiful bride who disappears on the night of her marriage feast would certainly indicate an association with later events and suggests once more the care with which one needs to treat these early years. As is the case with most adults, Janes could not free himself from the tendency to confuse time sequences and to read into portions of his childhood events that, though emotionally running in similar channels, were separated by considerable gaps in time. A careful exploration of his early years therefore must deal not only with the problem of his tendency to fictionalize his home and childhood in an effort to idealize his past, but with an equally obvious jumbling of events that became parts of subsequent emotional packages. While we may question the degree to which a boy of seven, just learning to read, understood the nuances of Samuel Roger's poetry, or the child of five, for that matter, felt the depth of grief expressed in Janes' fictional account of his sister's death, it is clear that the growing Janes was troubled by death and found emotional release in poetry, and that the mature Captain was subject to similar feelings and indulgences.

Tutelage under the gentle and dignified Mr. Everhard came at a crucial juncture in Leroy's development and allowed him at least temporary relief from the mounting difficulties in the home. "That year," he later wrote of his close association with Mr. Everhard in 1844, "marked a great change in me physically. Nature in me began to triumph over the evil conditions of climate and perhaps other causes of which no one was aware." And with growing strength of body came stamina of mind. "I was quite a new boy indeed, before I was fully seven years old. Weakness that had made me shy and passive, gave place to vigor that made me adventuresome."[51]

But the image of the vigorous new boy that showed itself in the school context must be juxtaposed to experiences that suggested a different picture. Janes wrote of the same period: "I had begun to spend much of my time at my Aunt Kitty's. My father was absent most of the time on public business. My mother was never strong after a severe illness she had had. So I was encouraged in my visits to my good Aunt, who always practiced upon the adage, 'if you wish to make a man (or a boy for that matter) love you, feed him.' "[52] While Aunt Kitty was soon to perform many of the functions of a surrogate mother, and Mr. Everhard and subsequent teachers may well have been surrogate fathers, there is a quiet note of estrangement that runs through these observations. What is not precisely indicated is the source of this estrangement. Here again we face the issue of confused time sequences. Although the Everhard school can be documented for 1844, there is evidence that the experiences that encouraged his visits to Aunt Kitty's did not fully materialize until 1845.

The year 1845 was difficult in the Janes household. In October his mother gave birth to twins, and in the wake of the delivery she became increasingly preoccupied.[53] Such "preoccupations" no doubt encouraged his visits to Aunt Kitty's. On the other hand, his mother's silent protests were well known and had resulted in earlier adjustments. What was disturbing about 1845 was the fact that the grave and courtly father, who had served to balance the emotional mother, began to give way under new and unexpected pressures.

By the mid-1840s Elisha Janes had become increasingly active in the abolitionist movement. Southern Ohio was one of the major spawning grounds for antislavery sentiment, and the debates that were subsequently to rise to national prominence often had their first airings in the local Presbyterian churches of the region in which New Philadelphia was located. In fact, the outstanding voice of Free Presbyterianism, which split from the Old and New Church divisions of the Presbyterian Church over the slavery question in 1847, was the Rev. Joseph Gordon, who started his career as an outspoken abolitionist while teaching school in New Philadelphia in 1844.[54]

By 1845 Joseph Gordon, Thomas M. Finney, the pastor of the local Presbyterian Church, and Elisha Janes became the leading spokesmen calling for an end to the Church's "shameful avowal of pro-slavery principles."[55] The position they maintained was that "God has made of one blood all nations of men," and as a result all human beings are endowed with rationality and have an equal right to freedom. Under the circumstances slavery was "entirely inconsistent with Christian character and profession," and consequently, "no person holding slaves, or advocating the rightfulness of slave-holding can be a member of this body."[56] Joseph Gordon, in particular, felt that the question of slavery could best be solved through the Church, and not through political action.

Janes later told his students in Japan that his father's commitment to the abolitionist movement taught him the importance of living for a cause, and that his father's involvement in the movement had come at great personal cost. A part of that cost became all too apparent in 1845. It was in the spring of this year that Gordon, Finney, and Janes' father were to take the locally developed position on slavery to the General Assembly of the Old Church division of the Presbyterian Church in Baltimore. The consequences of that act were to be dramatic for the Janes family as well as for the Church. Given the lasting impression that this incident made on the young boy, it is best to relate it in his own words.

"It was a great event to one, at least, of the household, that spring of 1845," he wrote, "when the head and hero of the little domain set out with the taller and almost equally beloved and honored pastor of the little church, Thomas M. Finney, as delegates to a certain historic General Assembly about to meet in Baltimore. To this hour the impression of that parting is as vivid as if it had been yesterday. And across the expanse of years vibrate distinctly as then the sensations of pained suspense and bewilderment which signalized the father's return to his worshipper."[57]

Janes went on to describe his father's experiences in Baltimore; the refusal of the General Assembly of the Presbyterian Church to consider a petition of the Scottish Presbyterians on the issue of slavery, and the decision of a small portion of the Assembly, chiefly members of the Ohio synods, which included his father and the local pastor, to enter an official protest and walk out of the session after "the great body solemnly declared that Slavery should be 'no bar to Christian communion.' "

The result was a clear schism leading to the establishment of the Free Presbyterian Church, which maintained that the owning of slaves was a "bar to Christian communion." Elisha Janes, Thomas Finney, and several local figures were to play prominent roles in the abolitionist rebellion against orthodox Presbyterianism, and their return to New Philadelphia to initiate such a movement appears to have resulted in further controversy.

What followed, Janes tells us, was "persecution, denunciation, and ecclesiastical hounding. The pastor and his Elder were driven from the church which they had been chiefly instrumental in founding and sustaining." Several of the Colonel's friends were arrested for failing to abide by the fugitive slave laws. "Political excitement," Janes wrote, "was envenomed by religious rancor, as everybody knows from that time on to the close of *that* particular phase of the Irrepressible Conflict. If the experience has been one that plowed deep into the conscience of the nation and planted therein seeds of a whole new order of moral and religious sanctions, it may well be understood that the primary schooling which it imparted to the boyhood of Ohio in its earliest stages of that nation developing experience, must have been searching and determinative of character."

Janes later pictured himself as having become a firm abolitionist as a result of the stories his father brought back from Baltimore, including a vivid description of slaves being shipped South. But here too one has to separate subsequent interpretations from actual events. The young boy's concerns seem to have involved more complex and personal issues. He wrote:

> The father's absence had made the streets of the neighboring village, and the choicest haunts of the big farm, places of solitude and desolation to his longing heart. The absence of a week or two had seemed to be an age. And on the return a stream of callers, with their anxious and sometimes tumultuous greetings, punctuated by serious controversy, and ominous forebodings, had swept him out

of notice. All day long he had been a silent satellite to the paternal sun hardly expectant, but hopeful of sometime fathoming the meaning of it all. At length, overlooked and weary of the vain endeavor, he had fallen asleep on a sofa in the corner of the parlor, accents of the last of the solemn consultations in which the talented and noble pastor and a few trusted friends remained to participate still prodding his ears.

It was certainly later than midnight, and may have been long after that hour, when he was awakened by sounds to which his ears were even more unaccustomed. They were sounds of manly grief: expressions of a mighty reaction, sighs of recognition, welcoming a new set of soul-stirring convictions, groans of a wounded and remorseful conscience. The surprise of the father over the discovery that he had an auditor, this later while, equalled the perplexity of the son over a circumstance, next to one, the most memorable and momentous of his entire childhood.

The incident, as Janes related it, was important not only for the way it penetrated the conscience of the nation, but for the way it affected the psyche of the young boy. There was definitely a traumatic quality to the experience, which, along with the death of his sister and the mother's rejection of the organized Church, remained the most significant and troubling events of his childhood. Moreover, in the whole structuring of the experience we can sense his attempt to deal with this period of his life in a detached, historical manner. The effort to explain his father's actions within the context of the antislavery movement, particularly those aspects of the movement that involved the father and family in mounting controversy, serves as a means of covering the more direct emotional consequences of the event. The detached, almost abstracted, third-person perspective through which the incident is narrated is itself revealing of a continuing need to control the impact of what had been, and remained, an inner crisis.

But what had occurred? Is this not another portrait of the ideal father, the hero jousting against the forces of injustice and bigotry, and in the process becoming an even more venerated figure of courtly Christian character and Washingtonian integrity? Certainly the first impression one gains is just that. And yet, the true impact of the whole occurrence seems to have involved the problem aired in the final paragraph—the curious situation in which the sleepy child, unnoticed and unattended by his elders, awakened from his slumber to find his father in the throes of an emotional display for which he was totally unprepared. To have caught the cool, rational, and intellectual father, who was not without criticism of the emotional mother, in a display of tears and groans, and to have done so from a position of concealment, not only stripped the father of his hero status, it also stripped the child of the security of the clear role model that he needed to countervail the pressures of the preoccupied mother. What was worse, it proved the fallen hero to be deficient in precisely the area in which the boy felt most vulnerable. As Erik Erikson pointed out some time ago, one of the deepest conflicts that a child can develop is the hatred for a parent who has served as the model and executor of the superego, but who in some way was found trying to get away with the very transgressions which the child could no longer tolerate in itself.[58] Erikson found such experiences to constitute major sources of adult pathology, and in the case of Janes, too, the foregoing experience seems to have ushered in a period of intense turmoil that was to have lasting consequences.

Despite the restructured history, and all subsequent efforts to restore the broken pieces of the ideal father in the family shrine, the damage could not be undone. For young Leroy, as the mature Captain recalled, the consequences were a "veil of misty confusion in the ethical theories and moral sanction of the home which a boy's intelligence, however precocious and alert, must needs discern, but failed to penetrate or clear away." What the boy increasingly felt was that a conflict was on in the world in which an "enlightened but natural sentiment" struggled against "a whole set of arbitrary codes, authoritative traditions, and logical definitions of right and wrong." Indeed, the struggle between what Janes defined as "what is right, true, and just, as between human beings by reason of their humanity" and concepts of right and wrong "based on temporary and artificial principles of expediency" was to preoccupy him for years to come.[59] It is quite clear, moreover, that with the passing years there were distinct periods of his life during which he oscillated between the enlightened but natural sentiment of his mother and the authoritative traditions and logical definitions of his father. If his efforts to penetrate such ethical ambiguities and clear them away in later years were to prove no more successful than they had been in his youth, they also remained the source of the particular dynamism of which his work in Japan was to serve as a good example.

The ethical ambivalence that the adolescent Janes found in himself was not without immediate consequences. On the one hand his autobiographical notes indicate an effort to identify with the antislavery cause, which was to dominate the father's attention for the next decade. Indeed, there was a note of obvious excitement in his recollections of the farm's role as a station on the underground railroad and over his first encounter with black travellers on the path to freedom. However, it is an exaggeration to see the family solely concerned with the abolitionist cause. To a large extent life went on as usual. While some in the community may have ostracized the Colonel for his stand on the slavery question, there were many others who continued to look to him for leadership in agricultural innovation and in such areas as his efforts to bring the railroad to New Philadelphia. If there was any change, it rested largely in the son's perceptions of the father's role within the family, and in the disturbing implications that such changed perceptions held for his attitudes toward the home and its head. Although Janes cites his father's frequent absences as one reason for their changed relationship, the growing alienation that emerged between them may well have been the responsibility of the son as much as the father. Unable to deal with the home environment, the boy continued to seek refuge beyond its limits. While the shadows that engulfed the farm became deeper with the years, there was still sunlight at his Aunt Kitty's.

In contrast to the silent mother and increasingly estranged father, Janes tells us that his dear aunt was esteemed and loved by everyone.[60] Having been left the old Cryder home, she provided a generous table for the professional men of the gradually expanding town. From her father she had inherited a frontier generosity and a distinct disdain for the materialistic urges that prevailed around her. Even the mature Captain recalled the joy that tingled through him as he performed the ordinary chore of calling guests to dinner at her house with a large bell. "O the delight of making such a sonorous resounding noise," he wrote, "of filling the atmosphere of the whole 'square' with a din to which all, everybody, young, old, idle, busy, must give attention." The effect of the experience was heightened by the "savory smell of steaming viands which I had encountered in passing from the kitchen to the front door; the vision of my good and pretty aunt, whose coral lips never in all her 71 years uttered even one harsh or angry or reproachful word to any one, begging me 'not to go away but to stay for dinner'; the kindly chattering of lawyers, merchants, and other great men as they passed, while I swung the heavy bell back and forth so as to extract the greatest amount of sound it was capable of uttering—O that was life, joyous, profound!"[61]

The warm joyousness that we see here is in distinct contrast to the increasingly cool and distant tones in which the family home is treated. The need for attention, for adult companionship, for usefulness, all these seem to have become accentuated in distinction to their loss at home. And if one reads such passages as the above from the inverse perspective of what they indicate to be transpiring on the family farm, we are made privy to a growing loneliness and isolation on the part of the youthful Janes.

Such feelings were to find emotional release in his conduct. The need for attention, which on the one hand found joyful fulfillment at his Aunt Kitty's, could also lead to expressions of a less positive sort. "Setting fire to the Knisely's Carpenter shop," "knocking out windows in Lutheran Church," and "taking nut off teacher's buggy for having been punished unjustly" are one-liners in his autobiographical notes that suggest conduct verging on the delinquent. "Cutting off the milk thief's (cat's) paw, 'for mother,' " may have been one way of gaining the notice of the inattentive and troubled lady, but one suspects that this was not the type of help that the "saintly" woman of "boundless sympathies" desired. "Cutting off pigs heads, 'for father,' " may have served a more important domestic function, but here, too, one senses a certain cruel violence that involved more than a mere performance of chores.[62]

While such notes in Janes' recollections indicate a tendency toward deviant behavior that was to reemerge in subsequent periods of emotional stress, one must be careful to place this conduct in its proper perspective. Janes was later to write next to the list of these events, which included the discovery of his father's tobacco box and a jug of whiskey out on the road, "Being a man!"[63] And to a certain extent they were just that. Like other children, Janes explored the limits of his adolescent environment, fought his youthful battles against self, and home, and sought to become a man. Although occasional outbursts of emotional dissatisfaction demonstrated the particular difficulties of the home environment with which he wrestled, such experiences seem to have represented momentary lapses—more indicative of future than present trouble—and indeed the maturing boy's life was to become more concerned with study than with exploits of the type mentioned above. This was particularly true after 1850, the year in which A. C. Allen came to New Philadelphia and Leroy experienced what he described as an "intellectual awakening."[64]

In the decade from 1840 to 1850 the population of New Philadelphia tripled from approximately 500 to just under 1,500.[65] While still little more than the neighboring village, to which Janes referred, the town was beginning to develop sufficient financial resources to address itself to a number of issues of public policy. The gradually expanding circle of lawyers whom Leroy encountered at his Aunt Kitty's was the direct result of the newly built Court House, which overlooked the center of trade and traffic in the central square. Influential legal figures, such as John A. Bingham, who subsequently served six terms in Congress, had commenced practice in the county seat in the 1840s.[66] Bingham served as district attorney of Tuscarawas County from 1846 to 1849. As a former sheriff, Elisha Janes maintained close contacts with men such as Bingham.

Moreover, as a Whig and a Republican of considerable local influence, he followed the careers of promising local lawyers, which included not only Bingham, but another prosecuting attorney from a neighboring county, William R. Sapp, who was about to embark on a congressional career.[67] In both cases Elisha Janes' support was to bear dividends for his son. But the law represented only one side of New Philadelphia's growing public concerns. Education, which for more than ten years had received little more than lip service, and which in the case of Leroy's early experiences was far from systematic, now moved to the forefront of public priorities. In 1850 a new school district was established. In the same year a board of education was elected and a new school built. At the head of this school stood an able principal, A. C. Allen, who one local writer noted in the 1880s "is yet remembered for the thorough discipline he established in the schools."[68]

The Allen Union School, as Janes wrote of it, was divided into three grades.[69] The curriculum of the highest grade included physiology, history, algebra, natural philosophy, and rhetoric. Under Mr. Allen's careful supervision Leroy expanded his intellectual horizons, and he wrote with excitement of having "learned to *read*!" "Reading," moreover, does not appear to have meant the mere mechanics of reading, but a direct involvement with books and the new world of ideas that they opened to his imagination. Young Leroy soon became an avid student of classical history and institutions and an ardent follower of heroes. Napoleon Bonaparte and George Washington were two of his favorites, and he reports dreaming of both.[70] A rudimentary study of Latin and Greek was combined with an exploration of Pope's Homer and Wiffen's Tasso. He also pursued his interest in poetry, beginning a life-long fascination with the romantic poets: Burns, Byron, Shelley, and Wordsworth. Wordsworth was also a favorite of his mother, who particularly liked the "Ode on Immortality."[71] Like his mother, Janes found consolation in such poetry, and success at school did much to alleviate his volatility. By the 1850s signs of deviancy had largely disappeared. Successful peer relationships were underscored by the stirrings of a childhood romance with a girl named Josephine Ferrel. But here again we have only the briefest of glimpses. "Love of J.F." is quickly paired in his recollections with the "rigors of recitations" and other elements of school life.[72]

Having finished with A. C. Allen's Union School in 1853, Janes was ready for the next step in his preparatory education. The Albany Manual Labor Academy to which he was sent by his father was typical of the small, transient schools that mushroomed in Ohio and other Western states in the mid-nineteenth century. Usually the product of a single teacher, often emphasizing manual labor as a means of supplementing the meager financial resources of the students, and in most cases closely associated with a particular religious position, these schools were grassroots centers of learning for many an American child.

There is some evidence that Janes' father intended to prepare him for the ministry. At Albany the headmaster was Joseph Gordon, and the dominant ideological position was that of Free Presbyterianism. By 1853 Joseph Gordon's reputation as a fiery orator and abolitionist editor of the *Free Presbyterian* had attracted considerable attention both in and outside Ohio. Albany, as Leroy was soon to discover, was clearly a reformist institution.[73]

Free Presbyterianism, as Gordon hammered home in his sermons and articles, advocated radical reform. "The great want of the present age," Gordon wrote, "is a living *practical* faith."[74] To the majority of America's nominal Christians, he insisted, Christianity "is an abstraction," nothing more than a "Sabbath garment" to be "thrown aside the rest of the week." As Gordon saw it, any "true religion includes genuine reform." "True religion," he noted, "is supreme love of God, and equal love of man." As such the true Christian could not shut his eyes to social and political problems. "To reform is to reconstruct, to re-model, to re-form or make over that which has been marred or broken," he wrote, "man's whole nature, physical, mental, social and spiritual, is marred and broken." If man and society lay in ruins, it was the responsibility of the Christian, he felt, to reconstruct the shattered powers of both. Hence the true Christian must be a genuine reformer. "The Christian," he wrote, "is, from the nature of the case, a radical reformer." Radical reform, moreover, meant a commitment not only to the transformation of the inner man, but to the great issues of the day, which for the 1850s were those of slavery and intemperance.

The selection of Albany as a center for Free Presbyterian activity was no accident. Towns and villages in which Free Presbyterians had churches or schools were invariably stations on the Underground Railroad.[75] Albany, situated in the southeastern corner of Ohio facing the West Virginia and Kentucky borders, was strategically located. Moreover, both Joseph Gordon and Janes' father cooperated in the Church's efforts to aid runaway slaves. By 1853, in the wake of the Fugitive Slave Laws, their resistance had merely hardened. While Janes' later recollections placed him squarely on the abolitionist side, and while the Christian position he was to take to Japan two decades later bears a striking resemblance to Gordon's concept of the Christian as radical reformer, Leroy does not appear to have shared his father's enthusiasm for the Albany Academy. "Too much ism and philanthropy, too little science and learning," he recorded in his notes. Even before the Academy came to a sudden halt in 1854, Leroy had declared it fundamentally unsatisfactory.[76]

On the other hand, too much ism and philanthropy and too little science and learning have to be placed in their proper perspectives. That the Albany Academy was preoccupied with the antislavery cause, no one can deny. And yet, despite his ambivalence, it would be equally hard to deny that the young man from New Philadelphia shared many of the fundamental values that motivated the school's mentor. In fact, Joseph Gordon, in spite of his ism and philanthropy side, was a first-rate teacher and a sound academician. Moreover, his teaching forte lay in the field of mathematics, not theology.[77] That Leroy learned more than he cared to admit at Albany was underscored by his matriculation at the United States Military Academy a few years later. West Point's admissions standards were extremely demanding, and few cadets could hope to survive its rigorous five-year program without a thorough preparatory education.

The problem with Albany, therefore, may have had less to do with the school and its headmaster, than with Leroy's inner tensions. Too much ism, as Janes subsequently used the term, usually meant too many rules and restrictions on his freedom of conduct. In later years this judgment was often reserved for sectarian orders of the Church, but at Albany it seems to have been extended to the school as a whole. Given the fact that Albany, like other sectarian schools of its kind, stressed a high morality that was to be combined with subservience to authority, it may be fair to argue that Albany helped to stimulate the growing tension between Leroy's inner quest for freedom and the concomitant need to deal with authority in the outside world. Leroy had been sent away to Albany at the wishes of his father, and the academy simply extended to the broader public sphere the struggle which had begun at home over the authoritarian demands of the father and the "enlightened but natural" sentiments of the mother.

To what degree the adolescent Janes pursued his dreams of Napoleon and Washington with more concrete images of a future military career remains silently concealed between the lines of his autobiographical notes. It is clear, however, that he was not prepared to pursue the clerical hopes his father entertained for him, and that the Colonel was not prepared to support his son's military dreams. Indeed, despite its militancy on the slavery question, Free Presbyterianism was decidedly pacifistic in orientation. "War is opposed to the spirit and principles of the Gospel," Joseph Gordon wrote in the *Free Presbyterian*. "It is everyone's duty to labor for the abolition of war and the war spirit," he insisted. As Gordon announced to his students, "war is one of the Devil's favorite agencies for the ruin and misery of men." Moreover, Free Presbyterians objected to the financial burdens that military expenditures placed on the people of all nations. "The army and navy of the United States," Gordon wrote, "costs the nation eighty per cent of all public revenues." That cost, he liked to point out, was "higher than any other nation on the globe."[78]

In what was clearly a curious contradiction given Janes' later career, it should be noted that the United States Military Academy at West Point served as one of the principal targets for the Free Presbyterians' antiwar stance. Joseph Gordon was an implacable foe of the Academy, which he regarded as a colossal waste of money and a seat of privilege. "The Military Academy at West Point has cost the nation more than four millions of dollars," he railed in the *Free Presbyterian*, and he noted with irony that, "each cadet receives, besides a gratuitous education, twenty-eight dollars a month for the privilege of being educated at public expense." Even a single lesson in target shooting, he liked to emphasize, cost the nation fifty dollars.[79]

On the other hand, twenty-eight dollars a month and a free education probably struck the ears of the Colonel's son with a different impact than Joseph Gordon intended. West Point's education and financial support may well have suggested a means not only of satisfying his inner ambition, but, more importantly, of dealing with the ultimate authority and financial control of his father. If Janes' eyes turned toward West Point after 1854, they did so quietly and with unannounced intentions. So far as he was concerned, Albany settled only one matter, and that was the overriding conviction that he was not meant for a career in the Church. While his father was adjusting himself to this new reality, Leroy was quite content to settle on an interim compromise.

With the closing of the Albany Academy and Leroy's return to New Philadelphia, that compromise became a legal apprenticeship. As a former sheriff and a close political associate of lawyers such as John A. Bingham and William R. Sapp, Janes' father appears to have proposed a legal career for his son. Consequently, in the latter part of 1854, Leroy entered the offices of John A. Bingham to read law.[80]

Janes' arrival at the Bingham office corresponded with a period of considerable excitement and activity. In the autumn of 1854 Bingham ran for Congress on the Republican ticket and was elected to the first of six terms in Washington. For Leroy, political campaigns, as his notes indicate, were fascinating and exciting events that brought forth some of the same joyous enthusiasm he had demonstrated earlier in his visits to Aunt Kitty. And yet, Bingham's sudden departure left Janes' training largely in the hands of a partner. In the wake of the campaigning came the reality, and drudgery, of law books. "Law by day, history by night," Janes recorded dispassionately in his notes.[81] But while he was willing to give law its due attention, his predilections clearly ran to history, and to philosophy, which was soon added to his evening studies.[82] Although Janes was willing to bide his time, he had not forgotten his heroes—Washington and Napoleon—nor had his taste in reading abandoned Tacitus and the romantic poets for legal treatises. As the months passed, West Point's silhouette seemed to be expanding on his horizon.

By the spring of 1856 Leroy had made up his mind. The law was not for him. Despite his father's initial reluctance to support his desire to pursue a military career, Janes had slowly won him over to his side. At least by the opening months of 1856 his father was no longer adamantly opposed to such a possibility.

Fortunately, with the election of John A. Bingham and William R. Sapp to Congress, the family was blessed with a dual path to a much coveted West Point appointment. On February 13 Sapp wrote to Colonel Joseph G. Totten, the inspector of the Military Academy, requesting him to send two copies of the Regulations for Cadets and asking him to enter on his book the name of "Leroy L. Janes as an applicant from the 15th district." "I will make the nomination by the first of March," Sapp added.[83] Early in March, Sapp formally wrote Jefferson Davis, the Secretary of War, nominating Leroy to the Academy. And on April 3 Janes replied to Davis: "Sir, I have the honor to acknowledge the receipt of your communication of the 15th inst. informing me that the President has conferred upon me a conditional appointment of Cadet in the service of the United States, and to inform you of my acceptance of the same."[84] Two months later Janes traded his boyhood in the Ohio hills for the life of a grey-coated West Point cadet.

CHAPTER II

LIFE AT WEST POINT

FOR THE YOUNG MAN of nineteen years who arrived at the West Point wharf in late June 1856, the next five years were to become an all-encompassing experience.[1]

By the 1850s the United States Military Academy was in the midst of its Golden Age. Established some sixty years earlier to train officers for the Army, West Point had matured into an accomplished institution of higher learning, offering not only a thorough military education, but a sound academic program. In fact, in the fields of engineering, science, and mathematics the Academy was unrivaled in the country.[2]

Situated on a level tableland above the Hudson River some fifty miles north of New York City, West Point found itself, as Charles Dickens observed, in a "beautiful place," the "fairest among the fair and lovely highlands overlooking the North River."[3] The Academy not only had grown intellectually, it had also expanded physically. The half-dozen ramshackle buildings that once squatted on the plain beneath the distant hulk of the Revolutionary War bastion, Fort Putnam, had given way by the mid-1850s to a series of solid Tudor structures that now spread over much of the plateau. From their castellated towers cadets looking north on one of the region's crisp, cold winter days could see the distant town of Newburgh as it rose above the river and sparkled in the early morning sunlight. To the east they faced Constitution Island, the cedar-bedecked jut of land from which Washington's troops had once tried to impede British access to the upper Hudson with a chain across the river.

Unlike most nineteenth-century colleges and universities, as Janes soon discovered to his satisfaction, West Point had left behind the prevalent pattern of Greek and Latin studies, moral philosophy, and Christian apologetics—the "too much ism" side of his critical evaluation of Albany—for the expanding fields of physics, chemistry, astronomy, geography, and geology. If there was a driving force behind West Point's education, it was mathematics. At the Academy mathematics was taught as the practical underpinnings of all scientific studies and not merely as a means to "sharpen the intellect, to strengthen the faculty of reason, and to induce a general habit of mind favorable to the discovery of truth and the detection of error," as one Yale report put it.[4] The ultimate emphasis of West Point's education was to prepare cadets for careers in the applied sciences and in civil and military engineering. It was West

Pointers more than any other group that spurred America's technical advance westward in the form of roads, canals, and railroads.

But dreams of glory and empire were a long way from the more mundane reality of West Point's day-to-day existence to which the young westerner and his fellow new arrivals were soon introduced.

"Hey Animal, what's your name?," was the opening greeting for most prospective cadets as they stepped off the boat at the West Point Landing.[5] After climbing the slope from the river to the Academy, newcomers were immediately advised to "report" to the adjutant in the library across the plain. Here they signed in, had their appointments confirmed, and were ordered to quarters. Almost everywhere they were already being barked at: "Follow me," "Stand at attention," "Take off your hats," and always it was "Sir!," "Yes Sir!," and "No Sir!" As Janes soon learned, prospective plebes—"Animals"—were quartered in the "Area," a four-storied quadrangle where they were assigned two to a room, told to memorize several sheets of regulations posted over the fireplace, and advised to prepare for the entrance examinations that would be administered in the next few days. For Janes, as for other West Point cadets, the entrance examinations were the first of a series of trials that did not end until he received his much prized commission in the spring of 1861.

The entrance examination was in fact typical of the whole West Point system as it had matured under Sylvanus Thayer, the superintendent of the Academy from 1817 to 1835.[6] A broad-minded educator and strict disciplinarian, Thayer pushed West Point in new academic directions and assembled a brilliant faculty in mathematics, science, and engineering. He was a firm believer in the idea that mastery of a subject meant the ability to present any portion of it orally to a public forum. Long after the departure of the Father of the Academy, as he came to be remembered, his system, including its public examination structure, remained intact. Janes later paid Thayer a quiet compliment by exporting much of the system to the Kumamoto School for Western Learning in Japan.

Yet Japan was hardly a part of his consciousness in the summer of 1856. Janes and his fellow applicants were confronted by more direct concerns. The academic qualifications of each were soon rigorously tested. But first came a thorough physical examination. By the 1850s the weakness that had once made him shy and passive was clearly a thing of the past. School life in New Philadelphia and Albany had added to his vigor and stamina. Now in his twentieth year, Janes had matured into a handsome and well-proportioned young man. Physically he stood close to six feet and weighed just under 160 pounds.[7] Like other western students he was possessed of a certain freedom of gait and carriage that marked his Ohio origins. His face sported clean lines, warm light brown hair, and a slightly dimpled chin. If his face showed any particular signs of distinction they rested in his intense blue eyes, which revealed a sparkling potential for both humor and anger. The surgeon's verdict was soon in hand, he was physically fit for duty. But was he mentally prepared for the Academic Board?

Despite occasional claims that West Point's entrance examinations were deliberately lenient to admit as wide a spectrum of cadets as possible, and thereby ward off the prevalent nineteenth-century criticism of West Point as an elitist institution, there is little evidence to indicate that this was the case in the 1850s when Janes arrived. Aware that on average only two out of three would survive to join the entering class, there were few prospective cadets who failed to watch nervously as the members of the Academic Board walked from their residences to the Academic Hall attired in their blue dress uniforms and fringed epaulets. As candidates entered and emerged one after another there were the inevitable queries, "Was it hard?" "Was it easy?" Some thought the former, particularly appointees from the western states whose preparatory educations were not as advanced as those of their eastern counterparts. Others insisted on the latter, although the majority agreed that the man to be feared most was Albert E. Church, the head of the mathematics department. "There never was a colder eye or manner than Professor Church's," one cadet noted.[8]

Soon it was Janes' turn. Entering the examination room he was confronted by a semicircle of desks. Behind each sat a member of the board, "brilliant in blue and gold." In the center he observed Richard Delafield, who had just returned to the Academy to replace the popular Robert E. Lee as superintendent. To Janes' subsequent regret, Delafield possessed none of Lee's charm and gallantry. A small man with a large, protruding nose, Delafield had a nervous and suspicious disposition. Near him sat the much feared Church, and a few desks away, what may well have been West Point's most brilliant nineteenth-century graduate, William H. C. Bartlett, who in four years at the Academy stood first in every class and never received a demerit, and who had since become professor of natural philosophy and one of America's foremost astronomers. On the other side sat John W. French, the chaplain and professor of geography, history, and ethics. And on the periphery there were the assistant professors and instructors, including First Lieutenant O. O. Howard, who assisted Church with mathematics. John A. Bingham's 1857 appointee to the Academy, George A. Custer, recalled that he was given specific instructions regarding Howard, whose religious sincerity and tough questions were already widely known. "Be sure to attend his prayer meetings—especially before exams," Custer was warned by another cadet.[9] There is certainly no indication that Janes, any more than Custer, shared Howard's Christian sympathies. What Janes relied on before the board was his experience—he was older than many of his fellow appointees—and his background in mathematics, which prepared him for Church's and Howard's questions. Successfully parrying their thrusts, he was at last told that he had passed, a triumph he shared with 72 of the 101 candidates examined.[10]

On July 1, 1856, Janes was officially admitted to the Fifth Year Class which was destined to graduate in 1861.[11] Like other plebes, his first six months were provisional, two in the summer encampment and four in the classroom. Now military life began in earnest.

If his education in New Philadelphia and Albany exposed him to a high morality and an equally high degree of subservience to authority, he was soon to discover that West Point was not to be outdone in these respects. As one West Point official observed, the Academy "exacts of every individual rigid conformity to its standards ... it stands *in loco parentis* not only over the mental, but the moral, physical and, so to speak, the official man. It dominates every phase of his development ... there is very little of his time over which it does not exercise a close scrutiny, and for which it does not demand a rigid accountability."[12]

The summer encampment, during which West Point cadets moved out of their barracks and into a tent city on the plain, was generally regarded by upperclassmen with some relief. Just the opposite was true of the plebe class, for whom "camp" meant not merely prison discipline, but almost continuous hazing at the hands of the upperclassmen. The routine of camp life in which Janes participated in the summer of 1856 was described in detail by his classmate, Henry A. du Pont, in a letter to his mother. He wrote that cadets rose at 5:00 A.M., policed the grounds until 5:30, drilled until 6:30, prepared for inspection and then ate breakfast at 7:00, went to parade at 8:00 and to artillery practice at 9:00, policed again, ate dinner at 1:00 P.M., attended dancing class from 3:00 to 4:00, policed again, and went to infantry drill at 5:30, to evening parade and inspection at 7:00, to supper at 8:00, and to bed at 9:30.[13]

Such a life was, as one cadet noted, "too much like slavery" to suit him.[14] But the schedule does not fully depict the pressures under which most newcomers found themselves. Everywhere they encountered a myriad of rules and customary restrictions, and always there was the incessant "drumming" that called them to meals, to sick call, to assembly, to drill, to parade, and even, in theory, to sleep. All had now met the "dread instructor" whose portrait was presented to the Dialectical Society by cadet Jack Garnett in the summer of 1859 in a bit of typical student verse:

He shouts out, "Stand attention, sir!
    hands close upon your pants,
And stand erect. Hold up your head!
    There—steady! don't advance,
Turn out your toes still further,
    look straight toward the front,
Draw in your chin! Throw out your chest!
    Now steady! Don't you grunt."
Says the Instructor "Where's my pen?
    This old one doesn't suit me."
"There it is, sir." "You hold your tongue!
    How dare you talk on duty?
I'm not surprised to see you quail
    and flutter like a partridge,
But soldiers' mouths must only open
    when they tear a cartridge."[15]

Intimidating as the instructors may have been, there were others to be watched out for, particularly the cadets of the Fourth Year Class who were waiting for their chance to pass on "favors" received. Hazing, while not yet the serious problem it became after the Civil War, was widely practiced and quietly condoned at the summer encampment. Rarely allowed more than seven hours sleep, neophyte "campers" frequently found even these precious moments disrupted by unsolicited visitors who rudely dragged them from their bunks. Knowing how to accept such acts in silence, Janes, like Custer, later became something of an expert at returning the "favors" he had been rendered.

Life in camp came to an end with more beating of the drums at the close of August. But first cadets were treated to a brief respite from the strict routine of camp life. On the closing night of the summer encampment a grand ball was held. On this occasion young ladies who came to West Point from the south and New York City to avoid the summer heat were treated to an elegant affair which began at nine in the evening and lasted until four the next morning. Janes and his fellow classmates were thereby granted a golden opportunity to put their dancing lessons to good use. That the handsome Ohio cadet cut a smart figure in his white dress uniform is not difficult to imagine. While the memories of Josephine Ferell were now confined to the distant past, West Point in its own restricted way provided at least some possibilities for a new adventure of an amorous kind. It is possible that Nellie, the woman he later married, joined him for one of these dances in a subsequent summer.

The romance of a late August evening with its music wafting over a silvery Hudson may have cast a momentary spell on many a cadet and his belle, but the reality of the Academy's routine soon reasserted itself. The next morning the summer tents were struck. Now a less elegant ritual ensued. As fellow cadets gathered around each tent armed with clubs and brooms, two cadets would take hold of the corners and at the proper moment would jerk up the floor. "Instantly about a thousand and one rats would go scampering about in every direction," one of Janes' fellow West Pointers wrote home; "then comes the fun, and such a yelling, chasing and slaughter of rats it never was my fortune to behold before."[16] Given Janes' childhood experiences it is not difficult to imagine him gleefully participating in such a "hunt."

By the first of September Janes and his fellow provisionals were back in the barracks. At least here they were no longer five to a tent. Each was now paired with a roommate and assigned to austere but adequate quarters. The daily routine involved rising at 5:30, studying from 6:00 to 7:00, going to class until dinner at 1:00 P.M., then studying from 2:00 to 4:00, writing letters or reading from 4:00 until supper at 6:00, and then further studies from 7:00 until 9:30 when tattoo sounded, and rooms were inspected for lights out at 10:00.[17] While the emphasis in the summer encampment had been on the physical aspects of an officer's military training, the focus now shifted to the academic side.

West Point's educational program in the late 1850s still followed the basic Thayer system. The only major change involved a brief experiment with a five-year, rather than a four-year, program—an experiment that ended with Janes' class. Under Thayer's curriculum cadets concentrated on mathematics, English, and French during their first, or Fifth Class, year. Mathematics included algebra, geometry, trigonometry, and mensuration. English included geography. Mornings were devoted to math and afternoons to French and English. The same subjects were continued in the second, or Fourth Class, year, but in addition cadets received instruction in drawing. In mathematics they added analytical geometry, calculus, and surveying.

By the Third Class year cadets reached the most difficult portion of the curriculum. During the first term they spent their mornings on natural and experimental philosophy (physics), and in the second term on acoustics, optics, and spherical astronomy. These were all Professor Bartlett's specialties. Afternoons were given to Spanish and drawing, Saturday mornings to English composition. In their Second Class year the emphasis was shifted to ethics, chemistry, and drawing, in addition to the military subjects of infantry, artillery, and cavalry tactics. The major focus of the First Class, or final, year was on civil and military engineering, mineralogy and geology, and law and literature. Classes tended to be weighted differently. Mathematics and natural philosophy were counted at three times the value of English, French, drawing, and chemistry.[18]

By the 1850s West Point's merit system was well in place. Thayer's dictum, "every day in every class," referred not only to his firm belief in the method of daily recitations, but in the careful daily grading of every cadet in each of his sections.[19] Instructors were required to keep meticulous notes. Every aspect of a cadet's conduct, both in and out of the classroom, was carefully noted and recorded. Merits and demerits were incessantly totalled to create the ultimate profile and position of every class member. The results were publicly posted. Not only were cadets divided into sections by their rankings, they daily marched to classes and were often seated according to their class standings.

Some of the results of this structure were positive. As one of Janes' fellow cadets wrote home, "little favoritism is shown and everyone starts with a fair chance to excel in his classes."[20] On the other hand, the result was a highly competitive spirit. Cadets striving for top positions worked exceedingly hard. The course of study was difficult. Cadet Henry A. du Pont, who graduated at the top of Janes' class, noted that the Academy was at least twice as difficult as the University of Pennsylvania.[21]

Not all the effects of the West Point system were positive. Another cadet observed, "there is a lurking selfishness hanging around cadets," and with grades posted weekly, every man is to some degree "jealous of his neighbor."[22] Moreover, given the fact that each cadet's future military career depended on his final class standing, there was good cause for such concerns.

As cadets were well aware, no one could stand at the head of his class without a sound talent for mathematics. In this discipline southerners and westerners were usually no match for those from the East. Indeed, for many a cadet mathematics became an obsession. As one of Janes' upperclassmen wrote home, "I am always thinking of Math—I have a nightmare every night almost of it.—Gigantic X's and Y's, +'s and -'s squat on me—and amuse themselves in sticking me with equations, and pounding me on the head. . . ."[23] Another cadet put it more directly: "God damn all mathematics to the lowest depth of hell!!" he inscribed on the fly-leaf of his calculus textbook.[24] Fortunately for Janes, his earlier training stood him in good stead. Algebra, geometry, trigonometry, and mensuration were fields in which he possessed a considerable background. French was new to him, but West Point's emphasis was only on a reading knowledge of the language, and this at a very rudimentary level.

The real test for Janes and his fellow plebes came with the January 1857 examinations that ascertained their competence and determined their admission as regular cadets. Like other Fifth Class students, Janes was fully conscious of the importance of these examinations and worked hard to have his subjects under control. For Janes, as for his fellow classmates, Christmas of 1856 was hardly a joyous occasion. All anxiously awaited the first week of January. Nor was their sense of anxiety relieved by an official notice warning that all students not found proficient in the coming examinations would be asked to settle their accounts and prepare to go home.[25] Fortunately Janes passed, and in the first week of February he and his fellow survivors took the oath of allegiance to the United States in the West Point Chapel and received their cadet warrants. At last they were no longer provisionals.

By the second half of his first year, as the Academy shed its mantle of winter snow for the verdant tints of a burgeoning spring, Janes was successfully adapting to the West Point routine. Recitations at which he was asked to declaim on any portion of the day's assignment were now treated as if they were little more than part of the normal daily pattern. With spring came outdoor drilling in infantry, cavalry, and artillery tactics. The lithe young westerner, once fond of breaking colts, was now given an opportunity to exploit his background to its fullest advantage. An excellent rider, Janes shared the enthusiasm of his fellow Ohio underclassman, George A. Custer, for the flying artillery. Galloping along with artillery horses was both exciting and dangerous. Artillery steeds were difficult to control and caisson spills, in which gunners went sprawling, were not uncommon. In a letter home Custer observed that on such occasions cadets were sometimes "seriously hurt and not infrequently killed."[26] The latter was clearly an exaggeration. Both Janes and Custer seem to have survived without encountering any serious mishaps.

While spring took them out of doors it also brought the June examinations and the annual Merit Roll rankings. The June examinations were by far the most serious for every class and were conducted before the Academic Board and a Board of Visitors that solemnly scrutinized all cadets and their replies. Responsible for virtually any question an instructor or visitor might pose, all cadets entered these examinations with fear and trepidation. For Janes the result proved once more positive. With others he could write home with a sense of exaltation and true gratification. "I was examined today and passed."[27] When the Merit Roll was posted he found himself twenty-sixth out of a class of fifty-nine, a respectable if not overly distinguished position.[28] For most cadets merely surviving the first year was a triumph. Janes had much to be thankful for.

By the end of his Fifth Class year Janes had met with some successes in adjusting to West Point's academic program and enjoyed certain aspects of the Academy's military training. He continued to revere Napoleon. And the scientific side of his personality, which he identified with the rational tradition of his father, was supported by the ideas of Locke and Rousseau to which he was introduced as a cadet.[29]

There were, however, broad areas of West Point life to which he never adjusted. The absolute submission to authority that West Point demanded, the stultifying rigidity of the Academy's schedule, and the constant surveillance by the staff too closely resembled his father's rigid Calvinism to suit his tastes. For one who had come to West Point listing his mother, not his father, as "parent or guardian,"[30] *in loco parentis* of the Academy's kind did little more than rekindle the conflict between authority and freedom that had troubled his earlier years. Moreover, the Academy provided little support for the side of his personality that found sustenance and solace in the poetry of Burns, Byron, Shelley, and Wordsworth. West Point had no room for poets.

Janes was hardly the first to discover this. Two decades earlier Edgar Allan Poe had found West Point intellectually stagnant and spiritually stifling.[31] "Why prayest thou thus upon the poet's heart, Vulture whose wings are dull realities?" Poe had written in a West Point sonnet titled "Science."[32] It was bad enough that the Academy's regulations forbade cadets to "drink, play cards or chess, gamble, use or possess tobacco, keep any cooking utensils in their rooms," or "participate in any games," "leave the post, bathe in the river, or play a musical instrument,"[33] the rules even went so far as to state that "no cadet shall keep in his room any novel, poem, or other book, not relating to his studies, without the permission of the Superintendent."[34] Little wonder that Poe simply walked out of the Academy one day never to return.

Unlike Poe, Janes had not yet resolved his inner turmoil in favor of a bolt for freedom. And yet, like his mother, he countered forced submission with his own inner protest. By the Fourth and Third Class years his response to West Point's rigidity was clearly documented in his growing list of demerits. In his first year he had done remarkably well by keeping his delinquencies to a mere forty-three.[35] Cadets were permitted to accumulate up to a hundred demerits per six-month period before dismissal actions were initiated against them on grounds of conduct.[36] Some demerits were almost inevitable.[37] Upperclassmen enjoyed tricking newcomers into costly errors. One favorite prank was to insist that a plebe had inadvertently put on the cap of another cadet. As the uninitiated cadet took off his hat to make sure that it was his own he was immediately reported for being improperly dressed.[38] Just learning to execute the drill manual correctly was no simple matter, and the slightest hesitation or unwarranted anticipation could lead to further reports. Then there were the normal problems with a tight schedule that required a fine sense of timing if repeated latenesses were to be avoided. A matter of lost seconds could mean additional reports. With instructors and upperclassmen constantly looking for mistakes it was the rare paragon of virtue such as Robert E. Lee and William H. C. Bartlett who carried out the superhuman feat of surviving without a demerit. Most cadets were happy to keep their demerits within reasonable limits.

Janes' first-year reports revealed the normal miscues of the Fifth Class student.[39] "Not wheeling properly breaking into platoons at parade—one demerit." "Wash bowl not inverted at inspection—one demerit." "Late entering Mathematics Academy—three demerits." "In hall of barracks without coat or cap at 9:45 A.M.—one demerit." "Endorsing excuse on wrong end—one demerit." "Not executing manual properly at parade—two demerits." "Late at reveille roll call—one demerit." "Room not clearly swept at inspection—three demerits." "Neck comforter in quarters—three demerits." And so forth.

The average cadet chalked his early reports up to experience and avoided similar mistakes in later years. Academy-wise cadets tended to project a profile of decreasing delinquencies in their Third, Second, and First Class years. With Janes the pattern was reversed. In his second year his demerits jumped from 43 to 120. By his fourth year they stood at 180. And in his final year they reached 188. Indeed, in his final six months, Janes' demerits stood at 99, just one shy of the unpardonable 100.[40]

It is quite possible that by his final year Janes was flirting with expulsion. What the reasons for this were are not entirely clear. It does appear, however, that unprepared to simply walk away from the Academy, as Poe had done, Janes sublimated his confrontation with the rigidity of West Point life into conduct that was unacceptable to the mores of the institution. To what extent this was a projection of methods he had already developed in dealing with his father, we can never fully determine, but there are some curious patterns to Janes' demerits.

By 1860 and 1861 Janes' delinquency record included numerous entries that suggest a deliberate repetition of offenses. On December 9, 1860, he was reported "Late at breakfast"; on December 10, he made a point of being late again. On December 18, he received a demerit for "Not keeping dressed after having been spoken to marching from dinner"; the following day he committed the same infraction.[41] At West Point "taking a nut off the teacher's buggy for having been punished unjustly" may not have remained a realistic possibility, but there were other forms of resistance to authority.

The repetition of offenses represented one side of the pattern. On the other stood an open rejection of basic West Point values. If the ideal cadet was punctual, properly dressed, and carefully groomed, Janes developed a code of conduct that was distinctly his own. As his delinquencies indicate, he was incessantly late—to reveille, to breakfast, to parade, to inspection, to church, and finally, what few cadets could be accused of, "late marching off duty." In the area of dress he flouted the normal proclivity for neatness. "Coat not buttoned," "belt twisted," "shoes not blacked," "waist plate out of order," and "collar out of uniform" suggest the degree to which he refused to conform to dress ideals. His grooming was no better. Again and again there were reports for "hair not cropped" and conduct that was regarded slovenly—"hands in the sleeves of overcoat marching from breakfast," "overcoat soiled with mud," or simply "slip shod at reveille."[42]

Janes' resistance took other forms as well. While Thayer's rules had strictly forbidden the use of tobacco and alcohol at the Academy, a slight modification had been initiated on the smoking front by the time of Janes' arrival. Cadets who received written parental permission were allowed to smoke without punishment, but those without parental consent could be reported on the slightest suspicion. The absence of a signed permit did not inhibit Janes' indulgence. "Tobacco smoke in quarters" became a common entry on his list of demerits.[43] And in a curious way the discovery of his father's tobacco box, which had been a part of the process of becoming a man, was to remain a source of contention between Janes and his father, as well as between Janes and the Academy.

Drinking was another matter. The consumption of alcoholic beverages was strictly outlawed in the Academy's regulations. Cadets guilty of such a violation were subject to dismissal.[44] By the time of Janes' arrival at the Point, even the one exception to this rule, the liberal use of alcohol on the Fourth of July, had given way under the reforming zeal of the temperance movement. And yet, as in other areas, the official tightening of West Point's screws did not necessarily lead to enthusiastic compliance on the part of her cadets. Clandestine drinking mushroomed.

Spirited by nature, hemmed in by regulations, and largely deprived of normal social intercourse, many West Pointers found relief in sneaking off to local taverns. Clearly the most famous of these was Benny Havens'. Years earlier Benny Havens had been part of the legitimate West Point scene as a seller of coffee and cakes, but a willingness to provide thirsty cadets with "rum flips" soon got him into trouble with the authorities and led to his banishment from the Academy. Benny's response was to relocate just south of the school's jurisdiction, and until well after the Civil War his cabin was a favorite hangout for adventuresome cadets who sought a few hours release from the Academy's iron life.[45]

Benny was a fine storyteller, and his wife an excellent cook whose roast turkey and buckwheat cakes were as renowned as her husband's way with a bottle. Benny's deep sympathy with cadet life, his willingness to listen and give advice, and the genuine warmth of his place—which went beyond the warmth of the alcohol served—endeared both the cabin and its owner to generations of West Point cadets. Even the critical Edgar Allan Poe remembered Benny as the "sole congenial soul in the entire God-forsaken place."[46]

After-hours visits to Benny Havens' involved cadets, as Janes was well aware, in a constant cat-and-mouse struggle with their supervising officers. In what became an ongoing game, cadets tried to outwit their superiors, who were constantly in search of new strategems of their own. But despite temporary lapses, cadet ingenuity seems to have prevailed. There were generally sufficient numbers of cadets at the cabin to join in rousing choruses of "Benny Havens, Oh!" the cadets' favorite drinking song:

> Come fill your glasses, fellows, and stand up in a row;
> To singing sentimentally, we're going for to go;
> In the army there's sobriety, promotion's very slow,
> So we'll sing our reminiscences of Benny Havens, oh!
> Oh! Benny Havens, oh! oh! Benny Havens, oh!
> So we'll sing our reminiscences of Benny Havens, oh![47]

For Janes, who had previously chosen the conviviality of his Aunt Kitty's boarding house to the cool rigidity of the family farm under the Calvinistic paternal control of his father, Benny Havens' cabin clearly sided with his search for freedom. Here he could once more find a brief respite from the overbearing inflexibility of cadet life.

It is difficult to determine the extent to which Janes became a Benny Haven's regular. In later years he suppressed this phase of his life, and as a staunch, almost violent, opponent of intoxicants of all kinds, he wrote little about this aspect of his West Point career. There are, however, some clues that Janes' years as a cadet distinctly contradicted his later stand on the issue of alcohol. Whisky, far from an object of disaprobation, was often explicitly lauded in his writings. By the autumn of 1858, after the much looked forward to summer furlough between the Fourth and the Third Class years, Janes entered the difficult mechanics course of William H. C. Bartlett. On the fly leaf of Bartlett's mechanics text Janes scribbled the following lines, which suggest that his mind was not always on the professor's lessons or his demonstration models:

> Those ivory balls are fine toys
>   And Water's Bart's fluid you see,
> But the ball I love is a billiard ball,
>   And Whisky's the fluid for me.[48]

Unlike some cadets, Janes was not prepared to take solace in the Academy's beautiful setting, or in the wishful singing of "Army Blue":

> We've not much longer here to stay,
>   For in a year or two,
> We'll bid farewell to 'Cadet Gray,'
>   and don the 'Army Blue.'[49]

Janes' consolation continued to come from visits "south of Fort Putnam," the euphemism that was generally recorded in the delinquency records of cadets discovered in the vicinity of Benny Havens' cabin.[50]

As might be expected, Janes' mounting confrontation with West Point's authoritarian structure affected not only his delinquency record but also his class standing. Every cadet's position was determined by his academic achievements as well as his deportment. With rising demerits, Janes displayed an inverse academic slide. In 1858 he finished thirty-third out of a class of fifty-two. The following year he was forty-fourth out of fifty. The next year he dropped to forty-fifth. And in his final year, perhaps due to Nellie's influence, he managed to pull himself up to thirty-seventh out of a graduating class of forty-five.[51]

One of the curiosities of nineteenth-century West Point life was the deference shown by cadets for both the top and bottom of the Merit Roll. While those at the top were respected for their superior intellects and academic accomplishments, those at the bottom, the "immortals" as they came to be known, were admired for different reasons. Like aerialists performing a high wire act, Janes, Custer, and the other immortals were always one step away from disaster. The more deliberately and consciously they played their role, the more they appealed vicariously to the fantasies of their less daring classmates. Attractive as both polarities were to the prevalent American respect for intellectual prowess and independent action, it is hardly surprising that many of West Point's leaders came from the polar extremes of their classes. Judged from such a perspective, Janes' demerits, particularly the ninety-nine of his final six months' period, could be regarded as a tour de force leading to peer status, as well as a subconscious flirtation with disaster.

While Janes' testing of West Point's limits was an important component of his cadet experience it was not an all-encompassing, morose preoccupation. The piercing eyes could sparkle with humor as well as anger. Nor was he a dunce. West Point's curriculum demanded a high level of competence from all cadets. Janes' subsequent years of teaching at West Point and in Japan demonstrated his ability to master the subjects at hand. If there was a problem it stemmed from a propensity to work below his natural abilities, and to amuse himself in idle conversations with fellow cadets, as his reports indicated.[52]

Unwilling to treat his studies with the diligence of a Henry du Pont, Janes was nevertheless quite willing to provide original interpretations of his own. Next to one of Professor Bartlett's expositions of a basic law of physics, Janes wrote, "It is on this principle that the cheat of loaded dice is founded."[53] On another occasion he noted, "The Professor ought to be reported for 'washbowl not inverted.'"[54] This had been one of his own first demerits at the Academy. Occasionally his humorous asides took the form of verse, and often it was "Old Bart" who became the source of his inspiration. In response to Professor Bartlett's efforts to instill in his students an understanding of the principles of mass and velocity, Janes penned the following lines in his mechanics textbook:

> Professor Bartlett owns a very fine horse,
> This horse's name is "Living Force";
> He drives him almost every where,
> But chiefly round the M.V. Square (mv^2)[55]

Years later, in Kumamoto, Janes was to march his own students through the world of physics and the laws of mass and velocity squared. Moreover, he was to see his own vision of a "Living Force" behind these laws that was to change the lives of many of his young charges.

Despite the sustaining power of his humor, there were signs of a mounting inner crisis. While the sparkling eyes and carefree public posture tended to suggest an attitude of nonchalance—the perfect devil-may-care performance of the ideal immortal—the inner costs of that performance were great. The self-conscious rejection of his father's Calvinism may have been easy for a rebellious son, but breaking the subtle psychological ties to that Calvinism was another matter.

Even at West Point there were signs that he had absorbed more of his paternal legacy than he cared to admit. It is, of course, possible to read his delinquency record as indicative of his earlier struggle against authority, which had broken out at home and was now extended to the *in loco parentis* position of the Academy. On the other hand, there were some distinct contradictions to his behavior.

For example, Janes demonstrated a peculiar fondness for the study of ethics. In fact, ethics remained his strongest academic field.[56] And yet, his strange performance, his delinquencies and his prowess in ethics, underscored the difficult middle position in which he found himself. Unwilling to be bound, he was at the same time incapable of becoming free. Having opted for the side of rebellion, he found it increasingly difficult to sustain that rebellion without great inner turmoil. Somehow, despite all his efforts, he still could not penetrate the misty confusion that had shrouded his earlier years. Externally he had become something of a hero, internally he continued to have doubts.

Emotionally a rebel and intellectually committed to a search for truth, Janes' years at West Point reflect the contradictory elements of his personality that were to influence so much of his life. Head and heart were pulling him in different directions. On the one hand stood the world of reason and scientific clarity, the world of Locke and Rousseau and Bartlett's mechanics, on the other the uncharted realm of emotions and feelings, the world of natural sentiment he identified with Wordsworth and his mother's deep, emotional religiosity.

As an institution, West Point and the education it dispensed clearly sided with the rational and scientific, and consequently pressured him to move in these directions. On the other hand, as we have seen, such pressures were not accepted without an inner protest. Unknown to others, Janes was quite literally an emotional aerialist engaged in a desperate high wire performance that had nothing to do with the type of act that fascinated his fellow cadets. Having already experienced the emotional turmoil as a teenager of tilting in the direction of his mother as a result of his father's failure to sustain his carefully balanced posture, he now felt himself drawn in the opposite direction.

Compelled to recognize in himself an attraction to values he identified with his father, he was hardly pleased with the discovery. Indeed, increasingly conscious that the very qualities he disliked in his father were part of his own make-up, Janes began to direct the anger and criticism, once reserved for the father, against himself. To what extent this process was part of an effort to avoid giving in to either of the polarities of his personality, to avoid the psychological pain of his earlier experiences, or to overcome the guilt that such a tilt instilled in him toward the mother, we can only conjecture. What is clear is the fact that Janes' final West Point year was far more troubled than his carefree stand suggested.

Despite the distinct silence with which he subsequently treated this period of his life, there is some evidence that hints at the inner turmoil to which he was subject and which eventually contributed to his conversion. One of the puzzling features of most of Janes' later unpublished, semiautobiographical novels is the distinctly negative treatment reserved for the youth and early adulthoods of his principal male characters.[57] In one such work, in which the hero is brought up under the strict Calvinist supervision of his clergyman father, Janes writes: "The solitary boy with nothing to do, Greek and Latin to study, and the ministry of a similar creed and congregation his only prospect in life, at sixteen grew impatient, at seventeen rebellious, and at eighteen reprobate." Running away from home, the boy indulged in a life of dissipation from which he was eventually rescued through a severe illness and the ministrations of a young lady with whom he falls in love and under whose guidance he is converted to a new understanding of Christianity.[58]

What this theme, and its frequent repetition, indicates is that Janes' rebelliousness, both as a teenager and as a West Point cadet, was accompanied by a considerable sense of guilt. Moreover, that guilt became increasingly difficult to bear. In a revealing letter written to his mother some years later, Janes reviewed his youth and early manhood, showing that his external nonchalance concealed a deeper preoccupation with the type of "lurking selfishness" that other sensitive cadets identified as the dark underside of the West Point system.

The prevalent values of his generation, he wrote, were all too frequently a basic avarice. Such values emphasized "toiling and slaving, and *craving*" in order "to *get* and to *have*." The dominant concern of everyone was "getting on in the world." And "getting on," he wrote, meant "getting more titles to property." For American young people, he felt, the great lesson "in the very air around them" was to "get rich," "live easy," and believe that "you can do anything with money!" In the process, he wrote, "the sense of right and wrong, the generous enthusiasm, the love of learning, the glimpses the soul begins to take, the spiritual questionings, the aspirations for everything noble or great or true so easily kindled in young natures died out, became obscured in the dust of the hot pursuit of the all-conqueror gold, and in getting to the top of the heap."[59]

Janes' West Point years tend to suggest a certain affinity for the prevalent values of this generation. As a cadet he hardly conformed to the image of the "poor fellow who loves knowledge, and meditates on righteousness," which he later pictured to his mother as a more appropriate role model. There was as yet little evidence of any deep religious commitment. But the distinct before-and-after contrast of his subsequent evaluation indicates that his final years at West Point spelled the beginnings of a change in attitude that prefaced his subsequent conversion to the type of Christianity he was to take to Japan.[60]

If the years 1860 and 1861 marked a gradual transformation in the life of cadet Leroy Lansing Janes leading to a personal crisis a few years later, these years also witnessed an expanding national confrontation

that led to the outbreak of the Civil War, into which he was soon cat-
apulted as a fledgling officer in the Union Army.

As we have seen, the national debate over slavery and secession, which
had grown with each decade after 1830, was one in which Janes' family
had played a prominent part long before he reached the Academy. Despite
the strong sense of community among the cadets and the purposeful
isolation of West Pointers from the outside world, by the late 1850s it
was increasingly difficult to quarantine the Academy against the prevalent
political forces and the increasing pressure to choose sides. With John
Brown's raid on Harper's Ferry in 1858, West Point was thrown into
confusion. Tempers mounted and political arguments became common.
One southern cadet hanged John Brown's body in effigy, while another
challenged Emory Upton, an outspoken abolitionist, to a duel.[61]

The Upton fight revealed the degree to which political passions and
sectional divisions had reached the flash point.[62] Upton's unconcealed
support of the abolitionist position and his years at Oberlin College, a
school most southerners associated with the antislavery movement, marked
him as a special object of derision for many southern cadets. One of
these, Wade Hampton Gibbes of South Carolina, conscious of Oberlin's
willingness to admit both female and black students, accused Upton of
intimate relations with a black coed at the college. Unprepared to accept
such an allegation, Upton called for an apology. When none was offered,
he challenged Gibbes. In a fight, celebrated by classmates as "the battle
of the century," Upton and Gibbes went at each other in one of the rooms
of the First Division shortly after dinner on a cold December evening at
the close of 1858.[63] Fortunately there were no serious injuries, but as the
incident illustrated, it became increasingly obvious that neither the efforts
of the superintendent nor those of moderate cadets could stay the Academy's involvement in what Janes described as the Irrepressible Conflict.[64]

With the election of Abraham Lincoln to the presidency in the fall of
1860, North-South tensions reached the breaking point. A month before
the national election West Point cadets held their own presidential poll.
Under the supervision of several southern cadets an "election box" was
set up. Of the Academy's 278 cadets, 214 registered their preferences.
Ninety-nine voted for the Southern Democrat, John C. Breckenridge, 47
for the Northern Democrat, Stephen A. Douglas, 44 for the Constitutional
Union candidate, John Bell, and only 24 for the Republican, Abraham
Lincoln.[65] Ohio cadets were among the leading Lincoln supporters and
Janes, who in later years always had a portrait of Lincoln in his study,
joined his fellow Buckeyes in announcing for the president-to-be. In an
institution in which southern sympathies were deeply ingrained, support

for Lincoln and his party required not only courage but a willingness to defend one's views with more than words.

As might be expected, the November elections did little to alleviate the sectional divisions at West Point. As rumors of secession spread, cadets paid increasingly careful attention to letters and newspaper articles that arrived from home. On November 19, just thirteen days after Lincoln's victory, the first break in West Point's ranks took place with the resignation of cadet Henry S. Farley of South Carolina.[66] A month later South Carolina seceded from the Union, followed in rapid succession by Mississippi, Florida, Alabama, Georgia, and Texas. Even before Lincoln's inauguration the effects of the secession crisis were being widely felt at the Academy. By the end of December the remainder of the South Carolina cadets had departed. With them had gone several young men from Alabama and Mississippi. As more and more southern states withdrew from the Union in the winter and spring of 1861, the West Point exodus expanded. Eventually sixty-five of the Academy's eighty-six southern cadets resigned.[67]

One of the favorite pastimes of Janes and those who remained was to speculate on who would be leaving next. Cadets were not the only ones to make difficult choices. Many of their officers and teachers found themselves equally torn between their army and sectional loyalties. In some cases the choice was easy. In January Captain P.T.G. Beauregard took the place of Richard Delafield as superintendent of the Academy. When approached by one troubled cadet for advice, Beauregard is recorded to have replied: "Watch me; and when I jump, you jump. What's the use of jumping too soon."[68] With such counsel it is hardly surprising that Beauregard lasted a mere five days as superintendent. When word of this reached Washington he was quickly replaced by the more trustworthy Delafield.[69] It was the same Beauregard, one has to add, however, who after "jumping" took command of the Confederate forces in Charleston, and under whose orders the opening volley of the Civil War was fired on April 12, 1861.[70] Pulling the lanyard on the cannon that fired the first shot at Fort Sumter was the former West Pointer, Wade Hampton Gibbes.[71]

With the firing on Fort Sumter, West Point's drums took on the distinct sound of war drums. On the very evening of the day that Beauregard's orders and Gibbes' enthusiastic compliance inscribed themselves once and for all in the annals of American history, Janes, Emory Upton, and their fellow northern cadets gathered in one of the Academy's rooms to sing "The Star Spangled Banner" with such intensity that it could be heard at Constitution Island across the river.[72] Morris Schaff, one of the Ohio cadets, recalled that this was the first occasion on which he saw the southern contingent cowed. "All their northern allies had deserted them, and they were stunned."[73] The following day there were patriotic speeches by many of the Academy's professors, including several of southern birth. A few weeks later, under the direction of the new superintendent, Major Alexander H. Bowman, all cadets were ordered to sign a new oath of allegiance to the United States.[74]

By the latter part of April, the Civil War dominated life at the Academy. Southern cadets were leaving the Academy on a daily basis. Those who remained, northerners and southerners alike, found it difficult to concentrate on their studies. Many West Pointers shared the general public opinion that the war would be of short duration. Quite possibly only one gigantic battle would be fought, after which the victorious side would march on the capital of the losers, seize it, and restore order. Convinced of such a scenario the Academy's cadets, particularly those of Janes' class, which was scheduled to graduate in the summer of 1861, were increasingly anxious about their confinement at West Point.

Books and examinations meant little when every potential Napoleon dreamed of leading his own company or battery into action. Letters from southern cadets, reporting their rapid rise in the ranks of the Confederacy, did little to assuage their discontent. Many cadets looked upon war as a golden opportunity. With daring and a little luck they might well secure a captaincy, or even a colonelcy, ranks that peacetime officers rarely achieved before middle age. Hearing that midshipmen at Annapolis were being allowed to graduate early to enter the war, Janes and his fellow classmates petitioned the Secretary of War to accelerate their graduation and order them to active duty.[75] To their delight the request was granted. The June examinations were advanced to May, and on May 6, without the normal graduation ceremony, or the three months leave granted by the Regulations, the class of 1861 graduated and was immediately ordered to Washington, to train the volunteer army that was assemblying there to defend the capital.[76]

Janes had deeply mixed feelings during his final six months at West Point. Like Custer he was restless. A part of that restlessness stemmed from the inner turmoil to which he was subject. And yet, much of it could also be attributed to a sense of ambition and the compelling need to make something of himself. In the spring of 1861 he had not yet rejected the success values that he regarded typical of his generation and which he was subsequently to encourage among his students in Kumamoto. Moreover, West Point, despite all protestations to the contrary, was indeed an elitist institution. Graduates of the Academy, as Janes was well aware, could look forward not only to significant military careers, but also to important positions of public trust and responsibility. As he reached the end of his five-year struggle and could look beyond the

Academy's walls to the glowing prospects of a bright future, he was overwhelmed by a sense of achievement that had eluded him previously. With graduation virtually at hand came a sense of pride and accomplishment. The mere realization that they had survived, while more than half of their fellow entrants had fallen by the wayside, provided Janes and his classmates with a strong sense of camaraderie and a solid esprit de corps.

Despite the moodiness and occasional volatility that continued to find reflection in his delinquency record, Janes appears to have differed little from his classmates. For all of them, the outbreak of war imposed a new and deep sense of immediacy that transcended personal concerns. Faced with the realization that he would soon be called upon to utilize his classroom learning on the battlefield, Janes' academic performance improved significantly. In spite of his overwhelming delinquencies, he managed to pull himself up nearly ten places in the Merit Order by the final May examinations. What is more important, he seems to have earned the respect of the Academic Board. For most West Point cadets, commissions were heavily determined by their Merit Roll standings. The top five graduates of each class were assured positions in the Corp of Engineers, the Army's elite branch for West Pointers. After the engineers came ordnance and artillery, which was followed by cavalry, and at the bottom stood the infantry. Immortals almost always found themselves recommended as second lieutenants to infantry regiments. Graduating thirty-seventh in his class of forty-five, Janes too should have been assigned to such a unit, but to his surprise and delight he was ordered to the artillery, the only member of the bottom twelve of his class to be granted such an appointment.[77]

On May 7, 1861, Janes and his fellow classmates, now duly graduates of the Academy, left West Point for New York City. Here they remained just long enough to outfit themselves as officers. Janes purchased the appropriate uniform, including an officer's pistol, sword, and spurs. By six o'clock of the same day, now dressed smartly in a blue dress uniform that enhanced his well-conditioned twenty-four-year-old's frame and sparkling blue eyes, he climbed aboard the first available train for Philadelphia and Washington. Like others on the train speeding toward their destinies, Janes was determined to make a name for himself. Little did he or his classmates realize as they narrowed the distance between themselves and the nation's capital what the full effects of the coming months and years would mean for them and their country.

CHAPTER III

WAR, LOVE, AND CONVERSION

THE TWENTY-FOUR-YEAR-OLD JANES who sped to Washington with other members of his class was thoroughly optimistic. As he later wrote, he entered active service in 1861 at the outbreak of the war in possession of an unusually powerful frame and robust constitution. "My every organ and faculty was to the best of my knowledge in perfect condition, and I was full of enthusiasm and ambition."[1]

Like other members of his class, Janes' task in Washington was to train the many citizen soldiers who flooded the capital in response to President Lincoln's May 3 proclamation calling for a volunteer army of forty thousand men. By the end of May Janes was fully occupied drilling and fitting out the 1st Rhode Island Battery of Light Artillery to which he was assigned on detached duty from the Second U.S. Artillery.[2] Commanding the Rhode Island Volunteers was the tough and crusty former West Pointer, Colonel Ambrose E. Burnside, whose name, through a dyslectic twist, was to be long associated with his style of bewhiskered visage. A photograph of Burnside and his officers taken in the summer of 1861 reveals that the Colonel was not the only individualist in his command. Standing behind Burnside—the only member of the assembled group of officers who appears to have refused to take off his cap—one can find a jaunty Janes, whose flashing eyes and pose tend to underscore that the defiance of his cadet years had not entirely dissipated under the pressures of the approaching conflict.[3]

By early June, Janes' efforts to prepare his volunteer battery for action were rewarded by a quick promotion from second to first lieutenant.[4] As the North and the South squared off for their first major confrontation at Bull Run, he left behind the safety of Washington for service in the field. Here the official record speaks for itself:

> In operations in the Shenandoah Valley, June to Oct., 1861; on sick leave of absence, Oct. 21 to Nov. 26, 1861; in the Defense of Washington, D.C., Nov.–Dec., 1861; in Defense of Ft. Pickens, Fla., Jan. to May, 1862; on Quartermaster and Commissary duty at Pensacola, Fla., May to Aug., 1862; as Aide-de-Camp to Brig. General Arnold, Sep. 1862, to Mar. 24, 1863; and on sick leave of absence, Mar. 24 to July 4, 1863. Served: at the Military Academy, 1863–65, as Asst. Instructor of Infantry and Artillery Tactics, Aug. 29,

1863 to Aug. 5, 1865,—and Asst. Professor of Geography, History, and Ethics, Sep. 1, 1863, to Oct. 10, 1864; (Captain, 2nd Artillery, June 15, 1864); in command of Company at Ft. Stevens, Or., Oct., 1865, to Dec. 1867. Resigned, Dec. 9, 1867.[5]

While this list of dates and places presents the formal record of Janes' military service, it reveals little of the personal odyssey that marked these years and significantly affected his subsequent career. In determining the impact of the Civil War on his physical and emotional health we have to turn to other sources.

In 1874, some thirteen years after the Battle of Bull Run, Janes penned a letter from his school in Kumamoto to a woman he addressed as "My Dear Anna." In this letter he tried to explain why he had not written her in three years. Shortly after arriving in Japan, he noted, "a little book of Susan's came which has its own share of this delay to bear." He thought the book was "intended to have just that effect." It was one in which the names of "Fanny, Leroy, *Nellie*, Hattie—are used." Whatever the purpose, it inspired "silence in me, and for a time pain." In consequence he felt the book to be "unworthy of Susan."[6]

Janes' reference to Anna and Susan, particularly to the latter's book, deserves closer scrutiny. Susan Bogert Warner and Anna Bartlett Warner were hardly strangers to the mid-nineteenth century American reading public.[7] In 1851 Susan Warner published *The Wide, Wide World*, a novel which became a major best seller in America and Europe. This was the first American novel to reach a circulation of more than 100,000 copies. Later in the 1850s Susan added another best seller, *Queechy*, and her younger sister Anna published *Dollars and Cents*, which also ended high on the Putnam lists. In the decades that followed Susan and Anna Warner were to write more than eighty-five novels, essays, and short stories. Susan's rise to prominence with *The Wide, Wide World*, a work which superseded even Harriet Beecher Stowe's *Uncle Tom's Cabin* (1852) in initial popularity, made her one of the major figures in the "feminine fifties," a decade in which, to quote the opinion of Nathaniel Hawthorne, America was "given over to a damned mob of scribbling women."[8]

The Warner Sisters, as they were generally known, lived with their father, Henry, and their Aunt Fanny at Constitution Island, the jut of land across the Hudson from West Point. Henry Warner had started his career as a successful lawyer in New York City. He had acquired Constitution Island as a result of a speculative venture undertaken by his brother, Thomas Warner, who was chaplain and professor of geography, history, and ethics at West Point from 1827 to 1837.[9] Although the site was initially intended for a summer retreat, financial setbacks in the 1840s forced the Warners to give up their New York home and settle at the island on a more permanent basis. It was the same financial necessity that eventually led Susan and Anna to make efforts to supplement the family's meager income through literary work.

Janes' familiarity with the Warners was hardly accidental. The history of the Warners, like that of the Janes family, was closely associated with the upper reaches of the Hudson. Two generations earlier, Leroy's grandfather, Roger Janes, had married Elizabeth Warner, the daughter of William Warner, for whom Leroy's older brother was named. William Warner's younger brother, Jason, was Susan and Anna's grandfather. In short, Leroy, Susan, and Anna were distant cousins.[10]

That Janes was familiar with Constitution Island can be readily ascertained from his letters. Writing from Kumamoto in 1875 he observed that his thoughts centered "more and more around West Point and the Island." "What an iron life those five years were, dear Anna," he wrote, "and yet, what sweetness and tenderness fill all the other two and a half years of my association with West Point." "And dear Susan and Anna," he confided, "no one on earth knows aright of this but you at the Island."[11]

Janes' correspondence indicates a particular closeness to Anna, and it is easy to presume that the Warners, who lived in considerable isolation and often suffered from an intense loneliness, were only too delighted to receive calls from their West Point cousin. Indeed, had it not been for later tragic circumstances we would probably know a great deal more about his years at the Academy and at the Island.

About Janes' first wife, Nellie, who was closely associated with these years, we know less. Although Janes specifically identified Nellie with Susan's novel, he rarely mentioned her. We do know that her real name was Helen Frances Robinson, and that her father, Eleazer Robinson, was a well-to-do manufacturer of Quaker background. She married Janes on December 11, 1862, and died of consumption at her father's home on December 15, 1864.[12] But even these few details would not have been recorded if the Commissioner of Pensions, after a futile search of the Department of Army records, had not insisted that the family provide affidavits in reference to the "conjugal state of this officer" while on active duty from 1856 to 1867.[13]

The only direct historical evidence of Janes' feelings for Nellie are found in his letters to the Warners. From Kumamoto he wrote to Susan and Anna: "You know I spoke not much to you of Nellie—there seemed to be not much call for words about her, when we had occasion to recall those days sometimes. But dear Anna and Susan the memory has come back to me very often of late with an overpowering sense of loss. That gentle nature, so mild, so sweet, so tender, yet with a power all its own that made it so strong, so ardent, so prevailing, which drew me to it just twenty-five years ago, calls out to me again from the nearer past, and my heart has stopped more than once recently to answer the call."[14]

"Dear Anna, there are houses in that mountain town where she lived that to this day will have the places in them where she sat pointed out to you and remembered as almost sacred." Houses of the "poor," the "lowly," and the "suffering," he elucidated. It was Nellie's Christian faith, Janes felt, that expressed itself not merely through a "love of the poor," but in a "strength and hope inspiring influence," a "lifting up," and "cheering away" that was "strangely in contrast with the mild manners, and the delicate frame that exercised it." And he observed that much of his life, "these ten years under God," had been strongly influenced by her faith and inspiration. Janes was convinced that Nellie was somehow with him in his work in Japan. As he wrote, "she sympathizes with me in it all," and he added, "I have the evidence" for this "in my own heart."[15]

Except in his letters to Anna and Susan, Janes never mentioned his first wife. In none of the many official forms he was required to fill out did he list his first marriage.[16] Moreover, in 1868 Frederic Janes published *The Janes Family*, a thorough and comprehensive genealogy. In this work the children of Elisha Janes are clearly listed. The marriages of Leroy's brother William to Julia Chapin, and that of his sister Ellen to L. A. Anderman, which took place in 1862, are accurately recorded. Leroy, for his part, is listed as a "teacher at West Point," but there is no reference to his marriage![17] What is equally strange is the fact that Elisha Janes submitted autobiographical sketches to at least three prominent local history publications in which he recorded the names of his children and their spouses. The only marriage for Leroy that is recorded is to "a daughter of Dr. Scudder" in "San Francisco."[18]

The concealment of his marriage to Helen Robinson, who so dramatically influenced his later years, is difficult to explain. But as their romance inspired one of Susan Warner's novels, we have at least a fictionalized version of their relationship.

In 1868 and 1869 Susan Warner published a two-volume novel, *Daisy*.[19] *Daisy* narrates the story of a young southern heiress, Daisy Randolph, whose father and mother have gone abroad for the father's health, and who is sent north to attend a finishing school in New York City. Daisy is a devout Christian and her religious beliefs have convinced her that slavery is wrong. In fact, she has quietly made up her mind that she will not manage her estate as her father and uncle have, using slave labor, even though this may mean her economic demise.

Possessed of a delicate constitution, Daisy is described as constantly in precarious health, and it is for this reason that her guardian, Dr. Sanford, decides to take her to West Point for the summer, where the air is cool and dry, and she can escape the New York heat. In searching for a southern cousin, Preston Gary, who is also a cadet at the Military Academy, Daisy encounters another cadet, Christian Thorold, with whom a romance unfolds. Cadet Thorold invites her to several summer dances, takes her to Old Fort Putnam, and begins to fall in love with her. This is rather troubling for Daisy, for Christian, despite his name, does not entirely share her Christian convictions. Moreover, she feels tempted by the spontaneous joy she experiences at the hops and in being with Christian. In an effort to deal with her inner turmoil she decides to terminate her relationship with Thorold and refuses to attend any more of the West Point dances. Dr. Sanford soon helps by taking her back to New York.

But Christian is not ready to forget her. Through fortuitous circumstances the two meet again in New York at the home of his distant aunt, whom Daisy has come to know independently. This meeting takes place shortly before Thorold rushes off to war. On this occasion he declares his love, and Daisy, apparently overcoming her reluctance of the previous summer, pledges herself to him, insisting only that he should properly request her father's approval for the marriage.

Before Christian can do this, the war has swept him and other members of his class to Washington, where he is described as busily training artillery volunteers. Daisy soon follows him in the company of Dr. and Mrs. Sanford. After a brief and concealed courtship in Washington, Christian is ordered to take his battery cross-country to General Patterson. When Daisy inquires, "What is General Patterson doing?" Christian answers, "I suppose he has to keep Johnston in order."[20]

As Christian is swallowed up by the campaigns of the Civil War, Daisy temporarily leaves the United States to visit her mother and father in Europe. While abroad she constantly awaits the arrival of Christian's letter to her father asking for her hand—a letter which has gone astray, but which finally arrives a year late. After returning to the United States, Daisy hears that her cousin, Preston Gary, has been seriously wounded and rushes to the hospital to care for him. At the same hospital she also encounters Christian Thorold, who has not been wounded, but who is suffering from internal injuries which the doctor declares are far more serious than those of Preston. In the end, the previously healthy and robust young officer wastes away and dies in the army hospital, while the delicate Daisy survives to devote her life to a career of Christian service.

Like other Warner novels now mercifully confined to the dusty shelves reserved for nineteenth-century didactic Christian fiction, *Daisy* is of minor literary importance. The Warners were far from powerful creative writers, and by the 1860s both sisters relied heavily on stories told them by others, from which they culled their characters and situations. Increasingly rigid in their Christian faith, they rationalized this approach as representing a certain discomfort with fiction and an attraction to a more honest approach to literature in which the didactic impact of slightly fictionalized real-life accounts could achieve its maximum impact.[21] Given this approach, it is not surprising that most Warner characters remain wooden and unconvincing. Moreover, this is particularly true of male characters, for whom the isolated spinster sisters possessed few models.

Mabel Baker, a knowledgeable student of the Warners' novels, has recently written that in Christian Thorold, Susan Warner produced "the only male character in any of her writings who does not demand more than a headlong suspension of disbelief in order to be tolerated much less credited as anything but a manikin whose presence is required for structural balance."[22] Baker concluded that Thorold must have embodied a cadet Susan had met at West Point many years earlier while her uncle Thomas Warner was chaplain at the Academy. Baker's failure to identify Janes as the model stems understandably from the vengeance with which Susan and Anna eventually rubbed out every hint of their relationship to their cousin.[23]

Nonetheless, Janes did serve as the model for Thorold. Christian is presented as the son of a northern farmer and land owner.[24] Daisy first meets him on the omnibus coming up from the West Point landing. As she watched him walk into the library after a brief conversation, she noted, "he was tall, very erect, with a fine free carriage and a firm step."[25] A few days later she met her friend from the omnibus again, noting, "I think we liked each other at this very first moment. I looked up at a manly, well-featured face, just then lighted with a little smile of deference and recognition; but permanently lighted with the brightest and quickest hazel eyes that I ever saw. Something about the face pleased me on the instant. I believe it was the frankness."[26]

Despite Susan's poetic license, which transformed his naturally blue eyes into hazel and at the same time shifted his origins from Ohio to Vermont, it was precisely Janes' eyes that fascinated Susan as much as others who knew him. Daisy tells us, "Mr. Thorold's eyes were dancing and flashing and sparkling with fifty things by turns; their fund of amusement and power of observation were the first things that struck me, and they attracted me too."[27]

But Daisy's attraction is described as transcending Christian's gaze. "There was a wealth of life in him, that delighted my quieter nature,"

Daisy records, "an amount of animal spirits that was just a constant little impetus to me; and from the first I got an impression of strength, such as weakness loves to have near. Bodily strength he had also, in perfection; but I mean now the firm self-reliant nature, quick at resources, ready to act as to decide, and full of the power that has its spring and magazine in character alone."[28]

Drawn in the years following Janes' conversion, the portrait of Christian Thorold bears the stamp of Susan Warner's rigorous Christian polishing, which glosses over a good deal of what we have already observed as part of Janes' less idealized West Point record. In fact, there are several occasions in the West Point portion of *Daisy* when the historic Janes reminds us more of Preston Gary, Daisy's somewhat dishevelled southern cousin, than of Christian Thorold.[29]

Caught up in the events of the summer of 1860, Daisy finds herself amidst the mounting tensions between northern and southern cadets at the Academy. Reminded that she is the daughter of a southern gentleman, she is constantly advised by her cousin to avoid Yankees, who he insists are a "mean set."[30] Daisy later hears of a fight between Thorold and southern cadets of Preston's disposition. Indeed, it was not long, Susan writes, before "unlovely and confused visions" appeared before Daisy which focused on "quarrels between the people where I was born and the people where I was brought up."[31]

With the outbreak of war the correspondence between Janes and Christian Thorold becomes even more distinct. Daisy soon receives letters from Washington, where Christian has been sent after a hurried and accelerated graduation from West Point. The letters tell of his "drilling raw soldiers," being "in the saddle all day," and feeling "very happy."[32] Before long she follows him to Washington with the Sanfords. In the quiet weeks before the storm of war erupts their romance blossoms. Daisy notes, "Mr. Thorold and I had walks continually together."[33] Fearful that her father would not approve of her marriage to a northern officer, she tries to convince Christian not to ask for her hand until the war is over. But he regards such an approach as cowardly.

During those brief June days of 1861 Daisy tried to spend as much time as possible watching Christian drill his battery of light artillery and went for walks with him after he finished his day's work. "The extreme gravity of the time and the interests at work, lent only a keen and keener perception of their preciousness and sweetness," Susan writes.[34] As Daisy was only too aware, "any day our opportunities might suddenly come to an end; every day they were welcomed as a special fresh gift. Every evening, as soon as Mr. Thorold's engagements allowed it, he met me on the avenue, and we walked until the evening was as far spent as we durst spend it so. I basked in the sunshine of care and affection which surrounded me, which watched me, which catered to my pleasure, and knew my thoughts before they were spoken. We were both grown suddenly older than our years, Mr. Thorold and I; the coming changes and chances in our lives brought us to life's reality at once."[35]

But the precious moments were not to last. Soon Major Fairbairn (Burnside?) informs her that things are "Getting to be serious earnest," and that he feels it would be best for her to leave Washington. "Beauregard is making ready for us at Manassas Junction," Fairbairn adds, and he has his doubts about what the outcome will be.[36] Later the same day Christian hastens to the Sanford's hotel to tell Daisy that he has received orders to take his battery of light artillery to General Patterson, and that he must leave within the hour.[37]

Here Susan's fictional account synchronizes perfectly with the historical record. Janes was indeed ordered, as he later wrote, to take his volunteer battery of light artillery (1st Rhode Island) into the Shenandoah Valley just prior to the first Battle of Bull Run to join up with General Patterson, who was to prevent Johnston from joining Beauregard.[38] Civil War historians have often argued that Patterson's failure to prevent this crucial link up cost the North the Battle of Bull Run, and, as we shall see, this campaign was also to prove extremely costly for Janes.[39]

And yet, before following Janes into the Civil War, we must pursue the question of Nellie somewhat further. If the portrait of Daisy that Susan Warner paints in her novel is in fact based on Helen Robinson, as Janes' letter from Kumamoto tends to suggest, then there remains the question of historical reliability. In the novel it is Christian Thorold who dies, and Daisy who survives, when in real life we know the opposite was the case. This contradiction can be understood only in the context of 1868–69, the years in which Susan Warner wrote and published the second volume of *Daisy*. What is important at this juncture is the fictionalized description of Nellie that is suggested by Susan in her novel. If Nellie was the daughter of a southern plantation owner, an heiress to extensive lands, a devout Christian, a confirmed—if quiet—abolitionist, and a young lady well-educated in northern schools, why did a northern landowner father, a Christian and abolitionist, not welcome her with open arms into his family? Indeed, if the historical evidence we now have is correct, which challenges Nellie's southern roots but confirms her father as a wealthy man—the leading figure of the city in which he resided—it still remains extremely difficult to explain why the marriage was not accepted by his parents or recorded in the Janes family genealogy. Why, for that matter, should Janes himself never have mentioned the marriage in any of the appropriate documents?

It is possible that we shall never fully unravel this mystery. In fact, Janes has added to the problem. In his later writings the Captain suggested a version of this relationship that defies both the Warner account and the historical record as we know it. Janes' story is certainly intriguing.

In his novel, "Out of Stony Lonesome,"[40] which like his other fictional works was never published, Janes presents the usual scenario of a young man given over to a life of dissipation, from which he is converted to new values through illness and the kind ministrations of an appropriate heroine. As we have seen, portions of this novel are distinctly autobiographical. But like other of his later writings it contains little to recommend it as literature. If Susan and Anna had trouble in creating convincing characters and personalities, Janes was light years behind his cousins in creative literary talent. Quite frankly, the one redeeming feature of the insufferably dreary didactic writing of his final years lies in the fact that its creative portions are so palpably contrived and stiff that interesting passages are invariably the result of direct personal experiences that have been subjected to the thinnest of fictional veneers.

Given Janes' letters to Anna in which he identifies Nellie with his conversion, "these ten years under God," it seems advisable to examine the manuscript of "Out of Stony Lonesome" with greater care. Reading through the initial chapters of the novel, in which a Mr. Ransom tells his life story to his granddaughter, even the dedicated reader will find himself struggling with ennui over the author's interminable lessons. But suddenly he finds himself wide awake! What has aroused his attention is not the personal history of Grandfather Ransom, but the introduction of a second personal history, which, like Susan's depiction of Christian Thorold, prompts the reader to spring to life with curiosity and to turn the folio pages with anticipation.

Having finished with the background of his hero, Janes depicts him "emotionally dejected" and "physically ill" on a canal boat from which he is taken with a raging fever to a nearby school house. His fever soon turns to delirium. Coming out of his delirious state he has no idea where he is or how long he has been there. "Never can I forget," Janes has him observe, "the deep impression which my first conscious view of the material world about me presented to my mind. I had lain in a prolonged sleep, near the open window that faced the magnificent avenue of mountain peaks, as the lofty hills appeared for the moment to be . . . I was entranced. I covered my face with my hands, to adjust my consciousness of returning life, to assure myself that it was not all a dream." He was "half afraid," Janes wrote, "to look again upon the transcendently impressive scene, so sublime, so beautiful, so ecstatic, to his unused faculties." "It was as if I had been born again in mature manhood," he observed, "with the innocent and tender sensibilities of an infant, and the ripened capacities of middle age, so intimately blended as to obliterate for the time all recollection of my former self."[41]

If the foregoing scene reveals the emotional impact of Janes' illness, the joy of having survived, and its close relationship to a spiritual conversion he underwent in its wake—all historical events that we shall soon encounter—it also introduced, as he wrote, a "face and form that haunt me to this moment like a dream of ineffable goodness and beauty."[42] That face, he tells us through his hero, belonged to the schoolteacher at the "Lone Lock School House." And it was under her care that Ransom was nursed back to health through many weeks of a slow recovery. "Pale but beautifully proportioned," that face hovered over him, Janes writes, "the eyes and the hair that waved itself into immense and glossy folds, were both dark, ample, and glowing with the kindly but subdued expression of superior womanhood. The cheeks and lips, and perfect, pearly teeth, the whole contour in short of face and neck and figure," he added, "bore an impress of a rare and wholesome beauty that completely stole my weakened sense from me, and of matured character that humbled me into silent wonder."[43]

Days pass and Janes' protagonist falls in love with the schoolteacher. After detailing his own past, with all its failings, he is about to ask her to marry him, when she explains that she, too, has a past that needs explaining. It is at this point that we start reading with greater speed and concentration.

> I am from the middle south, my name is Mary. My father's name was Grayson. I never saw, to know, my mother. She was an octoroon. My father and master took me from my mother's arms before she died, with a sworn promise to raise me as his own. He was young then. He married. Other children, five in all, came of that marriage. I was reared by the new mother as her own child under a promise my father exacted, he having told her all, previous to their marriage. Her promise she kept religiously. His, he fulfilled to the letter.
>
> I was educated at home, at the North, and in travel abroad. But I loved the home life. My tastes were, above all, domestic. My three halfbrothers and two halfsisters were just the reverse in most of their inclinations. This resulted in my being placed in a manner above them in the management of the household when my stepmother died. That was the fatal mistake my well meaning father made. My three stepbrothers grew up in uncontrollable license. They were much away from home in the society of fellow roysterers. My two step-

sisters were very proud. They grew up gay, giddy fashionables. I taught them all they would learn, and as our father grew old and helpless—early for one of his years—I was the more frequently tainted with my sixteenth of alien blood, as a reward for my endeavors. An angel could not have been more conscientiously devoted or dutious or helpful.

I had all the vigor and stamina of my father's young manhood, and a share of his fine mind; for I delighted in books, and craved every form of knowledge. I had the healthy and strong physical development of my mother which only the blast of a yellow fever epidemic could subdue. I inherited her features, her refined and happy disposition, and—the curse of her slave extraction. My brothers and sisters were of the mold of their mother, a consumptive. I always thought that my father paid with his life for his relationship to my stepmother. Anyhow, almost from the beginning of that connection a strange weakness seemed to have seized upon his vitals.

When my father too died, I felt that under the circumstances the burden of my obligations had been discharged. The brutal treatment of the boys became intensified, under the fear that I might have been preferred in the will, as I certainly had been in life. But there was no will, and there was no property left to quarrel over. If legal provision for my freedom had ever been perfected the proof of it must have been surreptitiously destroyed. My father had made a modest provision for me, in cash, while it was still within his power; and his paternal injunction, "waste not, want not," served through sheer habit of obedience to keep it in tact against the hour of need.

That hour came when I overheard my stepsisters, in secret, discuss plans for turning me into a gold and silver provision for their pressing needs.

Gathering my effects together I shipped them North in my own name, which had been my father's also, and with no concealment whatever. Accustomed to the writing of "passes," in due form, I prepared one for myself, for which indeed I had no occasion. It was never once demanded of me. Then, in broad daylight I travelled Northward, by the usual conveyances. Abandoning the stage coach, somewhere in this reputed land of freedom, I sought rest, with my slender effects, on the Canal Packet that eventually brought me to this solitary retreat. To the good "Captain" of our last boat and the equally kind manager here I owe my immediate engagement to teach the Lone Lock children. Here I have been over two years. No one knows, nor shall know, my history till the curse of slavery is cancelled in the blood of the coming revolution. I am taken as a widow with a past too sorrowful to be intruded upon.[44]

It is not long after this revelation that the protagonist of Janes' novel marries the schoolteacher. Later in the same work we are given a glimpse of Mary Grayson's graveside in the cemetery of a mountain town where she lies buried between her two infant children.

Was Nellie the daughter of an octoroon slave and a southern plantation owner? Is this the reason a cloak of silence surrounds Janes' first marriage? Moreover, is this the reason why his family refused to recognize the marriage, and why the Captain never mentioned it in any official communications in later years?

It remains difficult to say. While Janes' novel suggests some unexpected possibilities, the evidence for any such conclusion remains highly speculative and defies at least the surface reading of the historical record.[45] Helen Robinson, if we can trust the documentation we have, was the daughter of Eleazer Robinson and Cornelia Wells.[46] While the Robinson family did have a middle south connection, Eleazor and his family clearly stemmed from the North, and barring a silent adoption for which we have no evidence, Nellie, too, appears to have been born in Pennsylvania.

Janes' direct comments on Nellie further complicated the issue. In his letter to Anna in 1875 he noted that he had been attracted to Nellie some twenty-five years earlier.[47] Given his weak memory for dates it is not safe to interpret this statement too literally, but it would suggest that he had met Nellie sometime before his arrival at the United States Military Academy in 1856.[48] In fact, if we were to adjust the "twenty-five years" to "twenty years," the period of their initial meeting would fit neatly between his year at the Albany Academy and his matriculation at West Point. It is precisely for this period that there is a brief reference in his autobiographical notes to an "incident at Oberlin." What occurred at Oberlin we are never told. Certainly Janes never attended Oberlin as a student.[49] And yet Oberlin was a leading abolitionist institution, and this school was to become an issue at West Point precisely because allegations were made that certain northern cadets had fraternized there with coeds of black descent. Historians of the Academy have usually associated these rumors with unwarrantable charges made against Emory Upton, which led to the fight already mentioned. What Susan Warner's novel indicates, however, is that Janes, or to be precise Christian Thorold, his fictional counterpart, was also involved in the fighting that erupted over such tensions. Janes was a close friend of John I. Rodgers, Emory Upton's roommate and second in the celebrated duel, and it is conceivable that the original rumors included allegations against Janes as well as Upton.[50]

There is one portion of Janes' letter to Anna that seems to underscore the interpretation he presented in his fictional account. Writing of his efforts to transcend the racial prejudice common to most Westerners living in Japan in the 1870s—efforts which may well have aided his particular effectiveness as a teacher in Kumamoto—he noted that it was his relationship with Nellie that was chiefly responsible for his own transformation. It was Nellie, he wrote, who "showed me how first the unlovely may become lovable, and how the barriers we are oft to call natural, become no barriers at all, but one broad field of love." It was she, he added, who "made it possible for the interest that constrained me in Maryland, in the children of the negro sabbath school to deepen into love for them." And it was the same influence, he insisted, that kindled in his heart "a love, a genuine love" for the "yellow skinned" Japanese with whom he worked in Kumamoto.[51]

Whatever the mystery surrounding Nellie may have been, and much of it remains, it is clear that she played an important role in his conversion to Christianity and that her deep personal faith and early tragic death were to have a profound effect on his later years.

If Nellie served as one catalyst that led to his inner transformation, the other was the Civil War.

As the twenty miles of bloodied Virginia countryside starkly demonstrated, Bull Run rudely dispelled all notions of a quick and easy victory for either side. The battle's reality, its thousands of injured, maimed, and dead, seriously undermined the romantic notions with which most northerners and southerners had entered the conflict. For West Pointers such as Janes who had rushed to Washington seeking "promotions or a coffin," the specter of the latter, once little more than a dim possibility, began to loom with new and menacing proportions.[52]

The fatal thing about Bull Run, as the northern general McDowell later wrote, was Patterson's inability to keep Johnston from joining Beauregard.[53] It was precisely Patterson's inaction, his unwillingness to attack Johnston without reinforcements, that led to Janes' hasty departure from Washington with his Rhode Island Battery. With Bull Run lost, and the Union Army retreating toward Washington, it was only a matter of time before pressures at the northern end of the Shenandoah Valley would also increase. It was here that Patterson and Banks were to try to take the remaining northern forces across the Potomac River at Harpers Ferry. Janes' newly arrived battery was almost immediately thrown into action to cover the retreat.[54]

In dealing with his Harpers Ferry experiences, it may be best to let Janes speak for himself:

Returning out of the Shenandoah Valley in July 1861 with the Army under Patterson and Banks retreating before General Joe Johnston's greatly superior force, the 1st Rhode Island Battery which I had drilled at Washington and fitted for the field, and to which I had been temporarily attached by a special order, was of the rear guard of that army. The weather was intensely dry and hot, and I worked day and night to secure the retreat of that army. When *it* was safe across the Potomac, I was left behind insensible from sun stroke. To the best of my knowledge I lay four or five weeks so exposed and secreted with such attention only as could be conveyed across the Potomac into a town picketed by Confederate Cavalry. Thence I was removed in stealth by Major Hall, and conveyed in a hospital car to Frederick City, Md. and to the Camden St. Hospital at Baltimore, Md.[55]

While there is some confusion as to whether Janes fell from his horse insensible on the road to Harpers Ferry, or whether he collapsed while walking, there is no question that he was gravely ill, and at least for several days in what appears to have been a deep coma.[56] John I. Rodgers, Emory Upton's roommate and Janes' close friend, penned a letter to his mother on August 2 in which he expressed the general concern that all held for her son's life. According to Rodgers, Janes had been feeling unwell for several days, when on Sunday, July 28, while walking to Harpers Ferry, "he began to feel sick, dizzy, and everything appeared black before him." Unable to go any farther, he was "carried into the Wager House," an inn, where he remained insensible. When Rodgers visited him four days later Janes had difficulty in recognizing him and an attending surgeon thought him "still dangerously ill." Rodgers shared the surgeon's opinion that the following day should show a marked change either for the better or for worse. Rodgers naturally hoped it would be for the better, but added cautiously, "if it is for the worse, you will receive notice before this arrives by a Telegraphic Dispatch." "If the journey is not too great for your strength," Rodgers advised, "it would be better for you to come to your boy . . . and if he gets worse . . . you must come instantly."[57]

Janes' mother later wrote that for the next two months she could get no information on her son's condition or whereabouts.[58] The reasons for this were as Janes stated. Shortly after Rodgers wrote his letter Harpers Ferry fell to the southern side. Janes, who was secreted away in the Wager House, was literally abandoned by his northern compatriots. Meanwhile the effects of sun stroke were compounded by a severe case of typhoid fever. The few stealthy reports that found their way across the Potomac were not encouraging. On one occasion he was reported dead.[59] And indeed, he seems to have hovered between life and death for a good part of August. It was only in the final week of that month that he improved enough to be secretly conveyed across the river, and then on to Frederick, Maryland, where he was temporarily hospitalized before being moved to Baltimore.

Janes' experiences at Harpers Ferry, his struggle with sunstroke and typhoid fever, were but the start of a remarkable physical transformation. Within a matter of months the robust young cadet, once so fond of the active life, had become a virtual invalid. When he returned home at the orders of his doctors for a period of rest and recuperation in October 1861 his mother found him in a "very reduced state of health."[60] His sister Mary described him as a "physical wreck."[61]

But Janes' physical disabilities had not yet tempered his overriding ambition, or—as his mother saw it—his "martyrdom to duty."[62] Rejecting the advice of his military surgeon, as well as that of the family physician, Dr. Richards, Janes waived much of his prescribed sick leave to rush back to join the Army of the Potomac in the defense of Washington. Early in 1862 he accompanied his battery to Florida and served in the defense of Fort Pickens. Rodgers, who served with Janes in Florida and Louisiana in 1862 and who was with him until his return to Washington in December, the month in which he married Helen Robinson, commented on his disintegrating health. "He then appeared to me to be a man," he wrote, "of debilitated and generally enfeebled constitution, who had lost the power of resistance to climatic diseases of that locality, particularly malarial diseases, diarrhoea, etc."[63]

Janes' marriage to Nellie did not improve his health. In the spring of 1863 he was once more dangerously ill. At Aquia Creek, in Virginia, as the Army of the Potomac was preparing for the Chancellorsville Campaign, he was "no longer able to walk or stand."[64] Under the circumstances he was brought to the Robinson home in Uniontown, Pennsylvania, where he was nursed by his wife. Nellie's sister, Emma, wrote, "he was at that time in an extremely enfeebled condition, suffering from chronic diarrhoea and rheumatism, and aggravated forms of malarial poisoning." By May his condition was worse, "his mother was sent for to come from Ohio to my home, as the case of Lieut. Janes appeared to be very serious, if not hopeless."[65]

Janes' mother, hearing that his life was in danger, arrived in haste. "I never saw such a change in a man who had once possessed a powerful constitution," she observed. "He was so weak as to have congestive chills and suffered greatly from ulcers and neuralgic pains."[66] During one of the bombardments he directed from Fort Pickens in the spring of 1862 the hearing of his right ear was totally destroyed, and that of the left seriously affected. Janes regularly complained of headaches and roaring and ringing noises, which he attributed to his partially destroyed left eardrum, and which his mother wrote caused him more trouble than the deafness of his right ear. He described his own symptoms as "excessive nervous prostration," "sleeplessness," and "neuralgia," not to mention the "semiparalyzing effects at intervals of the tumor" on his right shoulder.[67]

Frederick C. Robinson, Nellie's uncle and an examining surgeon for the Army under whose care Janes was officially placed in the spring of 1863, reported that he was still suffering from a variety of ailments, and while he thought the Lieutenant capable of reporting to Washington in "ten days, or two weeks," he cautioned that he could recommend him only for light duty and not for active duty in the field.[68] Given such physical limitations Janes was temporarily assigned to the draft depot in Trenton, New Jersey, on mustering duty, and on August 11, 1863, he was ordered to West Point as assistant instructor of infantry and artillery tactics and assistant professor of geography, history, and ethics.[69]

While serving as a teacher and instructor at West Point Janes' physical condition remained precarious. Edward S. Dunster, who later became a well-known member of the University of Michigan medical faculty, treated him at this time. He observed that Janes often suffered from attacks of rheumatoid neuralgia and various other ills, which he felt were the results of exposure and arduous service in the field. "From all these exposures and injuries and from his recurring illnesses," Dunster wrote in conclusion, "he remained in his condition of marked nervous prostration and seriously affected in strength and health during my supervision of his case."[70]

Janes' physical condition in the wake of his experiences at Harpers Ferry, Fort Pickens, and Aquia Creek is only too clearly recorded in the foregoing accounts of those who ministered to his physical needs and treated him professionally during the years from 1861 to 1865. That the war took a serious toll and transformed the physically able and ambitious cadet, a young man whom one of his neighbors described as "the picture of robust health," into a virtual invalid, a "completely broken" man as the same neighbor added, is all too obvious.[71] What is less clear is the shadow of emotional stress that runs through these same years.

Janes' complaints of "excessive nervous prostration," "sleeplessness," and "neuralgic disorders," his debilitating "headaches," "semi-paralysis," and "chronic diarrhoea," suggest not only general physical disabilities, but an intense emotional strain. It is quite possible that Janes' collapse into insensibility at Harpers Ferry and his inability to walk or

stand at Aquia Creek went beyond mere sunstroke and neuralgia. There
is considerable evidence to suggest that Janes' breakdown in the Civil
War was not only physical but also psychological. He had once been
traumatized by the death of his younger sister, and the war quickly
reopened old wounds. The escape from emotionally intolerable battlefield
situations into physical illness, temporary paralysis, or comatose states
has been well studied in reference to twentieth-century wars and their
combatants. That Janes too may have suffered from the type of war
neurosis that became evident among combatants in the First and Second
World Wars seems a distinct possibility.[72]

Within this context it is worth noting that Janes' fictionalized reinter-
pretation of his experiences, particularly his conversion experience, suggests not only physical ailments that led to the hero's comatose state,
but a marked degree of mental turmoil. Janes writes of the "mental
dejection" of his hero. He notes that the "delirium" from which he suffers
is not just the result of fever, but the "delirium tremens of the sin-haunted,
remorse pursued brain."[73] Speaking through his principal character he
notes: "I had violated the sanctities of humanity. I had offended against
mankind. I had brutally withheld the honor, service, and defence due to
all womanhood."[74]

As the foregoing suggests, Janes' fictionalized confessional account
indicates a deep sense of guilt that focused not only on his wasted youth,
but on what appears to have been a specific incident involving a woman.
Whether the incident described related to a particular individual, or a
scene he had witnessed during the war, we will never know. What is
clear is that he had failed to do the honorable thing and to live up to
the internalized standards of his upbringing. Here once again was the
basic confrontation of his youth between the values of his Calvinistic
father and the world of natural sentiments. If West Point had allowed
him to counter his inner tensions with bravado and thereby postpone
the mounting crisis, the Civil War brought such strategies to a rude and
precipitous conclusion. Lying insensible at Harpers Ferry, and subsequently incapacitated as a patient at Frederick and Baltimore, Janes seems
to have undergone a mystical religious experience. "To this hour," he
observes in "Out of Stony Lonesome," "I have been unable to define to
myself or describe in words the change that had come over me. Was it
all due to physical causes; was it the reaction of miserable memories of
my crude and unbalanced mind; was it the beginnings of remorse awakened by a nightmare of sin, leading back to vistas glittering with the
glories of a mother's love and a sister's innocence?" "Falling upon my
deadened senses at the moment when they were about to lapse into
unconsciousness," Janes writes, "there was room left in my mental state

for but a single reflection, namely, a vivid realization of ebbing life and hope, and the thought of a rescuing hand." "Out of what mixture of savage nature still rampant in my being; impressions planted deep in the plastic mind of my unhappy boyhood by my father's sermons, exhortations, and direct teachings; and the novelty of situations and circumstances in which both those latent influences were made to span the gulf of sinful associations which then intervened, the result I speak of came to be evolved, and transcends, as I said, all my powers of analysis and explanation."[75]

Janes' joy at having survived, his sense of having been born again in mature manhood with the innocent and tender sensibilities of an infant and the ripened capacities of middle age, as he wrote in "Out of Stony Lonesome," were clearly symptomatic of his inner transformation. Janes' new Christian self, the beginning of his ten years under God of which he wrote to Anna Warner from Kumamoto and which he associated with the war and Nellie marked a distinct turning point in his life. Janes was later to speak of this deeply emotional religious experience as the first of his "strange joys."[76] While he regarded these experiences as beyond analysis or explanation, they were, as we shall see, almost always the results of periods of heightened physical and emotional stress.

Although it can be amply documented from Janes' writings that an intense sense of guilt over having failed to live up to his father's Calvinistic values played a central role in his conversion, it should also be noted that the type of Christianity to which he turned was not the Calvinistic Presbyterianism of his father, but the highly emotional religiosity of his mother. This was particularly true of the experiences he associated with his "strange joys," during which he was far more attracted to the camp meeting values of his mother's frontier Methodism, than the more coldly rational theology of his Presbyterian father. It was as if, having been forced to submit to the father and the values he represented in the inner struggle that had already subtly surfaced in his last years at West Point, Janes now found it possible to temper his submission by choosing the side of his mother against that of his father.

Janes' position was clearly underscored in his fictional account. His hero, he tells us, being "sick of a life of sin" and repenting of being a "prodigal," determines to become a "Methodist preacher" to "save the world by word of mouth." Despite his conversion, he writes, he stood "at the very atipodes" from his father's "Calvinistic fatalism."[77] Indeed, it is important to emphasize the antiorganizational and antitheological biases that were a part of Janes' mystical religious experiences, for it was this element of his Christianity that was to lead to subsequent difficulties with the organized Church.

While Janes' condition of nervous prostration and other physical de-
bilities persisted during his two-year tenure as an instructor at West Point,
he was subsequently to remember these years as filled with sweetness
and tenderness. Such memories were clearly colored by his love for Nellie
and his close associations with the Warners, whose lives briefly blossomed
under the renewed friendship and shared Christian fellowship. But while
retrospect transformed these years into warm memories, they were also
years of intense personal suffering.

Nellie was hardly robust herself, and there is some evidence that she
was already ill with tuberculosis at the time of their marriage in 1862.[78]
If Janes' conversion and marriage provided a brief emotional indian
summer that was to allow him to bask in the sunshine of love and
affection, and provided a new sense of wholeness, the sunshine of those
months and years raced over West Point as if driven before a gathering
storm.

The shadow of Nellie's deteriorating health appears to have been briefly
lifted by the birth of a child. But renewed hope was almost instantly
dashed by increasingly dark and foreboding signs. "Not my will, but
thine O Lord," Janes penned on a note in one of the textbooks he was
using in the autumn of 1864, indicating his own sense of resignation.[79]
As the last bright leaves of the season were reluctantly plucked from
West Point's surrounding hills by the first cold winds of winter, the storm
was at hand. On December 15, 1864, Nellie died.[80]

CHAPTER IV

OREGON AND CALIFORNIA

T HE DEATH of his wife constituted a deep personal tragedy of Janes. His inability to deal with death, particularly the deaths of loved ones, had been dramatically revealed in his earlier years with the death of his younger sister. While the full details of his response to the loss of his wife remain concealed by his and the Warners' silence, there are numerous signs that his bereavement led to a period of serious emotional turmoil. Janes' reaction included a heightened sense of religious consciousness. But while he entered a period of intensified religious activity, his religious concerns contrasted distinctly with a more down-to-earth anger directed against the medical profession, which he held responsible for Nellie's failure to recover from her illness.[1]

Nellie's death raised other vexing problems. In the summer of 1865, with the reassignment of the Second Artillery, in which he now held the rank of Captain, Janes was ordered to the West Coast as commanding officer of Fort Stevens, Oregon.[2] This transfer came at an extremely inopportune moment. Worse still was the location of the new post. Oregon in the 1860s epitomized the untamed frontier with all its hardships and dangers. Founded only two months earlier on a long spit of land at the southern edge of the mouth of the Columbia River, the fort to which Janes was assigned was a long way from civilized society. Astoria, the nearest settlement, was eight miles away. The closest supply depot, Fort Vancouver, was 110 miles distant. While the Clatsop Indians of the district were relatively friendly, the same could hardly be said for the climate. One shallowly optimistic reporter described the region's climate as "pleasant and uniform," only to add in the next sentence that "fires are required nearly every day during the year." "What is called the rainy season," he added, lasted seven months, "from October through April," with more than fifty-one inches of rain falling during one such season of a previous year. The average temperature hovered at fifty-four degrees. Despite such conditions, he observed, "the health of the locality is good," explaining further that there were "no deaths" at the fort "except from violence."[3]

Had Nellie lived, Janes would have been faced with the difficulty of moving her to such an inhospitable location. Taking his infant daughter was out of the question.

During the summer months of 1865 Janes wrote several letters to the

Adjutant General requesting a three-month leave or a suspension of his special orders for that period of time. He tried to explain that he had never received the normal leave given West Point cadets upon graduation, and argued that he was "entitled to that leave." "I would further state that in consequence of recent domestic affliction," he wrote, "I have private duties that make most urgent demands upon me, and that without the delay asked the above orders will cause me great hardship and loss."[4]

Janes' reticence to communicate clearly during periods of personal crisis remained a life-long problem. On this occasion there is no indication in the Army records that he made any effort to explain his recent domestic affliction or his private duties. Unwilling to discuss his wife's death, as he had once refused to use the name of his dead sister for seven years, and unprepared to raise the question of his parental responsibilities toward his newborn child, Janes argued instead that he deserved such leave, and that even General Grant on a visit to West Point thought such leave appropriate for him. But such an appeal fell on deaf ears in Washington. "Not approved," General Townsend wrote across the bottom of his petition.[5]

While the care and placement of his child was of prime importance, there were additional reasons for his desired leave. In the wake of Nellie's death Janes had come to spend more and more time at the Warners. Susan and Anna were now his nearest and most intimate companions. Constitution Island, as he later wrote, became a consoling retreat from the bitterness of the world outside. The Warners' deep Christian sympathy, as well as their peculiar melancholy, seem to have suited his mood. To Susan, and particularly to Anna, he could unburden himself about Nellie. In the meantime, his companionship with Anna, who was nearly thirteen years his senior, seems to have reached the threshold of deeper feelings. This was particularly true on Anna's part, and it is quite possible that she took at least temporary care of his infant daughter. Janes, who may well have been searching for a new mother for his child, later wrote of "affection" and "trust" that were "pledged" at this time.[6] What these pledges consisted of we will never know, but at least one member of the family has subsequently written that there were promises of matrimony, and quite possibly an engagement before his departure for the West Coast.[7]

One additional insight into Janes' emotional state during the months between his wife's death and his departure for California and Oregon is available from a slightly different source. Janes' oldest daughter by his second marriage, Frances Elizabeth Janes, also became a successful writer. In a novel she published in 1918 titled *Nobody's Child* she constructed a husband and wife relationship that bears a striking similarity to that of her father and his first wife. Writing of the wife's death, she notes, "he would gladly have given his life for the girl who was his wife for less than a year, and over whom he had agonized with an intensity that had almost deprived him of his reason. She had born her child and had left him desolate. She seemed to have taken with her all his capacity for love." Later Ann, the fictional child, is told by her aunt, "your mother died when you were born" and it "almost killed" your father. "He loved your mother dearer than I've ever known any man to love a woman. Every time he looked at you it brought it back to him. We went through a lot of trouble, Ann—dreadful trouble. It was too much for him to bear, an' he just went away from it, out west."[8]

Although Janes quite clearly did not escape to Oregon as his daughter's novel suggested, there is clear indication in what she has written that Nellie's death took him to the brink of mental instability and that there was a good deal of "trouble" before his departure. It is quite possible that his ambivalent feelings toward his newborn daughter, that she both reminded him of Nellie and was somehow responsible for her loss, may well have been part of that trouble, as well as a source of subsequent guilt. Janes later intimated that his love for Nellie had been very special and that the feelings that had blossomed in their relationship were not to be revived in subsequent relations with others.[9] His daughter's concluding lines, "they were like that," referring to his family, "an affection for each other and a tremendous sense of duty, but only one love," may well have had its basis more in reality than in fiction.[10]

With the army's official refusal to grant him the desired three-month leave, Janes' requests for a brief "delay of departure until the next steamer" became increasingly plaintive and now arrived in Washington by cable from Fort McHenry, Maryland, where the Second Artillery was assembled for imminent departure to the West Coast.[11]

In the second week of August Janes was suddenly ordered back to the Military Academy as a witness in a court martial.[12] This was the opportunity he sought. His return to West Point allowed him to settle matters with Anna and arrange for the care of his child. On August 23 he cabled Washington that his previous objections no longer existed. The brief delay—which was finally granted—would allow him, he wrote, to see his father; a visit that was no doubt necessary to prepare the financial arrangements for the care of his child at the Warners.[13] In the middle of September, with his domestic matters finally cleared up, Janes boarded a steamer for the West Coast. On October 24, 1865, he assumed his duties as post commander at Fort Stevens, Oregon.[14]

Janes' two years at Fort Stevens constituted an extremely difficult period of his life. Years later he told his students in Japan that he found peacetime soldiering frustrating and meaningless, and consequently decided to leave the Army for a teaching career.[15] While life in Oregon may have generated such thoughts, particularly in the wake of his West Point teaching experiences, the situation at Fort Stevens was considerably more complex than this explanation indicated.

The climate at Fort Stevens was hardly conducive to the health of an individual who suffered severely from rheumatoid neuralgia, intermittent fevers, and general nervous prostration—all previously attributed to excessive exposure in the field. Given Janes' history, his deployment to the damp, cold, dreary isolation of the northwest corner of Oregon was either thoughtless or deliberately cruel. Supervising as many as a hundred men and trying to attend to their daily needs, dealing with the local native population on amicable terms, and at the same time completing a largely unfinished fort was a full-time task sufficient to tax the stamina and ingenuity of a healthy officer. For someone of Janes' physical condition it was overwhelming.

Pressured by duties and the wretched climate, Janes' health deteriorated further. Asahel Bush, a fellow officer at the fort and later a practicing physician, wrote that during his acquaintance with Janes, the Captain suffered from vertigo, faintness, and spells of partial blindness. He continued to be subject to severe neuralgic pains of the head, rheumatism that had now become chronic and severely attacked his knees, and many of his previous ailments. "As I look back on the condition of Capt. Janes as I then knew him," Bush later wrote, "I can but be surprised that he is still living."[16]

While Bush was concerned with the Captain's physical condition, others were more alarmed by his mental and emotional state. There is considerable evidence that Janes' conduct in Oregon became highly erratic and unstable. Attacks upon his junior officers became common and so intense that they were alleged to have led to several desertions, including those of his first sergeant and the fort's contract surgeon. "It appears that no officer can serve under him any length of time without personal difficulty," General Steele wrote to General Halleck in an official communication dated November 3, 1866.[17]

When a doctor of proverbially peaceful disposition was assigned to the fort, Janes is reported to have grossly insulted him before the entire company and ordered men ill in the post hospital to attend muster. Janes' bitterness toward the medical profession was often central to these attacks. Denigration was extended to the families of the officers involved. On the subject of his first lieutenant, William Barrow, and his family, Janes became particularly abusive, speaking to General Steele, the division commander, for three hours at a time "in a very incoherent manner, scarcely ever finishing a sentence, and sometimes breaking off in the middle of a word." At the same time Janes is reported to have become highly religious. General Steele's diagnosis was simple and straightforward. "The death of Captain Janes' wife and religious excitement has turned his brain," he wrote to Washington. "The conduct of Captain Janes as reported to me from other sources and now confirmed by General Steele," Major General Halleck wrote in a memorandum to the Adjutant General's Office, "leaves very little doubt of his insanity."[18]

While Nellie's death quite decidedly led to trouble, as his daughter's novel indicates, and Janes' physical and emotional stress seems to have resulted in a period of heightened religious activity, allegations of "insanity" of the type forwarded by Generals Steele and Halleck are often easier to make than to substantiate. Janes was hardly the first West Pointer to stress discipline. Ordering men ill in the post hospital to attend muster may not have been asking them to do more than he himself was being asked. And in Janes, under stress, there was a peculiar tendency to invert the golden rule—"do unto others as they have done unto you."

Given an understanding of the polarities of Janes' personality, his conduct in Oregon in 1865 and 1866 is not totally incomprehensible from the perspective of his inner self. Many years later he came to regard his strange joys as a form of intoxication, as deleterious to physical health as the alcoholic pleasures he had once experienced at West Point.[19] Under the circumstances prohibitionism of the spirit was to become as important a theme of his final years as was an earlier rejection of the products of his grandfather's still house. But Oregon was many spiritual leagues distant from the analytical insights that permitted the somewhat tenuous and often precarious maintenance of a safe middle position in his later years. In Oregon Janes' polarized conduct was hardly comprehensible to those around him. Extreme discipline, in and of itself, was hardly a crime in the Army. Nor for that matter was a certain degree of religious commitment. But the combination of both in their extreme forms aroused considerable antagonism from those with whom he worked. Surgeon Steele may have put it most kindly when he noted that the Captain's "official acts" were truly "singular."[20] It may be safe to conclude, therefore, that despite its later potential for greatness in the Japanese context, Janes' blending of authoritarianism with intense emotionalism was an unfortunate one in the U.S. Army. For generals such as Steele and Halleck this mixture was overly volatile, and following the latter's memorandum to Washington it was only a matter of time before Janes was ordered before a Retiring Board formed under the special orders of General Grant and headed by General McDowell. The board met in San Francisco on April 23–25, 1867.[21]

The stated purpose of all military Retiring Boards was to determine the mental, moral, and physical condition of an officer when allegations questioning such qualifications were brought against him. Individuals brought before such boards were subjected to careful physical examinations. Evidence and testimony supporting allegations of "incapacity" were presented to the board and submitted to cross examination. After careful review the board could declare an examinee either "fit" or "unfit" for duty. Retirement at the hands of such a board generally meant an officer's transfer to the Army's inactive list, which, while removing him from his command, allowed him to remain in the Army on the disabled list with some financial compensation.

Leaving aside Janes' mental state, there is certainly a considerable body of medical evidence that suggests that his physical condition warranted such a retirement. It is therefore somewhat surprising to read the decision of the board that was forwarded to Washington by McDowell on April 26, 1867, which concluded that, "after mature deliberation on the testimony the Board found that Captain L. L. Janes, Second Artillery, is *not incapacitated for active service.*" Surgeon Robert Murray, the Board's chief examining doctor, testified that on the basis of his examination he found the Captain "in good health, and free from disease." Surgeon C. C. Keeney was even more explicit in his testimony. "After thorough examination of the Captain," he noted, "I find no impairment of his mental or moral faculties, or any defect in his physical qualifications." Moreover, when Janes was asked by the board, "Are you in your own judgement at this time able to do the active duties of your office in the field?" he replied with a clear "I am."[22]

In reading the records of the Board one is struck by a marked about-face by many of the principal witnesses. General Steele, who in November 1866 had written to Washington that "Captain Janes had done some things at Fort Stevens, if he is rightly informed, too contemptible for an Officer of the Army to be suspected of unless insane,"[23] now said, "I do not know that I know anything now that incapacitates him; at one time I thought that he was partially insane, and wrote to General Halleck to that effect."[24] Urged to elaborate on his earlier opinion, Steele replied, "his conduct was strange in several particulars. People said 'he was crazy' and I was told that he had been deranged for some time owing to the death of his wife and religious excitement." "When I wrote the letter to General Halleck," Steele added, "I had seen very little of Captain Janes except that he came to my quarters one evening and entertained me till a late hour of the night with abuse of Lieutenant Barrow and his family, his language was sometimes incoherent in this respect, that he would not finish a sentence, sometimes breaking off in the middle of a sentence, and sometimes in the middle of a word, going on to some other point. I know of nothing else that would lead me to suppose that he was insane, except what has been told me by Lieutenant Barrow, Doctor Steele and others."[25]

William Barrow testified that he knew "nothing to incapacitate Captain Janes from active service."[26] Only Doctor Steele retained certain reservations. He continued to regard Janes' acts as singular and added that "he appeared to be very irritable and suspicious, often forming opinions from merely suspicion of acts of others."[27]

In the end the board seems to have relied more on the medical testimony of Surgeon Murray, who in reply to Janes' question whether there could have existed a "lasting or otherwise serious disqualification in him during any recent period of say three to six months?," replied, "there could not have existed a lasting, but there may have existed a serious one, during the time mentioned."[28] What the findings of the board indicate is that by the spring of 1867 Janes had been able to come to grips with the problems that resulted from Nellie's death. Janes' handling of his defense, his statements and questions before the board, as well as his general demeanor all suggest that he was fully in control of himself. In fact, in defending himself against General Steele's accusations, he showed considerable skill as a defense attorney, revealing that his early legal training had not been wasted.

While the board's judgment that he was fit for duty jeopardizes any hasty conclusions that his appearance before it resulted in his resignation from the Army, Janes later suggested that the two events were indirectly related. He wrote:

At about the date of my resignation, I was known to be suffering and in such a way as to be considered by a superior officer, General Fred Steele, as a subject for retirement. I am no longer concerned as to his motives. But the fact remains that but for the offensive and cruel form in which this judgement was couched by an officer who knew nothing of my history, I should now be still in the Army and on its retired list. Immediately before my resignation I was ordered before the Retiring Board convened in San Francisco and presented by General Steele as broken in health and incapacitated for active service. But when the Board, whose medical chief was Dr. Murray, afterwards Surgeon General of the Army, under the presidency of General McDowell, learned the cruel and unwarrantable grounds alleged, namely that I was mentally deranged, they refused their sanction to the outrage—I was returned to duty.[29]

Saving himself from charges of insanity therefore required his return to Oregon for which he was physically ill-prepared. Janes later saw this predicament as a "wrong" and a "cruel injury," which left him no choice but to sacrifice his valuable commission as Captain of Artillery in order to save his health.[30] But in his letter of resignation, which was dated November 23, 1867, there is no mention of the state of his health or any physical incapacity. "On account of family bereavement and death and consequent filial duties," Janes wrote, "I have the honor hereby to tender my resignation to take effect February 1st, 1868."[31]

Janes' decision to resign from the Army was made in San Francisco, a city which had become increasingly important to him. Having been ordered there in the spring of 1867 to prepare himself for the Retiring Board, he had used the opportunity to make new contacts and renew old friendships. Among these were close ties with the Howard Presbyterian Church and the family of its pastor.

Henry Martyn Scudder, the clergyman who headed this church, was, as one writer observed, "a personality who loomed large in the life of the community."[32] A formidable preacher and remarkable organizer, Scudder had dramatically expanded the church physically as well as socially and culturally. Scudder's sermons epitomized the expansive, confident, and messianic mood of mid-nineteenth-century American Protestantism. "With Christianity for our religion, Republicanism for our form of government, the highest social, civil, educational and spiritual welfare of the multitudinous millions under our benignant sway for our aim, and with the examples of lofty national virtue for the residue of mankind," Scudder thundered in one of his sermons, "shall we not do much to usher in the day of millennial glory?"[33] Scudder, who had spent several years in India as a missionary, was now preoccupied with "civilizing" the West Coast. "What the Puritan with his Bible and school books did for the region east of the Rocky Mountains," he hammered home, "we should do for this state, and for the whole coast." "Erect the church and the school house," he concluded with enthusiasm, "and it matters little what quality the opposing force may be, or what populations may rally against us; we shall prevail."[34]

While Janes devoted himself to the schoolhouse with an equally messianic vision a few years later, Scudder's focus remained on his churches. In 1867 he moved the Howard Presbyterian Church to a new building on Mission Street, an edifice which appropriately towered over its surroundings and contained an auditorium that could seat 1,300 worshippers.[35] "Dr. Scudder's New Church," as the newspapers quickly labeled it, became something of a topic of conversation in San Francisco. The dedication service, on January 6, 1867, the day on which orders were dispatched to Janes to appear before the Retiring Board, was "crowded to the doors," and, as one observer noted, "beautiful and dignified, with depth and power."[36] A less charitable newspaper reported that as the Reverend Doctor's style "partakes largely of the melodramatic," and as it appears that the congregation has taken to applauding his main points, "it might not be inappropriate to finish the interior in the style of a first-class theater."[37]

Dramatic and theatrical as he may have been, Scudder followed the advice he gave to other preachers: "Be short and lively. Load up before you enter the sacred desk. Fire at point blank range. Make an impression, if you can, inside of thirty minutes; if not, ask God to give his blessing, and—close."[38] Such a formula seems to have suited the mood of his San Francisco parishioners. There were rarely empty pews at the Reverend Doctor's church on Sunday mornings. Years earlier, Susan and Anna Warner had heard Scudder preach in New York; Susan had noted in her diary: "Charmed! Something like the preaching I like—something like apostolic times."[39] As Janes would later agree, few could remain ambivalent about the Reverend Doctor's flamboyant oratory.

Scudder was also a popular lecturer and cultural leader. The Howard Social and Literary Circle, the cultural arm of the church, appealed to a broad audience, and its monthly programs of music and readings were well attended. In 1867 the Literary Circle introduced its own publication, the *Howard Quarterly*, which soon boasted that it had faithful supporters not only in "Sacramento, Placerville, Nevada, and Washington Territory," but among "outside barbarians" in "New York and Philadelphia."[40] Music, of which Scudder was particularly fond, played an important part in the life of his church. Concerts were regularly held, "sometimes in the church, sometimes in a public music hall." These were, as one writer noted, "programs of great classical music," which were "rendered not only by professional artists, but also by members of the church choir" and were "greeted by full houses."[41] Scudder's flair for the dramatic also resulted in a certain fascination with spectacles. In 1866 the church held a week-long "Ladies Fair," which was followed in 1867— two weeks after Janes' appearance before the Retiring Board—by a "May Festival."[42] These affairs were usually designed to raise funds for the church. Indeed, expansion, construction, and money raising were among Scudder's marks of genius, and given his achievements there were few who begrudged him the $6,000 annual salary that made all this possible.[43]

It is not clear that Janes was familiar with the Scudders before his arrival on the West Coast. On the other hand, the Warners' contacts with Henry Martyn and his wife dated to the 1850s, and it is therefore likely that they recommended the Doctor's church to their cousin, who shared their taste for apostolic preaching. Given the stated purpose of the Social and Literary Circle, "to introduce strangers and make them feel at home," Janes soon found himself welcomed into the Howard community.

Janes' new spiritual home, a Presbyterian rather than a Methodist church, one must emphasize, was perhaps symptomatic of his own retreat from the extreme emotionalism that had overwhelmed him in the wake of Nellie's death. Scudder's expansive, self-confident, even occasionally arrogant, self, which projected itself from the pulpit on Mission Street on Sunday mornings, was not too distant from the Calvinistic Presbyterian self of Janes' father. At the same time the Doctor's love of the dramatic, his fondness for music and poetry, and his fascination with spectacles were sufficiently emotional to be identified with the religious legacy of Janes' mother. In mid-passage between his inner extremes, Janes found in Scudder the ideal spiritual father who could assist him in redirecting his personality toward constructive ends. Janes' ability to transcend his earlier troubles, to put his life in order once more, and to convince the Retiring Board that he was fit for active service, was therefore closely linked to his association with the Scudders.

Janes' attraction to the Scudders was not, however, limited to the Reverend Doctor and his wife. It was, in fact, Henry Martyn's oldest daughter, Harriet, or Hattie as she was known at home, who interested him most. Susan Warner in her novel, *Daisy*, suggests that Christian Thorold met Daisy and a young schoolmate, Faustina St. Clair, while he was still at West Point.[44] Since Hattie is one of the individuals mentioned in his letter to Anna from Kumamoto in which he chided Susan for writing about his earlier experiences, it is possible that Faustina was modeled on Harriet, and that they had known each other before her father's transfer to San Francisco in 1865.[45]

Susan describes the young Faustina as well-bred, self-assured, and somewhat haughty. A gifted and able student, she excelled in writing, frequently winning the school's annual composition award. A born leader, she was much devoted to dress and appearances. Susan, who made a clear distinction in her writings between spiritual and physical beauty, described her as handsome in a physical sense. Given the stylistic need for character contrasts, Susan's creative portrait of Faustina was no doubt overdrawn. But a close examination of a photograph of Harriet taken in San Francisco in 1867 when she was twenty suggests certain parallels.[46] In the mature Hattie we are confronted with a firmly set mouth, penetrating eyes, and a well-proportioned nose. The total effect of bearing and demeanor indicates the same aloofness, breeding, and self-assurance that had been the trademarks of the fictional Faustina. Moreover, her dress, grooming, and appearance all reveal concerns typical of Susan's characters. And yet, it is in the mouth, in its partially concealed petulance, that one finds, as Susan wrote of Faustina, "something hidden, which took the shape of an advantage gained."[47]

About Janes' romance with Harriet Scudder we know only sparse details. As a leading member of the Howard Social and Literary Circle and the coeditor of the *Howard Quarterly*, Harriet had ample opportunity to meet Janes socially. Given what Susan has written, Janes was no doubt happy to renew an old acquaintanceship. For Janes, improved in spirits, "life had begun to seem worth living again," and to be certain, in the company of the lively and witty, and one might add eminently eligible, Harriet it seemed particularly so.[48]

While Janes and Harriet became good friends, there is no evidence to suggest that he was contemplating marriage when he resigned from the Army in November. As his letter to the Adjutant General's Office stated, it was his "filial duties" stemming from Nellie's death that necessitated his decision. Thoughts of "filial" responsibilities could not help but send his mind winging off to Constitution Island and his abandoned daughter. Moreover, in doing so, it is hard to imagine that he had forgotten his promises to Anna.

On the other hand, such promises had been made during a period of intense emotional stress. In the interim, time and distance, and the fairer emotional climate of San Francisco, had intervened to weaken his commitment. Janes later wrote of a breakdown in communications between himself and Anna that he regarded as a failing on his part in Oregon,[49] and many of Susan's subsequent novels reveal a preoccupation with undelivered letters that crucially affect her characters' lives.[50] What heightened the irony of the Warners' situation was the fact that Susan and Anna spent much of 1867 putting Leroy and Nellie's romance into the first volume of *Daisy*. Thus while they were living with him in their own vicarious manner and warmly awaited his return, Janes was about to embark on a different course.

The events of December 1867 and January 1868 remain perplexing. Janes initially contemplated a leisurely three-month conclusion to his military career. As he wrote to his superiors, the date of his resignation was to be February 1, 1868.[51] And yet, on December 4, 1867, he cabled Washington that General Halleck refused to let him "leave the Division" till the date of his resignation, and that under the circumstances he preferred to have it "take effect immediately."[52] The Army complied with his request, and his resignation was officially accepted as of December 9.[53] If Janes' initial resignation decision was the result of concern for his daughter—quite likely there had already been word of an illness—the acceleration of his need to "leave the Division" may have been in response to further disturbing news of her condition.

But if a hasty return to the East was called for, it is difficult to understand his decision to postpone his departure from San Francisco for over a month. Meanwhile his conduct suggested that his mind was not always on Constitution Island and his daughter. On December 12 he accompanied Harriet to Pescadero, a beach resort halfway between San Francisco and Santa Cruz. Harriet reported on this social outing in the form of a letter that appeared in the editorial column of the *Howard Quarterly*. "Winter in this corner of the globe," she wrote,

> presents a scene strangely incongruous with the pictures involuntarily drawn at the very mention of the season. Here, it speaks of south wind and rain, muddy streets and soiled carpets, india-rubbers and water-proofs, gloomy days and starless nights. Even the few cheering interludes of fair weather appear unnatural without the bracing cold and slippery ice of a northern clime. No crystal flakes are wafted gently down to form a pure snowy mantle, alike for roof and tree, barren wastes and choice gardens; but in their stead we have floods and impassable roads, blockaded valleys, and heights that cannot be reached. Instead of listening to the sound of merry sleigh-bells, and the happy voices of some active skating party, we hear tales of the sudden splashings and screams, besmeared garments and wry faces, if not of the sore bruises and broken limbs, of those who have been unceremoniously hurled into the mud from the top of some unfortunate stage-coach.
>
> During this California season of fitful drizzle and sunshine, it has been our lot to travel. The appointed day of departure proved to be one of sunshine above, and mud of a sticky consistency below. The journey was performed first by rail, then partly on horseback, and partly on the familiar old stage.
>
> Mounting our horses, quietly we sped our way through the woods and over the hills, until we reached the summit of a mountain whose position gave us a full view of the valley below, named Half Moon Bay Valley. In the distance there gleamed the ocean, bound by a sparkling fringe of foaming surf, and on either side of this fertile valley extended ranges of hills, whose bare, rounded forms and great waving folds proclaimed them truly Californian.
>
> At length, we reached a village called Spanish Town, a place

bearing all the characteristics of a Californian village. Treeless, low, dingy, dirty, in every way uninteresting and wretched. Here we were cramped within the partitions of a narrow stage. Packages of various dimensions and children of all ages were intermingled in a mass of confusion soothing to contemplate.

Finally, she added, they were "glad to be relieved of the tedium of the journey" by alighting "from the jolting vehicle, with a thankful bound, before the door of the hotel in this charming place, Pescadero."[54]

In Harriet's letter we are presented with a rather revealing "post card" portrait of its author. A keen observer and talented descriptive writer—qualities that were to serve her well in Japan—Harriet was habitually discontented. Beneath her surface wit and gaiety there lay a propensity for negative comparisons. A "merry," "happy," and "sunny" eastern winter is quickly contrasted to "gloomy days," "starless nights," and the inevitable "rain" of California. Her lack of sympathy for the "uninteresting" and "wretched" conditions of "Spanish Town" and its inhabitants did not augur well for a life among another racially different people of similar economic deprivation.

Moreover, unbeknown to the "kind hearted, good-natured, and talkative" Captain, who accompanied her, Harriet was subject to her own periods of emotional turmoil. Serious depressions were not uncommon, and on one occasion, as her father later wrote, she fell into a particularly "melancholy condition" believing that she had "committed the unpardonable sin." In this instance it had taken the Reverend Doctor and his wife a long time to free her from her "morbid state."[55]

While the journey to Pescadero occurred in one of her better moods, there are signs that even at such times she saw herself as living in a hostile world. At one point along the way, she noted in her letter she was "drearily looking down upon the stiff, deep mud" of the road when she noticed a "small spire of grass" that had somehow managed to survive among the wagon ruts. "It seemed wonderful," she wrote, "that it had been so carefully guarded from the crushing hoofs of horses, and from innumerable other forces that might have conspired to uproot and destroy it." For Harriet it quickly became transformed into "an emblem of purity in the midst of impurity and danger" and led to the inner prayer that she, too, might be "as pure and lovely as this little blade."[56]

Janes' outing to Pescadero was to prove even more revealing than simply providing us with a glimpse of Harriet. While Harriet was preoccupied with the environment and her inner self, Janes' motives for going proved somewhat different. Years later, when their relationship had fallen on more difficult times, Janes wrote to Harriet, "I loved you dear Hattie,

I loved you passionately all the time. Never a moment from the time I told you so at Pescadero Beach, to this hour, that I have not passionately, truly, and dearly loved you."[57]

If Janes declared his love to Hattie on this occasion and was planning to leave California for the East Coast to join his ill daughter as soon as possible, it is reasonable to assume that he would have quickly approached the Reverend Doctor and asked for the hand of his daughter. As the son of a well-to-do landowner and Presbyterian elder, a West Point graduate with teaching experience, and an individual of considerable bearing and good looks, Janes was certainly as eligible for the hand of the Doctor's daughter as most other well-educated young men in San Francisco. The nine-year age difference between the two was not regarded unusual at a time when marriages were often postponed until a man could support a wife and family.

Given the Reverend Doctor's love for the dramatic, his preoccupation with social standing and position, and his role as a leading figure of the San Francisco community, one might have anticipated some complaints about the need for haste and the difficulty of coordinating a year-end wedding with the busy Christmas season, but one would have expected a buzz of activity and preparations for a wedding that would have been appropriate in grandeur and style for the eldest daughter of one of San Francisco's leading clergymen. Moreover, anticipating her own departure from San Francisco and the church community in which she played such an important part, one might have expected Harriet to use the "Editorial Department" of the Howard Quarterly to bid farewell to her many friends.

To the contrary, the issue of the Howard Quarterly that included Harriet's "Letter from Pescadero," an issue that went to the printers shortly before Christmas and was released to the public in January 1868, contained not a single word of the editor's impending departure. Although there were to be no further issues of the journal, there were no indications of the publication's imminent demise. Instead, the editorial column carried a positive evaluation of 1867 and looked forward to a successful and expanded publication in 1868. In addition to an unsigned article by Janes on "The Evacuation of Pensacola," about which the editor wrote, "we hope to hear from its author again," there were several pieces that represented the first of serial articles, and in some cases the subjects of forthcoming articles were included. Certainly no one reading the Howard Quarterly would have received the faintest inkling that its editor was planning a wedding for January 2, 1868, and would almost simultaneously depart for the East.[58]

It is furthermore remarkable that in a society in which marriages and deaths received unusual attention and were frequently subject to extensive newspaper coverage, and in which the Reverend Doctor's church was often central to such articles, the marriage of his eldest daughter should receive only a cryptic three-line entry: "In this city, Jan. 2, at the Howard Presbyterian Church, by the Rev. Dr. Scudder, Captain Leroy Lansing Janes to Harriet Waterbury Scudder."[59]

What are we to make of this? If Janes told Harriet of his love for her on December 12 and planned an early January departure for the East, it is of course conceivable that it took Hattie several weeks to make up her mind, and that she found herself able to do so only at the last moment, thereby necessitating a hasty, and unannounced, wedding on the day after New Years. And yet, even if this had been the case, one would have expected the type of well-organized Scudder effort for which the Doctor was famous—and certainly a more extensive, and well-prepared, newspaper account. Then why the silence and haste?

In 1870 Henry Martyn Scudder wrote a letter to his daughter which suggests that Janes' marriage to Harriet had not started on a harmonious note. In that letter Scudder wrote: "When I left you [he had visited them in the fall of 1869], I said to Leroy and yourself that I took back all that I had ever said which had wounded either of you." He added that he had no intention to "reopen the whole controversy," and as far as he was concerned it was "ended forever." At the same time he pledged to send the young couple one hundred dollars a month in response to his daughter's question of what he now felt "inclined or disinclined to do."[60] In a later argument with his father-in-law, Janes recalled a scene at the Scudders, at which, he stated, the "terpitude of a falsehood" had been at stake. It is not often, he pointed out to the Reverend Doctor, "that even a kind Providence arranges the records of its inception and utterance for the vindication of truth." "Throughout your fuming and fretting in the parlor of that house," Janes wrote, "I sat silent. But twice only I broke that silence. I uttered a calm, solemn, explicit, comprehensive denial, which eternity has taken note of and will vindicate."[61]

Was Janes' marriage to Harriet the result of a classical case of entrapment? Was this an instance of an outwardly innocent but inwardly wily daughter of a straight-laced Protestant minister luring a handsome and interested Army captain to a beach resort where undue liberties were taken? Did the confession of these liberties to her socially sensitive and religiously conservative parents lead to a parlor scene in which a fuming and fretting minister demanded satisfaction in the form of an immediate marriage and hasty departure?

A cursory reading of the evidence available suggests just such a conclusion. But the situation may have been even more complicated. Janes' calm denials tend to suggest his innocence, and his first child by Harriet was not born until twelve months after their wedding.[62] But why then did he marry her under the inauspicious circumstances of the parlor scene described above?

One explanation, which Janes himself gave, was that he truly loved Harriet and that his decision to marry her had nothing to do with her father's pressures.[63] This, too, may have been only a partial explanation. His daughter, Bertie, who witnessed numerous bitter exchanges between Harriet and Janes at the time of their divorce in the mid-1880s, suggests in her novel, *Nobody's Child*, the possibility that Janes may have married Harriet because someone else, who should have "done the honorable thing," refused to do it.[64]

For Janes, as for others, guilt could serve as a powerful motivating force. As we have already observed, Janes was subject to an intense sense of sin and remorse at the time of his conversion, and this sense of guilt was at least partially attributed to "having brutally withheld the honor, service, and defense due all womanhood."[65] Given a chance to make restitution for his earlier failings, he may now have seized upon the inverse situation in which Harriet found herself as an honorable means of righting an old wrong. Having previously inflicted suffering, he was now prepared to accept suffering on another's behalf in order to make restitution. As Janes saw it, this was to be truly Christ-like.

Yet to be Christ-like, particularly toward Harriet, was often more than Janes bargained for.[66] As his cross became heavier, he registered his calm denials in the appropriate places. While the Reverend Scudder served as a proper target for such reminders, the Warners, who were never to recover from the shock of his marriage to Harriet, also deserved suitable hints. Janes wrote to Anna in 1874 that things were not always what they seemed. Hoping that "time and charity" had "soothed the hurt" left behind, he added that although he wished he could tell them all that he now knew about the past, he could not. He concluded simply that while God had put "too great a distance" between them for him to ever "show" her anything again, he wanted to "tell" her that despite all impressions to the contrary, he had never violated his Christian trust which he associated with her and Nellie, and that despite confusing appearances he had remained "what you thought me, what you wished me to be."[67]

While time and charity may have served to soothe the hurt, there is no question that the Janes' arrival at the Warner home on Constitution Island in the middle of January 1868 constituted something of a surprise. In 1873 Anna published a short story in *Harper's* in which she discussed the experiences of a young lady who had become involved in a long engagement, only to read in a newspaper announcement one fateful day that her fiancee had married someone else.[68] Much of the short story concerns the young lady's subsequent struggle to transcend the inner hurt that this discovery produced. In response to the suggestion that "things do die out," Anna wrote, "not out of some natures. The color is there as long as there's a thread of the stuff left to show it; though maybe it is all hid away and never *does* show to human eyes." Anna's solution, as both the short story and the biographical details of her life suggest, was to devote herself with greater intensity to her religious calling. Carrying out the "will of God," she wrote, "seemed to be the one thing life had left her."[69]

On the other hand, the publication of her story in *Harper's* may have represented her own effort to reach Janes, to whom she had sent letters in 1871 and 1872 without a reply, and it suggests that despite the content of her story she had not totally made peace with her fate. In fact, the concluding line of her story is strangely out of context. Asked by one of her young listeners whether her fiancee, John, could ever do such a thing to her, Anna has the narrator reply with a short laugh, " 'John' never does—it's always 'James!' "[70] As the villain of the story is named Seth, none of this makes sense, unless, of course, one considers the possibility that Susan and Anna read of Janes' marriage in the most widely distributed San Francisco paper, the *Daily Alta California*, which made the common mistake, writing "Captain Leroy Lansing James to Harriet Waterbury Scudder" in its brief wedding announcement on January 3.[71]

If signs of hurt feelings were to persist into the middle of the 1870s, one can only imagine that the hurt, hidden away as they may have tried to keep it, was intense on the part of the Warners. While Anna was obviously the chief sufferer, Susan was equally bitter, and even the kindly Aunt Fanny and Father Warner were not unaffected by feelings of regret.[72] Why Janes decided to bring Harriet to Constitution Island, which was hardly a suitable site for a honeymoon, can be explained only by the condition of his daughter. The fact that Janes and Harriet boarded with the Warners for the next nine months was, therefore, closely linked to the state of his critically ill child. Indeed, it seems reasonable to argue that what held the whole intolerable situation in check for both sides was the overriding concern for the child.

What was wrong with Janes' daughter remains part of the whole mystery surrounding Nellie's life and death. But there are hints that she suffered from a lingering ailment that gradually sapped her strength and eventually brought about her death.[73] It is, of course, easy to imagine that as she wasted away in the summer months of 1868, tensions at the Warners mounted. There were certainly plenty of reasons for recriminations on both sides. Susan found it all too easy to blame Janes for jilting Anna. Meanwhile, Janes was not without his own complaints. Frustrated by his inability to help his dying child, he seems to have lashed out at the Warners. Harriet, against whom much of the Warners' hidden hurt was directed, appears to have been uncomfortably caught in the middle. And Anna simply suffered in silence.

September brought the inevitable. Not yet four, Janes' daughter died. For Harriet and for the Warners there was at least the sense of relief that the long struggle was over. But for Janes there was once more trouble. Harsh words ensued. Some of these were directed at Harriet as well as the Warners. Janes later apologized to Harriet for the "bitter expressions" and for the sadness and wrong which his poor ill nature had wrought.[74] To the Warners he wrote from Kumamoto, "When I think of Aunt Fanny much self reproach is mingled, as it must be, with all my recollections of five years ago." He asked Anna to "please assure dear Aunt Fanny from me that with all these feelings and all these memories there springs up in my heart the reassuring reflection that God is infinitely just as well as loving, and loving as well as just." His image of Father Warner, he added, would always remain that of the old man's "weary frame leaned against the jam, the tears on his face!"[75]

While Anna may have suffered in silence trying to reach the inner resignation that allowed her to see the whole tragedy as "God's will," Susan was less inclined to follow such a course. In the hours of escape from the submerged tensions of the home that Susan could marshal in the name of keeping the family financially solvent, she repaired to her tent under the cedar trees to write. Now into the second volume of *Daisy*, she was to use the fictional world of Christian Thorold and Daisy Randolph to carry out her own subtle revenge on Janes.

Having followed the "truth" of Christian Thorold's life into the Civil War, to the hospital where he lay ill with disease under Daisy's care, Susan decided to end her relationship with her fictional character by allowing him to die. If this was a violation of the historical reality of Janes and Nellie's romance, it was a confirmation of the reality in which Susan found herself in the summer of 1868. By allowing Christian Thorold to die, Susan symbolically cut her ties with her cousin. Unable to confront Janes openly over the deep hurt he had inflicted on Anna, Susan resorted to the world she knew best to communicate with him. There are few more poignant lines in Susan's writings than the closing page of *Daisy* in which she speaks through Daisy, but for Anna, what was to become the "truth" of Anna's life. "People may love truly and love again, I suppose," she wrote, "I have no doubt that *men* may; but I think not women. Not true women, when they have once thoroughly given their hearts. I do not think they can take them back to give again. And mine is Mr. Thorold's."[76]

As Janes' silence in Kumamoto underscored, the arrow that Susan directed at him did not fail to strike its mark.

CHAPTER V

INVITATION TO JAPAN

WITH THE DEATH of his daughter, Janes took his wife briefly to New Philadelphia, where their first child Frances Elizabeth was born on December 27, 1868.[1] The birth of Fanny seems to have helped him to deal with the earlier loss. In the spring of 1869, ready to take up a new career, he moved Harriet and his infant daughter to Saint Denis, Maryland, where they settled on what his father described as an "old plantation."[2]

For Janes the Maryland years came to be associated with national and personal reconstruction. Moreover, important as they were on the American side, they were also crucial years in the history of Japan, where unbeknown to the Captain the forces that led him to spend many of his later years in the land of the rising sun were well under way. Events in Maryland were therefore curiously tied to those in the Far East. But of this he remained largely ignorant.

Life as a gentleman farmer was not always easy. Elk Ridge Farm was hardly a "plantation" in the common meaning of the term. Moderate in size, its land was largely of marginal quality. While Janes inherited traces of his father's land hunger, he seems to have lacked the Colonel's astuteness in judging the financial potential of the commodity, and his farm remained a precarious venture.[3] But there were advantages. Elk Ridge's beautiful setting overlooking the Patapsco River, and its easy commuting distance just nine miles southeast of Baltimore, made it a desirable location for the homes of Baltimore's prominent professional families who enjoyed the amenities of country life. Elk Ridge boasted one of Maryland's exclusive hunt clubs. Fox hunting, as Janes' daughter described in one of her novels, was a favorite local pastime that allowed socially ambitious doctors and lawyers to mix with the local landed aristocracy, whose estates, such as Caleb Dorsey's "Belmont," remained living monuments to a bygone era and a fading way of life.[4]

Janes later wrote that the region's "health inspiring climate" was its only attraction to an immigrant from the North.[5] Otherwise there were few benefits. While Harriet may have enjoyed the Ridge's social opportunities, Janes' two-year residence in Maryland as a "carpet-bagger," as he put it, only confirmed his earlier feelings about the baneful effects of an economic system based on the exploitation of one group of human beings by another.[6]

At the same time, having regained his health and emotional equilibrium, he also rediscovered his vigor and ambition. Both quickly became part of a new sense of mission. Years earlier he had rejected Joseph Gordon's brand of Free Presbyterianism, the Albany Academy's dominant emphasis on the Christian as radical reformer. Now he found himself standing squarely with Gordon, and with his father-in-law, Henry Martyn Scudder, arguing that the true Christian's responsibility was to be a reformer. Christianity should not be some abstract Sunday garment to be put on once a week and confined to the church, but should combine, as Gordon had put it, the "supreme love of God" with the "equal love of man." Such a faith required the believer to look beyond the mere personal aspects of his religious experience to the broader problems of the community. Gordon's dictum that to reform is to reconstruct and make over that which has been marred and broken, which included not only man's nature but his social and physical environment, fell on far more sympathetic and understanding ears in 1870 than it had in 1854. For one who had repeatedly jousted with life's trials, and his own ill nature, Janes found in Gordon's teachings a renewed hope not only that the inner man could once again become whole, but more importantly, that no matter how imperfect that man might be, inner reconstruction should be combined with a greater public role.

Janes admitted that he derived a certain zest from the inevitable animosities that an ancient slave breeding community directed toward "all and sundry who had had any share in 'setting at naught' the craft by which a few 'had their wealth,' and many their poverty, and the denuded soil its blight."[7] "I had begun to feel," he wrote, "from what I saw about me, that the war had been only the chopping-down process of the western 'clearing.' I felt the inertia of the dead trunks of slavery and secession to erect a free and modern civilization on the exhausted soil of the old—or to be more than obstacles in the way of the capital and energies of the competent from other regions—and I saw the stubborn fidelity of the decapitated stumps to all that remained of the vitality of the lost cause, and to the resources that had sustained it through the fiercest conflict that ever tested the tenacity of man's attachment to good and evil, right and wrong, freedom and slavery." In short, "I had made my home in an inhospitable region," he concluded, "where to be, was itself a mission, and where to stay and to do or die, appeared to be a duty."[8]

Janes' two years in Maryland were to prepare him for his work in Japan in several ways. Life on his farm stimulated a renewed interest in agriculture with which he had had little contact for the previous fifteen years. Dealing with marginal land was itself a challenge. Informing himself of the latest farming techniques in an effort to turn his farm into a profitable venture, Janes was to perpetuate the family tradition of agricultural innovation, which had led to his father's prominent position as president of the Tuscarawas County Agricultural Association. As in other areas, Janes' intellectual and scientific approach to farming, his familiarity with voluntary associations that were designed to encourage and spread such an approach, and his conviction that agriculture must serve as the foundations of a modern industrial state allowed him to serve as a useful bridge between the American transformation of the 1820s and 1830s, in which his father and grandfather had played their part, and the efforts to build a modern Japan in the 1870s.

More importantly, while life in Maryland inspired a new consciousness of the Christian as radical reformer, the setting under which these sentiments blossomed was to do its part in subtly preparing him for the task that awaited him in Japan. In Maryland Janes was ·confronted by an environment that bore some interesting parallels to the situation he would encounter in Kumamoto. Convinced of the South's need to move toward a new society and an industrially based economy if it were to become modern and remain a part of the American mainstream, Janes became only too conscious of the forces that inhibited such a transformation. The strength of entrenched ideas and a venerated aristocracy, traditional patterns of education and an established cultural style, the submerged hatred of a domestic population for conquering outsiders, all these served to limit the potential reformer. America, too, had its dying old regime and its arch conservatives. Having lost the open battle, these groups were now preoccupied with rearguard actions of a more concealed type. While Janes pictured himself as rising to such challenges in the American setting, his writings also suggest a sense of frustration with the results of these efforts. Still, it would be wrong to assume that he did not learn a great deal from these lessons. Pent up energies that were stifled in the American environment were soon to express themselves in Japan.

Engrossed in his farming, Janes remained unaware of the forces that were about to pull him from his Elk Ridge Farm halfway around the world to Kumamoto. But Japan had undergone momentous changes in the three years since his resignation from the Army. We may presume that, like other Americans who followed current events, he was at least familiar with the broader outlines of what was happening in the Far East. That he was aware of American efforts to establish relations with Japan, which culminated in the Perry Expedition of 1853 and the signing of the full commercial treaty under the American consul, Townsend Harris, in 1858, seems unlikely given his youth and personal preoccupations at Albany and West Point. On the other hand his contacts with the Warners, who were mission-minded and closely affiliated with that segment of the American church that called for the "opening" of Japan, not for trade, but for the preaching of the Gospel, may well have exposed him to information and interests not available to others.[9] It is likely that he encountered his first Japanese at the Howard Presbyterian Church in San Francisco, where a well-attended Japanese Sunday school class was in place in the late 1860s.[10] And it certainly would have been difficult for him to have missed the headlines announcing the Meiji Restoration, or more precisely the "Abdication of the Tycoon," which appeared in the January 2, 1868, issue of the *San Francisco Evening Bulletin*, which also carried his wedding announcement.[11]

By 1870 Japan had embarked on a new course. Directed by a group of young and able samurai, the new imperial government was rapidly turning its back on the old order. Conscious of their nation's backwardness and the dangers of the international environment, Japan's new leaders were predominantly concerned with national survival and with the task of transforming their country into a powerful and viable modern state.

Equality with the West was Japan's ultimate goal. But those directing the Restoration were well aware that achieving this goal required an almost complete transformation of Japanese society. Such a transformation would have to include not only the destruction of Japan's age-old feudal system, but extensive borrowing from the outside world. As the Meiji Emperor's Charter Oath made amply clear, the evil customs of the past would have to be discarded, and knowledge sought throughout the world.[12]

The first decade of the Meiji period therefore presented a major challenge. To develop a viable new Japan the former political system would have to be dismantled and a new economic and political order built to take its place. The environment for such changes remained precarious. Moving too quickly against the old order would inevitably invite internal reaction and possibly civil war; moving too slowly might elicit aggression from abroad. What was clear to the majority of Japan's new leaders was that Japan could reach its ultimate goal only through a balanced development of national wealth and power, and that to achieve these Japan would have to rely not only on its internal energies and resources, but on extensive assistance from abroad.

It was this search for foreign expertise that brought Janes to Japan in 1871. But here something further needs to be said about the domain that issued his invitation, and the legacy of its most important thinker who prepared the groundwork upon which the Captain was to build during his years in Japan.

In 1870 Japan was still in transition from the old to the new order. Just two years into the Restoration, the new administration ruling in the name of the boy Emperor, Meiji, was largely preoccupied with consolidating its power. Feudalism, in the form of its symbolic manifestations, the daimyo and their domains, was still in place. Hardly a united nation, Japan continued to be divided into some 250–odd domains, each under the control of its largely autonomous lord, and while the majority of these had been convinced to return their domain registers to the Emperor in the summer of 1869, their new appointments as governors of their territories indicated the token nature of what was largely a cosmetic change. Four of the greatest of these domains, all from the southwest, had spearheaded the Restoration.

But there were other powerful lords. And while most felt the winds of change sweeping Japan, which included Japan's need to turn to the outside world, few were certain of where the new Japan would lead. To them the cohesive Restoration, as historians would look back upon it, seemed far from cohesive. Intensely competitive, they often looked at their world from the perspective of their particular territories. Sensing on the one hand that Japan's survival required a national effort, they remained equally preoccupied with their own role and position in the newly emerging national order.

The Higo domain, in whose castle town, Kumamoto, Janes and his family were to reside from 1871 to 1876, was typical of Japan's larger feudal territories. Under the able leadership of the Hosokawa house, Higo had established a national reputation for staunch conservatism and for the bravery of its samurai. A *tozama* or "outside" domain, which was barred from the Tokugawa government's inner administrative circle, Higo had nevertheless developed close ties to the Shogunate. Two and a half centuries of friendly relations allowed Kumamoto's lords to retain independent control over Japan's fifth largest territory.[13]

Higo's conservatism and its ties of friendship to the Tokugawa inhibited its participation in the Restoration. By 1870 it was all too obvious that it was Higo's neighbor to the south, Satsuma, and its neighbor to the north, Hizen, as well as the nearby domains of Chōshū and Tosa, that had seized the initiative in transforming Japan. Having risked the most, they received the largest rewards. To the more astute of Higo's leaders, including the daimyo, Hosokawa Morihisa, it was all too obvious that their domain was being bypassed in the rush to create the modern state.

But how was this course to be stemmed? Kumamoto's conservatism had created a powerful legacy. The domain was well aware of growing shogunal weakness and the need to give in to Western pressures in the 1850s. Nor was it exempt from the deteriorating economic circumstances that plagued Japan's feudal domains, which persisted in relying on agriculture in an age of increasing commercialization. Unfortunately the Higo leadership found itself incapable of new responses. Unwilling to support those calling for the overthrowal of the Shōgunate in the 1860s, it was equally incapable of adopting new economic measures. In most areas Kumamoto's answer to the tide of change sweeping Japan was to shore up the old order and to rally to the banners of orthodoxy.

In Higo, as elsewhere in Tokugawa Japan, orthodoxy meant the Chu Hsi brand of Neo-Confucianism which served as the ideological underpinnings of the Japanese feudal state. This philosophy was firmly entrenched in the domain academy, the Jishūkan. Moreover, it was the conservative School Party that ran Kumamoto politics until 1869.[14] To members of this party the formulas of the past were sufficient. Trapped in the parochial world of their domain, obsessed with the traditional approach to reform, which stressed frugality and retrenchment, sumptuary legislation, and a renewed emphasis on earlier spiritual values, these men were little prepared to lead the territory through its unprecedented political and economic crisis.[15]

Higo's efforts to maintain domain solvency through traditional methods weighed increasingly on the lower strata of the samurai class. At the same time the renewed emphasis on feudal restrictions also affected another group that shared certain interests with the lower samurai. Like other Japanese domains, Higo included a group of rising farmers. By the middle of the nineteenth century this group saw economic opportunities in the changes that threatened the feudal structure.[16] Members of this class combined a respect for feudal status—some even managed to buy their way into the lower samurai ranks—with growing dissatisfaction over feudal restrictions that limited their talents and opportunities to a narrow and confined arena. Both groups developed a common concern for practicality. While the lower samurai had such attitudes forced on them by the struggle to survive amidst the combined pressures of inflation and reduced stipends, the rising class of wealthy farmers found in such an approach the formula for their growing economic well-being. Moreover, both groups rallied to the banners of a dissident Kumamoto samurai whose ideas were central to the Restoration, and, indeed, to bringing the Captain to Japan.

Janes never met Yokoi Shōnan, Kumamoto's brilliant contribution to the Meiji Restoration.[17] One of the most original thinkers of his generation and a principal ideologue for the movement that brought the Meiji Emperor to power, Yokoi was cut down in Kyoto early in 1869 by reactionary samurai who opposed the Restoration.[18] Like many of his activist friends he was never to witness the fulfillment of the Restoration he had engineered. But Yokoi's ideas remained very much alive. Incorporated into the Charter Oath by one of his pupils, they played a central role in steering the new Japan to look abroad while concentrating on reform at home.[19] In Kumamoto they led to a revolution that is often referred to as the Restoration in Higo.

Although Yokoi came to be seen as a Kumamoto hero after 1868, this was hardly the case earlier. A turbulent figure whose ideas clashed with those of the School Party, Yokoi spent most of his life in exile from the domain, or under virtual house arrest while at home.[20] Born in 1809, he became one of Japan's first intellectual leaders calling for an end to seclusion. Convinced that the nation's blind adherence to a policy of isolation would lead to mounting confrontations with superior Western military power, the consequences of which might well be defeat and humiliation, he wanted Japan to deal more realistically with the outside world. Yokoi argued that the Japanese had fallen far behind the West in science and technology, and he urged Japanese leaders to drop their unfounded prejudices about foreign "barbarians," and to learn freely from them by opening the country and sending students abroad.[21]

An early advocate of the formula that proposed to combine Japan's Confucian value core, or Eastern ethics, with Western science and technology—a formula that was to be an essential feature of the Kumamoto School for Western Learning at the time of Janes' arrival—he later came to argue that other cultures maintained their own ethical "ways."[22] One of the few Japanese scholars of his generation to take an active interest in Christianity, he was particularly concerned with the role that this religion played in modern Western societies.[23] Virtue, he liked to point out, was not an Eastern monopoly. Nor were virtuous men confined to China and Japan.[24] George Washington, he proclaimed to those who saw all Westerners as "barbarians," was worthy of enshrinement in the same pantheon as the Chinese sages, Yao, Shun, and Confucius.[25] Insisting on one occasion that if anyone would send him he would "cross the Pacific and urge the Americans to promote cooperation between Japan and America," he followed this up by secretly sending his nephews Saheida and Daihei to the United States in 1866.[26]

Yokoi was a firm believer in practical learning. In distinction to the School Party, which maintained an orthodox approach to education, he was convinced that Japan's feudal elite, confronted by a set of rapidly changing conditions at home and abroad, had grown increasingly abstract in deriving solutions to domestic and foreign problems. Rather than concern themselves with the practical issues of reform, orthodox Neo-Confucians tended to be absorbed in classical studies that bore little relationship to the contemporary world. By contrast Yokoi became outspoken in insisting that education must deal with practical matters and with the substance of current problems.[27] With the followers of the heterodox scholar Wang Yang-ming, he argued that a student should study a problem until he was convinced that he had discovered the right solution; then he should be prepared to sacrifice his life to see it implemented.

Yokoi's emphasis on practical learning, which he taught in Kumamoto at his school, the Shōnandō, in the 1840s and 1850s, became increasingly attractive to the lower samurai and wealthy peasant who had reason to be concerned with practicality. Thus, while Yokoi's reform ideas were vigorously opposed in Higo by the conservative School Party, and Shōnan himself spent much of the 1850s away from Kumamoto attempting to implement his reform program in another domain, his legacy of practical reform continued to receive active support from a small but devoted group of followers who identified themselves as the Practical Learning Party.

The ultimate triumph of Yokoi's party came only in the wake of his death in 1869. Fully aware of the degree to which the Restoration was passing it by, particularly after Yokoi's death, and at the same time more than ever conscious of its precarious economic position, the Kumamoto domain was ready for a major transformation in the closing months of 1869 and early 1870. In an environment ripe for change, the Practical Learning Party, led by two of Shōnan's principal disciples, Tokutomi Ikkei and Takezaki Sadō, seized the initiative. Hammering out a sweeping reform plan, they set in motion changes that were designed to accomplish in Kumamoto the transformation that was already well under way at the national level.[28]

Tokutomi and Takezaki called on the domain lord, Hosokawa Morihisa, to return from Edo and take direct charge of affairs in Kumamoto. In addition they put forward a series of proposals designed to alter radically the old order. In a frontal attack on Kumamoto's feudal heritage, the Practical Learning reformers called for a complete revamping of the domain's administrative structure, the firing of a large number of domain bureaucrats, and the closing down of various traditional offices. The Restoration in Higo showed no distinction for rank or status. Boldly suggesting that the Hosokawa house give up its traditional privileges, which included its hawking preserve and private lands, the reformers insisted on strict financial retrenchment, the abolition of miscellaneous taxes, and the abrogation of domain debts. In a radical break with the concept of hereditary status and position, they called for public election to all major posts and the establishment of a two-chamber domain legislature. Moreover, in a financial, as well as symbolic, gesture, designed to underscore the reform program as a whole, Tokutomi and Takezaki proposed razing Kumamoto's massive castle, which, like many of Japan's impressive "white herons" of the seventeenth century, had become a white elephant.[29]

Echoing Yokoi's emphasis on education, particularly his long-stressed need for a broader knowledge of the outside world, the Practical Learning reformers proposed a complete revamping of the domain's educational system. In their eyes, the Jishūkan was largely superannuated and, like the castle, an expensive but useless monument to the past. What Kumamoto needed were schools to teach its young men the secrets of Western wealth and power upon which Kumamoto's as well as Japan's future rested. Yokoi's followers saw in these educational proposals a potent means of uniting domain and national interests. By annually selecting Kumamoto's brightest minds, training them in the knowledge of the West, and infiltrating them into the national administration, the domain could not only serve the nation, but also recoup its lost influence and position.

With Hosokawa's return to Kumamoto in May 1870 and the appointment of his younger brother, Nagaoka Moriyoshi, to the position of chief councillor in June, the Restoration in Higo began.[30] Using the Practical Learning Party's proposed reforms as a model, the "two brother princes," as Janes later referred to them, threw their full weight behind an all-out effort to transform Kumamoto into a modern and progressive territory.

The Jishūkan and other traditional offices were disbanded, and the School Party's long-standing hold on Kumamoto politics was broken. A new mood of optimism and excitement seems to have swept through the city. Coming two years after the national Restoration, this mood was brimming with impatience.[31] With the chief members of the Practical Learning Party appointed to positions of responsibility, the cry "We Must Civilize!" which Janes remembered echoed from the highest echelons of the domain's administration down to its lowest representatives, was given its first articulation. While Janes later wrote that this cry always fell on his ears with the "thud of a weighty obligation," it no doubt struck those who issued it with an equally demanding challenge and sense of responsibility.[32]

Having attained power, the Practical Learning Party's hopes for a new school system that incorporated Yokoi's emphasis on knowledge from abroad became a realistic possibility. By the summer of 1870 an Office of Western Learning had been established in Kumamoto.[33] Under this office two new schools were proposed. The first was a medical school that could train doctors and surgeons in the arts of Western medicine.[34] The second was a more general school for Western learning, or Yōgakkō, which, it was hoped, would produce the type of Western specialists who could advance Kumamoto's interests at the domain and national level.[35]

As the reformers envisioned them, both schools were to be placed under the supervision of Western teachers. In the case of the Yōgakkō there was the further conviction that the teacher should be an American. Yokoi Daihei, who had recently returned from his studies in the United States, was particularly persistent in this opinion. Although ill with tuberculosis he worked assiduously with other members of the Practical Learning group, such as Nonoguchi Tameyoshi and Yamada Takesuke, to convince the domain leaders to establish such a school.[36]

And yet, to invite Westerners to teach in Kumamoto was not without risk. In 1870 there was no guarantee that the fragile coalition of domains that directed the national transformation in Tokyo would hold together. Civil war was the ultimate harbinger that overshadowed the early Meiji years, and domains such as Kumamoto were keenly aware of such a possibility.[37] Worse still, Kumamoto harbored one of Japan's most violently outspoken antiforeign groups, the Shimpūren, or League of the Divine Wind, which was fervently dedicated to the preservation of Japan as a sacred land free from the baneful and sullying influence of outsiders.[38] In a world of two-sworded men, many of whom were committed to violence, guaranteeing the safety of anyone—Japanese or Westerner alike— was no easy task.[39] At the same time, Kumamoto was familiar with the fate that could befall a domain that was responsible for the life of a foreigner. Less than a decade earlier, British warships had destroyed much of Kagoshima, the castle town of neighboring Satsuma, in retaliation for the death of an Englishman at the hands of Satsuma samurai.[40]

By the summer of 1870 the initial reluctance of Hosokawa Morihisa and Nagaoka Moriyoshi to invite Westerners to teach in Kumamoto had been largely overcome by the arguments of Yokoi, Nonoguchi, and Yamada. Convinced that waiting for antiforeign sentiments to die out in Kumamoto was like "waiting for China's great Yellow River to run clear," Kumamoto's domain reformers decided that the best policy was a frontal attack on the old order.[41] Unwilling to accept the Practical Learning Party's radical proposal for razing Kumamoto's castle, the "two brother princes" were nevertheless willing to erect alternate symbols that could publicly underscore the domain's new course.

Having accepted the idea of Western learning they were determined to dramatize its importance to the general public. Plans for the new school included not only a Western teacher, but a complete set of Western buildings—with an impressive house for the school's foreign headmaster. Given the fact that there was not a single modern, or Western, building in Kumamoto in 1870, and indeed, that there were no carpenters or workmen capable of constructing such buildings in Higo, one can readily imagine the symbolic impact of this decision.[42]

Shouldered with the responsibilities of transforming the reformers' vision of a new educational order into a viable reality, Nonoguchi Tameyoshi was hurriedly dispatched to Nagasaki to search for an appropriate teacher and to hire carpenters and workmen capable of undertaking the construction of the new school buildings.[43] The latter he apparently found readily available in Nagasaki: domain records for the fall of 1870 show the new school complex rapidly taking form above one of the stone-walled ramparts of the inner castle compound.[44] Given its prominent location the new school attracted a great deal of attention. As objects of curiosity and conversation, the school buildings were closely scrutinized by Kumamoto's citizenry, who were fascinated not only by their Western design, but above all by their glass windows, which were the first to be seen in the city and, like many of the building materials, imported from Nagasaki.

However, finding an appropriate teacher for the school proved more difficult. Neither the daimyo nor the Practical Learning reformers were willing to hire the average Westerner who passed himself off as a "teacher" in the treaty ports.[45] Yokoi Shōnan had stressed character development as one of the most important tasks of education. A teacher's responsibility was to nurture such character development in his pupils. Thus, even though the education of Kumamoto's young men was to be entrusted to a Westerner, Yokoi's followers were convinced that this Westerner should be a man of high ideals and noble character. What they wanted, as one of them later recalled, was an American samurai.[46]

Given the dangerous environment, and the fact that the "Restoration in Higo," like the national Restoration, incorporated a strong element of military self-strengthening, Kumamoto's reformers were unanimous in desiring an American "military man," preferably a retired army officer.[47] Yokoi Daihei, who had been impressed with the quality of American teachers during his studies at Rutgers and the United States Naval Academy, was firm in this conviction.[48] The domain, he insisted, should hire the right man, preferably a military officer, and it should be prepared to pay such an individual a handsome salary to come to Japan to teach.[49] The splendid house that Nagasaki craftsmen were erecting not far from the school buildings in the winter of 1870–71 confirmed the degree to which Yokoi's ideas had been accepted by his fellow reformers. Meanwhile, Yokoi and Nonoguchi were officially instructed to hire the appropriate Westerner. As in other areas involving Kumamoto's reforms, plans for the school and its teacher, once made, were accompanied by a sense of urgency and impatience. Kumamoto's students of Western learning, who had earlier gone to Nagasaki, were immediately recalled to join the new school. A staff was appointed, and entrance procedures, including a graded set of examinations, were announced.[50]

To find an American teacher Yokoi and Nonoguchi approached Guido Verbeck, the pioneer missionary of the Dutch Reformed Board in Japan.[51] Verbeck had come to Nagasaki in 1859 shortly after the Harris Treaty opened the ports to foreign residence. In the decade that followed he had made a reputation for himself as an excellent teacher, a man of high integrity, and a friend of Japan. By the mid-1860s he had taught some of the most important Restoration leaders. Iwakura Tomomi, Soejima Taneomi, and Ōkuma Shigenobu all numbered themselves among his pupils. He later recalled that he taught each of these men the "New Testament" and the "American Constitution."[52]

Verbeck's first contacts with Higo came in 1864 when Nagaoka Moriyoshi visited him hoping to solicit his help in purchasing a Western steamer for the Kumamoto domain.[53] A year later Yokoi Shōnan dispatched his nephews, Saheida and Daihei, to study English under his supervision. In their company came other Kumamoto students of Western learning, including Nonoguchi and Iwao Toshisada, with whom Janes later worked.[54]

Verbeck shared Yokoi's vision that the Japanese should look to the outside world for the skills upon which a new society could be established. "I quite agree with you," he wrote to the Reverend John M. Ferris, secretary of the Board of Foreign Missions of the Dutch Reformed Church in New York in 1867, "that the best way for Japanese to get a knowledge of foreign learning is to send for teachers and master mechanics to come here and teach them."[55] At the same time he was convinced that Japanese should also be sent abroad to study. In 1866 he helped the Yokois get to the United States—the first of several hundred Japanese students for whom he wrote letters of introduction.

By the summer of 1870 Verbeck had moved from Nagasaki to Tokyo. Now teaching in the newly established "Imperial University" (Kaisei Gakkō), he had become a central link between the Restoration leadership and the outside world. Having long suggested that Japan should send a major embassy abroad, he was on the verge of performing his most significant historical act: serving as the chief planner for the Iwakura Mission, the embassy which took a large number of government leaders and students to the West in 1871 and further convinced the Japanese of the need to modernize along occidental lines.

Although seriously ill, Daihei made the arduous journey to Tokyo to consult with Verbeck in the summer of 1870. Both agreed on the importance of the Kumamoto appointment, and that the right man be found for it. On August 20 Verbeck wrote to Ferris indicating the need for "a young man to go to the Prince of Higo's county."[56] Endorsing Daihei's request, he wrote, "I consider that this placing of good Christian men in various parts of the Empire will operate as a very useful auxiliary to our main object, the Christianization of this nation."[57] "I should like to prove to them, the Japanese," he wrote shortly thereafter, "that our country produces honest and honorable men outside of our order who will yet stand by us."[58] "The government of Higo would like to get an ex-lieutenant of the Army"; moreover, they "would prefer a married man with his wife."[59] "The salary mentioned," Verbeck pointed out, "was from $2,400 to $3,000," a year. But, "if the man comes with his wife it ought to be $3,600." Underscoring Kumamoto's haste he told Ferris that the teacher was "desired to come so as to be here by the end of December."[60] By the following mail he repeated his request. "One general teacher of English and the sciences, if possible an ex-military man and married to a *sensible*—excuse the necessary comment—wife for the Prince of Higo's school," he wrote, adding that the conditions were to include a three-year contract, a salary of $250 or $300 a month, and a house.[61]

Kumamoto's hopes for the speedy arrival of their American teacher were to be severely tested. Ferris, who usually responded to Verbeck's requests with dispatch, seems to have had difficulty in locating the appropriate military man for the Kumamoto appointment. In March 1871, some three months after the hoped-for arrival date, Verbeck wrote to Ferris that the man "who is most anxiously waited for is the man for Higo." "The plans for his school and residence," he advised, "are made and awaiting his approval." Verbeck noted that a month earlier Nonoguchi, "one of my former scholars," arrived in Tokyo "to receive the expected man and to escort him to their country. The Prince too is continually inquiring for him. They seem to feel that every day he delays is a loss. But I trust by your kindness we shall hear by this month's mail *who* and *when*."[62] Two months later Verbeck observed that the Kumamoto delegation was still in Tokyo awaiting their man. Frustrated by the slow response to their offer, Kumamoto's reformers improved the proposed contract. Transportation funds, which were not originally included, were now added, and a graduated salary, which moved from $300 a month in the first year to $400 a month in the third, was proposed.[63] And yet, despite such improved terms, June came and went with no candidate. As late as July 20, Verbeck wrote to Ferris, "what of a man for Higo? They begin to feel very uneasy under the delay. If I only had the promise of a certain man and his name and possible time of coming—something *tangible*."[64]

Kumamoto's proposal was not as neglected as the slow monthly communications across the Pacific suggested. Ferris, who had broad connections in the church, was actively searching for the right candidate. Showing Verbeck's letter to various leading clergymen, including Henry Martyn

Scudder, he hoped to find an appropriate Christian officer. Nor was he alone in this quest. Daihei had also requested his brother Saheida at Annapolis to conduct his own search.[65]

Janes later wrote that the offer to teach in Japan reached him in Maryland "early in the spring of 1871."[66] In his book, *Kumamoto: An Episode in Japan's Break from Feudalism*, he observed that the "call made a considerable circuit in our service; and finally came to me through General Grant, then President, who personally urged its acceptance."[67] While the reference to Grant's personal efforts now appears an embellishment of old age, the observation made in another manuscript that "application had been made to the War Department at Washington, to a general officer or two in New York, and to West Point—at least for information" may suggest the course set upon by Saheida.[68] Janes was quick to add, however, that "almost the only effective means of making such an application at that time" was through the church, and as a result, he noted, "this invitation came every step of the way from Japan to myself through the hands of missionaries and missionary agencies."[69] It was in fact Henry Martyn Scudder who first thought of his son-in-law when he was shown Verbeck's letters in the Dutch Reformed Board offices in New York and suggested the former captain to Ferris.[70]

Ferris's initial transmittal of Kumamoto's proposal was, as Janes wrote, "quickly declined."[71] In 1871, he admitted, he "had little knowledge" or "means of knowing" about Japan, and that while he fancied that he knew much of a "generally conclusive nature" he soon learned that what he knew was largely "distorted, prejudiced, and false information."[72] To Janes, as to many Americans, Japan seemed a remote, hostile, and inconvenient place—hardly an acceptable location for a man with a wife and two young children. Nor was he the first to balk at such an offer. Griffis, Verbeck's biographer, who at the latter's request eventually went to teach in Fukui, recalled that "going to the turbulent Japan of that day, beyond treaty limits at least, seemed like venturing into Central Africa or into the regions of eternal ice."[73] Griffis, too, quickly declined Verbeck's initial offer. He futhermore observed that no one would insure the life of "one going inside Japan," and that most American businessmen thought him extremely naive to trust the Japanese to abide by the financial terms of his contract.[74]

Janes had further reasons to be concerned. After the emotionally trying summer of 1868 and the birth of Fanny in December of that year, Hattie had gone into a severe postpartum depression.[75] The arrival of Katie, her younger sister, who lived with them at Elk Ridge Farm for a good part of 1869, helped to improve her spirits, but with the birth of their second child, Henry, in April 1871, Hattie seems to have had a recurrence of the earlier problem. Janes subsequently wrote that "the gentle and highly intelligent mother of our five children [two were to be born in Kumamoto] was compelled to endure, through life, the burden of a constitutional infirmity, returning with increasing severity after every recurring confinement."[76] Worried about Hattie's health, he took her to the nation's leading gynecological specialist, Dr. Marion Sims, the founder of Woman's Hospital in New York, under whose care and treatment she remained for several weeks.[77]

At the same time the offer to go to Japan was renewed from various directions. Ferris, Henry Martyn Scudder, and Hattie's Uncle Joseph, who was pastor of an influential church in Brooklyn, all encouraged Janes to go. Kumamoto's added financial inducements enhanced the attractiveness of the offer. Despite his continued efforts, Elk Ridge Farm was far from a successful financial venture.[78] Growing family responsibilities may have made the prospects of a substantial monthly salary and the potential for a tidy nest egg in three years outweigh the dangers of a distant foreign assignment.

It would be wrong, however, to regard Janes' decision to accept the Kumamoto offer as solely the result of pecuniary concerns. Equally important was the psychological dimension. Life in Maryland had allowed him to recover his health in both an emotional and physical sense. The turbulent inner transformation that had begun with the war and with Nellie was now largely complete. Elk Ridge provided a quiet atmosphere for contemplation, observation, and preparation. For Janes, periods of quiet introspection were often followed by outbursts of energy and activity. Whether he adhered to a standard manic-depressive cycle is difficult to establish, but it is clear that he was capable of long and intense periods of sustained physical activity. In some cases this activity accelerated, as if driven by inner forces, and eventually culminated in one of his "strange joys." Although Janes' Christianity was the product of a quiet period of introspection, it became thoroughly action oriented. In Maryland his potential as a radical reformer had been inhibited by the environment. Japan suggested new possibilities. Moreover, it was just such possibilities that were implied by Ferris and the others who encouraged him to go.

Buoyed by the rising mood of his inner reconstruction, the Christianity Janes was to bring to Kumamoto was not only action oriented, but, following Gordon's dictum that true religion should combine the supreme love of god with the equal love of man, it stressed the need for daily application in spheres that ran far beyond those of the church. The Christian's task, as Janes saw it, was one of daily involvement in the society around him. The Christian as reformer was an individual, Janes later observed, for whom "action, effort, thought, pre-vision, courage, science, the spade and pick, tile, cement, and pure water, *are* prayer, praise, and sermon, and a bit of heaven—that is, *life* and *happiness* are imported to replace hell and death."[79] As Janes viewed it, the equal love of man implied social reform. To believe in heaven and rest, he later wrote, while passing without notice over the festering heaps of our own filth, be it moral, spiritual, or physical, is to make a mockery of truth, Christ, and God.[80]

While Janes' strong social orientation, including his antisectarian biases, were later to serve as points of contention between himself and the organized church, it would be wrong to overlook this dimension of his faith at this stage of his career. Moreover, it was precisely this aspect of his Christianity that was to make him unusually effective in Kumamoto. Janes' layman-centered Christian reformism, in which daily action was far more important than Sunday sermons or theological debates, was to find a particularly receptive environment in Kumamoto. The domain's impatience and urgency for change, the whole quest to civilize and to enlighten, blended well with his own impatience to transform the world in the image of his Christian reformist ideals.

Janes' rising self-confidence furthermore echoed the expansive, assertive, and messianic mood of post-Civil War American society, particularly the American Protestant Church. It was this mood that attracted large congregations to the sermons of his father-in-law, Henry Martyn Scudder, who demonstrated more than usual gifts in blending the themes of national and religious mission. Moreover, despite their later estrangement, Janes shared many of Scudder's sentiments.

Describing his thoughts as he travelled with his wife and two young children from New York to San Francisco by train in the summer of 1871, Janes observed that his decision to go to Japan was less the result of a religious call than a "cheering and inspiring sense of opportunity and a determination to meet it." Fully as committed a nationalist as Scudder, he had become convinced that "a man of right mind and character and will, can serve his *country* and promote its welfare and honor amid foreigners abroad to better and more distinguished purpose than lost in the masses, or submerged in the indifference of selfish pursuits at home."[81]

But Janes' nationalism was also tempered by higher ideals. As he sailed out of the Golden Gate on August 1, 1871, accompanied by Horace Capron, Theodor Hoffman, and Leopold Müller, all fellow employees of the Japanese government who would leave their marks on modern Japan, Janes observed that his thoughts of duty also began to expand. Echoing a theme that was common to Scudder's sermons, and which had sent American missionaries to the remotest parts of Asia, Africa, and the

Middle East, Janes noted: "What would our Union, our Republican Institutions, our Liberty, our Enlightenment be, were they the whole, and all, for the sake of one people alone?"[82]

And yet, Janes was no crude chauvinist. While radical reform implied transforming the world in the American image, he was also conscious of the fact that Christianity possessed the potential for transcending nationalism, in the name of broader ideals that could be identified as universal. Using his free hours aboard the "splendid steamship America" to think about the task he would soon confront in Japan, he observed that as the ship headed into the vast Pacific his own "impulses of patriotism" broadened "until they embraced in one view of duty and responsibility the solidarity and common interests of the whole human race." Conscious of the degree to which his Christianity was carried by his feelings of patriotism and the American idea of manifest destiny, he nevertheless believed that Christianity's role was to serve higher ends. As he wrote, "there is but one remove, one step of progress, from the sentiment of patriotism to that of humanity, from the concept of countrymen, fellow-citizens, to that of mankind. But it is the mightiest that man ever makes in his views of human relations and human destiny." "And it is the peculiar glory of American institutions," he added, "that the step is more easily made, and the position more invincibly maintained, by the American than by the man of any other land on earth."[83]

If Yokoi Shōnan sought to universalize the way of Yao, Shun, and Confucius beyond the four seas, as he wrote in his farewell poem to his nephews bound for America, the thirty-four-year-old captain heading for Japan was no less intent to achieve the same goal for his practical Christianity.[84]

CHAPTER VI

YOKOHAMA, EDO, AND KUMAMOTO

T HE WORLD of Meiji Japan that Janes entered on August 24, 1871, was one of turmoil and change. A year to the day after his disembarcation even the "good ship America" was nothing more than a burned out wreck beached on a spit of land in Yokohama harbor. "Poor dear old 'America,' " Janes later lamented, equating the ship's demise with the aborted impact of "liberal American thought and impulses" with which he had descended the gangplank full of optimism at the bustling wharf of Yokohama. And yet, the accidental fire that destroyed the world's largest wooden steamer, the finest in her class, as he remembered her, was a minor occurrence in the momentous events that were sweeping Japan in the first decade of the Meiji era.[1]

Yokohama, the port to which Janes was introduced by Nonoguchi and the welcoming Kumamoto delegation, was itself symptomatic of a nation in transition. With a history of less than a dozen years, the town had grown into the leading foreign settlement. Situated on a narrow tongue of land protruding into Edo Bay across from Kanagawa, the officially designated Treaty Port, Yokohama's superior deep-water facilities, greater security, and the government's desire to have Westerners settle there resulted in a growing population of businessmen and traders who flocked to the port in search of an Eldorado of quick and easy profits.[2]

By 1871 such hopes had not yet been dashed for a majority of the foreign settlement. Indeed, a sufficient number of men had struck it rich in the Japan trade to inspire a steady flow of new arrivals. Members of old and established trading houses such as Jardine Matheson & Co. or Dent & Co., who had expanded their field of operations from China, were joined by a broad array of lesser merchants, shopkeepers, traders and treaty-port adventurers. As Japan's dominant window to the West, Yokohama served as the rubbing edge between occidental and Japanese civilization, and, as some observed, life at the rubbing edge was often less than salubrious. In the first year of its existence five members of the community fell to the murderous assaults of Japan's anti-Western samurai, who regarded the very presence of Americans and Europeans an intolerable insult to their divine land and Emperor.[3]

By the 1860s Yokohama had developed into what one writer called "the Wild West of the Far East."[4] To be certain there were parallels between the port's expansion and the mushrooming goldrush towns of California and Australia. Nor were their similarities confined to the single-storied clapboard buildings, dusty streets, and houses surrounded for protection by wooden palisades. Life in Yokohama was risky, fast, and often lived on the edge of the law. Early edicts inveighed against the "furious" and "careless" manner in which horses were raced through the settlement's streets to the danger of its pedestrians, and the reckless "discharge of firearms, whether by night or day," which were, no doubt, equally lethal in their misuse.[5] Largely a male society, Yokohama soon catered to the usual male vices, which it would seem were more readily understood and accepted by the Japanese authorities, who were long familiar with the largely samurai world of Edo, than by the Western diplomatic corps and the missionaries, who bemoaned the low moral state of the place. Excessive drinking in the settlement's numerous saloons, a fondness for games of chance, and easy access to houses of ill fame troubled those who, like Janes, hoped that the West had more to offer the Japanese than whiskey and fast horses. "The moral tone of the European community is very low," an American observed, "in the majority of cases a young man settles down to a life of license and shame. The prevalence of this custom would seem incredible to you folks at home."[6] Others, like the pioneer American missionary S. R. Brown, were less inclined to single out Europeans. "Drunkenness is fearfully prevalent," he wrote of the American community.[7] And Verbeck himself, writing to Ferris, noted: "The temptations in this country are fearful, and many a one has fallen who would have been safe as iron at home."[8] As the bishop of Hong Kong, who visited Yokohama in the 1860s, put it: "There is a sense of negligence and discomfort throughout the whole place and everything was in a state of transition towards something which it was hoped would be improvement."[9] Certainly in the eyes of the missionaries there was much that needed improving.

Kumamoto's invitation stipulating a married man clearly had its source in Verbeck's and Yokoi Daihei's disdain for the prevalent treaty-port type. Moreover, both were well aware that Higo's staunch conservatism posed unusual dangers for any Westerner. Verbeck, who was no stranger to the potentially violent environment in which he lived and worked, and who combined circumspection with a carefully oiled and loaded revolver which he always carried in his right coat pocket, knew what could befall a Westerner who overstepped Japanese feelings of propriety.[10] Only a few months earlier two of Verbeck's teachers at the Kaisei Gakkō had been terribly mutilated by an assailant whose ire they aroused while fraternizing with several Edo "ladies."[11] Given the normal temptations

1. Janes' mother, Elizabeth Cryder Janes

2. Nellie, Janes' first wife?

3. Officers of the First Rhode Island Volunteers during the Civil War

4. Barracks at Fort Stevens, Oregon

5. Henry Martyn Scudder

6. Harriet Waterbury Scudder, Janes' second wife

7. Kumamoto Castle, early 1870s

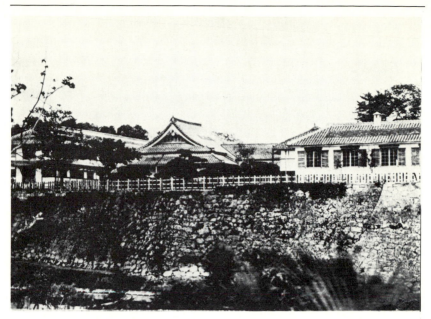

8. Kumamoto School for Western Learning

9. Janes Mansion, Kumamoto

10. Study of the Janes Mansion

11. Zen Temple near Kumamoto where Janes spent summer of 1875

12. L. L. Janes, 1885

13. Janes' home in San Jose, California

14. L. L. Janes and family with Ebina Danjō and Chiba Toyoji, 1908

that were to befall even Griffis in Fukui, neither Verbeck nor Yokoi was prepared to take chances with their man for Kumamoto.[12] For the Prince's school they wanted neither a "professor," as the riffraff treaty-port teachers were euphemistically known, nor a bon vivant bachelor whose personal peccadilloes could lead to a confrontation with far-reaching regional, or even national, consequences.[13] One can well imagine Nonoguchi's sense of relief as he watched the Janes family land on Japanese soil. Waiting for the better part of a year had been trying, but with Verbeck's help the Kumamoto reformers had found their man.

In 1871 there were certainly few who looked upon Yokohama and Tokyo with the eyes of the Prussian observer, Hermann Maron, who ten years earlier described life in the shogunal capital as dreary, apathetic, and lacking in the "quick pulsing life of Europe."[14] The surface elements of the momentous changes underway in Japan since 1868 were readily apparent to anyone like Janes who was to transit through Yokohama and make the four-hour journey by stage to Yedo, as most Westerners continued to call the city despite its new name, Tokyo. All along the route there were signs of the Meiji transformation. The railway, making its first experimental runs from Yokohama to Kanagawa, the telegraph, which had fascinated the Japanese when Commodore Perry set up the initial apparatus and lines along the beach at Uraga, and the brisk stage traffic, managed by the Australian gold-field firm, Cobb & Co., were only the dominant external indications of more profound changes at work in the government and society.[15]

While Janes' recent arrival deprived him of the perspective to judge the pace of the transformation around him, this was not the case with his counterpart, Griffis, who had arrived somewhat earlier. Returning from Fukui in 1872 Griffis wrote:

> Tōkiō is so modernized that I scarcely recognize it. No beggars, no guardhouses, no sentinels at Tsukiji [the foreign concession], or the castle gates; city ward-barriers gone; no swords worn; hundreds of yashikis [mansions] disappeared; new decencies and proprieties observed; less cuticle visible; more clothes. The age of the pantaloons has come. Thousands wearing hats, boots, coats; carriages numerous; jinrikashas countless. Shops full of foreign wares and notions. Soldiers all uniformed, armed with Chassepot rifles. New bridges span the canals. Police in uniforms. Hospitals, schools, and colleges; girls seminaries numerous. Railway nearly finished. . . . Gold and silver coin in circulation. Almshouses established. . . . An Air of bustle, energy and activity prevails. . . . Old Yedo has passed away forever, Tōkiō, the national capital is a cosmopolis.[16]

Perhaps the most cosmopolitan spot in Tokyo in the early seventies was the Yedo Hotel. Located in the Tsukiji concession, the hotel, a rambling two-storied Victorian structure mounted by the ever popular cupola and weather vane, was situated along the waterfront and separated from the bay by a prettily laid out garden. Boasting eighty "nicely furnished apartments in an airy cheerful European building," the hotel had been built with government support and designed to accommodate members of the foreign community who had been permitted to take up residence in Tokyo in 1869.[17] Sporting the usual entertainments of bar and billiard room, the hotel had become something of a social center and counted among its permanent lodgers the American and Spanish consuls. It was here, safe behind its broad wooden palisades, that Europeans and Americans visited, discussed current events and politics, and arranged business deals with Japanese agents. It was also here that Janes, like many of his fellow foreign employees, lived for several weeks while the details of his contract were worked out and officially recorded.[18]

The Captain's arrival in "Yedo" coincided with one of the most significant changes of the early Meiji years. On August 29, 1871, the government declared an end to the long-standing domain system under which Japan had been divided into some 260 feudal territories. In place of the old domains and their lords, a centralized prefectural system was established under the control and supervision of the imperial administration in Tokyo. The government's most direct attack on feudalism to date, "the abolition of the domains and the opening of the prefectures," as the act was known, confirmed the general pattern of consolidation that followed the Restoration. The suppression of military opposition was succeeded by careful planning for a national structure designed to facilitate the economic and political modernization of the country as a whole.

The new army and police, both uniformed in Western dress as Griffis observed, were only among the more obvious external symbols of the intended transformation. Tokyo's signs of Westernization, while increasingly visible, were not always easy to decipher. Much of what occurred in the early Meiji years was, as Janes liked to reiterate, "symbolic," which for him meant external and shallowly rooted, and there was certainly some truth to this assessment in areas such as dress. The adoption of hats, coats, and shoes, or other symbols of modernity, gold watches with appropriately long and ostentatious chains, "bat wing" umbrellas, and the ubiquitous cigarette—so much of the color of treaty-port life—involved little more than surface transformations, which, given the Japanese taste for the novel, new, and up-to-date, could be discarded as easily as they had been adopted.

But intriguing as the environment may have been, Janes' initial concerns were with his contract. He was aware of the "rapidity with which changes followed on the heels of innovation in Japan." And he observed that there was an initial proposal for a "military school" in Higo. However, in "the brief interim elapsing between the start from America and the arrival at Tokyo the privilege of establishing military schools and colleges in the provinces of the former Daimios was withdrawn by imperial decree." "The change," he added, "was in conformity with the centralizing policy of the Revolution itself, and probably had nothing to do with the specific case of the Prince of Higo."[19] Most importantly, he thought, "it nipped in the bud" what he later described as "any latent, ulterior motives which *may* have lain concealed beneath the project of a distinctly Military Academy."[20] And he pointed out that this was particularly fortunate in that it was Kyushu schools, most notably the "military academy" established by Saigō Takamori in Kagoshima, that later became seedbeds for the bloody rebellions of the late 1870s.[21]

Despite the obvious change in national policy, Janes writes that it "was not allowed to interfere in any essential particular, either with our wishes, or with the plans of the Higo friends of the new departure in the line of Enlightenment."[22] Given the altered conditions there seems to have been some anxiety about whether he would be willing to go to Kumamoto. Moreover, there was the further problem of general jurisdiction between the old domain and its "Prince," and the newly opened prefectures in which most "princes" became governors, but in which their administrations were closely controlled by the central government and its various departments. By the time Janes arrived, Foreign Ministry approval was required for all contracts. Such approval also necessitated a consular letter of recommendation for each prospective teacher. In addition, the Ministry of Education now came to assume national responsibilities for hiring instructors even at the local level.[23]

"Under the circumstances," Janes writes, "much consultation and several conferences both with the officials of the Mombusho (Department of Education) and the Imperial Government, and with the Elder prince of Higo and the representatives of the provincial government sent to welcome and escort us to Kumamoto consumed a week or more at Tokyo."[24] In the interim his contract was worked out. Stipulating a three-year term, a monthly salary of $400, transportation to, but not from, Kumamoto, a "Western style house" free of charge (he was to be responsible for food and furnishings), liberal sick leave, and appropriate vacation time—a month in summer, two weeks at Christmas, and all Sundays—the terms of the agreement were, as Verbeck wrote to Ferris, "much better . . . than at first offered."[25] Janes was favorably impressed with Verbeck, whom he met in the company of Nonoguchi. "Mr. Verbeck is doing a noble work here in his present position," he noted to Ferris, ". . . the work of *two dozen* missionaries. . . ."[26] The feeling of respect appears to have been mutual. Seeing Janes in Tokyo, Verbeck offered him a teaching position at the Kaisei Gakkō, although he had earlier written to Ferris that he could not "retain him here."[27]

It seems likely that Verbeck, sensing the quickening pace of centralization, was more than ever aware of the difficulties of sending Western teachers to isolated interior locations for extended periods, when the cultural and intellectual currents of the new Japan were flowing toward the capital. Griffis, with whom he corresponded, and who had been in Fukui for less than a year, typified the problem. Lonely and feeling himself deserted by his best pupils, who used the abolition of the domain as an opportunity to leave their castle town for Tokyo, he already pined for a chance to return to the "cosmopolis."[28] In any case, Verbeck offered Janes a choice. In the meantime the Captain appreciated the quiet good sense of the men from Higo, who, far from pressuring him, calmly awaited his decision. "It was easy to see," Janes wrote, "the earnestness of the desire of the men in control of Higo . . . although most anxious over the decision and eager to avoid the frustration of their cherished plans, no great demonstration of these was made until a decision had been reached. Then they were, one and all, overjoyed, happy, hopeful."[29]

Janes himself was pleased with the outcome. "Nothing could have been more cordial or grateful than the greeting we received from all classes of officials and others at Tokyo," he observed.[30] On September 11 he wrote to Ferris:

> I have the satisfaction of informing you of our safe arrival in Japan and the entirely satisfactory adjustment of our business matters. We go to Higo, as originally contemplated. This evening the red tape of the contract is wound up, and in the morning, God willing, we go to Yokohama and next day sail for Nagasaki. We prefer to go to Higo, finding the opinions expressed at our last interview quite confirmed. Mr. Verbeck is quite positive in his counsel recommending it. The country is fairer, the position far more independent, the field of work larger, and newer, no lady society, it is true, nearer than Nagasaki, neither, however, are there the rivalries and jealousies and divisions to encounter which I fear distract more or less even the missionary society of these parts, where European influences have had longer sway and larger temptations and more corrupting phases of society must be encountered. From them all we turn very willingly away.[31]

Janes later elaborated on his decision to go to Kumamoto, stating that "it was determined by my dislike of the commotion, noise, and formalities of a political capital, and confirmed by my resolve to maintain personal independence and the authoritative control of all forms of partisan, political, military, and especially religious machine government and mandarinism."[32] Unlike Griffis, Janes entertained no great fondness for the cosmopolis:

A few days observation convinced one who is interested in the question of environment, who looks steadily beyond the surf and froth of passing political contentions towards the ocean of deeper meanings and mightier forces beyond, who has proved the necessity of physical health to the promotion of healthy and fruitful intellectual worth, that Tokyo at that time was about the most undesirable place in Japan, at least, as a place of exile from home. Its social and political atmosphere, like that of its dusty thoroughfares, was filled with grit from the grinding attrition of the diplomatic, commercial, and international contact of two antagonistic civilizations. Its swampy levels, and wretched drainage, and the boggy shore fronts of its shallow bay, insured malaria and other undesirable conditions both epidemic and endemic. . . . And finally, a week's touring among its temples and other few historical monuments exhausts personal interest and serves only to sharpen the appetite for change, and to quicken the desire for a nearer and less superficial acquaintance with the ancient and actual life of Japan.

So little cause of regret over this decision have I ever felt, that no subsequent temptation has succeeded in overcoming that early feeling of repugnance to a scene which is still the leading center of windy strife, of ridiculous ceremonial, and of grotesque experiments in fashion in all the land. And in spite of all that has been untoward and trying, a feeling of inexpressible gratitude and satisfaction animates my review of the past, as I contemplate the fruits of that freedom and independence of action which resulted from this decision at Tokyo over twenty-five years ago. For its special effect was to make every resolutely progressive and enlightened spirit in Higo— handful as they were among the mass of reactionaries—not well disposed merely to the foreign helper, but trustful, cordial, and in their own behalf enthusiastic.[33]

With the decision made, Janes was in a hurry to depart. Avoiding a banquet that was planned in his honor by the former daimyo, Hosokawa Morihisa, a "declination" that must have startled the "good Prince,"

Janes later explained himself by noting that he felt strangely at odds with the common Japanese custom of feasting at the inception of a project, which inverted the Western tendency to "feast accomplishments."[34] Anxious to start his new task, he took the first opportunity and boarded a Pacific Mail Line steamer for Kobe and Nagasaki. From Kobe he penned a quick line to Ferris ordering fifty sets of McGuffey's readers, Guyot's geographies, Ray's arithmetics, and Webster's "blue backed" spellers and definers.[35]

Once more underway, sailing through the Inland Sea, he was struck— as if for the first time—by the beauty of Japan. Having described Yedo as dirty, dusty, and the most undesirable place, he now grew positively lyrical about the scenery. "It is the privilege of a lifetime," he wrote, "to pass in review of a combination of sea, island, sky and temperature so transcendently beautiful, so indescribably sublime . . . a combination more entrancing than the unaided imagination or even dreams ever pictured."[36] Only the islands of Greece and the Aegean were comparable, he felt, and in both cases he was convinced there were lessons to be learned from the relationship of the natural setting to the civilization that emerged therein. Echoing Buckle's theory, which linked the concept of environment with national character, Janes wrote, "I drew many a positive and, as time proved, correct inference from what I saw at every step of the beauties which nature had spread with studied prodigality everywhere in Japan." "Were these beauties of natural environment less striking, less wonderful in their composition of the ultimate elements of the earth, foliage, wave, sky, and temperature," he underscored, "Japan and her people would not stand where they do today in the realm of art and manners."[37]

Janes reached Nagasaki only to find that although "we were but fifty miles distant from our inland home as the bee flies, in actual point of time we had accomplished but little over half of the journey from To-kyo."[38] In Nagasaki Janes met Henry Stout, the missionary who had taken Verbeck's place as representative of the Reformed Church. Stout recalled Janes' enthusiasm and his "distinct and far reaching plans" for the school, which, given Stout's more subdued personality and his view of limited possibilities in the Japanese environment, "seemed almost chimerical."[39] Despite differences of temperament and personality a warm friendship developed between the two men. Nagasaki served as Kumamoto's gateway to the outside world, and Stout was to act as an important intermediary for the many requests that Janes sent to San Francisco, New York, or more distant centers in Europe.

Janes left Nagasaki with his family on the night of September 26. "Our only means of reaching Higo, save by the long detour of a week's travel or more," he wrote, "was by a wretched little craft which a thrifty British trader had palmed off upon a company of Japanese capitalists as a veritable 'steamer.' "[40] The Wheezy tub with its bent piston rod, which had already stood more wear and tear of sea life than any man living, was in for a further test, Janes noted, as it rounded Cape Nomo, crossed the Amakusa Straits, and tried to head into the mouth of Shimabara Bay. Having managed ten miles in six hours, the tub now ran into the dual forces of an incipient storm and the emptying tide of the bay. As a result the craft stood stock still, and no matter how much the captain tried to force on steam there was no visible effect and the craft seemed to hang in mid air with no hope in sight but a change in tide. The situation was not without its dangers. "To have shut off steam" or to have given up the contest, Janes observed, would have sent the ship "into the trough of the vicious current and consigned her to a watery grave." The Japanese captain, "a junk seasoned salt," as Janes described him, suddenly awoke as if from a frozen dream and arose full height to the occasion. "He gave an imperious command," Janes recalled, "tiller and rudder responded. With full steam on, the turn off shore was made; and the *Nomo* shot down that incline as if pursued by sea-god and dragon of the storm. The plunge at the foot was perilous in the extreme, but the age of miracles never is past so long as man and the elements conspire to work them." The ship survived.

Safely in the lee of Shimabara Point, the party spent the night and much of the next day hoping for better weather. Like many nineteenth-century Westerners, Janes was decidedly unenthusiastic about the Japanese diet. He happily recalled that the family's hampers were freshly filled in anticipation of a start of housekeeping in Kumamoto, so that neither he, Hattie, or the little ones were "reduced to a diet of raw fish and krauted radish which the crew of three boys and our worthy Captain offered up in appreciation of the good god *Yebisu*."[41]

The next day the odyssey continued with "rain and spray and an occasional sea threatening to engulf us," Janes wrote, and finally in the wee night hours of September 29 the Japanese captain's "cats eyes" perceived something of which Janes and Hattie soon became equally aware. "We were, indeed, at length running under the lee of a great headland that overlooks the mouth of the Shirakawa." "That was our port," Janes was relieved to record, and the tub at last came to a standstill knee-deep in the ooze of the estuary. "Poor dear lame Nonoguchi" was soon assuring them that they were now safe and that they should get as much sleep as possible in preparation for the following day. The *Nomo*, still a mile from the Kumamoto landing, would have to wait for the morning flood tide. Meanwhile runners were dispatched to inform the appropriate officials of Janes' arrival. As the dawn of his first day in Higo broke, Janes observed that the roar of the surf along the stone-revetted seawall was the only reminder of the night's terrors. Indeed, if the situation twelve hours earlier had been ominous, that of the morning, he noted, "was bright with promise."[42]

Harriet described what followed:

> We had a delightful day for landing. Boats crowded with people— men women and children—surrounded the steamer whenever she stopped, to get a look at the wonder of wonders, a white man and woman, and children with flaxen hair! How they looked and laughed, and looked again in perfect amazement. The little ones are the great attraction, the Japanese being extravagantly fond of children.
>
> First, we were conducted off the steamer into a long rowboat with great ceremony by our two officers. The boat was fitted up with a canopy above, blankets beneath, and two chairs of state. This boat took us up the river to a place called Oshima, about an hour's sculling. Here the banks were lined by crowds of spectators who were kept in perfect order by a military and official force who awaited our arrival. We were introduced, conducted up the bank to an inn, and again introduced to a very high official, the second after the Prince. Then we were treated with the fruits of the land, all kinds of native cakes, and very curious omelettes.[43]

"Kumamoto," she continued, "is about four miles above Oshima, right up the banks of the Shirakawa, or here and there across garden lands and rice paddocks." "The trip was made in a *norimono*, baby and *amah* had one, I another, and Fanny a third." "A *norimono*, I must explain, is a light, lacquered, box-like vehicle built like a tiny cabin and swung from a long lacquered beam, hollow and of the lightest wood. It looks massive, and excites one's compassion for the coolies who bear it on their shoulders; but the whole affair is lighter than other loads they are accustomed to bear." "Ours were evidently from the Prince's collection, being right royally ornamented with gold plate, gold lacquer, and very fine brocade." Harriet particularly liked the "softly gentle and graceful" ride of the palanquin. As curious about the world she was entering as the Japanese were about her and the children, she observed that she "kept both latticed slides open and the heavy brocade curtains up all the way to Kumamoto."[44]

Peering out of her *norimono*, she liked what she saw. "The country was beautiful, our path ran along the riverbank through fields of waving rice and millet and past the neatest market gardens of sweet potatoes and radishes, egg plants and turnips."[45] As might be expected, Harriet was thoroughly impressed by the sumptuous ritual of the procession that made its way from Oshima to Kumamoto. The Practical Learning reformers, determined to impress the Kumamoto public with the significance of Janes' arrival, lost no opportunity for pomp and ceremony. Janes' entry into Kumamoto resembled that of a Japanese feudal lord. As Harriet described it, the procession was "led off by two heralds" whose duty it was to "warn off the counter current of bullock carts, pack animals, cows, ponies, bulls, and throngs of men, women and children who had come to see the sight." Following the heralds came a guard of mounted samurai. Next came Janes riding on "the sleekest of black ponies," which had been sent him by the Prince, and behind him Harriet and the children in their palanquins. The family was followed by Nonoguchi and Takezaki Sadō, each riding in their own *norimono*, and they in turn were followed by a company of foot soldiers bearing muskets. In the wake of the soldiers there came a "straggling line of officials, attendants and citizens a quarter of a mile in length."[46]

"It was not long," Harriet wrote, "before we began to enter with martial music the thronged streets of Kumamoto itself. The people looked more miserable and much poorer than in the open ports. . . . It made my heart ache to see the expression of hopelessness on so many faces. . . . Soon our *norimono* were set down on the pavement in front of the house we were to occupy. This rambling structure was situated past the bridge over the wide moat of Higo castle. Here all the host of townspeople were stripped off the official procession for none were allowed to pass the bridge. . . . This temporary house of ours is perched along the crest of the inside wall of the moat, nearly fifty feet high, I should say."[47]

Safely inside the inner castle compound, it soon became apparent to Janes and Harriet that the mounted guard and company of musketeers had not been merely for show. No one was certain how Kumamoto would respond to the arrival of a foreign family, and the Practical Learning reformers were not about to take chances. Even within the castle precincts this was only too obvious. "We were first taken through a room filled with guards and rows of muskets," Harriet wrote, "then through a couple of rooms in which were bowing officials of various grades. Next we entered the house proper, consisting of five rooms fitted up in a sort of European style; a dining room, two bedrooms, a pantry and a bathroom, the kitchen being separate."[48] The Janes mansion was still awaiting its final touches and these were temporary quarters.

Meanwhile the reformers were concerned that their visitors maintain a low profile. "For three days," Harriet observed, "we were the guests of the Prince in our own house." "Three boys of rank waited on us at table, and a host of officials and retainers kept guard about us." "In fact," she lamented, "we were as carefully guarded as prisoners in a penitentiary, though such highly honored guests." "The third day after our arrival," she wrote, "the Prince visited us and gave us a dinner with all his principal officers. The ceremony was something almost painful; but, of course, we were equally ceremonious and polite, and after all spent a pleasant evening."[49]

Harriet liked Nagaoka Moriyoshi. "The Prince is an intelligent man and very anxious to learn," she wrote, "with his interpreters he has frequently come to take supper with us." Of the Practical Learning reformers and other Japanese she met during her initial weeks in Kumamoto she observed: "They are truly patriotic men. How often the Prince has said, 'I hope we shall be civilized,' 'I want Japan to be civilized.' " Thinking about the Japanese she added: "They are far in advance of other nations of the East in many things, but they do not seem to be at all a religious people, like the Hindoos, for instance." And yet, she continued, "they are beginning to court Christian civilization, and are more impressed by American institutions than any other." In conclusion she noted, "I think they are striving to imitate our liberal spirit."[50]

Janes, for his part, felt rather uncomfortable in his role as "foreigner in Higo," who was to be "looked at and feasted and courteously entertained." Preferring to be at work, he found the period of waiting most intolerable and used the first opportunity to break away from the round of ceremonies and the throng of attendants to get a good look at his new environment.[51]

"From whatever direction Kumamoto is approached," he observed, "there is one object that continues to fill the eye, whether it touches the mind of the beholder or only excites a passing wonder. That object is the great castle."[52] Janes had reason to be impressed. Built by Katō Kiyomasa, a leading general of the late sixteenth century, Kumamoto Castle ranked as one of the four great castles of Tokugawa Japan. Riding into the city from Oshima, Janes was struck by its sheer size and symbolic power. There it stood, the center of all attention, he remembered, "tier upon tier, and story upon story . . . a stupendous pile of wooden structures, gabled in every direction, tiled, crested, and pointed with dolphin finials, their tails in the air three or four hundred feet above the moat."[53] Its outermost defenses were "more than five miles in circuit; its loftiest tower rose nearly four hundred feet above the waters of the ditch."[54]

In the fall of 1871 the castle was still filled with its armory of medieval weapons. Making his way through the lower halls and up the wooden staircase that connected the different levels of the *donjon*, Janes was fascinated by the massive wooden beams supporting the central structure. The view from the uppermost room was magnificent. Looking down he could see a covered bridge with windows that ran sixty feet above the ground and led over the moat to the Prince's residence. The residence itself stood in the middle of a beautifully laid out garden that was covered with peach, plum, cherry, and evergreen pine trees. The garden was dotted with artificial mounds, ponds, and water courses that were filled by pipes from the main river. Although now somewhat in disrepair, as were the interior walls of the keep, the scene still suggested the power and refinement of Japan's feudal age.[55]

Looking out farther, Janes recorded, "one could see most of the large, compact province of Higo. Round the magnificent valley at the center of which, on a lofty ridge of volcanic tufa, stands the castle, encircling mountains make an inspiring sweep," he wrote, "with the ever active volcano, Aso-no-Yama, rising sentinel like at the farther border of the circuit." "Over this amphitheater of historic activities," he observed, "a cloudless canopy of blue rested like a reminiscent dream." It was not difficult, he thought, "to picture the host of toilers gathered from every district in Higo and from neighboring provinces breaking soil and chipping the soft lava within the bounds which Katō Kiyomasa himself outlined for the stupendous structure."[56]

"Happily for me that day," he explained, "it stood less as a monument to his genius than a record and exponent of one of the most significant and picturesque of the greater human institutions and as a monitor of things that must be borne in mind in the work about to begin."[57] Janes liked to emphasize that "pyramids, temples, and castles" were "not what they seemed." As he saw them, "they are the mute statues of human institutions. They are dashes of emphasis and exclamation points in the history of human progress." "Long after the passing purpose which they first served is lost," he emphasized, they remain signposts of the "moral and intellectual development of man." As such they are less "inspiring" in the "line of their past purpose," he underscored, than in "the significance of their promise" and "the assurance which they one and all imply of human power and of future progress."[58]

Janes later wrote that his early experiences and impressions were both favorable and challenging. He admired the Japanese for having materially effected "in a brief three years" what it "took England seven centuries to fully secure." At the same time he insisted that the Meiji Restoration, important as that event was as a symbolic break with the former feudal system, represented the "merest formalities of a beginning" toward a new order of "reconstruction." "The courtesy, the self-control, and seeming simplicity, the gentility, the love of nature and of beauty, the feeling for art, the patience, the patriotic fervor, and above all the newly awaked passion for learning," Janes wrote, excited his sincere admiration. And yet, these very qualities, he felt, threw into marked relief the latent tribal and national traits that centuries of feudalism had implanted as the natural order in Japan. "The old system," he observed, "was still there rooted in traditions, precepts, customs, sanctions and habits of thought that had the force and tenacity of religious convictions." Moreover, "viewed in the light of our Western civilization almost every feature of the system had a sinister and vicious aspect." Fascinated by the scene, Janes concluded that while feudalism and those allied with it had fought its first open battle with modern civilization and had been defeated, it was not by any means vanquished. From his perch it appeared to him that under his very feet "lay the prime obstacle to every forward movement in Japan."[59]

Looking down, Janes was struck by the general poverty that prevailed in Kumamoto and which seemed to stand in stark relief to the better economic conditions he had seen in Yokohama and Tokyo. He was distressed that the loudest sounds he heard upon entering the city, once the martial music had stopped, were the cries of beggars who lined every bridge he crossed. Moreover, he was outspoken in his criticism of the feudal order. The castle itself clearly stood as a symbol of what was wrong. "Poverty prevails," he wrote, "from the lair of the chief baron down to the horde of beggars that throng the highways because production is left to the least competent of the community, who toil in terror and starve while the proceeds are born off to the castle to furnish the feast for idle rioters." It seemed to him that little had changed. There were the samurai, "bare-headed and bare-legged, clothed chiefly in the sash or girdle in which were thrust his two villainous swords!" Not far away he saw the other half of the spectrum, "the parasite of the soil, the slave of the system, leading a manure-laden pack pony, or himself harnessed to his lumbering, wooden-wheeled cart!"[60]

Unlike some Western visitors to nineteenth-century Japan, such as Lafcadio Hearn, who saw in Japan's feudal heritage positive elements which they contrasted to the growing problems of Western industrial society, Janes had few good words for Japanese feudalism.[61] For Janes, who was an ardent believer in the concept of evolutionary progress, and who had drunk deeply from the wells he described as the "higher order of liberty, enlightenment, and individualism," feudalism represented the arch enemy. It was feudalism, he insisted, that dwarfed the Japanese mentally and physically. "Feudalism has no use for science and enlightenment," he stated, "hence, that all-enveloping pall of ignorance under which sickness and pestilence breed as fungi in a dense shade." "The aim and end of feudalism is to produce an ideal state of stagnancy," he wrote on another occasion, "and in the sphere of mind and morals, stagnancy as effectually produces mischief as it breeds poison in the fetid pool."[62] To Janes, looking out over Kumamoto, the effects of feudal stagnancy were everywhere apparent: in the social system, in the political order, in the physical condition of the people, and even in their taste for food and dress.

The Prince's dinner had underscored the problem. To see men, "grave and good, of noble blood and princely authority, fill themselves with flakes of absolutely raw fish, soy, beancurds slightly broiled, and krauted radish deftly cut for the chop-sticks into finger length morsels, crisp and malodorous—all on a broad and deep preliminary basis of boiled rice," caused him to speculate on the relation of a people's dietary habits to the "moral, intellectual, and physical stamina of its individuals." No one in Kumamoto, Janes wrote, seemed to be capable of the simple observation that a "diet of dirty sea salt—salt fish, salt radish, salt egg-fruit, salt plums, and salt soy—means a briny and pickled moral state and a desiccated, scurvied condition of every organ and tissue of the body." The Japanese, Janes was convinced, were salt poisoned, and this led to other "abnormal hankerings quite as inimical to health and to average bodily children and mental development." The Japanese fondness for raw fish, Janes insisted, was responsible for the "prevalence of the disease of leprosy" in Japan.[63] Moreover, he subsequently noted, "when children and adults alike come to take a ravening delight in the acrid acids of green sloes and of all other indigenous fruits in their primitive condition and unripe state, where is the motive for improvement of these fruits, or for the importation of those varieties of the most luscious and wholesome?"[64]

From the start, then, Janes was determined to mount a campaign against what he regarded as the "semi-savage appetites" of the Japanese he met in Kumamoto. Wasting no time to fire the initial salvo in his war against the old order, Janes invited the Prince and other local authorities to the first of his civilizing dinners. Using his temporary quarters as a base for a private propaganda campaign designed to exhort the virtues of the nineteenth-century American home and to demonstrate the advantages of Western culinary skills, he presented his assembled guests with an all-enveloping "rice pilau," which was "thick studded with seedless raisins and steaming with the savory essence of chicken." On the "snowy summit" of this dish were placed "two plump pullets," and at its base "abundant accessories suitable" to it. What Nagaoka Moriyoshi, the younger brother of the former Kumamoto daimyo, thought of the pilau, we can only leave to the imagination. However the dinner did afford him an opportunity to display his dexterity with knife and fork, something he had been secretly practicing with one of his interpreters, and gave him another occasion to pronounce the inevitable "We must civilize!" Needless to say, raw fish was not the cause of leprosy, as Janes thought, and there have always been those, including the good-natured Prince, one suspects, to whom raw fish could be as savory a dish as a rice pilau. But as Janes saw it, he had taken his first step to rid the country of the causes that had so dwarfed a whole nation physically and intellectually.[65]

Janes recalled that the refrain "We must civilize! We must civilize!" soon echoed from the top echelon of the domain's administration to its lowest representatives.[66] "The tone with which this formula . . . was flung into the air was such as to rouse in me only admiration and pity," he wrote, "while the feeling that I had the whole community at my back as clients and wards, from the Prince of the Province down to the beggars on the bridges, caused the spirit of devotion and determination to grow hot and constant within me from the culminating moments of our reception to the last hour of our stay in Kumamoto."[67]

But the question remained by "what process and means?" "Where was a beginning to be made? How was the race with reaction to be run under circumstances so peculiar?" "Look in whichever direction a conscientious person might," he lamented, "the difficulties in the way of any adequate returns seemed calculated to benumb effort and appall resolution."[68] There seemed to be so many obstacles. Not only was there the castle and its feudal past, which "hourly frowned despair" at him, but a multiplicity of other problems, major and minor, from frustrations with the incomprehensible Japanese language to the administrative inscrutability of those who brought him to Kumamoto, that had to be dealt with and overcome.[69] "Never had I felt more the need of the knowledge of men," Janes wrote, "never had I been so utterly severed from those supports to duty and endeavor which are so common to us at home as to be rarely recognized, never so hopelessly puzzled for means and methods of fitting an alien undertaking to so strange and uncongenial an environment." "Our entry upon the scene," he added, "had very poignantly impressed me with the necessity of carefully studying the situation before ever a stone was stirred toward the erection of a temple to the new order of enlightenment and progress." "Indeed far more forcible is the need for precaution and circumspection," he concluded, "when one is dealing with mind and moral character and the prejudices instilled by ages of counter influences rather than with material obstacles to material undertakings."[70]

While Janes had his doubts they involved only the question of where to begin, not the course to be pursued. For the Christian as radical reformer Kumamoto, and Japan as whole, presented unlimited opportunities. What shaped Janes' work in Kumamoto was not his doubts, but his unswerving conviction of the rightness of what he advocated as a reformer. Riding the wave of his own inner reconstruction, a wave which was not without its manic dimension, Janes had no room for ambivalence, half-way measures, or compromise. As he saw it, the world was remarkably clear. Almost everything around him was stagnant, backward, and in need of transformation. Moreover, Janes saw that transformation in scientific, not simply religious terms. Given the Practical Learning Party's own preoccupation with science and technology as a means of overcoming Japanese weakness, Janes' convictions were not without a sympathetic echo among the men with whom he was to work in Higo.

What Janes was to demonstrate in Kumamoto was the fascinating way in which his personality, the source of so much suffering in the American context, could combine with the unique flavor of the local environment. In a curious way the two suited each other. Despite his many prejudices, Janes could, and did, become a driving force for reform. As the all-embodying representative of Western civilization, he was called upon to play the hero, to make rules, to dispense advice, and to innovate. His introduction to Kumamoto, riding into the city in a procession befitting a major daimyo, clearly underscored local expectations. It was precisely Janes' "absolute fearlessness and assumption of superiority," and his ability to "out-samurai the samurai," that earned him lasting respect from the Japanese with whom he worked in Kumamoto. The missionaries later commented on his "impressive and imperious personality."[71] Nor were they alone in such an evaluation. One native pointed out that in comparison to Janes, "an everyday missionary would have looked like a penny candle flickering and fading before a typhoon."[72]

Janes brought to Kumamoto all the assumptions of superiority that a white man in the nineteenth century harbored toward orientals, but he also bore an unswerving belief and confidence that there were no innate racial reasons for Japanese backwardness. Freed from the shackles of feudalism, and enlightened by modern science, the Japanese possessed the same potential for "ushering in the day of millennial glory" as did Westerners. Nellie's legacy, to see men everywhere as pretty much the same, was therefore to make its own significant contribution to his work in Higo.

More than anything he wanted to get underway, but he also wanted to do his work in his own manner. Three weeks of feasting seemed more than enough to initiate him to Kumamoto life. In fact, he had already made certain crucial decisions. Among these was the all-important question of language. Making it amply clear that he was not going to work through "interpretation" in Kumamoto, he had "relieved" the two interpreters the domain had hired on his behalf in Tokyo—the first, a Mr. F, the day after his arrival in Kumamoto, and the second a few days later.[73] The length of the "feasting" may well have constituted an effort on the part of the Practical Learning reformers to size up their man and to determine how to deal with his independence.[74] Janes quotes Nonoguchi telling him in his own quaint English: "Please you, be patience, after a few months all will be ready. Then you can have *new interpreters*!"[75] Moreover, he recalled that having dismissed his interpreters, "a look and feeling of suspense began to take the place of the jaunty, hopeful, and rather childish expectations" of the men who had brought him to Kumamoto. "When my impatience and desire to be 'at work' were expressed," he recorded, "anxiety and amazement replaced their doubts and uncertainty."[76]

On the surface it seemed to Janes that "there was no thought whatever of anything's being done toward the direct advancement of the undertaking which had brought me all the way from America—for months." "How could there be?," he noted, "were not all the premises littered with lumber and chips for a vast space within that end of the moat and walls which enclosed the castle?" "The buildings which were to accommodate the school and ourselves," he emphasized, "existed only in the proud imagination of our Japanese friends . . . there seemed to be small prospect of anything tangible appearing above ground for the space of at least a year."[77]

On the other hand, Janes did not hesitate to involve himself in the construction project. Seeing the largely completed "Janes Mansion," he insisted that it be provided with fireplaces and a chimney. He recalled that it was "at once proposed to send immediately to Nagasaki to import materials and mechanics." But he insisted that the work could be done locally under his personal supervision. Using the available volcanic stone, "suitable holes were cut in the porch floors below and above, and through the ceiling and roof overhead." Then showing the Japanese builders "how to lay stone up to a plumb line" the fireplace and chimney went up with dispatch and with a sturdiness that defied the "fiercest typhoons" and "scores of earthquakes." Having earlier marked the absence of a single chimney or smokestack in the city as he gazed upon it from his perch atop the castle, Janes, who, like Hermann Maron, associated belching smoke with the quick pulsing life of industrial Europe and America, was pleased to have struck another blow for "civilization" and "enlightenment."[78]

Despite such diversions, Janes remained undaunted in the desire to be at work in his school. He begged Nonoguchi to trust him and to give him a temporary shelter large enough "to accommodate the fifty-odd students, who had crowded upon the scene and were waiting their turn in the novel venture" with far more "patience" than he himself possessed.[79] Finally, in what was clearly a far-reaching decision, the reformers agreed to let the foreign teacher have his own way, and the search for an interim location was undertaken.

"Half a mile or more from the site chosen for the school buildings," Janes wrote, "there rose the central citadel [of the castle] which crowned the five mile circuit of Cyclopean walls. Nearly half way toward this landmark, perched high up above even the level of the school grounds, and modestly ensconsed among the rocks and rock work, old camphor trees, and tufts of feathery bamboos . . . there stood a nearly deserted *yashiki*. It was the home of some female member of the Daimio's family—a princess—but whether the mother or sister of our Prince was not definitely stated. However, the whole household except for a servant or two, were away with the Prince's elder brother at Tokyo."[80]

"A few words from the Prince," Janes recalled, "caused this charming substitute . . . to be vacated and prepared for our use in less than as many hours." "The very next morning, I was asked to visit the place and see how it would answer." " 'Charming!' 'Thank you!'—and similar expressions of satisfaction, soon put the whole environment into a new but expectant state of equilibrium." The required accessories, including blackboards, were quickly assembled. And as Janes wrote, the "day of small beginnings" was at hand—the school was underway.[81]

CHAPTER VII

THE KUMAMOTO SCHOOL FOR WESTERN LEARNING

Small as its beginnings may have been, the Kumamoto School for Western Learning soon developed into one of the most important experiments in Western education in Meiji Japan. For the Practical Learning Party the school was central to its hopes for a "Restoration in Higo"; for the Captain it served as the means of realizing his own ideals. Powerful as the feudal forces around him were, they simply served to heighten his sense of mission. Having set his face against the "semi-savage appetites" of the Japanese he encountered in Kumamoto, Janes was ready to lead the younger generation in the direction of a new order.

With the start of classes in the mansion of the Hosokawa princess, the Captain was soon familiar with the forty-five students who composed the entering class. Both sides spent the initial days sizing each other up. The majority of the students had never seen a Westerner. Now they could observe one at close quarters and test the curious notions they had picked up about "foreign barbarians." There were those who maintained that "the legs of a foreigner were as straight as a bamboo cane and would not bend."[1] It was no accident, therefore, that one of the pupils carefully observed the Captain's legs, with the comforting conclusion that at least in this respect Japanese and Americans were more or less alike. Janes was not without his own preconceptions. Convinced that "man is pretty much the same the world over," he nevertheless found himself looking out over a sea of "black-eyed, heathen" faces.[2] But sensing the intensity, desire for learning, and thirst for Western knowledge that animated his class, he readily dropped even his religious distinctions. Impersonal "pupils" were soon transformed into "my boys."[3] Possessive and enthusiastic, Janes set himself to work.

He was now confirmed in the goals he had developed in his early sleepless nights in Kumamoto. As fully convinced as the Practical Learning reformers that the only solution to Kumamoto's feudal past was education and enlightenment, he differed only in the intended outreach of his program. As Janes saw it, "the education, the enlightenment, the progress in intelligence, which on the one hand will teach one class their duties and the policy of doing them, on the other will teach the masses to know their rights, inspire the courage and provide the means of maintaining them."[4]

The formal structure of the school was soon in place. By December Janes forwarded to the new prefectural government his educational plan, which called for a four-year program, an eventual enrollment of two hundred students, daily instruction of five or six hours, and a course of study that concentrated on a mastery of English as a means of acquiring the highest level of learning from around the world.[5] When the plan had been "fully outlined," "its inherent virtues and advantages explained," and its "feasibility assured," Janes recalled that "enthusiasm took a new bound," and "confidence was restored."[6] By the early months of 1872 the school's new facilities were in place. Ample dormitory space for several hundred students in Western-style rooms with bunk beds, a large lecture hall, and airy recitation rooms replaced the temporary quarters.[7] With these changes, Janes wrote, the foreign teacher "was willingly allowed to become an autocrat, in a mild way" within these precincts.[8]

While Janes pictured himself as an "autocrat, in a mild way," there were many among his students who saw him as "stern" and as a "rigid disciplinarian."[9] Ichihara Morihiro, a member of the first class, observed that in "the strictness of its rules and regulations . . . the school . . . was managed as though it had been a barrack of soldiers."[10] All aspects of student life were highly regimented. A myriad of rules governed student conduct from the moment they jumped out of bed in the morning to the instant they wearily lay down to sleep in the evening. Ebina Danjō has left us a picturesque portrait of daily life at the school.

The rising hour was either at five or six [depending on the season], and at the sound of a bell everyone had to jump out of bed. The breakfast bell rang at seven and everyone formed a line. Being led by one of the officers we entered the dining hall. In the dining room there were tables and no one was allowed to start eating before the others had begun. When the bell rang everyone started eating in unison, and when they were about through, the bell was rung again and the meal was finished. It didn't pay to eat slowly. When the bell was rung again, everyone got up as one body, and went out into the yard. In the yard we fell into ranks and facing East performed deep breathing exercises. Following this we broke ranks and took walks in the neighborhood of the school. Returning from these we stood before our rooms until the dorm chief addressed us with an English 'Good Morning!' After this we were allowed into our rooms. In a little while the class bell sounded, and forming another line we entered the classroom.[11]

Once they were seated Janes would enter with a "Good Morning!" of his own and the class would begin. Classes ran from eight to twelve in the morning and from one to four in the afternoon, with an hour off for lunch. During class hours no one was allowed in his private room, and attendance in the lecture hall was mandatory. Janes' method of instruction was usually to divide each class into sections, which he instructed personally in a separate room for an hour at a time. While not receiving personal attention, students studied by themselves. This lasted until four or five. In later years Janes' best students, particularly those of the first and second classes, served as instructors for the lower classes.

"After the evening meal," Ebina recalled, "it was all right to remain in the rooms, but the ideal thing was to go out into the garden for exercise. We usually went to bed at ten, but the bell rang half an hour earlier so that we might clean up our rooms and leave the lamps out in the halls. After ten an employee came to investigate, and everyone had to be in bed."[12]

If the regimen was strict so were the rules. Smoking and drinking were strictly forbidden. Punctuality was rigorously enforced. Students were not even allowed to use the school's toilets without first informing the dormitory officer, who inspected the facilities after use to make certain that cleanliness standards had been maintained. Woe to the student who failed to observe such regulations. Janes brooked no challenges to his authority. Those who did not care for the discipline, or the regimen, were asked to leave. Life became, as one student wrote, a "daily examination."[13]

Instruction in the school was wholly in English. Janes harbored no fondness for the Japanese language. The use of interpreters was, as we have seen, anathema to him. Moreover, he was appalled at the fact that it took most Japanese fifteen years of hard study to learn the mixture of Chinese and Japanese that lay at the core of traditional education. Given the need for rapid changes, the only solution, as he saw it, was to leave the Japanese and Chinese languages behind. English, the "all conquering" language, the noble tongue of "Clay and Webster, of Lincoln and Grant," he promptly insisted, should be learned by every student.[14] Fully confident that his wards could learn English in less time and with less effort than they expended on Chinese, he was also convinced that this was the best way of opening for them "the stores of knowledge they so hunger for."[15]

Starting with the first lesson, students were rapidly taught the alphabet, presented with one of Webster's blue-backed spellers, and instructed in the pronunciation of difficult English sounds by means of blackboard diagrams showing the appropriate positioning of tongue and teeth. Janes was a strict drill master and a firm believer in repetition. Even Nonoguchi, who remained in charge of the school, could often be seen limping along to and from the school muttering "e-l" "el," "e-l" "el," "j-a" "ja," "*the*," "*th*is," "*th*ese," with "only an occasional lapse into 'zis,' 'zese,' 'zose.' "[16]

After ten days of drill and practice Janes proceeded to daily examinations. In the first of these he failed several students and dismissed them from the school. Those who survived worked doubly hard to avoid a similar fate. One of the students recalled how these examinations made his "flesh shrink."[17] Another, Shimomura Kōtarō, who later became president of Dōshisha University, noted that students were soon required to memorize forty words a day. On one occasion, Shimomura remembered, Janes divided the boys in his class in two and dismissed the lower half from the school as hopeless. "You can imagine how I shuddered," he wrote, "when you learn that the line of demarkation was drawn between me and the next seat!"[18] Shimomura's hairbreadth escape resulted in the "utmost diligence." Thereafter he never failed to commit every word to memory, and even remembered the "order of the words as they appeared in the book."[19]

Every day Janes seated the students according to their academic standing. A poor performance might well mean moving to the very last seat, and a second lapse could easily result in dismissal. Of the thirteen students who accompanied Ebina Danjō to the school in the second year, only two survived.[20] Of the first class of forty-five, only eleven managed to graduate four years later.[21] Most of those who survived regarded Janes' methods "severe," but effective. The majority agreed that they did much for their learning powers.

Under such pressures the students' English improved rapidly and Janes started them on McGuffey's readers.[22] "Once we had come to the place where we could spell," Ebina wrote, "we were able to help ourselves."[23] With the readers came a copy of James C. Hepburn's new English-Japanese dictionary just published in Shanghai. At work on the readers the students noticed that the words they had taken such pains to learn to spell emerged again and again. It mattered little that the stories were childish to young men in their middle to late teens, what was important was their ability to read and understand them. Somehow, being able to read made everything interesting and all the work worthwhile.

For most of the boys McGuffey's simple stories with their distinct moral lessons constituted their first contacts with Western ideas. As a result every detail was weighed and evaluated. "When we read the first reader," Ebina stated, "we came to understand that Americans also possessed a moral conscience." Trained in the academies of Confucian scholars who emphasized the superiority of Eastern ethics and admitted a need to learn from the West only in the fields of science and technology, this was a "great discovery!" Reading further, Ebina was struck by the reader's efforts to instill humane attitudes toward animals in children. All this convinced him that Western sympathies were even more profound than Japanese, for these were things that "Japanese mothers did not teach their children."[24]

From a focus on the English language—spelling, grammar, and the readers—which occupied the students' first year, Janes moved them on to geography, history, and basic mathematics in the second. Algebra, geometry, trigonometry, and surveying took up the mornings of the third year; history the afternoons. In the fourth year mornings were given over to philosophy (physics), astronomy, and geology, while afternoons concentrated on chemistry, physiology, and English literature.[25] By the second year Saturdays were devoted to special subjects: composition, dialogues, declamations, and even speeches.[26]

Each of these fields broadened the students' vision. In geography "the whole world appeared before us in its entirety," one student wrote; in history there was the "idea of progress," which made Western history exceedingly interesting by comparison to the boring Chinese history he had learned earlier.[27] In geometry there was "logic," and in physics and chemistry the "air became alive" as students came to realize that "everything happened according to natural laws."[28] With growing enthusiasm among his students, Janes became equally enthusiastic about his teaching. "The changes I have seen," he wrote to Anna Warner in 1874, "are marvelous." The progress of his students, he added, is "simply astonishing."[29]

Janes' students were unquestionably talented. Kumamoto differed little from other parts of Japan where young men were quick to grasp the implications of a Western scientific education for both personal and national advancement. In the initial competitive entrance examinations more than five hundred students had vied for selection to the school's opening class.[30] Unlike Fukui, where the abolition of the domain led to an exodus of students in the direction of the cosmopolis, the Restoration in Higo seems to have had the opposite effect. Kumamoto's students, whether by choice or necessity, rallied to their former castle town and were fully prepared to shoulder the responsibilities of restoring not only their own, but the region's prominence in national affairs. At the same time, they shared the sense of national crisis that transcended regional politics.[31]

Nor was the domain parochial in its search for talent. The degree to which ability could cut through traditional feudal barriers and sectional animosities was amply illustrated in Janes' most brilliant pupil, Yamazaki Tamenori, who came from the northeast.[32] Selected by the governor of

Mizusawa prefecture (a former Kumamoto samurai) as one of the local students whose unusual aptitudes for learning could serve the nation, Yamazaki was introduced to Nonoguchi and Janes in Tokyo and accompanied them to Kumamoto. The governor's other choices, Gotō Shimpei and Saitō Makoto, the former a leading colonial administrator and head of the South Manchuria Railway and the latter prime minister of Japan from 1932 to 1934, show that he was not lacking in a discerning eye.[33]

Yamazaki and those like him who survived the daily examinations were unusually gifted young men. But in their enthusiasm they possessed a tendency to leap before they looked and frequently ran to extremes about almost anything that caught their momentary fancy. Later when they came to Dōshisha, Jerome D. Davis, their teacher, described handling them to be similar to "a man out West trying to plow his fields with wild donkeys hitched to his plow. He couldn't move them or stop them; all he could do was to hang on to the reigns as he was dragged around the field. When they rammed into a stump and came to a sudden halt, all he could do was roar."[34] While Davis was to have his troubles, this was not true of Janes, who soon earned his students' respect and in whose hands they became pliable. Whatever Janes may have lacked in academic brilliance, he was a remarkably effective teacher and leader in the Japanese setting.

In its rigid discipline, daily recitations, and constant ranking of its students—not to mention the scientific focus of its curriculum—the Kumamoto School for Western Learning bore striking resemblances to West Point. Nor were these the only parallels. The Higo school shared West Point's highly egalitarian structure, its fierce competitive emphasis, and its effort to develop individualistic leaders who were endowed with a strong sense of national mission. Moreover, if the school shared West Point's virtues, it also shared its vices. "A lurking sense of selfishness" was not confined to the banks of the Hudson. "We studied so hard," Miyagawa Tsuneteru wrote, "that we could feel the work tell on our health." While he looked favorably on the school's competitive structure, emphasizing with others that it resulted in a high level of performance, Miyagawa also frankly admitted that the system "had the disadvantage of producing envy and hatred among the students" and "divided them into parties."[35]

Kozaki Hiromichi remembered that the development of factions placed him under considerable pressures as assistant dormitory master responsible for the maintenance of Janes' "perfect order." During the third year, he recalled, "the discipline became very loose." Contrary to the regulations several students took up smoking, including the "son of Baron Hosokawa, a branch of our lord's family." "Among the students there were two parties," Kozaki noted, "the strict and the lax, which were at sword's points with each other." "Because of my office it was my duty to discipline them, but as the lax party included several students of great physical strength, and the sons of not a few wealthy and influential people, to administer summary punishment was not easy." In fact, trying to restore discipline seems to have led to a minor riot. As Kozaki recalled, one night "about midnight they raised a commotion in the dormitory and besieged my room, but I locked my doors and they were unable to break in."[36]

Janes was disturbed by such events. Using the history of the ancient Greeks, Miyagawa noted, "he told us that, among the causes, the envy and hatred which the Grecian states bore each other had been greatest in bringing about their ruin. He told us with tears that schoolmates should be kind and good to each other, and that they should not follow what the Grecian states had done." Miyagawa remembered that the students "were greatly moved" by Janes' zeal and "immediately cast off evil feelings" from their "hearts."[37] Kozaki recalled another side of the solution. Early the next morning, he tells us, those responsible were called up, "the heavier offenders were dismissed from the school, and the lighter placed in confinement." All, he underscored, received "proper punishment."[38]

Education, Janes warned the students, was like climbing a mountain, "one wrong step meant disaster." As a result patience and perseverance were required. Learning, he insisted, was a personal experience that he was "not able to teach." "You must do the thinking," he told the students, "I can act only as guide."[39] Mastery of a subject, for Janes, meant the ability to transmit what had been learned to others and to inspire them to think for themselves.

At the core of the school's educational program lay not only West Point's discipline, but the strong influence of Thomas Arnold's Rugby, with which Janes had become fascinated after reading Stanley's *Life* of Rugby's headmaster.[40] Arnold's muscular Christianity, his emphasis on character building, and even his insistence that enthusiasm and energy were more important in a teacher than high scholarship, seem to have struck responsive chords in Janes. Janes shared Arnold's goals of awakening the intellect of each of his pupils. He also shared Arnold's practice of teaching by questioning. Morita Kumando, himself later a teacher and professor at Dōshisha, recalled how Janes' method followed that of the "celebrated Arnold."[41] "His object in education," Morita wrote, "was to make the boys learn to improve their characters by their own efforts." "Mere bookworms were no object of his applause," he noted, "when, however, he found anyone whose intellect, feelings, and will were making united progress, there was no limit to his applause. His method of teaching was not that of simply pouring facts and ideas into the little heads of his pupils, which is often the case with ordinary teachers. On the contrary, he would only help to develop their mental faculties, arouse them, temper them, strengthen them." Morita added that, like Arnold, Janes considered the "development in his students' minds of patriotism, philanthropy, and religious belief" as the chief task of an educator.[42]

Many of Janes' students later commented on the degree to which their teacher worked to instill in them a sense of self-respect, self-worth, and self-effort. Ichihara Morihiro summed up the views of others when he wrote, "his object was to produce in the pupil's mind the spirit of self help, by which alone they could hope to become great and useful men." Janes not only prodded his students with questions; he was reluctant to answer any they posed. Instead he forced them to consider their questions until they were capable of deriving their own answers.[43] Ichihara recorded the quandary in which students unused to Janes' individualistic demands could find themselves. "There is an event," he wrote, "which I remember as if it happened yesterday. The Kumamoto hospital was in need of a new head doctor, and it was proposed to hire one of Captain Janes' relatives. He invited me to his house, and asked me what I thought about this proposal. I could not answer, for I was young and totally unaccustomed to being consulted on such important questions." "I felt ashamed for my inability to answer him." "The respect he paid me taught me that I must respect myself," Ichihara added, and "since that day I have always been careful to form opinions of my own on all important matters."[44]

Janes' effectiveness as a teacher was enhanced by his ability to understand the needs of individual students and to judge the personalities of those with whom he worked. As Ebina noted, "he was strict to some, and indulgent to others, modifying his method of teaching according to the character he had to deal with." "It is a matter worthy of utmost admiration," he added, "that he could discern the characters of his pupils and others without knowing a single word of Japanese."[45] As Ichihara saw it, he could be "mild and strict at the same time." "He would suppress by force the pride and conceit of one, and would give encouragement and consolation to the reserved and melancholy."[46] Most students admired his forthright and open approach to approval and censure. Shimomura wrote that if a student was making progress, Janes would "pat him on the head" and call him a "good fellow," but when he saw a student idle and neglecting his lessons, it was "fearful to hear him rebuke the boy." "Sometimes he could not contain himself and would smear the fellow's face with chalk."[47] The majority of the students agreed with Ichihara that "whether he praised or scolded us, he did it with all his heart, and we were always moved to our innermost being."[48]

It was clearly Janes' sincerity that made a deep and lasting impression on his students. While many commented on his extreme sternness in the classroom, his hardness, and even harshness, within the confines of his official duties as teacher and headmaster, they were also quick to add that he possessed a father's heart, was deeply concerned for their health and well being, and often treated them as if they were his children.[49]

For the sons of samurai, as the majority of the students were, the early Meiji years involved a difficult transition from the established values of the former feudal system, including its carefully delineated loyalty structure, to a more open, but often less charted, modern world for which the past served poorly as guide. Caught between two worlds, the young men of the Kumamoto School for Western Learning looked to Janes for new leadership. And yet, their conception of leadership was largely shaped by their early socialization as samurai. Despite Verbeck's assurance that there were no samurai in the United States, Janes' personality, demeanor, and conduct in Kumamoto basically challenged such an assertion. To samurai children the ideal warrior combined the strict discipline and hardness of fine swords with the soft emotional sensitivity of tears and fine poetry. To such individuals Janes' dual personality in which the rational educator, stern and strict disciplinarian, and firm advocate of science and technology could within the context of his home be transformed into the warm and affectionate father, the religious enthusiast subject to his strange joys, and a man capable of tears was not without a potential for greatness. Japanese heroes were made of such stuff, and if Janes looked upon the Japanese from the perspective of his American value structure, the Japanese were no less bent on judging him from theirs.

Janes' effectiveness in the school was influenced not only by his personality, but by an uncanny ability to sense the principal intellectual and political currents of the Japanese environment in which he worked. His emphasis on the development of a sense of moral wholeness, which expressed itself in public service, was readily comprehensible to students—as well as administrators—who shared the well-established Confucian conception that personal morality in the form of self-cultivation, and its extension to the family, prepared a man for the responsibilities of a public career and government service. In the mid-1870s, with the destruction of the feudal order and the privileges of the samurai class, efforts to preserve personal morality using the age-old categories of loyalty and filial piety became increasingly difficult. The result, as we shall see, was a moral reorientation. But that very reorientation was made possible by the fact that Janes' approach to education shared premises, which, for the sons of former samurai listening to him, resonated with harmony rather than dissonance.

While Janes' emphasis on personal effort and his attempt to instill in his students a consciousness that the future of their nation depended on their personal achievements had their sources in his own particular conception of the Christian as radical reformer, such ideas ran remarkably close to the mainstream of Meiji thought. Rugby's muscular minds and bodies, and West Point's rigid discipline, were in tune with the age, as was Samuel Smiles' dictum that "heaven helps those who help themselves." Nakamura Masanao's 1871 translation of *Self Help* rapidly transformed Smiles into a household word even in Kumamoto.[50] If Smiles became a dominant best seller in the early Meiji years and along with *Robinson Crusoe* provided new insights into how an island nation might be transformed, it was precisely Smiles' blending of personal and national interests that appealed to the Japanese samurai. "The worth of a state, in the long run," Smiles wrote quoting J. S. Mill, "is the worth of the individuals composing it." "The spirit of self-help is the root of all genuine growth in the individual," he added, "and, exhibited in the lives of many, it constitutes the true source of national vigour and strength."[51] Janes' position, despite its divergent origins, closely paralleled that of Smiles.

At the same time, the Captain's efforts to build self-confidence in his students involved a more subtle process. While he was well aware that modernization in Japan would require a component of Westernization, Janes objected to the unqualified Westernization of Japanese who rejected their national identity and the Japanese past in the name of a new modern and Western self. He was particularly critical of Japanese who despised Japan. Ebina remembered a conversation with his teacher in which Janes commented on a Japanese who had just returned from America and who indicated that he wanted to return to the United States because in Japan, he said, "houses were so small, food so poor, and everything so dirty and miserable." "It argues a want of patriotism," Janes told Ebina, "for a Japanese to wish to 'go back' to America, especially when he is not ashamed to speak badly of his own country before a foreigner."[52] Janes advised Ebina not to go abroad until he had come to know his own country better. On another occasion, hearing that a Japanese had referred to other Japanese as "savages," Janes warned Ebina: "You take care never to call your fellow countrymen savages or any other names no matter how wretched they may be."[53]

Yokoi Tokio, Shōnan's son, was similarly taken with Janes' efforts to counter the uncertainty and confusion of the early Meiji years with a strong emphasis on purpose, moral identity, and national mission. Janes' object, as Yokoi wrote, was to teach the students the advantages of working together, to help them to develop their personal faculties, and at the same time to instill in them a sense of independence that insisted on a "despising of foreign assistance and a relying on themselves." Finally, he added, Janes taught them to serve their nation through "practical work."[54]

Janes' dual approach, combining an emphasis on a thoroughly Western education with a demand for self-respect that included a strong identification with the nation, proved to be highly effective in the Higo setting. Kumamoto's young men, like many elsewhere in Japan, saw the early Meiji years in terms of destruction and dislocation. Ebina put it most succinctly when he wrote of the Restoration largely in negative terms: "As I was the son of a warrior family, I was deprived of the object of my loyalty, namely my lord, and even my attitudes toward my parents changed. The four classes became equal, but everywhere the gaining of influence resulted in a loss of manners. Art and music were destroyed. Confucianism which had ruled our lives for centuries was also destroyed and the writings of the sages were considered of no value. It was in such an age that I was raised, and I could not avoid being influenced by it."[55]

Ebina, like others of his generation, was troubled by the contradictory faces of the Restoration. Renovation and reform—the conservative effort to restore an imperial tradition, on the one hand, and the need to modernize in the face of an overwhelming Western military threat, on the other—were equally destructive to the world in which these students grew up and received their early educations. As a result, pride in Japan's unique past, even in Japan's imperial tradition and its restoration, was quickly short-circuited by the sense of inferiority that many Japanese felt toward overwhelming Western military superiority. As Janes realized, emulation and the need to overcome, pride and inferiority, were intricately linked in the Meiji samurai mind. The Captain's call for a strong sense of national consciousness on the part of his students, which went hand in hand with the school's Western education, therefore not only served to build self-confidence, but suggested to the young men under his supervision a remarkably effective way of transcending the paradoxical polarities of national pride and inferiority that lay at the heart of the Restoration.

As Janes saw it, a sense of "self esteem (in a good sense) is an essential to civilization" everywhere.[56] He agreed with Mill that the strength of a state depended on the worth of its citizens. Self-reliant, independent men were as important for the maintenance of the state in Japan as they were in the West. Moreover, Janes did not believe in innate Western superiority. As he wrote to Anna Warner, strip "active Christianity" from "European life and character, and civilization," and "there would be not so much left on which to base a claim of superiority."[57] Janes firmly believed that men of self-esteem endowed with a sense of national consciousness could use the tools of modern science and technology to help the nation turn its back on ignorance and superstition, and could enable the Japanese to achieve a level of civilization on par with that of the West. His confidence in evolutionary progress underscored such a hope. The millennium, in its secular form, in which "the spade and pick, tile, cement and pure water" were "prayer and praise," was as achievable in Japan as it was in Europe and the United States.

As appealing as Janes' vision of a new order based on the twin pillars of self-esteem and science may have been in the school, they do not appear to have elicited an equally enthusiastic response at home. Harriet, whose approach to mission work reflected more conservative attitudes nurtured during her childhood in India, did not share his views. Janes' method of teaching, which was designed to endow the Japanese with the tools through which they could unlock the secrets of the outside world for themselves, ran counter to her conception that the West had a truth, rather than a method, to dispense. When Janes suggested that she teach the sisters of the Yōgakkō students, she replied: "I do not feel called upon to teach these people. I do not believe in your 'science' and your 'knowledge.' It only puffs them up and makes them conceited, whereas they should learn to be humble, humble, humble."[58] Needless to say, Janes' judicious rejection of his wife's formula constituted a major reason for his success.

Interestingly enough, Janes was a firm believer in coeducation. On this issue he was willing to confront not only his wife but many of the Yōgakkō students. At the start of the fourth year he allowed two girls, Yokoi Shōnan's daughter, Miya, and Tokutomi Ikkei's daughter, Hatsuko, to join the entering class. Receiving the reluctant approval of the school authorities, he was warned by many of the students that this was a radical departure from the local mores and could lead to reprisals. "I tell you," he is said to have replied, "that if I am to lose my life in Higo, I would rather it had been done after this school was half filled with girls, for then my death would count for something and there would be such an awakening in this country as would make short work of this stupid prejudice against the education of women."[59] To Ebina, who told Janes that he never thought he would have to "come down" to being a "teacher of girls," he advised that he might think of the fact that his mother had "also once been a girl."[60] As far as Janes was concerned women were in every way as capable of learning and contributing to the new order as were men.

Janes saw the purposes of education as transforming individuals who as independent entities committed to universal values and seeking their own fulfillment would become the firm underpinnings of a modern state much as laissez-faire economists hoped through Adam Smith's "invisible hand" to transform self-interest into public good. The students with whom he worked, while less concerned with the issues of universal values and self-fulfillment, were equally committed to the goal of state service. Given the nature of the school and its original goal of producing statesmen through whom the domain could retrieve its lost position in national affairs, it is not surprising that, as one student observed, "the official air was in evidence everywhere."[61]

Most of Janes' students saw their training as a prelude to national political careers. Kozaki recalled that "discussions on the political situation of the day were long and fierce."[62] Exposure to Western ideas provided new possibilities. Long before others called for a parliamentary system, he observed, Saturdays were frequently devoted to planning a future cabinet. What Kozaki later chose to forget is that in these discussions he always reserved the premiership for himself.[63]

In some ways Janes catered to the political inclinations of his students. Convinced that Japan would soon establish a parliament, he advised them that learning the art of public speaking was of vital importance to anyone interested in modern politics. Students were taught the rules of debate, given speeches by Clay, Webster, Macauley, and Burke to memorize, and allowed to practice their oratorical skills on Saturdays—sometimes before the local citizens.[64] Given the fact that there was no tradition of public speaking in Japan, all this was no doubt quite new and exotic for both speakers and audience.[65]

While Janes saw the usefulness of public speaking and its future application to the political world, he was generally distrustful of politics, and he was hardly enamored of the overwhelming political preoccupation of those in the school. Students, as he saw them, were novices, unqualified to make mature judgments about national affairs. Even oratorical exercises at the students' level, he told Ebina, were more important for their spiritual significance and self-discipline than for any future political rewards.[66] Politics was an arena for adults. When one of Ebina's classmates criticized the Meiji government's position on the controversial proposal for a punitive expedition against Korea in 1873, Janes gave the student's paper a very bad mark and soundly scolded him for "presuming to know more than the nation's leaders."[67]

Worried about his pupils' political ambitions, and what struck him as a strong clannishness, Janes worked hard to turn them in new directions. It was at this time, Kozaki relates, that he started to lecture on world politics and pointed out the evils of clan government, as well as the need for a strong and united country. Such thoughts, Kozaki added, "changed the current of our enthusiasm and ere long we were going through the community talking of world currents, the abolition of the clan system, a united nation, etc., and all the time getting well laughed at for our pains."[68] Yokoi Tokio noted that in leading his students toward a "saner frame of mind" Janes was not above using sarcasm when necessary.[69]

Janes constantly tried to suppress the overwhelming personal ambition of his boys in favor of what one of them described as "a true love of our country and a resolution to work for it, placing ourselves in humble stations." Suggesting that he had his own ideas on humility, which combined self-respect with public service, Janes told them: "It would be a vain effort for you to place yourselves in high stations and call the people up to you. You must be humble and not hesitate to take on your shoulders the most disagreeable tasks, to push the nation up to prosperity."[70] With time, his lessons, foreign as they were to the young men who had been brought up to see themselves as a privileged ruling class, were taken far beyond the confines of the Kumamoto school. Tokutomi Iichirō (Sohō), subsequently one of Meiji Japan's best known journalists, and the leading spokesman for the younger generation of the 1880s and 1890s, proudly called his immensely popular journal *Kokumin no tomo*, *The Nation's Friend*, and its supporting association the *Minyūsha*, *The Friends of the People*.[71] While Tokutomi's attitudes toward Janes' Christian values cooled with the years, he, like many of his schoolmates, remained committed to the secular portion of Janes' vision and continued to see himself as a "self appointed staunch ally of the people."[72]

Trying to have his students devote themselves to the greater public good, Janes attempted to point them toward new ideals. As he wrote to Anna Warner in 1874, his goal was to "fit the students for the work of developing the country," to utilize "its untold and untouched resources for mining, manufacturing, shipbuilding, commerce, engineering, and agriculture."[73] For these Japan would have great need. Politicians were plentiful. What the country lacked were engineers and technical specialists who could devote themselves to the development of commerce and industry. Arguing that the economic development of Japan was crucial for both national strength and the improvement of the people's lot, Janes inspired his wards to dream new dreams. "The foundation of the prosperity of a country is national wealth and military strength," Janes announced to the students. "For the advance in strength of a country the most important factor is the development of industry. For Japan, in particular, the important thing is the encouragement of agriculture, mining, engineering, ship-building and mechanical arts."[74] "Politics," he added, "is the least important." In America, he assured the students, "politicians are generally inferior men." Moreover, "to become an official is the humblest of professions."[75] Such exhortations, Kozaki tells us, caused many of the students to find fresh aims for their careers. For a time he had Ichihara Morihiro, later the mayor of Yokohama, headed for medicine, Yokoi Tokio for the navy, Kanamori Tsūrin, who later lectured on political economy, for shipbuilding, and even Kozaki, reluctant as he was to abandon the premiership, for a career in mechanical engineering.[76]

While there were many pupils who made the transition from politics to commerce and industry, and subsequently from these to education and religion (the latter largely during the revivalistic phase of the school's final year), there were others who remained firmly committed to Janes' secular vision. Yokoi Tokiyoshi was typical.[77] Not only a gifted student, but subsequently a brilliant scholar and professor who spearheaded the development of scientific agriculture in Japan, Yokoi never accepted Christianity. But as Meiji Japan's most prominent agricultural specialist, and subsequently as president of Tokyo Agricultural University, he was to leave a deep and lasting imprint on the field in which Janes first aroused his interests. Yokoi's emphasis on the need to educate, to enlighten, and to lift up Japan's rural population, which became a life-long crusade, shows that Janes' lessons could be heeded and implemented in their purely secular form. As such they were no less endowed with a potential for reform that left its mark on modern Japan.

It must also be emphasized that education at the Kumamoto School for Western Learning was almost entirely secular. Janes' task as he saw it within the school was to educate, and not to proselytize. In writing about their experiences, most alumni insisted that the Captain "did not say one word about Christianity in the classroom."[78] While one may question the veracity of such an assertion after the Christmas vacation of 1875, when Janes appears to have become subject to an unbridled revivalistic fervor, it does seem to have been true of the earlier years.[79] If Janes used the school to push the students toward Christianity, it was through the indirect process of getting them to consider what lay behind the predictability of scientific laws, the orderliness of the universe, and the beauty and intricacy of the world around them. Such an approach was consistent with his rational and scientific conception of the Christian as radical reformer, the image that had allowed him to restructure emotionally in Maryland and convinced him to come to Japan.

Janes' respect for the secular nature of the school, and his reluctance to engage in proselytizing efforts during the initial four years of his tenure in Kumamoto, suggests the degree to which the carefully worked out compromise between his mother's emotional Methodism and his father's cool and rational Presbyterianism remained intact. And yet, Janes could certainly become revivalistic on other subjects. One of these was education.

Addressing his students, their parents, and an assembly of official guests at a banquet held at the close of 1874, the purpose of which was to commemorate the completion of his first contract and the decision by Hosokawa Morihisa to fund the school for an additional two years, Janes told the people of Kumamoto that during his first three years at the school he had not only tried to create an environment designed to minister to the growth of the best and noblest powers of mind and heart among his pupils, but that he had tried to establish "a school that would in due time contribute its share toward the development of the material resources, the mines, manufactures, and commerce of the country." He assured his audience that in the course of his work within the school his respect and love of the people of Kumamoto had grown steadily, and that, increasingly enthusiastic about the school, he had also greatly expanded his vision of the importance of education to modern life.[80]

"My friends," he announced to the assembled guests, "this thing we call education is the supreme friend of man—the hope of the human race—the source of power and permanency to government—the source of happiness and wealth, and the means of usefulness to individual men." "The mind of man is expanding with new ideas, and leaping forward to new efforts. His soul swells with the contemplation of what has been accomplished in these few recent years, and is all aglow with hope and action."[81]

The world, as Janes pictured it, was in the midst of an "educational revolution," which Japan could ill afford to ignore. Everywhere it was the societies that most broadly educated their citizens that were on the rise. Not only was this the chief source of America's expanding power, but the lessons from Europe were equally clear. Germany's recent victory over France was the result of an enlightened German peasantry fighting its uneducated French counterpart. France's elitism, he argued, was to cost it dearly. "If you enlighten, as for instance Paris is enlightened in the midst of thirty millions of ignorant peasantry, in the day of war and trial it counts for no enlightenment at all." The relationship of education to national power was abundantly clear. Even the Russian Tsar, Europe's least enlightened ruler, he noted, had become aware of the need for education, if "Alas!" only to produce "intelligent soldiers." It is because of Europe's and America's emphasis on education, he insisted, that they are ahead of the East.

All the great inventions, whether the steamship, telegraph, printing press, railroad, or electricity, not to mention advances in agriculture, industry, or business, Janes went on to tell his audience, were the products of education. "The cotton gin, the reapers and mowers, the sewing and knitting machines, the spinning jenny, the loom, the steam engine itself and the thousand other products of enlightened mind, to which its powers are applied—have these not demonstrated," he asked, "the profit of learning?" "They will yet convince governments by the potent argument of power and wealth, of the impolicy of devoting millions to armies and navies and hundreds to schools." "He will be counted an unsuccessful statesman before the close of this century," Janes warned his politically ambitious pupils, "who would perpetuate the reign of ignorance, with its accompanying poverty and weakness, and do it by the expensive hand of power."

"What," Janes next asked, "is the peculiar treasure of a government, the peculiar wealth of a nation, in its national capacity?" Rejecting the idea that the wealth of a nation lay in the richness of its land, plentiful harbors or in its mines, agriculture, and natural resources, or even in the numbers of its citizens, he emphasized that the true wealth of a nation rested in the "*intelligence* and *virtue* of its people," for, as he added, "wisdom and virtue are ever associated." "What is wealth but a curse without virtue?," he asked. "What is power but an evil, without wisdom to guide it?"

"O let the words go forth through this beautiful land!," Janes exclaimed with missionary-like fervor, "would you lay deep the foundations of its wealth, its strength, its grandeur? Would you draw to you the longing eyes of the less happy nations around you, along the Asiatic Coasts? Would you lead the civilization of five hundred millions of Asiatic people? Then learn, Oh! learn and heed the lessons which all history teaches. The cornerstone of the structure you would build must be intelligence and virtue, 'peace and enlightenment!' "

Janes advised his listeners not to trust in numbers—look at what happened to India—nor in natural resources—look at Spain, "one of the richest countries in Europe" and at the same time "one of the poorest and weakest." If there was a model for Japan to follow it was Switzerland. "Switzerland," he observed, "is a land of rocky mountains containing no minerals and possessing a most sterile soil. It lies in the heart of Europe and has no sea port. Its government is the freest, one of the oldest, and I may say the strongest in Europe. It has withstood the shocks of war and every attempt at conquest, longer than any other in Europe." The leading powers of Europe, France, Germany, Italy, and Austria, have "more than once sent their mighty armies to pull down the little Republic from its stronghold in the Alps, only to have them come back at last beaten and unsuccessful." "For more than four centuries, that little state nursed its liberties and its life in the lap of intelligence. The school system of Switzerland is the oldest . . . and best in Europe."

Appealing to the strong nationalistic sentiments of his listeners Janes observed: "Who is there that loves his country? I know that you are patriotic. But if that be a foolish question, let me ask, *what* do you love? Do you love the rocks and trees, and rivers and soil? There are rocks and trees and hills and valleys in all lands. The true patriot is a lover of men, of his countrymen." Underscoring his effort to get his students to devote themselves to public service, he noted, "how many show their patriotism by desiring to rule! How few are willing to teach, and to serve!"

The real threat to Japan, Janes emphasized, was not foreign invasion but ignorance. "If one were to come in here and proclaim that an enemy had landed on your coast and was preparing the conquest of your homes, I know what you would do. Father and son would go forth together and stand as an outer wall against such a foe. *That* conquest could not be made while you lived. But O my friends, there is an enemy abroad in this land, as in every land, mightier than armies, more to be dreaded, and harder to be fought than any invasion. It is ignorance! *He* strikes at the roots of a nation's greatness; he toils to undermine all its prosperity! It is his method to dry up the resources of the country, to blast and destroy through weakness; for if 'Knowledge is Power,' ignorance is weakness. He locks up the wealth of your mines. He paralyses the arm of the manufacturer. He steals the fertility from the farm, and sucks the life blood from all commerce. And this giant enemy has many allies. Disease is his ally. Intemperance is his ally. Poverty, prejudice, and crime are all marshalled under the banner of ignorance and do his work. Look around you. O look around you, and see the sorrow, the misery, the sickness, suffering, and death which the enemy of your people and of the race scatters broad-cast all over the land!"

"Have you no heart," he challenged his audience, "to feel for those who have enjoyed none of the advantages you enjoy?" "We call it a brave thing to die for one's country," he continued, "but is it not a braver thing to live for one's fellow men?" "O if the armies that have desolated the earth with war, and washed it with blood, had been armies under the glorious banners of 'Peace and Enlightenment,' what a different scene would the world present today! And if the treasures that have been lavished on fleets and armies, in fruitless conquests, and wars of ambition, if only a fraction of these untold millions had been spent in the cause of enlightenment, to the blessings of which the world is just awaking, how much less would now remain to be done to lift the race out of its degradation!"

In a long outburst Janes compared education with ignorance. "It is education," he insisted, "that blesses the race and the nation, and man. And ignorance is their curse. Education is the life of states, their vital principle. Ignorance is their dry-rot, their disease, their greatest burden, their heaviest tax. Education is the power of states. Ignorance is their weakness. Education soothes passions, softens prejudices. Ignorance inflames them all, cultivates hatreds and inspires revenge. . . . Education fertilizes the farm, multiplies workshops, builds manufactories, spreads the sails of commerce. Education builds ships. Ignorance wrecks them. Education builds hospitals and delights in healing; ignorance builds prisons and fills them. Education builds asylums; teaches the dumb to speak, the deaf to hear, the blind to see. Ignorance fills the streets with these children of suffering; and breeds with poverty to multiply them."

"Ignorance says to his son, 'you dishonor me if you learn more than I have been able to learn; be content like the bull or the horse to be led.' Enlightenment says to its child, 'my son let my old age rejoice in your prosperity. Go forward in the great race of life and win a glorious prize. Make me glad with the honors of your high career; and let my dying ears hear the praises and the blessings men bestow on the name you bear!' Ignorance will use no tools that have not on them the rust of time. Education teaches its votaries to make the best use of every advantage for the blessing of the race. Ignorance is stagnation, and stagnation breeds rottenness and death. Education gathers fresh life and new energy out of every acquisition and grows stronger by its own exercise. Ignorance is the offensive, slime-covered ditch, whose waters are poisonous, and whose smell is disease. Education is the mountain stream, springing pure as crystal out of the rocks, laughing in the sunshine, leaping to turn the wheels of industry, and drive the mills of progress, and spreading out to irrigate the fields of man's mind and heart and soul; to feed the roots of every noble impulse; and to make them fruitful in blessings to the race."

"Who would dam up such a source of infinite blessings?," Janes asked. "Who would shut down the gates, and turn the waters off, to waste in the ocean of ignorance." "He that would," Janes stated with disdain, "is an enemy of his country and of the race. Patriotism will disown him." On the other hand, "more than patriotic praise" will come to those who devote their lives to the enlightenment of others. "The reverence of minds set free from the tyranny of ignorance will be his rich reward." "The love of hearts that owe to him their highest motives and best hopes in life, will be to him, living, tribute which such hearts only can feel; and when he dies will mourn as none others mourn the departure of the friend of man." "Surely," he concluded, "such efforts are their own exceeding great reward."

What we have here is the essential Janes. Passionate, enthusiastic, fully convinced of the rightness of his cause and the purpose of his mission, he was caught up in a world-wide crusade that was as important for Meiji Japan as it was for post–Civil War America. Filled with the zeal of a secular missionary, he inspired confidence not only among his pupils but among the broader public. Propelled by the rising tide of a new sense of personal worth and usefulness that made him ever more optimistic, he instilled a similar mood in his listeners. "It is easy to imagine," Kozaki wrote, "how this kind of talk took hold of us and fired our imaginations. Our industrial castles faded out of sight, and we became enamored of education."[82]

Having moved his students from politics to industry, and from industry to education, Janes was only one step removed from the second half of his educational formula, i.e., virtue. While the educational emphasis of the school remained strictly secular, Kozaki noted that the move to education inspired new ideals, and although religion was generally discounted by the majority of the students as of no consequence, "some of the boys resolved to investigate it," and "asked the Captain to teach them the English Bible."[83] The consequences of these Bible studies were to be dramatic and deserve exploration in a separate chapter. What needs to be underscored here is that Janes' goals for the school remained consistent with the plans of the Practical Learning reformers to train young men in science and technology, and to prepare them for public careers through which Kumamoto's lost prominence could be restored.

If there were any signs that Janes hoped to achieve a different goal than that intended by his sponsors, particularly in the dominant emphasis on secular enlightenment, they remained largely undetectable before the winter of 1875. Janes may have hoped that some of his students would come to share his Christian ethical values and would become "Christian miners and mechanics" with time, as he wrote to Anna Warner in 1874, but the school's emphasis was on teaching them to become miners and mechanics.[84] As Ebina wrote, "he was always exceedingly careful to distinguish education and religion." "I never heard him speak of Christ in the classroom," he added, "it was only to the volunteers and in his own house that he preached the Gospel."[85]

At the same time, Janes objected to the Practical Learning Party's separation of ethical studies from the rest of the school's curriculum. The initial program of having students study the Confucian classics with Takezaki on Sundays particularly aroused his ire. Regarding himself well qualified to serve as "an example of sound morals" to his wards, he saw little that was worthy of emulation in the Neo-Confucian system, which he associated with the decadent past. Takezaki's Sunday lessons were soon quietly dropped.[86] Meanwhile, Janes renewed his efforts to convince the students that Western science was not devoid of ethical underpinnings of its own.

By 1875 the original goals of the school had been largely achieved. Kumamoto's Practical Learning reformers had much to be thankful for. While some of their reform ideas had suffered considerable setbacks within the give and take of prefectural politics, the school remained a positive expression of their reform ideals.[87] With the graduation of its first class in the summer of 1875 both sides had reasons to feel elated. Janes, who four years earlier had often been overwhelmed by the enormity of the task before him, was now confident and enthusiastic. He, too, had reasons to be proud. In their achievement, as well as in their mental capacities, he observed, his students compared favorably with "any class he had known at the United States Military Academy."[88] Their subsequent careers certainly underscored such an evaluation.[89]

While it is clear that Janes looked upon the school as part of his secular campaign to bring civilization and enlightenment to Kumamoto, and while it is equally obvious that the school became an extension of his personality, it should also be emphasized that in the Captain there was always the possibility that the rational educator could turn into the revivalistic camp preacher. As one student saw, the control mechanism that balanced Comte's practicality with Milton's idealism could run amuck in his Carlylian personality.[90] Under such circumstances what had been paeans of praise for an educational revolution could easily become a call for an inner revolution of a different order.

But if the rational side of Janes' personality could be overwhelmed on occasion by his revivalistic and emotional instincts, as the winter of 1875–76 was to show, such predominantly religious periods should not detract from the fact that he was also a secular reformer. Enlightenment through education was clearly one of the dominant themes of his work in Kumamoto. An improvement of the livelihoods of the people through the advancement of agriculture and industry was another.

CHAPTER VIII

YANKEE INGENUITY AND INITIATIVE

W̲HILE JANES' official duties centered on the school, his influence and accomplishments were to range far beyond the context of Kumamoto's educational enterprise. As he observed, the region provided numerous opportunities to pioneer and innovate. The Captain's role as agricultural adviser and technical consultant represents one of the most important, if least known, aspects of his stay in Kumamoto. Indeed, it was in this capacity that he moved beyond the closely guarded confines of the school, established wide contacts with the people, and made some of his greatest contributions to the prefecture.[1]

Janes' experiences in Kumamoto were unique in several respects. Few Westerners were allowed into the interior during the immediate post-Restoration years, and fewer still sought to reside there for any length of time. Janes was thus among a select handful of Americans and Europeans who saw the Meiji transformation from the vantage point of a provincial power center, and who experienced the early Meiji changes at the grass-roots level.[2]

From his position in Kumamoto Janes saw the Restoration as having opened up both a political and social rift. And it was into this rift that the men who brought him to Kumamoto hoped to wedge his school. Their aim, on the one hand, he wrote, was to make the break with the past complete. On the other, it was to secure "the forces and resources of science and enlightenment" to support "some undefined and vaguely yearned for new order and policy."[3] Janes' analysis was quite correct. But what he failed to add was that the use of wedges was not limited to the school. The very presence of the Captain, his wife, and children was part of the overall plan of the Practical Learning reformers to shift Kumamoto's focus in the direction of a major reorientation. As such, Janes' out-of-class expertise, and the symbolic significance of his family, were intrinsic parts of the reform plan. Quite apart from his personal motivation, the practical application of his conception of change and improvement was to blend nicely with the reform ideals of his sponsors.

To what extent Janes was prepared for these tasks remains open to question. Other than the personal experience he had gained on his father's farm and at Elk Ridge, he hardly qualified as an agricultural specialist.

But what Kumamoto needed was less advanced expertise than practical information. By experience Janes had become a good generalist with wide-ranging interests. Kumamoto's needs in the 1870s paralleled those of Ohio in the 1820s and 1830s, and the legacy of his family's role in the American transformation allowed him to function as a useful intermediary in Japan.

Janes' initial response to Japanese agriculture was highly favorable. He and Harriet had made their way toward Kumamoto through beautiful fields of waving rice and millet. Along the banks of the Shirakawa they had admired the neat market gardens of vegetables and greens. Considering his recent acquaintanceship with Horace Capron, he questioned whether Japan might not "send an agricultural commission to teach Americans," rather than have one "sent from the United States to enlighten Japan." But soon he concluded that his initial assessment represented a hasty and superficial view. Despite the intensity of the cultivation, he was surprised to find that fruits and vegetables were "coarse in texture . . . tasteless and innutritious." Japanese agriculture, he came to feel, was far too limited to a "comparatively few grains reproduced over and over again with no thought of improvement." Although manuring was carried out "to a high pitch," fruits and vegetables grew "too rank for flavor and quality."[4]

The lack of sympathy for Japanese cuisine, already observed, was soon matched by a severe disappointment with the products of Kumamoto's gardens. One of his Tokyo friends, Janes recalled, had warned him of the "necessity of a special provision of vegetables" that were "fit to eat."[5] He quickly agreed. At the same time he envisioned the chance of "ameliorating the conditions which affected the health and well being of the community and race." And as he pointed out, "within the school and without it, no opportunity was ever lost to press the importance of a sound physical foundation, and the means of attaining it, as the necessary basis of all improvements—whether intellectual, moral, social, material, or political." It took only a brief stay in Kumamoto, therefore, to "confirm an incipient purpose already formed." By the next steamer he sent off an order of seeds to Peter Henderson of New York that was ten times larger than required for his own use. The seeds arrived just in time for planting the next spring (1872), and as Janes remembered, "few investments were ever freighted with profounder satisfaction."[6]

Before the seeds could be planted, however, a plot of land had to be secured, and here Janes seems to have encountered some difficulties. The Prince, to whom application for a piece of land was made, could not understand why a foreign teacher would give thought to so insignificant and ignoble a thing as the production of vegetables. He insisted that he himself would furnish the Captain with sufficient vegetables every day. Janes would not accept such an offer, and finally a small garden plot was provided, "not more than a quarter of an acre," which stretched between the foreign house and the outer wall of the castle along the Shirakawa. The land was quickly cleared of its "bamboo-growth, shrubs, and rubbish" and put into a condition that would have gratified "the eye and requirements of a Peter Henderson himself."[7]

Next Janes encountered negotiations that he thought decidedly "oriental." Before the seeds could be planted a deputation of members of a newly organized "Horticultural Society," including Takezaki Sadō, its head, paid a call on him, saying that they had a small fund and would he help them to get started. Here was "face saving," indeed, he noted, and in turn offered the society a majority of the seeds he had ordered from New York. No, this they could not allow, but would he direct the planting in his own garden and conduct such experiments as he thought best, merely allowing them free access and the benefits of his instruction?[8] Janes was only too happy to comply.

"The seeds came," he wrote, "and a set of American garden tools from San Francisco. The former, but not the latter, were promptly divided and shared liberally with the Society with injunctions to observe my operations carefully so as to repeat them in the garden space on the outskirts of the city, which they had already secured for planting and experimenting of their own. Then there was planting indeed in seedbeds and in the open for the production of plants in some variety to be given away and distributed."[9] The enterprise seems to have been off to a good start.

> The season, the soil, the work of my excellent Betto—destined to become an intelligent expert gardener—everything was auspicious. Everything seemed to grow as if it had felt the watering and nourishing of fervent desires. Pease went promptly into the ground of both gardens; but not the solid shot of the native shops, which had been proven capable of resisting the solvent power of twenty-four hours boiling, and whose texture defies the digestive effects of anything more yielding than a pair of granite mill-stones painfully kept in motion by a pair of strong arms. Onion sets of various sorts were also planted to replace the leek-like fibrous stalks, which, once seen as they are drawn from soil sodden in the all prevalent vehicle of typhoid fever and eaten to the very leaf tips in a watery soup which would have no flavor without them, become an object of just abhorrence to civilized sensibilities. These foreign sets were induced to resume their globular growth and prove to the onlooking member-

ship of the Society that evolution is a factor to be considered in the production of onions as well as of men.[10]

In addition to the peas and onions, cabbage, cauliflower, and lettuce plants were grown and widely distributed for trial in other parts of the prefecture, where Janes reported they did well. By the time he left Kumamoto he had added okra, sweet corn, potatoes, tomatoes, turnips, melons, and peanuts to the local vegetable supply.

Janes' farming interests harmonized well with those of Takezaki Sadō and other members of the reform group. Many of Yokoi Shōnan's followers stemmed from the top rungs of Higo's village society, the *gōnō* or wealthy peasant class, and this class, as we noted earlier, had risen to a position of prominence through the commercialization of agriculture. Men from this background were quick to respond to new stimuli, and, as Takezaki suggested, were delighted to find in Janes not only a teacher who could introduce their sons to the secrets of Western science and technology, but an agricultural "specialist" whose expertise might help them to utilize new opportunities for their personal and regional advancement.

With the garden bearing its first fruits, Janes and Harriet organized the second of their civilizing dinners. To demonstrate the advantages of Western cooking and American materials, "the only dish prepared from Japanese sources was a savory fish from Shimabara Bay—a *tai*"; and this "was not stewed out of sight and savor in soy, nor yet served alive and raw, but stuffed and baked in 'foreign style.' " "There were none of the heavier meats," he recalled, "for none were obtainable in the province. Their place was taken by a couple of young chickens fricasseed without the American addition of cream gravy—no cream or milk being available within thousands of miles." "But they were flanked" he continued, "by snowy potatoes from Oregon, by cauliflower creamed from a can of condensed milk, by 'egg'-turnips and green peas dressed with butter from San Francisco—all produced from the Kumamoto garden as was also the crisp and appetizing salad of lettuce. The rest was a simple Indian corn pudding, which drew ocular and eloquent tributes of approbation from the rotund little Prince."[11]

" 'No use! No use!' " Janes quotes Nagaoka Moriyoshi lamenting at the end of the meal. " 'We can make the vegetables, but my people can never cook them this way.' " The Prince's exclamation was followed by a pause, and then by the observation: " 'You give us the vegetables, you must teach us to cook them!' " But soon he was despondent again. " 'Then we have none of these knives, no silver spoons and forks, no tables and chairs, none of these many things—I don't know what you call them—to cook (serve food) with. Our women know only how to boil rice, and broil salt fish; to cut up *daikon*, and stew seaweed in soy. I am too full—I am satisfied (placing his plump little digits over his abdomen, which, in the East, signifies all we mean by 'heart' and 'mind'), but I am very—unhappy! You must help us! You must help us! And we will civilize—we will civilize!' "[12]—an exclamation which the good Prince had long since learned by heart from the gray-haired Takezaki.

As the result of his experiences with gardening, and with the backing of the Prince, Janes' contacts with the Horticultural Society, and with the soon-to-be-organized Agricultural Association, were deepened and officially endorsed. Convinced that Japanese agricultural development must precede industrial growth, Janes began to lecture at the school on the importance of agriculture. His lectures, translated by three of his best pupils, were published in Tokyo in 1873 as a small volume, *Seisan shoho*, or *An Introduction to Agricultural Production*.[13]

"The first step in advancing the agriculture of a nation," Janes wrote in the introduction, "is to expand the production of its native products, and to select those which are most valuable among them." There was no point, he felt, in producing new products for which there was no market. It was only as markets developed, and here Kumamoto should make special efforts in Nagasaki, that the extensive growing of new crops would become profitable. Meanwhile, it was better for the Kumamoto region to concentrate on the development and improvement of three traditional products with well-established and growing markets—rice, silk, and tea. By specializing in these products Kumamoto could reap the greatest gains and prepare the groundwork for further agricultural and industrial growth.[14]

Janes had the highest respect for Japanese rice, which he exempted from his criticism of other Japanese agricultural products. At the same time he was convinced that rice production could be increased with better farm-tools, such as deeper cutting plows and harrows, and by opening up new lands through the use of such tools.[15] Silk, he felt, offered the greatest possibility of becoming an important cash crop in Kumamoto. Higo, he thought, was particularly well suited to the growing of mulberry trees vital for sericulture. More important, with China entering a period of unrest, Janes felt that Japan would soon have a golden opportunity to become a major world supplier of silk. Kumamoto, he contended, should prepare for such prospects by embarking on an extensive program of sericultural development. Students should be sent to Italy and France to study the art of silk production. In the meantime mulberry trees should be planted and allowed to mature, and an extensive campaign to educate the local farmers in methods of silkworm raising should be spearheaded by the prefectural administration.[16]

One of Janes' fundamental arguments was that a rational program of increased agricultural production would result in the development of secondary industries. Sericulture would lead to spinning and weaving, and the development of a silk textiles industry. Tea also represented a traditional product with foreign trade potential. Here he warned local producers to be especially careful to raise the quality of the product. Instead of settling for quick profits, only the best Kumamoto teas should be sent abroad in boxes clearly marked with their Higo origins. Higo producers should become proud of a label that stood for quality, and such quality teas, he felt, would make significant inroads into the world's tea markets. Tea, Janes furthermore pointed out, was an area of agricultural production in which profits from the product and from its processing all accrued to the local community.[17]

Janes' little book was the first treatise by a Westerner residing in Japan specifically directed toward agricultural development. It was also a rare example among subsequent works that directed itself to the development of a specific region. The full impact of the book is difficult to judge, but its objectives were clearly in line with the goals of the Jitsugaku reformers, who were as much in search of wealth as they were in search of power. Men such as Tokutomi Ikkei and Takezaki Sadō shared Janes' view that Kumamoto would have to pull itself up by its boot straps, and that this pulling would have to begin with the development of what they had. His book clearly fit the general mood of the day, and it was no accident that the goals of Takezaki's Kōunsha (Janes' "Horticultural Society"), organized in the same year, were specifically to develop the production of silk and tea.[18]

Silk and tea, of course, did become Meiji Japan's leading exports, providing a good portion of the foreign exchange necessary to modernize the country. Moreover, rice, silk, and tea became the three pillars of the Kumamoto economy. Janes' role in this was not insignificant. Nor was it confined to his garden and book. As Tokutomi Kenjirō noted in his biography of Takezaki Junko, Sadō's wife, the relationship between Janes and Takezaki grew increasingly intimate.[19] Both thoroughly enjoyed farming. Students often observed him in the fields with Takezaki inspecting some favorite project. On occasion he became so absorbed in these ventures, they recalled, that he lost all sense of time.[20]

In keeping with Janes' advice, Takezaki and his society devoted their energies to the propagation of the silk industry. On a former samurai parade ground at Kubonji, they planted Kumamoto's first mulberry field.[21] At the same time, Nagano Shumpei, one of Takezaki's disciples, began to raise silkworms and Takezaki's father-in-law, Yajima Chūzaemon, and his wife Tsuruko, opened the Midorikawa silk filature in 1875—the only mechanical silk reeling plant west of Osaka in the 1870s.[22] Kawada Seiichi, one of the Tokutomi in-laws, sold his swords and books to build the region's first silk weaving establishment.[23] By 1885 Kumamoto produced 10 percent of the nation's total silk output.[24] Takezaki also followed Janes' advice on tea. In fact, it was about this time that he began to use the penname, "Sadō" (Tea Hall), identifying himself with the product.[25]

Janes' work with Takezaki's Horticultural Society was only one of his many out-of-class efforts to improve the living conditions and livelihoods of the local residents. Writing to Anna Warner, he noted that the studies of the school were quite familiar and required no undue preparation. This allowed him to spend a good deal of his time on tasks involving a variety of voluntary organizations, and on "outside, secular, and practical" projects. Tokutomi Kenjirō later observed that what the Meiji government had sought to achieve in the development of Hokkaido, Janes, Takezaki, and those working with them were to accomplish on a smaller scale in Kumamoto.[26]

Janes wrote of those days: "It was as if all life's little learnings," its "teachings of experience," and "much that had never entered into the mind of the poor teacher" had been called to Japan "to undergo the challenge and quizzing of a remorseless committee. . . . The very atmosphere crackled with questions, surcharged, as it was, with the electric tensions of change and novel needs . . . nothing available for the purposes of inquiry, either learned or honestly humble, whether in the heavens above or the earth beneath, or in the waters under the earth, seemed to escape the summons of this manifold scrutiny." "Prince, priest, prowling tradesman; official, farmer, and incipient manufacturer; Buddhist, Confucianist, Shintoist, Rationalist, Materialist, Idealist, and the man without a creed; officers from the garrison, and veterans who had fought gallantly in the revolutionary war just ended; parents of my boys, with presents of eggs packed in tea leaves, or boxes of *yabekakki* figs, each," he observed, "took his turn to satisfy his curiosity, ventilate a theory or a scheme, solve a difficulty, secure counsel, or impart a warning, and in all cases to present a polite and wordy tribute of gratitude, well calculated to keep the door of access and inquiry open for the future."[27]

"Advice, information, and practical suggestions," Janes liked to point out, "were eagerly sought upon the inauguration of a great number of undertakings which made that period of five years memorable in the history of the Province for enterprises of progress and profit—petty and important. All were alike momentous in the eyes of their promoters!"

"And whether it was the awful innovation of breeding and fattening pigs for pork in the midst of people chiefly Buddhist by religious profession," he exclaimed, "or the establishment of the *Sei-in*—or local senate —for schooling the people in the privileges and duties of constitutional government, the *Senshi* (foreign teacher) was supposed to know somewhat or something that might facilitate and encourage the enterprise."[28]

In 1872, Janes tells us, the inevitable committee, this time from the Agricultural Association with Nonoguchi leading the way, approached him with what he thought was a most peculiar request, which dealt with the means and methods of dying cotton fabrics. "We have dyes from our crops of indigo which answer very well for the darker colors," the committee explained to him, "but we lack reds and yellows in their brighter shades, especially the reds. Such as we have are very expensive and limited in supply."[29] A part of the desire for brighter colors seems to have been the result of the Meiji Restoration's liberation of large segments of the Japanese public from the previously prescribed dress code. Janes noted that Nonoguchi and the other members of his committee were searching for new dyes that would enable the Japanese "natural love of striking colors to gratify itself without the impoverishing expense" of "fabrics hitherto chiefly found in the Shogun's palaces and in the *yashiki* or castles of daimios." In Kumamoto, he recorded, these had been dyed by means of vegetable dyes produced by a laborious and costly process from the various shades of balsams, or touch-me-nots.

Janes writes that his immediate response to the committee was to recommend the analine dyes just then coming into use in America. But the members of the committee, while aware of their existence, objected, pointing out that importing these was also exorbitantly expensive, and that there was as yet not a single coal-gas plant in Japan from which they could be produced. Now Janes was confronted by what can only be described as a typical Meiji request, one which he saw as emanating from a deeply ingrained trait of the Japanese character, that is, a spirit of self-sufficiency and independence: "Is there not some material from which the other two colors, the reds and the yellows, the former especially, can be made, which we can produce *ourselves* so as to make ourselves *independent* of *importations*?"

Janes suggested cochineal, but the cactus that feeds this insect could not be grown in Japan, and again there was the problem of the foreign product. Given the circumstances it seemed to him that there was only one product that would meet the Japanese conditions and that was madder. A "deliberate and painful" search for all information on the plant, its adaptability to soil and climate, was immediately undertaken by the Captain. This required time, which he tells us was "very irritating to the enthusiastic projectors." In any case, a local test was eventually proposed and Janes writes that "an order was made out and sent to Madame Villemin, Paris, successor of the late head of the leading seed house of France for eighty pounds of madder seed, to be sent first to the Allens at New York and by them to be dried, if need be, repacked, and shipped via San Francisco to Higo."

Meanwhile local preparations were made for the arrival of the seed. It was decided to make all information obtainable on the plant from reference sources available in the vernacular language for the use of Higo farmers. "The characteristics of the root and seed," he noted, "the processes of production up to the final stages of treatment of the crop, the manipulation and application of the coloring extract to its various uses in dyeing, and the mordants necessary: every essential item within reach was embodied in successive chapters of a little book. These were given as English dictation exercises for translation to the first class of the school. A committee of Chino-Japanese scholars with the venerable Takezaki san at its head, made a selection of a dozen of these exercises; and from these took the three that appeared to be the most perfect. Of these three a recension or combination was made and sent to Tokyo to be published for distribution with the seeds."

The arrival of the seeds and the publication of the pamphlet occurred almost simultaneously. The seeds were distributed to forty districts in the prefecture, two pounds to a district, and with each package of seeds went one or two pamphlets. Half of the seeds were to be planted the first year, the other half at a different season the following year. Janes felt this decision had been a mistake, and that a "concentration of effort under rigorous supervision would doubtless have produced more perfect results." The commercial growing of madder requires two or three years to allow the root to mature, then more time is required for drying and preparing the root for dyeing. "Three years' time," he wrote, "was a stretch of patience and foresight to which the volatile Japanese was at that time utterly unequal in any project which had not the support of his *Yamato damashii*." Scarcely was the madder seed in the ground, than the project on which Janes had spent so much time and effort was half-forgotten in the hatching of new schemes.

As the madder experiment illustrated, not all of his projects ended in success. While he obviously respected the gentleman-farmer of Takezaki's class who was prepared to be progressive, patient, and farsighted, he had few good things to say about the average Japanese farmer. As he stated on more than one occasion, he was struck by the "utter absence of enterprise among the farmer class," and by the "helpless, stolid subserviency to the routine and traditions of the past." "The Japanese farmer," he grumbled, "must be cajoled, coaxed, bought, and cheated, if need be, into sharing an enterprise with more blessings in it than in a thousand Hyaku Man Ben."[30] "The horse" could be "brought to the stream," he complained, but "no amount of reasoning could compel him to drink the strengthening and inspiring waters of progress."[31] Nor had the leadership's relationship to the agrarian sector resulted in much that was better. Except for the production of rice, he insisted, under samurai supervision "no plant or animal indigenous to Japan" had been "improved a single step beyond its natural state."[32] While such views were obviously extreme, overstated, and the products of personal frustration, they seem to indicate an agricultural sector divided between a progressive group of village leaders open to foreign stimuli and a mass of inert and largely poor farmers who in the wake of the 1873 land tax were all too often doomed to tenancy. Janes, who saw himself as a champion of humanity and of the common man, found himself, like many another reformer, annoyed by the inability of Higo's agricultural masses to understand his program in their behalf.

If madder ended in disappointment, there were plenty of successes. Janes' interest in fruit trees, shared by Takezaki Sadō, involved one of these. In the autumn of 1873 Janes started a campaign to encourage orange production in the Kumamoto region. From a group of wild orange trees on the shore of Shimabara Bay he procured two or three bushels of "gnarly, small and bitter oranges."[33] These, he recalled, became "the theme of many a discourse on the duty of planting, propagating, and improving this delicious fruit, which is so highly prophylactic of several of the most prevalent diseases in Japan." Other fruit trees were soon added. A number of foreign species were imported for Takezaki's "orchard," and one of the members of the reform party, Iwao Toshisada, established the prefecture's first vineyard using foreign grapevines.[34] Janes felt that "no single development of possible resources" had been more successful, or prolific in blessings to the people, than the effort that had begun with "orange culture" in 1873.[35]

Bread was another area in which Janes pioneered successfully in Higo. "Bread! Bread! Wheaten Bread! The Western 'staff,' not only of 'life,' but of civilization," he rhapsodized, "think of a whole nation living a thousand years without a solitary ounce of fermented bread! Think of a nation boiling all its cereals, millet, wheat, barley, and rice, into a sodden mass of indigestible starch; washing it down with a weak decoction of tannic acid and theine; and stimulating the indigestion of the obdurate mass with nothing more savory than salt—whether as the principle ingredient of soy, the pickle for plums, the solidifier of nature's bounteous supplies of fish, or the over-strong preservative of millions of tubs of krauted radish!"[36] Bread had in fact become the topic of conversation at a recent dinner at which the Captain had put his Golden Gate Flour to useful purposes. At the end of the meal Nagaoka Moriyoshi, Yamada, and Takezaki briefly consulted and approached him with a problem. "We have wheat," one of them said, "but I suppose it is very poor. Do you think it is possible that our wheat could be improved so that it would be fit for good bread?"[37]

Janes thought this request "so modest, so reasonable, and so entirely in line" with his "work and wishes" that he determined to help them. To avoid the effects of a possible failure he decided to experiment alone. After ordering three bags of wheat from the local rice merchant, which were delivered as three bags of barley due to Janes' faulty Japanese, the wheat finally arrived although "it was a sorry sight when opened up." What was wrong was not the quality of the grain, but having been thrashed on a dirt floor it was "covered with soil and pervaded by grit." To meet this problem Janes devised a means of washing it: "A large tub was procured, placed in the open yard and half filled with water. Sliding doors or shutters were brought from the servant's quarters, placed nearby in the full sunshine, and covered with tablecloths. Into the tub, a bag at a time the wheat was poured. The tub was kept full to overflowing so that the chaff, defective grains, and loosed soil could be carried off. When the water ran clear, the firm clean wheat was dipped out with a sieve, care being taken not to go too near the bottom where all the grit had accumulated. Spread in the sun the surface moisture was dried off thoroughly; and the grain, quite unaffected by the wetting, was as bright, plump and promising as could be desired."

Some days later when a picnic was proposed at the picturesque site of an old mill Janes seized the opportunity to take his wheat along and have it milled. In conditions that were "indescribably primitive," Janes had the miller run the wheat between his stones three times before he was satisfied with the product. After paying the miller "three prices for grinding one grist" Janes packed his "treasure" in his now empty Golden Gate Flour sacks and brought them down the mountain to Kumamoto. Here they proved to be a treasure indeed. As he wrote: "The bread made from that primitive form of practically 'whole wheat' flour, was the sweetest, most nutritious, and palatable ever served in our household. The outcome was so unexpectedly and entirely satisfactory that no more Golden Gate Flour was required in the solitary white man's household in the province of Higo."

The benefits of his discovery were soon transferred to the people of Kumamoto through the establishment of a bakery by a friend and protégé of Janes' cook. As the Captain remembered it, "cheap and good bread for all who desired to substitute it for rice and boiled barley was peddled through the streets of the city and suburbs, and the business rapidly became one of increasing importance."

Bread seems to have taken on a kind of amuletic and medicinal appeal in Kumamoto, which may well have been the result of the popularization of Janes' never-ending pronouncements on the relationship of a sound diet to health, and his emphasis on bread as part of such a diet. Tokutomi Kenjirō tells us that Takezaki Sadō, who suffered from various digestive ailments, was much taken with Janes' "health food diet," which in addition to the milk-of-magnesia the Captain supplied him seems to have done much to restore his physical condition.[38] Janes recalled that Takezaki became particularly fond of bread and of Gail Borden's condensed milk, which he liked to spoon on it directly from the can. With Takezaki's support bread was quickly accepted as a health food. As Janes wrote, "bread became a great boon to invalids, and when it is remembered that half of Japan was at that time dyspeptic, and the whole more or less afflicted with catarrh and rheumatism, there were customers enough to keep the peddlers on the trot." Much bread, he added, went to the excellent hospital the Prince established near the Yōgakkō.

The success of Janes' efforts to produce flour and bread seems to have involved him in another project with the Agricultural Association. Once again the formally appointed committee arrived. This time its purpose was to consult on how wheat production could be increased. The committee had the idea that they might turn the prefecture's less productive upland rice fields into wheat fields.[39] Janes thought this unnecessary since his rides on horseback through the surrounding countryside had convinced him that less than half of the easily arable portion of Higo was under cultivation. When he inquired why this was the case he was told that Japanese farm tools were "inadequate to the work of breaking the sod of such lands." "But the best of your lands naturally," he told the committee, "are those very plains . . . the broad rolling reaches beyond the sand plains, whose dense sod—while difficult to subdue—was proof positive of the natural fertility of the soil." "There is the place for all dry-land grains, for grapes, berries, and fruit without limit." The committee was not fully convinced. "But what can we do there," one of its members asked, "with our simple tools?"

Janes' opinion of Japanese tools was only one step removed from his evaluation of Japanese food. "Simple, clumsy, cruelly ill-shaped, ancient, worthless are all terms but poorly descriptive of every implement of the garden and farm then extant, from the uncouth pretence of a wooden plow, used to stir the mud of the rice paddy, to the back breaking thing that did the combined duty of spade and hoe." On the other hand, the committee was soon assured: "There are tools—and they are easily attainable—which will do that work of breaking up those sods, and corn—a grain which you do not know—with slight cultivation will make the surface as friable and easily tilled as your sandy vegetable fields. And as for your complaint about the wearing out of the rice lands and the growing necessity of the application of increasing quantities of artificial manures, it will be quite possible to extend the available resources for that crop by gradually bringing some of the rich soil, untouched by your cultivation, to the surface."

In keeping with his advice, the committee had the Captain order the necessary agricultural equipment from the United States. Some months later when he returned from the school to his house, he found the compound astir with excitement and curiosity as members of the Agricultural Association were examining "two chilled-steel plows," a "set of double harness," and a variety of hand tools, including hoes and mattocks, "which had all been unpacked and displayed for inspection with the care bestowed upon the curiosities of a museum."

On the first opportunity when there was no school Janes decided to demonstrate the art of plowing. In the company of the Yōgakkō students and the members of the Horticultural Society and Agricultural Association he led two horses to the "trial grounds" several miles from the castle. The spot, he recalled, was "admirably suited to make the severest test of the cutting and turning capacity of the plows." Unfortunately the horses would have nothing to do with the double harness, and consequently "when their hoofs were not lunging out viciously on either side, they stood doggedly still," refusing to move. "Here was a fine ending to a beautiful dream of progress!," Janes thought, until he was struck by another idea. With the help of two long ropes taken from nearby wells the students of the Yōgakkō were hitched to the plow. "Under simple instructions they drew away, and the foreigner at the plow had the satisfaction of seeing the tenacious sod turned over in a way to elicit a chorus of wondering ejaculations from the elders of the party."

"Laying out a 'land' with his eye and assuring his boys that this was the best of exercise for them, the plowman had the 'team' turn," Janes wrote, "and then laid a 'back-furrow' with a 'lap' that would have delighted the eye of a Nebraska prairy farmer with his six yoke team of oxen. Furrow after furrow was thus turned from side to side, until the demonstration was complete." And now before the eyes of all present there "lay the stubborn sod of their upland waste, between a sixteenth and an eighth of an acre of it, upturned and ready for the subduing crop of corn, or pease, or whatnot. This leading principle of American agriculture was carefully explained in detail to the elders before we left the ground, and then the foreign teacher felt that his task in that line was done."

As was to become amply clear, the lessons of that demonstration were not lost on the members of the two associations that had witnessed it. The lifting, turning, and deepening powers of the steel plows were quickly recognized. There was, moreover, in Higo a considerable area of land on which these virtues were to be fully displayed and demonstrated. "During all the remaining years of the stay in Higo," Janes recalled, "both in November, when, the water being withdrawn and the rice harvest concluded, the ground was put in order for the winter crop, and in the spring, when it was to be prepared for the rice plants, both plows were kept busy going from plot to paddock, hither and thither through the valleys surrounding the city, stirring and slowly deepening the surface soil in a way that had never been done since rice was first cultivated in Higo." Needless to say, the efforts of the Yōgakkō "team" had long since been displaced by two powerful bulls, which in the company of their coolie plowman could often be seen from the windows of the school slowly moving through the streets of Kumamoto with their steel plows "share up" on top of their huge saddles. "It was a sight," Janes remembered, "well calculated to move the curiosity of the townspeople, and to madden the topknotted malcontents to fury."

While the shiny steel plows aroused curiosity and opposition among the various segments of Kumamoto society, another episode, more perhaps in the line of animal husbandry than farming, must have aroused similar wonder and discontent. Janes addressed himself to this incident in his book on Kumamoto under the title "milk and meat."[40] Here again Janes became involved in a project which he saw as "one of the most substantial and beneficent contributions to the health, welfare, and happiness of the Japanese." This project began as an effort to introduce the people of Kumamoto to the virtues of milk by improving the milk-giving propensities of the native wild cows of the mountains of Higo.

Through Nonoguchi and a farmer he had befriended with seeds and plants Janes managed to obtain a "very fair specimen of the native breed," whose calf had died of an accident a few days earlier. And yet, no amount of persuasion by his servant could procure more than a mite of milk from this cow. Janes was temporarily tempted to give up the experiment, but sending her back would have set a bad precedent. The only alternative was to send for another cow, this time specifying some excellence as a milker. The second cow soon arrived and became celebrated in the neighborhood for providing from three pints to two quarts of fairly good milk a day. But the Captain did not forget the first animal, for which he had a secondary design. Encouraging his servant to feed the cow generously, he observed with a "satisfaction too profound for words" that a "fattening process" was "going on about the ribs and flanks of the animal." Of course there was not a word of his intentions to the servants or anyone else since this would have "exposed the foreign teacher to a form of execration difficult to control, and made him an aversion too intense to be withstood."

Meanwhile Janes was confronted by a secondary problem that was to aid his original plan. Under the pressure of three years of work the health of the students of the school seems to have deteriorated seriously. "Scurvy in an aggravated form," he noted, "was to an alarming extent decimating the attendance in classes and lectures, and filling up the dormitories with lamed, debilitated, and suffering invalids." One student came to him with "fingers stiffened," "limbs grating in the joints," and his "gums bleeding as he spoke," saying that he would have to return home. Upon investigation Janes discovered that over thirty of his students were suffering from similar difficulties.

Under the circumstances he decided to act. Going to Nonoguchi and Yamada Buhō, men he regarded as the most sensible officials in the prefectural government and long-time friends of the school, Janes told them that "there was no remedy for this particular evil but a radical change of diet." "Watery vegetables, lacking in the stimulating nutrients required, while prophylactic and favorable to health in the well and strong, would," he added, "by no means meet the requirements of such a situation." "Fresh meat," he asserted with a "positiveness that carried conviction and bore down all opposition," was the "only medicine," the "one remedial measure adequate to the occasion." This should be applied at once. When asked "how?" by the overwhelmed pair, Janes replied, "never mind how," adding that he would provide the "materials necessary." Permission, he recalled, was "reluctantly granted," although everyone but the lame and heroic Nonoguchi seems to have fled the scene "as boys do from that of the explosion for which they have arranged." Once it became known that one of the teacher's cows was to be killed, the servants in the compound, and even the husband of the washer woman, disappeared. "Not a soul, man or woman, even among those most deeply interested, could be found willing, not merely to lend a helping hand in the slaughter, but even to countenance the proceedings by his presence."

Faced with this dilemma, Janes had no choice but to go to the *eta*, the outcasts, or "not men," for help. Nonoguchi arranged for a visit to an *eta* village not far from Kumamoto. Janes remembered how surprised he was by this visit, finding the outcast community to be the "wealthiest and most prosperous class for their number in Higo." Arrangements were quickly concluded for sending two men to help Janes with the butchering the next day.

The day was a cold one in January. The two *eta* arrived on time, but then a problem arose. Nothing that Janes said or did could convince the two men to kill the cow. Butcher a dead animal they would, but "kill they would not." After meditating momentarily on the thought that "life is a mystery," but that he had to "hold to that which nature seems to demonstate," i.e., that "all life is for the promotion of the highest life," and that "the fit survive, and are served to that end by the faulty," the Captain solved his dilemma by a "well planted shot" from his old army revolver. The *eta* assistants doing their work "deftly" and "most satis-factorily" soon had four quarters of "prime beef" suspended from as many spikes cooling in the winter air. For his part, Janes finished his morning's work, not without a sense of "foreboding" however, won-dering what "echoes of outraged sentiment and deadly resentment it was sure to awaken in the community." But he concluded "there was no backing down."

Having finished with the butchering, and having in the process stirred up the outraged Shimpūren members "who gathered below the main hall and recitation rooms of the school to look up, exchange sentiments of execration, twirl their fans, and predict doom," Janes set about to aid not only the ill Yōgakkō students, but to invite the leading prefectural administrators to another of his civilizing dinners. Once more he became involved in the subtle effort to "impress these founders and sponsors of a new order of things in Japan of the righteousness of their cause, the boundless beneficence of their policies, and the sacredness of their mis-sion." As Janes reflected, all this was done "over roast beef from a herd of cattle on one of Japan's thousand hills," potatoes and grapes "all the way from California," and good bread "from flour brought in abundance from the mill by the waterfall on the Higo mountain." Confronted with such a repast, he argued, "the mind of the stolidest Japanese must needs broaden a little to the larger implications of political economy, and to the humanitarian interests and possibilities of the brotherhood of man implied in commerce!"

While the officials were feasting, the students in the "barracks" were presented with a huge cauldron, in fact a washboiler, filled with as savory a soup as "ever gladdened the palates of the famishing." The soup was in essence a great stew with "huge pieces of flesh and bones," to which had been added "chopped cabbage, onions, a few precious potatoes, and tomatoes from the garden." In addition there was added "rice enough to give that body to a dish which suits the generous nature, and a pepper pod or two to make it familiar to the native eye and taste." The quantity was such that there was nearly a quart for each student.

The stew, Janes noted, accomplished the "miracle" of "absolutely perfect medication." "From the first sip the scurvy patients began to take heart." No one refused the "treatment," and within a few weeks of this and a similar diet "not a trace of salt poisoning, or scurvy, remained to threaten or interrupt the work of the school." As Janes observed, "the general health of the entire body of students underwent a change for the better that appeared to the eyes of some among themselves to be miraculous."

Janes' "treatment" was thereafter repeated at regular intervals. Despite public opposition on the part of some of the "baser sort," as Janes saw them, and public nonchalance on the part of the leadership, which was "secretly much gratified," beef came to be regularly butchered and eaten in Kumamoto, particularly at the Yōgakkō. As the circle of consumers grew, so did the value of the wild cows in the hills around Kumamoto. With time the prices became so high that it took a strong "hint" from the proper official quarter to bring them down again.

While the general public of Kumamoto continued to regard the eating of beef as offensive to their Buddhist sensibilities, beef, like bread, appears to have acquired a certain medicinal significance. As word of the Yōgakkō "treatment" spread, Janes remembered, it was not long before a Japanese vendor appeared at his door, a "jerked-meat huckster . . . grinning all the way down from his top-knot to his toes." From his reference to the word "byōki" (illness) and from his desire to thank him for something that was not entirely clear, it suddenly dawned on Janes that the man was "peddling beef, not as a butcher, but as a physician," and that he had come to thank his foreign benefactor for his new line of work and growing good fortune.

In time regular meat shops made their appearance in Kumamoto, and genuine efforts were made to improve the quality of the Higo herds through the importation of foreign breeding stock. Janes' advice and efforts in behalf of animal husbandry were not limited to pigs and dairy cows. Chickens, which regularly appeared at his dinners, were also ordered for breeding purposes from the United States.[41] Furthermore Janes helped Takezaki import American cattle, which were intended not only for the butcher shops, but for the establishment of a dairy industry.[42] Takezaki, as Janes recalled, soon gave up Gail Borden's "tin cow" for the real thing. Kenjirō noted that his uncle took not only to milk, but to butter—which he began to produce on his own—and to the American chickens and eggs to which he was introduced by Janes.[43] Later, in his portrait of Uncle Noda, a leading character in his novel *Footprints in the Snow* modeled in part on Takezaki, Kenjirō observed: "Uncle stuffed himself with eggs—and with hens. So many of the latter did he eat, in fact, that eventually Aunt announced a 'constitution' for the birds, and laid down (to Uncle's dismay) that except on festival days or when we had visitors, he was not to go beyond a chicken a month."[44] While fictionally exaggerated, Kenjirō's depiction of Uncle Noda captured Takezaki's qualities as agricultural innovator and developer. Moreover, Takezaki's achievements were considerable. By the time he left Kumamoto, Janes wrote, there was not only an ample supply of milk and beef in the city, but Higo milk and beef were being shipped to Nagasaki, fulfilling his original vision for the development of the region's agricultural industries.[45]

While the Captain and his family's role was highly public, life in Kumamoto also had its private and more personal dimension. At times it was difficult to separate the two. As Kumamoto's only Western family it was hardly possible to opt for anonymity or a low profile. Janes, Harriet, and the children were stared at, pointed to, and discussed wherever they went. Moreover, those in charge of the family's welfare and well being were constantly torn between an overriding need for security and a desire to use the Captain and his wife to further their reform ideals.

The prominent location of the school and the foreign teacher's residence made all this amply clear. Indeed, if there were any doubts, they were quickly dispelled at the time of the school's inauguration ceremony. As if to spread the significance of that event far beyond the walls of the castle, the trunk of a tall cryptomeria had been mounted halfway between the school and the Janes mansion. Topped with a large rising-sun flag, itself a symbol of the newly united nation, it was draped with tier upon tier of gaily colored lanterns which glowed brightly at night. To the people of Kumamoto watching the ceremony from a distance it seemed that a "veritable pillar of fire had arisen in the West," which they interpreted as an omen of momentous changes.[46]

The general interest of the community was displayed a few days later when the Captain and his wife decided to hold an "open house." More than a thousand curious visitors lined up to be admitted.[47] As Janes noted, "the house . . . was held simply in trust, and administered as a means of persuasive education. Throughout the five years of its occupancy, gate or door was never shut to the eye or feet of respectable curiosity." For the purposes of "education," he wrote, "the free and open display of every room and every appliance was always accompanied by candid and sympathetic answers to questions, with full explanation and information." "To this result every little item of our household economy contributed a recognizable share. The beds and bedding were often overhauled at the desire of 'visitors'; and the purpose of a raised bedstead, variable quantities of cover, pillows, and clean sheets was explained. Then the table service would be outlined, the mysteries of knives, forks, carving and courses, and their relation to foods and nutrition made known, while the cook, who had been painfully initiated in the formal mysteries of his vocation, stood simpering by, explaining, on demand, the secrets of his bread-oven and the various paraphernalia of an American cooking-range." "On all these visits," Janes added, "the sootless, scentless, cleanliness of the papered walls—snowy white even at the end of five years of use—was viewed in connection with the perfect ventilation and equability of temperature which the blessed chimneys alone enabled us to secure."[48]

Janes' enthusiasm for Western architecture and its "lessons" was matched by a disdain for Western writers like Lafcadio Hearn who praised the simplicity of the Japanese house. "The impractical idealist, the *ennuye* tourist, and the briefed renegade from the higher civilization of the West, all in turn dilate on the convenient and beautiful 'simplicity' of the Japanese homes and home-life," he wrote. But for Janes simplicity was not in itself a positive value of civilization, which, as he pictured it, was on an ever upward march. "Civilization is to man what evolution is to all life," he insisted, "a process of endless differentiation and integration." "Human progress, which is not only the destiny but the duty of the human race," he added, "is in its healthiest stages when in sympathy with the fundamental principles of evolution; when it is occupied in disintegrating and eliminating this maudling affectation of simplicity, and in revealing the higher beauty which inheres in perfectly adapted complexity."[49] In Janes' eyes the Western house and home was important precisely because it demonstrated so clearly the advantages of complexity and integration.

Whether the people of Higo understood his Social Darwinistic lesson is hard to determine. What is clear is the fact that they remained inquisitive, and that they came to see and listen. "Sooner or later," Janes recalled, "almost every town and considerable village in the province was represented in the list of visitors to the 'foreign teacher' and his home." Occasionally there were those who came incognito. On one such visit a Shinto priest from near Mt. Aso came and "looked furtively at everything" and made "frequent excursions to the window . . . to be sure that he was free from observation." At other times, Janes noted, even "the leading representatives of the party of reaction," the Shimpūren, visited the house—"sullenly observing, inspecting, and questioning," to the great anxiety of those in charge of the foreign teacher's safety.[50]

On the other hand, Janes had long since made up his mind that the only course to be pursued in Kumamoto was a frontal attack on those who disliked him. From the outset he had dismissed his guards and had ventured out alone on horseback—on some occasions with one of his children in the saddle before him—to tour the region around the city. The Captain's openness and boldness, coupled as it was by a sense of courtesy and a respect for Japanese patriotism, appears to have earned him the grudging approval of even some within the Shimpūren. Years later Ebina Danjō observed that there were those within this organization who called for Janes' assassination—as the leaders of the progressive party accurately feared—but that the leadership would not support this plan.[51] Janes was convinced that it was his "fearless disclosure of honorable motives" and his "desire to *serve* a community that stood much in need of just such service" that postponed the general outbreak of dissatisfied samurai violence, and that when it did occur, two weeks after his departure from the city, it "was shorn of half its danger." At the same time he admired his "brave associates," some of whom were later killed, who lived with their own "haunting fears" of being cut down at any moment. "Those men," he later wrote, "never knew the extent to which their constancy and courage endeared them to their foreign coadjutor!"[52]

But while Janes saw himself living on a "castled island" in the midst of an "agitated, tumultuous sea" nearly a hundred miles from the nearest open port, an environment that was not without causes for anxiety, he was once again to contrast such an external world with an idyllic home and family life.

"The home," he wrote, "was new from the foundation up, fresh, bright, and clean. Thanks to the kindly forethought and generous disposition of Prince Nagaoka the house was ample in size, very roomy, cheerful, and conveniently appointed, and well calculated in most respects to make a delightful home. It was of two high stories with tall pillared verandahs along the front and half way back on both sides, above and below. It must have been very strongly built to stand unshaken by the score or more of earthquakes and three or four terrific typhoons which more than once played such fearful havoc within and around the city during the five year's period of our occupancy."[53]

"The view from the upper verandah," Janes noted, "was widespread, and if not inspiring, at least very interesting."[54] Built on an elevated plateau, the house looked down on the maze of Kumamoto's winding streets. The family could see the bustle of daily life, the vast array of shops and houses, and the thousands of city dwellers going about their everyday affairs in ways that could not help but be quaint and curious to their foreign eyes. Although the color of the visual scene could be turned off and on at the discretion of the viewer, Kumamoto's olfactory delights were another matter. Janes had a list of nemeses: "manuring," "*daikon* tubs," and "hot wax for the stiffening of hair"—all inescapable under the right wind conditions.[55] But the view of the distant mountains and bay were beautiful, and from the dining room the family could look out on the silhouette of Mt. Aso, whose occasional eruptions and showers of ashes provided excitement and, as Janes saw it, suggested the "instability of things" in Higo.[56]

Life in the Janes mansion, despite its fish-bowl qualities, seems to have gone on pleasantly and with some comfort. "From four to six of the best natured and most efficient of servants did much to reconcile us to the isolation," Janes recalled, "they made the premises lively, and the life far from lonely."[57] With a cook, washer woman, and several attendants for the children, Harriet was relieved of most of the housekeeping duties and had time to devote herself to her own interests. These involved not only the education of her children, but her own form of service to the community. In keeping with the Prince's request, Harriet devoted herself to teaching the Japanese to cook in the Western manner. Tokutomi Kenjirō recalled that Takezaki Junko and her husband completely shifted to Western cuisine, which Junko learned to cook under Harriet's supervision, and Kenjirō was particularly struck by the wonderful taste of "delicious roast beef."[58] Harriet's lessons in the home arts were not limited to cooking. Janes firmly believed that Japanese apparel, "that piles a mountain of stuffs about the waist, leaving the limbs, head, neck and chest exposed to all weathers," was on the lower rungs of the evolutionary ladder and, like so much he encountered in Kumamoto, in need of reform.[59] Harriet seems to have shared these views and responded to the challenge by teaching the ladies of the district to sew Western clothes, particularly flannel shirts, of which Janes was fond and to which Takezaki took with equal fervor. While the Captain introduced steel plows and other farm equipment to the region, Harriet seems to have been responsible for the introduction of the prefecture's first sewing machine.[60]

"My greatest pleasures," Janes wrote to his mother in 1876, "are in my work, and my children." "I am inclined to think that if we took as much care, sensible care, of our children, as many do of their pigs and calves, more of them would live and grow to usefulness."[61] Many of his students also noted that Janes' few free moments were usually spent with his children. To these, two daughters, Lois and Eunice Ann, were added in 1873 and 1875.[62] "This baby [Eunice Ann]," Janes wrote home, "resembles Hattie more than either of the others. They all have somewhat different features as they develop. Little 'Lois' . . . is a dimple. Her hair now is exactly the same as Fanny's when we left America. Yesterday, as she was walking from me, I seemed to see again little Fannie's sunny head."[63]

"The children are all growing," he wrote, "but Fanny is becoming quite large and tall for her age. She is as active as ever and climbs like a cat. Almost every day she has some new feat to display for my approval when I come in from my work. The other day she shinned up a bamboo tree ten or twelve feet til she was almost hid in the feathery foliage . . . last evening she had in two little low-class boys both bigger than herself to whom she was displaying herself as a jumper. They would climb successively upon the wall seven to eight feet high, and jump, having (or leaving) straws on the ground as markers. Then it was turning somersaults (summersets), and then climbing into a catalpa tree from the wall to have a chat with the neighbor's boy." Meanwhile Lois was "pulling up Phloxes that had gotten scattered in the grass, with one little star-like flower on the top of each, and planting them in 'her own' little bed." Henry was "in the back yard 'taking care' of his two pups, two kittens, two ducks, and six chickens." His son, he wrote, was "passionately fond of 'stock.' " All the children, he emphasized, were in excellent health and spirits. "Good plain, but *nourishing*, *substantial* food in abundance, plenty of sleep, not less than ten hours in twenty four, a daily wash all over, and flannel clothing, chiefly, have, under God's good care and blessing, hitherto kept our children healthy, strong, rosy skinned, and growing," he reported home with considerable satisfaction.[64]

Janes' letters from Kumamoto tell us less about Harriet. In fact, they are unusually silent about her. While the incident dealing with the education of girls indicated that there were substantial differences between the Captain and his wife on matters of educational and religious policy, there were other indications that, despite the positive image Janes tried to convey, there were issues that seriously divided the home, and that Harriet's postnatal problems had not entirely disappeared. Writing to Anna Warner in 1874 Janes observed, "The children are quite well and so is their mother now, though Hattie has had a time of ailing too."[65] In a subsequent letter he quietly compared Nellie with Hattie, indicating that he preferred the former's "humble strength" and "the power of humility (blessed virtue!)."[66] In another letter he wrote that *he* had as yet nothing to complain about in Kumamoto, but that he had heard plenty of complaints from others.[67] Nonoguchi, who saw much and said little, simply stated that there were arguments in the household and that these were generally well known and taken for granted.[68]

Janes and his wife's differences sometimes expressed themselves in curious ways. One of these involved the visit of the Meiji Emperor to Kumamoto in 1872. Searching for an appropriate place for the Emperor to stay, the Kumamoto authorities suggested the Janes mansion. At the start the Captain seems to have supported this proposal, but a few days later he returned, suggesting to the prefectural leaders that it might be an "injury to the prestige of the country" to have so "august a personage lodged in the home of a foreigner." The reason for the about face is not clear, but it is possible that Harriet was less inclined to give up her house for the imperial entourage. Those responsible for the Emperor's visit were quick to see the correctness of Janes' advice and attributed the decision to his prudence.[69]

The Emperor's visit was an important social and political event in Kumamoto. The records show that he made a point of visiting the Yō-gakkō, personally greeted Janes, and listened to an English recitation by two of his students. Afterward he toured the garden, where Janes presented him with flowers grown from American seeds—a gift that was warmly received by the monarch. What is also recorded by the ceremony-conscious Japanese is the fact that Janes appeared before the Emperor in his everyday clothes—suggesting his general disdain for pomp and ceremony—but that his wife, dressed "in full formal attire," showered the Emperor with flower petals from the second story verandah of their home.[70]

Despite the comfortable house, life in Kumamoto was far from easy. The sense of isolation, broken only by the arrival of the monthly mail bag, the lack of privacy, which could be relieved only by a few picnics to the Hosokawa's private *Suizenji* garden, closed to outsiders for the occasion, and a constant need for caution living among a people with a "special repute for hot-headedness, quarrelsomeness, and anti-foreign prejudice" all took their toll on nerves and spirits.[71] Even simple outings were made unduly complex. Janes had initially brought two rickshas from Tokyo, the first to be seen in Higo, but they soon attracted "so much invidious curiosity, and entailed such trouble in procuring men to draw them that they had to be abandoned."[72] Instead the family made its limited excursions in *norimono* and *kago*, which always involved a series of bearers and an official procession, usually with Nonoguchi in the train.

While Janes tried to shield the family from undue anxiety, it was not always possible to gloss over the turbulent times in which they found themselves in Higo. The outbreak of the Saga Rebellion in February 1874 ushered in one such period.[73] As Janes wrote to Peter Carter in New York:

> Unusual events have occurred in our vicinity since I last wrote. But I have no inclination to detail them: the risings, the brutal butch-

eries by the insurgents, and the final beheadings. It seems to me such fruitless bloodshed all around. But I suppose there is a purpose in it all, and that the nation reaps the fruits for good in one way or another soon or late. The fighting and open rebellion did not extend within the limits of this Ken and city, though the old warrior class with their longest swords and daggers thronged the streets like a disturbed hive of hornets, and at one time for a month continuously, there were from one to three and even more fires every twenty four hours, sometimes two and three houses burning in opposite quarters of the city in the dusk of the evening and at nearly the same time. This was a new experience to me. We live in the heart of the city on a slight elevation. The common people, merchants, and unmilitary classes had become so sensitive to the cry of "fire" (Hie-e-e! Hie-e-e!) that the quick tolling of the great copper bells, would stir them, too, into intense excitement. Towards the last of that month of daily conflagrations, the sound of gathering feet, as the throng pressed from every quarter toward the burning buildings, had fairly a weary, melancholy, fagged note in it. It has been a miserable winter for the poor people and not a pleasant one, altogether for us. But the school has not been intermitted for a day. . . . You will agree with me though that it makes up-hill work of the sort I am trying to do here—these barbarous distractions.[74]

Such pressures took their toll on the family. Later evidence suggests that life at the Janes mansion was not always harmonious, particularly for Harriet, who suffered from a growing sense of isolation. Nor was the Captain exempt from his own anxieties. Overwork and stress, as we have already observed, were always a threatening combination for Janes. He had arrived in Kumamoto much restored in health. As his students recorded, he was "full of spirit, muscular, and stoutly built"; he was "fat and blooming, had piercing eyes, and was frank and open minded."[75] Several commented that he never missed a day in the school—except that on which his second daughter was born. All remembered his spirit and energy, and the vigor with which he threw himself into the local projects. These included the agricultural efforts already discussed, and the ordering of a variety of equipment, which ranged from Japan's first printing press to operate outside the treaty ports—imported from New York—to stereoscopic pictures and their viewing apparatus so that the local citizens could get a graphic impression of the outside world. Responding to the thousand and one minor requests for information, advice, and service, Janes had increasingly full days.[76] The Captain's students later saw his outburst of activity as typically "American."[77] And yet, pleasurable as he found his work, it tended to become all-consuming.

What few of his students realized was that Janes' manic propensities were exacting a greater and greater toll. Moreover, it is difficult to understand his highly emotional religious phase, which was to play an important part in their conversion to Christianity, without noting this change. Writing to Anna Warner in 1874 Janes declared that he had been ill most of the latter part of the previous year,[78] and in April 1875 he complained of severe headaches: "I do not know what this headache confliction of mine means, but dear Anna, I am prepared for all it may bring. This attack has been the most persistent and severe of any I have had. From about the first of the month, for seven or eight days, there was scarcely a moment that I remember of respite from the pain of a torturing headache, day or night—and for days since, such a sensitiveness that has been a continual warning off from all brain exertion."[79] Subsequently he complained about "acute bowel troubles," "rheumatism affecting seriously my eyes and head," and "a general state of prostration."[80]

By the summer of 1875 the whole family was in need of rest. Harriet was pregnant with Eunice Ann. Janes wrote, "the heat of succeeding summers was being felt more and more." He himself was worn out and in need of change. As a result a search was made for a retreat in the hills outside of Kumamoto "sufficiently elevated and not too difficult of access."[81] The site selected was a place named Iwado in the highlands nearly due north of the city. "Here quarters were secured," Janes wrote, "in the temporarily vacated abode of a chief official functionary of a little old temple, who for a consideration, gladly consented to occupy apartments in the temple itself."[82] The place was spruced up. Nonoguchi supervised the laying of new mats, the grounds were put in order, the rock work repaired, and a new bamboo pipe was laid so that the little lakelet in front of the cottage could be kept full of fresh water from a mountain spring.

The expedition to Iwado started out in the usual fashion with the Captain in front on horseback, Nonoguchi next in a *kago*, then trailing behind a *norimono* for the mother and one for the nurse with the baby, and still another for one of the two older children, whichever was not seated on the pummel of the Captain's Civil War saddle, followed by a select group of "official attendants," as Janes described them, or more precisely samurai guards who were "thought imperative on account of the troubled state of the times." These were followed by a string of bearers carrying all the supplies for an extended stay.[83]

"The whole day of our departure and ascent," Janes wrote, "was perfect in every feature of temperature, light, and delightfully refreshing breezes."[84] The latter soon freed the company from "the disgusting odors of city and suburban life in the 'land of repulsive smells,' " and substituted for them the "sweetest sensations" of the "exhalations of mountain pines and cryptomeria, lichens, and ferns."[85] Janes found the cottage at which they arrived a very charming place with delightful grounds. The temple was located near a lovely spring. Just beyond was a mountainside covered with stone statues of Buddha's "five hundred disciples," or *gohyaku rakan*, and a little beyond this a large dark cave: "a deep, cavernous passage," as Janes wrote, "that had been painfully hewn into the rock directly under the seats of some of the more prominent *rakan*. Entering, you pass through an outer room, then a second darker one, and find yourself at the portal of a dungeon-like recess in the farther wall, in the presence of the Buddhist Prince of Hell."[86] Janes paid little attention to the cave, but thoroughly enjoyed the cool and refreshing environment. "Iwado," he recalled, "was hid from our view by a grove of tall and plumey bamboos, within whose embrace our cottage and its pretty grounds were perched."[87]

But even here it was difficult to leave anxiety behind. Immediately upon their arrival, Fanny disappeared. Janes went through "two or three hours of agony" thinking she had been abducted by some of Higo's malcontented samurai who by the summer of 1875 were, as Janes described them, "a prowling, bare-legged, top-knotted, bristle streaming, starved horde ... which at that time infested the streets of their chief city like a swarm of hornets whose nest was being disturbed and destroyed. Every fellow of them certainly looked like a born assassin." The whole group he summed up as "incarnate worthlessness, sloth, and disgruntled ferocity!"[88] The very atmosphere, Janes emphasized, "was redolent of civil commotion and sanguinary strife." "In fact," he observed, "the insurrectionary forces had already been organizing and secretly drilling for months." The instability of the situation was heightened, he felt, by the fact that large numbers of the priesthood had been drawn into the same vortex by the loss of their officially sanctioned positions and financial support. It seems that the expedition had encountered some difficulty in securing porters. "To be seen in the service or train of the foreigner," Janes wrote, "subjected even servants to ridicule and scorn."[89] Fortunately, Fanny's disappearance was soon explained. Following lunch she had decided that the Prince's *norimono* would make a lovely place for a nap. Quietly asleep she had been carried halfway back to Kumamoto by the returning bearers before they realized they had an unwanted passenger.

A few days later Janes was to experience a more serious encounter.

His youngest child had taken ill and needed medicines left in Kumamoto. Janes decided to return the nine or ten miles to the city alone, and in haste. As he wrote:

> Refusing attendance so that I could make the trip as quickly as possible, booted and spurred I mounted my staunch little pony and galloped off. Half way down the mountain trail, I saw before me two samurai approaching up the steep. They were of the two-sworded class and had their short swords in their sashes. I believe without law or leave. They were of the swarthy and sinister class that never concealed the intensity of their aversion from the eye of the hated foreigner. As I slacked up to take counsel of my defenses, the two also paused, turned toward each other and consulted. Before I reached them the one on the inner side of the narrow way laid his hand on the hilt of his sword while the other laid hold of his sword arm as if to restrain him. It was my opportunity. Dropping my left boot from its stirrup, I drew back my leg to put all the force I could command into the kick I had determined to deliver full into the fellow's face. But upon the movement, the spur of that boot caught violently into the flank of my pony in an unaccustomed spot. The animal leaped as if I had meant him to, knocking the two malcontents off the trail, and he never stopped until I was certainly clear of peril for the time. Reckless and angry, I turned and shouted derisively at the ugly figures who stood staring at me. As my spur jingled, the man who had intended to strike dropped his eyes in quick alarm to my foot. I have never doubted for a moment that the fellow was suddenly seized with the idea that I had some weapon in or on my boot.[90]

Procuring the needed medicine, Janes returned across the rice fields and up the same mountain trail, thinking that the men he had encountered earlier would long have left. "Nearing the very spot where the encounter had taken place," he wrote, "I was struck with consternation to see the whole passage-way filled with a well-dressed throng of precisely similar characters armed with short swords. What should I do alone with no weapon more than a pen-knife on my person! As usual I concluded, in that speedy way one does when there is no time to reason, that the boldest course was the safest. I rode straight forward compelling the crowd to give way right and left as I passed."[91] Iwado was reached in safety, and baby was well in a few days.

Nonoguchi, it appears, took longer to recover. Hearing the story of Janes' experiences he was in consternation for the Captain's safety and his own position. "Besides," Janes concluded, "an international tangle at that particular time was the last thing to be desired."[92]

Nonoguchi's concern was not without good reason. What Janes does not mention and seems blissfully unaware of is the fact that Iwado was one of the holiest shrines of the Japanese samurai tradition. For it was in the cave at Iwado, just past the granite statues of Buddha's disciples, that Miyamoto Musashi, Japan's greatest swordsman and a legend in his own time, had spent his final years meditating and writing *The Book of Five Rings*, the mystical treatise on swordsmanship that many Japanese samurai regarded as the "bible" of their cast and profession.[93] For a Westerner to camp on such a site seems reckless, if not downright foolhardy, and one cannot help but wonder how the Practical Learning reformers could have permitted this to happen. Janes was never to know how truly lucky he had been that his choice of a summer retreat did not end in bloodshed and a major international tangle.

CHAPTER IX

CHRISTIANITY

WHEN JANES arrived in Japan in 1871 Christianity was still strictly proscribed. Sailing from Nagasaki to Kumamoto the Captain and his wife were able to get a brief glimpse of the Shimabara Peninsula. It was in a dilapidated castle on this neck of land that Japanese Christianity made its last stand in the rebellion of 1637–38, bringing to a full stop a promising chapter in the history of Christian missions which had begun with the arrival of the well-known Jesuit, Francis Xavier, in 1549. Extensive Japanese conversions to Christianity eventually ushered in a period of reaction, which reached its climax in a frenzy of cruel and fanatic anti-Christian persecutions in the first three decades of the seventeenth century.[1] By the 1640s, with Japan officially "closed," the Christian movement was dead—the Church outlawed, its flock exiled, imprisoned, or martyred, and its priests expelled, killed, or forced into apostasy. For the next two hundred years Tokugawa authorities remained ever vigilant, carefully watching for any violations of the government's anti-Christian edicts. Most Japanese were periodically required to affirm their opposition to this "pernicious faith" by treading, or more literally trampling, on one of the Church's sacred symbols—the cross, a bronze relief of Christ, or the figure of the Virgin Mary.[2]

Kumamoto's anti-Christian sentiments were no less deeply ingrained than those of the Shogunate. Katō Kiyomasa, who built Kumamoto castle, was widely renowned not only as a fearless general but as an implacable foe of Christianity.[3] Moreover, the Hosokawa house, which succeeded to the domain in 1632, was equally fervent in its anti-Christian sentiments. It was in fact an ironic twist of seventeenth-century history that Hosokawa Tadatoshi, whose mother Gracia had been one of the best-known Christians of her day, served as the leading lord in the campaign to eradicate Christianity at Shimabara in 1638.[4]

As Janes recalled, the legacy of such attitudes was still obvious in Kumamoto in the early 1870s. Officially little had changed since the Restoration. "From across the moat, over which the series of five recitation rooms was perched, it was no more than a stone's throw," he wrote, "to the stone platform over which a government bulletin board was supported, high in the air, so that the densest crowd could have no excuse for not seeing and observing. On it, within plain view of the window of every recitation room still hung . . . that edict which had, for two and a half centuries denounced the 'hateful Christian religion,' and decreed death as the sure penalty either of accepting and practicing that form of belief, or of harboring a believer, or even of concealing the whereabouts of any who believed."[5]

As the continued use of the proscription board indicated, attitudes toward Christianity had been little altered by the transfer of government in 1868. While Westerners in the treaty ports were allowed to pursue their religious interests and callings—Protestant and Catholic missionaries had been among the first Westerners to take up residence in the concessions—natives who displayed an interest in such teachings were far less graciously treated by the authorities. When, with the establishment of a new Catholic church in Nagasaki, thousands of "hidden Christians," who had preserved their faith underground, reemerged to worship openly, they were rudely persecuted and exiled not only by the dying Tokugawa regime, but more dramatically by the early Meiji reformers, who in their effort to give Shinto a new place in national affairs adopted a firmly anti-Christian stance.[6]

Despite the protests of Western diplomats, government repression continued.[7] Shortly before Janes' arrival the teacher of an American missionary had been arrested and imprisoned in Kobe on grounds that he possessed a portion of the Bible in Japanese.[8] Like many another early Meiji prisoner, he did not live long enough to be brought to trial. Object lessons of this kind were not lost upon the missionaries. Verbeck, for one, quickly sensed the need for caution. As he wrote, the mere mention of religion in the presence of a Japanese could lead to strange behavior: "his hand would almost involuntarily be applied to his throat to indicate the extreme peril of such a topic."[9] Under such circumstances it is hardly surprising that at the time of Janes' coming there were still less than ten baptized Japanese Protestants in the whole of Japan.[10]

Plain as the government's attitude toward Christianity was, there were less clearly stated reasons why even Kumamoto's Practical Learning Party was firmly anti-Christian. Despite Yokoi Shōnan's interest in Christianity, particularly in its ethical core, which he saw as central to Western civilization, his assassination, allegedly on grounds that he had become a secret believer of this "evil teaching," saddled his followers with the compulsive desire to cleanse his reputation of all associations with this foreign faith. Kumamoto's emphasis on a secular teacher and the domain's clear rejection of all missionaries expressed the Practical Learning reformers' continuing concern with this problem.

The efforts to separate ethical studies from the rest of the school's curriculum further underscored such concerns. Ethics were to be taught by Takezaki Sadō using Yokoi Shōnan's mixture of Chu Hsi and Wang

Yang-ming Confucianism. The educational program entrusted to the Captain dealt exclusively with the school's secular and scientific goals.[11] Kozaki, who had studied ethics with Takezaki, expressed the general feelings of the school's founders, as well as many of the students, when he observed that while they were prepared to sit at Janes' feet in order to study science and technology, they were convinced that they "could teach him religion, morality, and all other things spiritual."[12] Kozaki considered it a personal responsibility to "preach Confucianism" to the Captain.[13]

Janes seems to have heeded the advice of Verbeck and Stout on the need for caution. In keeping with his invitation, he determined that the best course of action was to devote himself purely to education and to the creation of a close personal relationship with his students. If there were grander plans, as he had intimated to Stout, these found no room for "railing accusations," "denunciations of the heathen," or "invidious comparisons," which would have "wounded a just though very mistaken pride."[14] Indeed, for the first three years of his stay in Kumamoto Janes made no effort to discuss Christianity, either within or without the school. While the threat of the proscription boards and the language competence of his pupils may have necessitated such an approach, there were other reasons as well.

The Christianity he brought to Kumamoto, incorporating the concept of the Christian as radical reformer, differed from that of many of his missionary counterparts in that its principal focus centered on service to the community, and not on proselytizing in the more traditional sense. The Christian's responsibility, as the Captain saw it, was to serve as a moral example and to help his fellow man in whatever way possible. For Janes, who had been particularly influenced by Renan's *Life of Jesus* and Seeley's *Ecce Homo*, the significance of Christ Lay precisely in his moral example and in his commitment to humanity. From such a perspective the education of the young, the utilization of science to improve the conditions of those around him, and the constant desire to be of help and service were in themselves prayer, praise, and sermon. This was a form of preaching, one student later observed, that did not require words.[15]

That is not to say that Janes could not become revivalistic. As we have already observed, the potential for another pattern, which closely paralleled his mother's emotional Methodism, was also inherent in his religious and psychological make-up. But while these forces were to become important during his final year in Kumamoto, they showed few signs of exerting themselves at an earlier date.

There is a further explanation for his initial silence. Janes was convinced that Christianity lay at the core of Western civilization, that it was central to Western ethics, and that its truths were confirmed by the laws of science and the natural world. In keeping with nineteenth-century theology, he firmly believed that God revealed himself not only through the Bible, but through his handiwork—the natural world. To study nature, science, and history was to read God's "other book." Given the school's preoccupation with science and Western civilization, and considering the profoundly anti-Christian environment in which he found himself, such an approach was ideally suited to working within local limitations and echoed his own scientific inclinations. Until the summer of 1875 Janes' effort to lead his students toward Christianity clearly adopted this indirect approach. Stressing the evidences in the world around them that revealed a higher force, the order and beauty of nature, the immensity of the universe, and the course of history, he prodded his students to consider the existence of a divine force that directed human destiny. As he wrote to Anna Warner, it was impossible to learn about God's world and know nothing about God. "And to know the God who made you—aright—," he added, "is to be a Christian."[16]

By the fourth year Janes had effectively led his students, particularly those of the first and second classes, into an ever-expanding and fascinating world. Taking advantage of the students' thirst for knowledge, he had trained them to think for themselves, to follow his hints, to question and explore, and to come to their own conclusions. Janes wrote home that he was well aware of "how absorbing that thirst could be" from his "own past life," and that he had exploited the increasing enthusiasm of his boys to show "how all knowledge at some point or other touches upon God, Providence, and the spiritual and immortal side of our being."[17] To Peter Carter he wrote, "you observe that in all this the Bible, Christianity, and religion, are not alluded to," admitting that his approach was somewhat different from Carter's evangelical expectations, but at the same time he reassured him that "this is really one of the fruitful mission stations."[18] Knowledge, without an understanding and appreciation of the religious value structure that lay behind it, Janes warned the students, constituted "but the dry husk, the chaff and straw— the living and life-producing part lies beyond!"[19]

Janes' efforts to reach his students through God's "other book" were not without success. Ebina Danjō recalled that one morning the Captain marched into the classroom with particular vigor and announced to the class: "The Universe is growth!"[20] Ebina thought this an exciting concept. If the universe were subject to growth, he speculated, then it must have some form of life, or indestructible spiritual essence. Not long thereafter, while working on geology, Ebina toyed with the idea of progress and evolutionary change, and he was pleased to hear from Janes that there already was such a scholarly theory.[21] Ebina was not the only one whose explorations of the natural world led him to conclude that there must be some "universal mind" behind the natural order. Miyagawa Tsuneteru shared Ebina's views and later wrote that it was his scientific studies that led him to Christianity. One day, while climbing Mount Hanaoka, where the students often went for exercise, Miyagawa thought of a sentence in his chemistry textbook: "There is no chance work in nature."[22] Meditating on this idea, Miyagawa concluded that there must be some great being who created the universe where such law and order prevailed, and that this creator must be what Westerners referred to as God. Even Yamazaki appears to have thought along similar lines. One morning, while washing his face alongside his dormmates, he blurted out inadvertently as if to himself, "Yes, God does exist after all." Yamazaki's admission was well received by Miyagawa and Ebina, who had come to similar conclusions on their own, but it aroused the ire of Kozaki, who glared at him and snapped, "What was that you said!"[23]

Sensing this growing interest among some of his students, Janes occasionally violated his own strictly maintained silence within the school to speak, if not of Christianity, at least of God in the Newtonian "clock maker" or "first cause" sense. On one such occasion, after demonstrating the Pythagorean Theorem in a geometry lesson, he became wound up and, as he later recalled, felt a tension he could not resist.[24] "Does it not occur to you as being a very significant fact," he asked the class, "that the proposition just demonstrated should always and forever prove equally true of all the infinite variety of right-angled triangles which you may draw, or even of which you may conceive?" "What is there in nature, or in the inherent quality of magnitudes and the mathematics of their dimensions, or in the constitution of mind," he continued, "that should leave established and maintained throughout the eternities past, present, and future, this absolute and unchangeable equality between the square of the hypotenuse and the sum of the squares of the other two sides?"

Faced by a bewildered and stolid audience, Janes seems to have warmed to the subject. "What is so palpably and provably true of the simple postulate propounded by this proposition," he added, "is equally true of every proposition in your Geometry. Whence this rigorous exactitude of relations, this uniformity of demonstrable truths?" Still no reply. Faced with an "impassive, gaping silence," he decided to press his argument further. "Why is it that the mathematical relations between the power and resistance in the theoretical use of the mechanical powers with which your Physics begins never in a single instance fool you with a failure? Why is it that the chemical affinities, methods and propositions of combination and resolution of your Chemistry remain always as mathematically true and invariable as the elements of this proposition and the demonstration of its truth? Your Geometry deals with magnitudes which may conceivably be larger than worlds, or systems large as the universe itself. The facts of chemical affinities and the constitution of matter, organic and inorganic, relate to molecules, to atoms beyond the reach of the microscope. Why is it that through all this endless chain of sequences, of tremendous forces incessantly reacting but never lost, of relations of magnitudes, weights, measures, causes and effects, the utmost stretch of human ingenuity is incapable of detecting a solitary interval or irregularity, a single mutilated or missing link?" There was still no response, Janes recorded, "not even one sympathetic look."

Now the Captain dropped his interrogative manner, planted himself firmly before the rows of students, and adopted a "coldly authoritative" and "didactic" tone. "Gentlemen," he said, "I will tell you why this proposition is not sometimes, now and then on convenient occasion, but always, invariably, and forever true. I will tell you why it is that cause and effect are so invariably linked that you may base the intellection of a lifetime on the fact and never once be disappointed. I will tell you why that which is true of your Geometry, is equally trustworthy of the phenomena treated in your Physiology, your Physics, your Chemistry. It is, it is because this world, this universe, is a scene of law and order. It is because law is so universal, and order so invariable, that there is no room anywhere, not a single atom, that is the abode or the object of chance. There is no such thing as chance in the universe of which you and I are mere atoms."

"And I will add to that, Gentlemen," Janes concluded, "that to my mind, this universal reign of law, order, and uniformity of cause and consequence, indicates the fact of an initial purpose, a one power commensurate with the infinite requirements, and intelligence of which I can conceive at all only through the analogies of my human mind as a Roman historian said of the God of the Jews, 'a great governing Mind' that guides and controls the whole frame of nature, eternal, infinite, and neither capable of change nor subject to decay!"[25]

This time, Janes tells us, there was a response. "Scarcely had the term 'God' been uttered, than a student on a middle bench, leaned forward, his swarthy face swarthier with anger, his eyes flashing, and his breath thick with emotion, and said, 'That is a lie, Sir. We do not believe that!' " The student was Kozaki. "You a Confucianist, worshipper of a Chinese sage who associated your teacher with your Emperor, your parents, and your friends in the regard and duty you owe them," Janes flared back, "you dare to treat me with such disrespect!"[26] The section, embarrassed by the exchange, quickly took matters in hand, and as Janes recorded, "convinced the hothead that his remark contained no argument." "If it be a lie," Janes added getting in the final word, "the salt of the earth today cherish it." Western civilization without God and Christianity, he assured the students, "would leave a civilization like your own." "And I knew full well," he wrote to Anna Warner, "that they were ashamed of their country's condition."[27]

The foregoing incident aptly illustrates Janes' approach in leading his students toward a Christian conception of God using the evidences of science and the natural world. In it we can also detect a fine sense of timing. Aware of the fact that natural leaders such as Yamazaki, Ebina, and Miyagawa had already come to accept the idea of God's existence, Janes was prepared to confront the broader group by using his authority to underscore what had largely been a silent commitment on the part of the former. At the same time he was ready openly to face opponents like Kozaki, who viewed themselves as spokesmen for the tradition. Indeed, in dealing with Kozaki, Janes showed not only that he could manipulate science and Western civilization to his advantage, but that he could use the tradition against his opponents. Kozaki, who had determined to preach Confucianism to Janes, suddenly found himself in a serious dilemma. Openly contradicting the Captain before his classmates, he had been forced to violate the basic Confucian dictum that required a pupil to defer to his teacher. Moreover, Janes had called him on this failure, thereby indicating the degree to which he violated the very ethical system he was defending.

Kozaki's dilemma, which entailed the need to defend the tradition against outside forces by violating a part of that tradition, was itself symptomatic of the difficult straits in which many of the students found themselves. Largely the sons of samurai, or wealthy peasants who emulated samurai values, Janes' students, who varied in age from twelve to twenty-two, had all been subject to the childhood education and socialization of the Japanese warrior. Based on the Confucian value system, this training had stressed the close relationship between ethics and public service, arguing that only the ethically upright man was capable of an effective public career. Ethics, within the world of the Japanese samurai, concentrated on filial piety and loyalty and were defined within the basic father-son and lord-retainer relationships of Japanese feudalism.

Neo-Confucianism held that personal morality, or self-cultivation, was an essential prerequisite for those who aspired to high public office. Moreover, while the nexus between politics and an unchanging natural order had been broken by some Tokugawa thinkers who argued that the sages, rather than transmitters of a fixed natural order and its laws, had themselves created that order to deal with the practical realities of their day—thereby allowing modern man to do the same—there were few late Tokugawa Confucian teachers who downplayed the need for self-cultivation, or personal morality.[28] Quite the contrary, as Japan entered a period of crisis the pressures in these areas seem to have mounted.[29]

While the need for a sense of moral wholeness remained a dominant concern of those who aspired to public careers, the Restoration and the abolition of feudalism did irreparable damage to the traditional ethical structure. Loyalty and duty, the dominant values of the Japanese samurai, were cut adrift from the lord-vassal relationship in which they had been carefully defined. In a world without lords, who was one to be loyal to? In a world without traditional guidelines, where did duty lie? Although many of Janes' pupils reflected the turmoil into which the Restoration plunged them, none more clearly illustrated the specific problems of his generation than Ebina Danjō.

Ebina had come to Kumamoto from Yanagawa, a small domain north of Higo, where he had been born into a samurai family and had received the strict upbringing typical of the warrior class. Early in childhood he had been taught the duties and responsibilities that were the inverse side of samurai privilege. The severity and self-discipline of such an upbringing were often extreme. On one occasion, for a minor offense, Ebina's father ordered him to prepare to commit suicide, but not to proceed with the act until he could return to witness it in person. Six hours later, after his thirteen-year-old son had had ample opportunity to meditate on his faults and test the quality of his will, he burst into the room announcing that the infraction was not bad enough for suicide. Little wonder that Ebina looked upon his father as a strict and stern disciplinarian.[30]

A gifted student, Ebina was selected at an early age as a study companion for the son of the local daimyo. This was not only an important honor, but a route to success and higher office. But just as Ebina appeared to be facing a bright future, tragedy struck. In the turmoil that followed the Restoration, Yanagawa castle was put to the torch, and the young lord was killed in the conflagration.[31] For Ebina the loss of the castle and his lord constituted a great shock. "When the castle burned," he later wrote, "for me Yanagawa domain was dead, and I suffered within myself a greater tragedy than the burning of the castle."[32]

The tragedy of which Ebina wrote was, in fact, one that many of his fellow students experienced with the Restoration and the abolition of the feudal system. The destruction of the feudal order meant the loss of the ethical underpinnings of the system in which they had been educated and socialized, and they naturally suffered from an extreme sense of dislocation. Ebina wrote of loneliness, isolation, and a growing lack of a sense of moral wholeness.[33] Forced to rely more and more on himself, he came to see himself as cunning and selfish, a man incapable of following the Way, and consequently unsuited for a public career. And yet, despite his sense of failure, he was not free from the demands of the old order. "I had within me a spiritual demand for loyalty . . . I wanted something to revere . . . I wanted again the morality of the Analects."[34]

Students of Japanese Christianity have long observed that many Meiji converts were former samurai. There are, moreover, those who have suggested that the largest number of such converts came from domains that were on the losing side in the Restoration.[35] And one prominent recent study has argued vigorously that it was the loss of status by samurai in such domains that led them to attempt to regain their lost positions and status through conversion.[36] What Janes' students in general, and Ebina in particular, suggest, however, is not so much a sense of lost status—all saw themselves heading for important public careers in a world that provided far greater opportunity than could be found in the feudal system—but an extreme sense of moral dislocation that had its roots in the breakdown of the former value structure.

While Kozaki and one or two others continued to find satisfaction in Confucianism and faithfully attended Takezaki's expositions on the Chinese classics, Ebina and others no longer found these discourses satisfying or effective in dealing with their sense of alienation.[37] Stout, who met some of the Kumamoto students in Nagasaki, noted that they were "restless, discontented men . . . looking out for some new thing, somewhat like the Athenians of old." In this observation he captured something of the troubled mood of the exsamurai boys under Janes' supervision. He noted, moreover, that from his conservative Christian perspective they were not particularly interested in "truth for its own sake," but in the application of Christianity to the broader needs of their society.[38] While this observation illustrates the basic differences in approach between Stout and Janes, it was precisely the latter's conviction that the Christian's duty was to serve the community that provided the avenue by which many of his students were able to make the transition from Confucianism to Christianity.

For young men such as Ebina the school's rigid discipline, the emphasis on ethics, which was part of Janes' regimen and which permeated the American textbooks they were using, and the Captain's efforts to get them to look through science and the natural world at ultimate causes, not only helped to deal with their sense of moral dislocation, but suggested new possibilities for a moral and ethical restructuring that maintained the strong public, or political, commitment that had been part of the Confucian ethical structure in which they had been socialized.

There were other areas in which his presentation of Christianity allowed close linkages with the earlier system of thought and values. Had the Captain initially presented his pupils with the concept of God typical of his more revivalistic moments, a highly anthropomorphic and personal being with whom direct human communication was possible, the gap between the Confucian conception of Heaven and such a God would have been insurmountable. On the other hand, Janes' presentation of the Divine through the "natural order" shortened the distance between Heaven and God. As Ebina noted, Yokoi Shōnan had come to interpret Heaven as more than merely "pure reason" and had argued that Heaven possessed "personal character."[39] Of course it is conceivable that Yokoi's studies of Christianity may have convinced him that if Confucianism were to be spread "beyond the four seas," as his poem to his nephews urged, its concept of Heaven would have to take on certain qualities that were synonymous with the Christian conception of God.[40] But as the students were to show, such a transformation of Heaven could also serve as an inverse path to Christianity.

Having quietly come to their own conclusions about God's existence several of Janes' students, including Ebina, Yokoi, Yamazaki, and Miyagawa, formed the nucleus of a group that determined to learn more about Christianity. Janes recorded an occasion on which Yamazaki, Yokoi, Ebina, and Ichihara approached him. "We have no religion now," Yamazaki began, "Buddhism is corrupt, and its priests are degraded." Shinto, he thought, was only "patriotism"—unacceptable as a religion because "it teaches only myths and fables." "Confucianism is no more than a few moral precepts," he continued, "it is good, but it does not inspire us." Worse still, it was Confucianism that led China to become what it was, "and Japan must be different!" Yokoi Tokio, Shōnan's son, now took up the appeal. Assuring Janes that their interest was purely personal and did not involve the school, he noted: "We are studying; we are learning. All this we owe to you." At the same time suggesting that he felt a disquiet with knowledge for knowledge's sake, Yokoi added, "but we lack motive except to know. Science we love, literature we love, but it seems selfish to heap up our little pile of knowledge, not knowing what to do with it and with no impulse or disposition to make use of it. Maybe it is the purpose and the duty of religion of some sort," he concluded, "to inspire and direct our use of what we learn." "What is it that makes the teacher so earnest, so determined, so devoted? Why should he come so far to stay here alone to teach us?," Yokoi asked for the group. "We want something of that kind in our natures, and think he can help us in that way as in so many other ways." Ebina was typically blunt in his inquiry: "Does the teacher think Christianity is what we need?"[41]

While the foregoing incident represents a reconstruction based on the Captain's notes and may include some later distortions, it certainly rings true in its basic themes. Many of Ebina's classmates shared his sense of dislocation, alienation, and loneliness. The Restoration had resulted in a distinct break with the past and had cast them adrift. Buddhism, Shintoism, and even Confucianism not only had lost their power to inspire, they had become associated, as Yamazaki underscored, with the problem of national weakness, and in the case of Confucian China, with defeat and foreign domination. As Janes observed in response to Yamazaki's concerns, "the uppermost thought in the mind of every Japanese of that day was—Japan." "In that land of fiery patriotism," he recalled, "self was always little enough thought of."[42] But self, too, was a problem, and in a way that was not anticipated by the Captain.

If loyalty and duty were the highest values of the old order, self-interest and selfishness were its greatest vices. To elevate the individual above the group was inconceivable in traditional Japanese society, and yet, such conduct was encouraged by the Western education the students received at the school. Individual decisions that clashed with the old order were sometimes necessitated by the force of change that swept the country. Ebina once more illustrated the problem. Forbidden by his conservative father to return to Kumamoto after his first years at the Yōgakkō, he broke with his family on the grounds that his training in Kumamoto was necessary not only for his personal future but for the future of the nation. Becoming an unfilial son, he gave up his birthright, but he was shouldered with a nagging doubt that his decision had been selfish—a doubt which further served to undermine his sense of moral wholeness.

As the previous episode indicates, Yokoi Tokio was subject to similar misgivings. Learning for the sake of learning was exceedingly selfish from the Confucian perspective. Moreover, his father had taught the Wang Yang-ming dictum that knowledge and action were inextricably linked. Knowing that something was right meant carrying it out. Knowledge meant practical application. But knowledge also meant a moral, intuitive understanding. During moments of national crisis such an understanding could allow the individual to defy the demands of tradition—it was this logic that Ebina used to break with his father and the rules of filial piety— but such actions constantly pitted the convictions of the individual's morally based perceptions against those of the broader community. A child who thought himself right, and his parents wrong, could defy the traditional values only if he were convinced that his moral perception of reality was superior to that of his elders. And yet, it was precisely in this area, in their sense of moral wholeness and the conviction that their moral uprightness allowed a clearer understanding of reality than that of the conservative older generation, that Janes' students were most vulnerable. It was here, in fact, that the Restoration had done its greatest damage, and that an effective restructuring was necessary. As Yamazaki told Janes, what they needed was "some kind of *living* inspiration," which could restore their sense of wholeness and usefulness' and allow their knowledge to be applied effectively in the interests of the broader community and their nation.[43]

In response to the foregoing request Janes announced a weekly Bible study at his house on Saturday evenings. These Bible studies were to become increasingly important for his students. Initially there was a good deal of hesitation in attending what was obviously a gathering devoted to a teaching still seen as wicked. But there was also curiosity. Janes' efforts to get his students to think for themselves were bearing results. While many supported Kozaki in the persuasion that God and Christianity were "a lie," there were others who followed the lead of Yamazaki, Ebina, and Yokoi, who argued that Western religion, and particularly Christianity, deserved careful consideration and study. And yet, the motivations of those who joined Yamazaki, Ebina, and Yokoi were often mixed. Some had originally gone to Takezaki about the propriety of attending such meetings and had been advised that they might go, not in order to become believers, but to seek flaws in this foreign faith. Many were interested in attending for the English practice the meetings afforded.[44] And there were those who went for less obvious reasons. Okada Matsuo found the Bible studies uninteresting, but enjoyed the refreshments that followed. Shimomura Kōtarō, who later earned a doctorate in engineering and became a well-known professor in this field at Dōshisha University, had heard that in Christianity there was something about a means of ascending into the sky. While nothing specific was said on this subject, Shimomura would watch Janes' face when he prayed at the close of each meeting. Deep in prayer, the whites of his eyes would begin to show, and Shimomura would give his thigh a slap in excitement, thinking that the mysteries of the ascension were about to be revealed.[45]

Janes' Bible studies were largely unstructured and employed his fundamental approach to education. Meetings were held on Saturday evenings and, as the number of those attending swelled to sixty by the end of 1874, in two sections on Saturday and Sunday evenings. The basic format was simple. Students were asked to read a chapter of the Gospels aloud, each taking a verse by turn. Ebina recalled that when a chapter was completed "that was it."[46] The Captain made no attempt to explain the content unless one of the students posed a question. If there were questions he provided various answers, but often there were questions to which he replied "I don't know" and let it go at that. Yokoi regarded

Janes' method of teaching the Bible "the most curious that could be imagined."[47] He further added that the Captain seemed in no hurry and appeared totally unconcerned about the students' conversion. When anyone asked him a particularly difficult question, he simply replied "study the Bible deeper, and your doubts will be cleared away." Occasionally he added that the matter was "a thing he could not understand himself, and that he would ask it directly when he stood before the Lord." For Janes the study of the Bible, like all other studies, was a matter of self-education. While he was prepared to serve as guide, the students would have to come to their own conclusions. "We studied the Bible for about a year," Yokoi wrote, "and were not without our doubts, but his ardent love and unchanging sincerity were living testimonies to the truth of the doctrines."[48]

Though many of Janes' students initially attended the Bible studies to find fault with Christianity, most were clearly influenced by his sincerity. The Captain's prayers at these meetings seem to have made a particularly deep impression on a number of the boys. When Janes prayed for the future of Japan and for the role that his students might play in it, tears would often run down his face. Most of the students kept their eyes open and were surprised to see a grown man shedding tears for them and their nation. When they realized that he was completely earnest in these appeals, they were often moved more deeply "than they cared to admit."[49]

In the meantime a number of the students had come to their own conclusions about Christianity. In May 1875 Janes wrote to Anna Warner: "There are twelve or fifteen of the boys, comprising the best scholars in the three upper classes, who in every way give evidence of confirmed, intelligent Christian faith, and a wish to make the most open and unreserved profession of it. I say this without having said a word to one of them on the subject of a formal profession." He preferred it this way, he wrote, and reported that he had added a regular Sunday worship service to the Bible studies. Attendance at this service had grown from "two the first Sunday to fifteen of the boys . . . several officers from the native garrison . . . and a lady, the mother of one of the medical students."[50]

By the summer and fall of 1875 Janes became increasingly enthusiastic about his Bible studies and his new Sunday services which, we are told, often lasted for more than three hours.[51] To these a weekly prayer meeting was added at the start of November.[52] Moreover, as his letters to Anna Warner showed, he found himself under mounting physical and emotional pressures which, as in Oregon, were transformed into a heightened and far more emotional religious consciousness. Evidence for such a transformation can be found not only in his increasingly emotional prayers, full of tears and a sense of anguish, which the students interpreted as sincerity, but in his presentation of God, which shifted from the coldly rational model of Newton's clock maker to a highly personal being with whom a direct and intimate human relationship was possible. This inner transformation on the part of their teacher was to be of great importance for Janes' students, for whom the more personalized image of God played a vital role in their quest to transcend the discontent into which the Restoration had plunged them.

Ebina typified the difficulties in which many of the students found themselves. Having accepted the concept of God in the sense of a "universal mind," which he saw as a transformation of the Confucian conception of Heaven, he found it difficult to feel any personal relationship between himself and such a God. In fact, earlier, when he had broken with his father, he had defended himself on purely Wang Yang-ming grounds, arguing that "Heaven sees my mind and will defend me."[53] But just as the education of the Yōgakkō pushed the frontiers of knowledge into the distant reaches of the universe, the God of that universe was equally distant and removed, and not apparently as approachable as Heaven. Ebina and many of his fellow students found such a deity intellectually stimulating, but of little consolation in their daily lives. And it was in this area that the students' real struggle was taking place.

As Janes recorded, "character, character, and again character became the favorite theme of all thought, motive and conversation."[54] Ebina, for one, saw life as a daily struggle with his passions, to which he attributed his sense of moral dislocation. "In trying to control my passions, though my attempts rose to heaven," he wrote, "they were not sufficient." And yet, as he added, "within my innermost heart there was the demand somehow to live a life of sincerity."[55] To deal with this problem and to develop their characters the students seem to have turned to the classical Confucian austerities—cold baths, exposure to the weather, sleep deprivation, and fasting. But these too ended in failure. "In Confucianism there exists a distinction between 'essential nature' and 'individual character,'" Ebina noted in retrospect, "according to Paul's thought it is a collision of reason and the appetites. Is reason established? Are the passions established? Reason is the demand of 'real character,' but it is hard to establish. Passions are not desired by 'real character,' but they flourish. Paul exclaimed, 'The good that I want to do, I cannot do, and the evil that I do not want to do, this I do,'" "Many were the times," Ebina added, "that I too had to cry out in this manner."[56]

Janes' new presentation of God, no longer as universal mind, but as a personal Lord to whom the individual owed loyalty, and with whom man could communicate directly through prayer, was to have profound effects on the exsamurai boys who gathered at his house to study the Bible. Ebina recalled a meeting that changed the course of his entire life. On this occasion the Captain ordered the students to stand for prayer. Ebina regarded standing a sign of assent. He thought it improper to stand if one could not agree with the concept of prayer. Moreover, Confucians stressed that it was inappropriate to ask anything of Heaven. In a quandary, he hesitated, suffering considerable inner turmoil. Finally, arguing that it was appropriate even for a Confucianist to stand, if the act indicated a desire to repay one's obligations to Heaven, he rose to his feet.[57]

Janes next announced that prayer was man's duty toward God. The word "duty," Ebina remembered, struck him "like thunder."[58] "In an instant," he wrote, "the light dawned on me. Ah! I had been neglecting my duty. I had done something unpardonable. If it were my duty I should bend my knee; I should bow my head; I should be willing to do anything. It was exactly because God had created me that it was a mistake for me to exist for myself. Just like the Ptolemaic world I was self-centered, while God existed in the periphery to be used by me. Then, however," he wrote, "God became central and I became like the world of Copernicus. My way of thinking changed in the same way that the ideas concerning the heavenly systems changed. When I reached this point I was completely and profoundly humiliated. . . . However, following God's command I became a changed person. I became a completely changed being. Speaking of the inner self, it was at that moment that I brought about the restoration of imperial rule."[59]

Ebina's conversion, like that of others among Janes' students, proved to be functionally effective. "Up to that time my conscience had no authority and my desires and passions were in control," he wrote, "but with the restoration of imperial rule, the authority was born in the conscience." "When I realized that it was my duty to make God my lord," he emphasized, "it was then for the first time that my conscience gained authority. I was exceedingly happy. This was the rebirth of my whole life. As for my faith, my conscience being bound to God, its power was restored." "What I had been unable to attain by sincere and wholehearted Confucian austerities, namely the control of the passions by the conscience," Ebina recalled, "this power I gained once I became attached to God." In summing up his conversion he wrote: "To me God became my lord and I became his retainer. We had a relationship based on a lord-vassal morality, and consequently I served God as a loyal servant. As for this experience it was one of rational religion," he insisted, "and I was quite unaware of being either forgiven or saved."[60]

While it must be recognized that the phenomenon of conversion often incorporates elements that are distinctly personal, and consequently defies indiscriminate extension to the broader group, Ebina's experiences do seem to have echoed the central dilemma in which the Yōgakkō students found themselves, as well as the process by which the Captain was able to lead them to a new sense of moral wholeness. Externally the destruction of the feudal system had been quick and complete. But internally, in the lives of those who had been socialized in its values, the destruction of the old order was more difficult. The demands of loyalty, the need for sincerity, the search for a sense of moral wholeness, all these were directly related to the Confucian ethical system and did not cease with the Restoration.

Pushed toward Christianity by the inner needs created by such values, former samurai such as Ebina, Yokoi, and Yamazaki accepted Christianity as a new means of dealing with the demands of the old order. But in doing so it would be hard to deny that the former values also vitally influenced their perception of this foreign religion. Janes' presentation of Christianity as a highly personal inner faith that was to find expression in service to the community blended well with the Confucian linking of self-cultivation with societal reform. As we have seen, such a blending facilitated a workable restructuring that allowed Ebina to become a Christian samurai.[61] Moreover, the re-creation of the former feudal relationship with God as Lord reestablished the power for moral action that many of the students had been seeking. And with single-heartedness of purpose restored, they were ready, as Ebina noted, to devote themselves to serving their country.

Janes quietly watched as other students underwent similar transformations. "There was an enlargement of the feelings of manhood," he wrote, "that presently became manifest." Still more noticeable was the growth of a "modest kindliness and mutual deference," and a "gentleness that gave a firmness of substance to the habitual polish of Japanese manners" that the Captain found "very affecting."[62] Ichihara underscored the metamorphosis at work in those who attended the Bible studies, noting that by the closing months of 1875 many who had originally gone to the teacher's house with skeptical eyes now became convinced that "Christianity was not a wicked religion, but that there was truth in it."[63]

With a growing circle of believers, including fourteen or fifteen of the best students, it was hard to keep the issues of Christianity out of the school. While Janes adopted a neutral and aloof stand and continued to see his role in the school as purely secular, the Christian students saw no need for such a separation of roles. Organizing themselves into a Christian association, they openly challenged their non-Christian counterparts. The latter found themselves increasingly at a disadvantage, and Kozaki recalled his own predicament. Still staunchly anti-Christian and a leader of the opposition, he was quite literally "dragged off" to one of the Bible studies by Miyagawa, Ichihara, and Ebina. Overjoyed to see him, Janes openly prayed for him at the close of the meeting while Kozaki glared at the Captain in dismay, and muttered to himself, "well you have a cheek." Moments later, when tears were pouring down the Captain's face, Kozaki, who still had no use for Christianity, found himself deeply moved by his teacher's "desperate earnestness."[64]

While Kozaki remained firm in his conviction that there was neither sense nor reason in religion, and that it was rank superstition to believe that God spoke to man, he gradually found himself bested in the open debates that now flared up among the students. Janes seems to have made an effort to direct his converts through a course on Christian evidence. And in the discussions that followed, Kozaki found that "they had laid hold on certain truths of which I was entirely ignorant." Forced to study in self-defense, he pored over Bushnell's *Nature and the Supernatural* and found its reasoning so convincing that he simply had to give up his former "loose and rambling style of argument." Swearing never to give in, Kozaki went to Janes and asked him for books that opposed Christianity. Told by the Captain that he had none, he was on the point of despair, when he recalled that he had read somewhere that Herbert Spencer could give him help and resolved then and there to use the first opportunity to go and sit at his feet.[65]

By December 1875 the issue of Christianity was clearly coming to a head in the school. While the number of those belonging to the Christian association swelled, so did ill feelings toward Christianity among an increasingly organized opposition. With the Christmas vacation upon them, a group of the Christian students went to the Captain to ask how they might best use their time during the holidays. Janes advised an "intense study of the Bible," and "prayer!" And this they seem to have done, for when they returned to the school in January they had a faith that "burned like fire."[66]

Almost immediately the whole school found itself immersed in a revival. None of the students, Kanamori remembered, was aware of what the term meant, but they became filled with a religious fervor that was close to madness.[67] Janes saw the phenomenon as the descent of the Holy Spirit on his work, and he was himself increasingly carried away by the experience.[68] Studies were forgotten as students gathered in groups of five or six to study the Bible and pray in the recitation rooms, in the dining hall, and in their private quarters. Prayer meetings often went on until dawn, as did Bible studies. Some students turned to midnight ice baths and to fasting to harden their faith and commitment. Many felt a compulsive need to preach the Christian "way" to those who had not yet converted. While only weeks from the normal term examinations, the school virtually "faded out."[69] Recitations were suspended, and even the usually circumspect Janes seems to have taken to preaching during school hours. On Sundays, to Kozaki's consternation, the audience at the Captain's house swelled to over a hundred, leaving not more than ten or a dozen students in the dormitory.[70] When the school authorities got wind of these developments, they reprimanded Janes and warned the students that the school was not to be used for religious purposes. He made an official apology and kept the students from using the classrooms, but this had little effect on their behavior. From then on, one of them wrote, "our preaching was not confined to the school, but found its way to the servants of the teachers, our kindred at home, and to the men and women on the streets."[71]

By the end of January many of Janes' pupils were ready to make an open and public declaration of their faith. The Captain himself seems to have urged caution in taking such a step, but on Sunday, January 30, about forty of the students assembled on Mount Hanaoka, the "Mount of Flowers," as Kanamori later called it, a favorite location to which the students usually repaired on Sunday afternoons for prayer and meditation. And yet, this was no ordinary gathering. Careful plans had been made beforehand. The students climbed up this wooded hill on the outskirts of Kumamoto in groups of threes and fours in order to dispel the suspicions of their irate opponents. They assembled at a designated rendezvous point—an ancient pine tree on which Katō Kiyomasa had long ago suspended a bell that tolled the hours for his castle builders below. Miyagawa, Kanamori, and Ebina had made their way to the "bell pine" by way of the Yokoi home, where they had picked up Tokio and the formal declaration that Furushō Saburō and Sakai Teiho had prepared for the meeting.[72]

When all arrived, they formed a large circle and a prayer meeting ensued. The meeting opened under Kanamori's supervision with Anna Warner's hymn, "Jesus Loves Me," which was one of Janes' Sunday morning favorites, and of which the boys were particularly fond. Yokoi Tokio next read from the English Bible the passage from John, chapter 10, "I am the good shepherd . . . ."[73] Following this it was Furushō's turn to present the covenant he and Sakai had composed. In a clear and firm voice he read out what was to be Meiji Japan's first formal Christian Declaration and the credo of the Kumamoto Band.

> In studying Christianity we have been deeply enlightened and awakened. The more we have studied it, the more filled with enthusiasm and joy we have become. Moreover we strongly desire that this faith

might be proclaimed over the whole Empire in order to dispel the ignorance of the people. For many of these have no idea of its beautiful content, and are steeped in ignorance and worn out ideas. This is truly deplorable and unbearable! It is consequently our duty as patriots to arise with enthusiasm, and with no concern for our lives, to make known the fairness and impartiality of this teaching. It is to this goal that we dedicate all our energies, and it is for this purpose that we have gathered here on Mount Hanaoka to endorse this covenant.[74]

Thirty-five of the students affixed their signatures and swore to uphold not only the main covenant but three subclauses that called upon all to be "brotherly in their relations to one another," to be "free to admonish," "ready to cooperate," and to "forsake all evil and turn to the good."[75] More importantly, all endorsed the call for solidarity. "Since at the present time the majority of our people are opposed to Christianity, the lapse from faith of even one of our number," Furushō had written, "not only invites the scorn of the multitude, but frustrates the very purpose for which we are banded together." Anyone giving up the faith not only would be regarded guilty of deceiving themselves and their friends, but was certain, he added, to be "punished for his sin."[76]

After a series of deeply felt and fervent prayers, the group climbed to the top of the hill from which they could look down on the city of Kumamoto and its castle. Here they bowed deeply once more as Ebina led them in prayer. Ebina recalled the proverb, "A castle that is set on a hill cannot be hidden." Suddenly he felt he knew what this expression meant. Fifty years later he could still remember the excitement he felt on that day.[77] For many of Janes' Christian students the Hanaoka Declaration represented the final act of their revolutionary break with the past. As Tokutomi Kenjirō later put it, "it was the Bunker Hill of Japan."[78]

When Janes was told of the Hanaoka Declaration he was quietly pleased. But he was also concerned about the large number of younger students who had signed the covenant. Sensing that this step would lead to a public confrontation, he wrote to Stout, "I have advised the younger and less instructed, as being possibly less stable, not to thrust themselves suddenly into difficulty."[79] At the same time he was taken with the "mellow, tender feelings of penitence, piety, love, and joy" that pervaded the school. Janes found the school's new mood as pleasant "as the breath of a May morning after a shower."[80] And yet, there were also thunderclouds on the horizon. For the men who had backed the school as Kumamoto's only hope for securing an influential position in national affairs, Janes' success in converting Higo's brightest minds to Christianity—

which in 1876 clearly made him the most successful "missionary" in Japan—was a dubious one indeed. The last thing the Practical Learning reformers and their allies wanted was an army of Christian converts.[81] Consequently pressures were almost immediately applied both at the school and by the families of the students to get them to recant. Within a few weeks a full-scale persecution of the Christian boys was underway.

Even before the storm fully broke, Janes seems to have become aware of his own precarious future in Kumamoto as well as that of his Christian boys. On February 7, 1876, just a week after the Hanaoka incident, he penned a letter to "Rev. Mr. Davis, Missionary, American Board (Care of any Missionary of the American Board) Kobe or Osaka, Japan." "You have perhaps never heard of me," Janes wrote in the opening portion of his letter to Davis, "and I am therefore permitted to say that I have been occupied in charge of a school which I established in this place somewhat more than four and a half years ago. My other work has been accompanied from the time when it was possible to speak of Christianity— about four years—with the religious instruction of my pupils; and indeed all my work has been inspired by the one aim of making it subserve the Kingdom of Christ, and so the highest welfare of those under my superintendence, and the large community influenced by them and the school." "At length," he continued, "there is the most abundant evidence of the presence and powerful influence of God's spirit throughout the work, the evidence, character and details of which it will be most gratifying to you to learn in due time."[82]

Of his school he wrote to Davis: "The school has an excellent reputation here and in Yedo. It has been my care to make the instruction most thorough as far as it extends, the course occupying four years. The first class graduated last summer. Another leaves in July next. Several of the last class . . . and a number of the class to graduate in July are Christians of deep and earnest convictions, and have openly for some time announced the consecration of their lives to the service of Christ and their poor people; and have put themselves into my hands, under God, to do with them as shall deem to me best to further the work of saving souls." "The material," he added, "I feel to be good." "None is too good," he thought, "but I doubt there is better today in Japan." "Do you want them?" "Can you better prepare them for the work of the Master?," he inquired of Davis, noting that he personally favored the "union movement" among the churches working in Japan and hoped that his students' future work would avoid the "narrow," the "little," and the "divided."[83]

Janes' letter made its way to Kyoto, where Jerome D. Davis and Niijima Jo were attempting to organize the American Board's first Japanese educational institution (later Dōshisha University). Davis recalled that the letter arrived as if "a word of God had come from heaven."[84] In the meantime the situation in Kumamoto had become increasingly troubled. "The awakening in the school, called 'the revolution in the school,'" Janes wrote to Stout a few days later, "has produced a profound sensation in the city and throughout the region." "There is much excitement and some disturbance, a good deal of downright persecution," he noted, "and many threats of more." Most of the converts, he reported, "stand fast" and "take the persecuting blows as they come." But two of his boys had already been "cast out from their homes." And all, he felt, were under a terrible strain.[85] Maintaining an aloof posture was now extremely difficult. "The concentrated aversion and hatred that should, humanly speaking, have been spread over four and a half years," he observed, "are crowded into these few days and weeks." The hotheads, who were not only his enemies, but the enemies of those who had created the school, he explained, would like to break it up. "And they may even be successful," he concluded pessimistically.[86]

Nor was opposition confined to those outside the school. There were opponents within as well. The events of January had dramatically split the student body. On the day that the Christian boys had climbed Mount Hanaoka to affirm their covenant, those opposed to Christianity had gathered at the Suizenji gardens to pose for a commemorative photograph and to reaffirm their own commitment to the Hosokawa house and to the values of the Practical Learning Party, which had created the school.[87] Led by Yoshida Sakuya they called for the expulsion of the Christian students as traitors to the tradition and the Hosokawa family. For a time there were those among the Christian group who thought they should accede to such demands, arguing that Christianity called for nonresistance and a turning of the other cheek. When Ebina consulted Janes on this issue he was assured in no uncertain terms that "non resistance" was a misunderstanding of Christ's teachings. Rather than give in, the Captain told Ebina, the Christian students should be prepared to fight! The result was a great debate. Held in the main hall of the school, with the anti-Christian group sitting on the right, and the Hanaoka group on the left, Ebina squared off against Yoshida Sakuya.[88]

Arguing that the Christian students had done nothing to bring shame on the school, that they represented the school's best and most hard-working pupils, that the search and respect for truth was the responsibility of all students, and that matters of faith were essentially private, Ebina challenged his opponents to find a single point of fault with the Christian students, and openly declared that there was no reason for them to leave the school. Yoshida's side found itself at a loss for words. Finally one of the students on the right shouted: "Believers in Christianity are unfilial! Christianity is a heretical way devoid of loyalty and righteousness!" "Such a statement," Ebina countered, "simply shows your ignorance about Christianity. It hardly deserves a reply."[89] By the time the debate had ended it was clear that the victory had gone to the Christian side. Demands for the expulsion of the Hanaoka group were dropped. And not long thereafter Yoshida appeared at Janes' house to declare that he too had become a believer.[90]

If calmer voices prevailed within the school, this was not the case beyond its confines. On March 4 Janes wrote to Davis that "my boys and I have been passing through unusual events, to say the least." They were in the midst of a "sharp," "vindictive," and "exciting" persecution, he reported. "I think the little colony is practically in tact; no lives have been taken, though that was threatened seriously enough; and there are no cases of *hara kiri* yet to report, though a mother in one family and a father in another took that method of driving their sons from the faith; their degradation was declared to be insupportable." "I grieve over my imprisoned Christian boys," he continued, "the physical strength of one is failing, and the unthinking persecutors may kill him."[91]

In the interim the situation in Kumamoto had indeed become precarious. As Janes was well aware, the good will that had been expressed toward him was closely tied to his accomplishments in the school. He had made them "like the school," as he had written to Davis,[92] but certainly no one in Kumamoto wanted the students to become "priests," as was now feared. As we have seen, members of the Shimpūren had been violently opposed to the school from the start and Janes' life had been in danger on several occasions before the winter of 1875. By the end of February 1876 antischool and anti-Christian anger seems to have crystallized into plots to kill the Christian students as well as the Captain. "Parties in the city are banded who swear the death of the Christian boys," Janes had written to Stout on February 28, "and the same interesting information is brought to me regarding myself. The beggars!"[93] Earlier he had told Fuwa Tadajirō, one of the Christian students, that he was quite prepared to "die an unnatural death in Japan."[94] And yet he was hardly willing to accept such a fate without resistance. Informed by his students on the evening of February 27 that they would all be killed that night, he is reported to have retorted, "very well, then you'll all be in Heaven tonight, and I'll be there with you! Get your swords and I'll get my revolvers." Thereafter he marched to Takezaki and told him that "if a single hair of these boys' heads is injured off comes your head first of all."[95] Fortunately for Janes, Takezaki, and the students, ample security was provided and all managed to survive the night unharmed. But it was not long before Nonoguchi conveyed to Janes the decision of the prefectural authorities that his services would no longer be needed after the expiration of his contract in October.[96] In the wake of the foregoing incident Janes wrote to Stout that he felt very tired. He noted that he had tried to shield Harriet from the general turmoil, but that incidents of this type made it difficult to keep her "measurably in ignorance" of the troubles they all faced. "I have not exaggerated the critical state of things here," Janes wrote, "and it needs little I am persuaded, to precipitate an explosion. The idle-class are babbling again, and the streets are full enough of swords."[97]

The persecutions intensified. Most of the Christian students were ordered home, where family pressures were exerted to get them to recant. In the case of boys such as Kanamori, efforts were made to have prior teachers modify their views. Kanamori had been a favorite pupil of Takezaki Sadō. His former teacher now told him that he had become a traitor to the sages. Kanamori countered by inquiring whether Takezaki had ever read the Bible. "Why should I read such rubbish?" Takezaki replied indignantly. Kanamori came back by pointing out that in earlier years Takezaki had stressed the need to "investigate and examine" all things, and that Takezaki should now adopt the same approach toward Christianity. Confronted by such boldness Takezaki could only sputter, "get out of here you idiot!" The uncompromising Kanamori soon found himself in solitary confinement at home; his books were burned, and he was forced to subsist on three small rice balls per day.[98] Little wonder that Janes was worried that his persecutors might kill him.

Yokoi Tokio fared even worse than Kanamori.[99] The very idea that Shōnan's son had rejected the teachings of his father for the religion of the West was enough to arouse the anger and despair of those who had worked so hard to dispel all rumors of Shōnan's association with Christianity. Takezaki's wife, Junko, went to Tokio's mother and told her to her face that she should commit suicide to atone for her son's conduct.[100] This would be the only way to restore her dead husband's honor. Yokoi's mother called him in and remonstrated with him, saying that she could not face her dead husband and that she had no other course but suicide. Tokio bargained with her for one more day, while he wrote to Ebina, who was still at the school, for advice. Tokio's letter ended with the line: "My cross is too heavy. Shall I bear it and cause my mother to die? Or shall I refuse it and be damned?"[101] Confronted by such a question Ebina had no answer. Hearing about the imminent suicide of this noble and gentle lady, the Captain decided on action. Dispatching a messenger to the prefectural offices, he requested that an official be sent immediately to the Yokoi home to "prevent crime." The arrival of the official seems to have turned the tide. The next day cooler heads prevailed at the Yokoi's family council. Faith, one of its members insisted, was a matter of personal choice. Yokoi Shōnan had himself insisted on this. All the family could do was to make certain that Tokio should never become a Christian minister. The compromise was accepted and the life of Tokio's mother was spared.[102]

Tokio's cousin, Tokutomi Iichirō, who was one of the youngest students to sign the Hanaoka Declaration, found himself in equally distressing circumstances. Years later, as the well-known journalist Sohō, he insisted that he had signed the Christian oath in blind obedience to the upperclassmen, that he had not really understood Christian doctrine, and that his relationship to Janes had never been close or intimate.[103] Moreover, in his popular autobiography he wrote little about the persecution of the Christian students. But there is evidence that Tokutomi, too, was subjected to intense family pressure to recant. Closely linked to the Yokoi house, and, more importantly, the son of one of Shōnan's principal disciples, Tokutomi was "called to strict account by his father, who told him that under no circumstances would Christianity be tolerated." Tokutomi's Western books were burned in a great auto-da-fé, as were those of his sister, Hatsuko, one of two girls Janes admitted to the school in 1874. Tokutomi was repeatedly reprimanded by his father. No wonder, Kozaki wrote, the poor lad had for a time to "bow his head to the inevitable."[104]

Tokutomi's position was clarified in a letter from Janes to Stout in which the Captain tried to illustrate the difficulties in which his boys found themselves by the end of February. "A boy, a member of one branch of the Ise [Yokoi] family on his mother's side," Janes wrote, "had become a Christian and I believe is one yet." "This boy was called for by his father who had been away on business in the countryside and ordered to renounce his Christian belief." "The boy declared he would not. He is but 13 or 14 years old. He escaped from the house and came to the school, or rather to my house to prayer meeting which was half over." "Learning the circumstances," Janes noted, "I advised him to go the next morning to his father, and assure him of his dutiful love, and willingness to obey him in all things *possible*, but cautioned him to beware being led or forced into any denial of Christ." "His father seemed mollified," Janes continued, "and allowed him to return to school, but last evening the father sent for the boy, and stated his determination to commit *Hara kiri*—suicide—before him, if he did not yield. The boy was overcome and led his father to believe that he had gone back to anything the father required. The poor boy, by name Tokutomi, is wretched, and is over in the school weeping."[105] Although Tokutomi later went, as

Janes recorded, "in the agony of his regrets and remorse and told his father, he had not and could not renounce his faith in Christ,"[106] the fact that he alone among the Christian students had been forced—if temporarily—to "bow to the inevitable" was to leave a lasting scar on the leadership-conscious and ambitious Iichirō, and may well have influenced his subsequent interpretation of this period of his life.

The experiences of Kanamori, Yokoi, and Tokutomi were shared by many of the Christian students. None of Janes' boys escaped persecution in one form or another.[107] To the pressures of friends, teachers, and family members were added financial inducements. Ebina remembered that he and many of his Christian friends suddenly found their stipends cut off.[108] Left without financial support they were at a loss what to do, particularly about food. Janes countered by allowing the students to cook their meals at his house and where necessary provided financial support.[109] Harassments of this kind ceased after word was sent from Tokyo that questions of religious belief were private matters not subject to state or school control.[110] By late March life within the school returned to its normal routine. Christian and non-Christian students buried their differences in favor of preparing themselves for graduation. The administration, having heard from the Captain that he had no intention of leaving Higo before the last day of his contract, made the best of a bad situation. Janes, in turn, returned to his role as secular educator and teacher.

By June he was able to report that things were "growing better and better" for his Christian boys. Some of the students "still suffer privations and wrongs at the hands of relatives and friends," he wrote, but the Christian band had gained "a substantial victory." "The trials through which all have passed," he observed, "have abundantly proved not only the firmness of their conviction and the strength of their faith, but the power of the truth itself to sustain in times of trial." Remembering the "intense feelings," "violent threats," and "intemperate rage" that confronted him in February, he wrote to his mother, "when the crisis came, I just made up my mind that it was to be the end with me." But now he was convinced that "the very violence of the spasm has seemed to work its own cure." "Things are calm again, and the patient is ashamed of himself."[111]

Janes was pleased to record that the persecutions had actually augmented the Christian band. Yoshida Sakuya, Fukushima Tsunanori, and Okada Gentarō, all original opponents of Christianity, had come over to the Hanaoka side. Yoshida soon found himself in the fiery furnace with the other Christians. Hearing that his son had become a believer, his father became extremely enraged and ordered him home. When Yoshida arrived he told him coldly: "Give up this faith. If you won't I'll have to kill you with my own hands!" Yoshida returned to the school to seek Janes' advice, and was told by the Captain that he should prepare himself for death. Like Ebina, some years earlier, Yoshida's samurai upbringing seems to have steeled him for such a possibility. Returning home, he calmly announced, "I am happy to die at the hands of my father. Please kill me as you wish." While saying this he bowed his head, presenting his neck without the slightest indication of anxiety or fear. Unable to bring himself to kill his son, the elder Yoshida found the situation intolerable. Yelling out "You Fool!" he struck him on the neck with the back of his sword.[112] Most of the Christian students sensed that they might be required to offer up their lives for their faith. As Shimomura recorded, the Christians often exchanged "cups of water" and "parted with tears" from those who were ordered home, fearing that they "might never see each other again."[113]

The fortitude, courage, and determination with which the Christian students bore up under such pressures made a deep impression on Kozaki and finally led to his conversion as well. One of the last students to join the band, Kozaki moved to Christianity very gradually. Later he wrote of the year and a half that he spent as a Christian inquirer as the unhappiest period of his life. Torn between the need to uphold the traditional Confucianism in which he had been raised and a growing attraction to Christianity, he eventually found the strain too great. "The rational part of me," he wrote, "rebelled against taking the decisive step; yet to turn away from Christianity and be content with Confucianism would leave my spirit of inquiry unsatisfied."[114] The result was a nervous breakdown.

In the wake of his illness Kozaki withdrew from his role as chief anti-Christian spokesman, but he was not yet prepared to become a believer. In fact, on the day the Christian students climbed Mount Hanaoka, Kozaki had been at Yokoi's house. Asked if he would join them in the declaration, he replied that he preferred not to climb the mountain that day.[115] While still searching for a way to transcend his dilemma, the persecution broke out. Kozaki was personally unaffected because of his anti-Christian reputation, but he felt sorry for many of his friends who were directly, and he thought unfairly, wronged. Above suspicion, Kozaki's house became a favorite gathering place for the Christian students. What started as sympathy soon turned into a deep respect for his Christian friends. Open assistance followed, and on one occasion he appears to have talked a despairing Kanamori out of suicide.[116] At the same time, seeing the strength of the Christians' faith, he noted that this "in turn aroused anew my spirit of inquiry" and "induced a state of mind favorable to belief."[117]

Finally one evening late in February Kozaki paid a call on the Captain at his house. Janes asked him if he had made a decision. Kozaki replied that he was still inquiring. "How long it takes you!" Janes lamented, "Unless you bring yourself at once to the decision of entering the life of faith, I am afraid you'll go on 'inquiring' all your life!" Janes advised him to pray directly to God. Then he quoted to him the verse from I Corinthians: "For who among men knoweth the things of man, save the spirit of man, which is in him? Even so the things of God none knoweth, save the spirit of God." He told Kozaki that "as a horse or dog however wise cannot comprehend man's mind, and similarly an ignorant or small man cannot understand the conduct of the learned and wise, even so we men can in no wise know the holy will of the omniscient and almighty, the supremely good and supremely loving God." Kozaki suddenly felt a veil slip from before his eyes. That night he went home and for the first time prayed with sincerity. The result was a "great awakening," he wrote, that led him to become a believer.[118]

Shortly thereafter Janes wrote to Stout that Kozaki had come to see him "overwhelmed," a few nights earlier, "and humbly and fervently announced himself a follower of Christ Jesus, and willing to do His commands and go where He should lead." "He was so subdued," Janes noted, "that I should not have reminded him of his original declaration . . . which he doubtless hoped I had forgotten." "But I did," Janes added, "just to confirm his faith, and forewarn him of what he may expect, that he may be forearmed!" "Poor fellow," Janes observed, "he had a long way to come down, and the descent was hard. But he is on the bed rock at last—the 'Rock of Ages.' "[119]

Kozaki, like Ebina, looked upon his conversion to Christianity as a fulfillment of the Confucianism he had studied in his earlier years. He liked to identify himself with the Apostle Paul as one who had been brought up in another religious tradition and had come to see the teachings of Christ as a perfection of that tradition. "In proceeding from Confucianism into Christianity," he wrote, he had "not rejected the one to replace it with the other." Commenting on the Kumamoto Band he later explained, "we embraced Christianity because we believed that it fulfills the spirit and real import of Confucianism."[120]

Ebina Danjō, Kozaki Hiromichi, and Yokoi Tokio were subsequently to become three of the leading voices of modern Japanese Christianity. As important pastors and publicists they played a central role in the intellectual life of late-nineteenth- and early-twentieth-century Japan. Moreover, they took to the Japanese public many of the values they had learned at Janes' feet: a firm individualism, a strong sense of patriotism, a clear commitment to independence, and the overriding conviction that the Christian as reformer should devote himself not only to the improvement of man's spiritual well being, but to the improvement of his physical conditions as well. If all three saw the roots of their Christianity in Confucianism and essentially became Christian samurai, a process which in some respects confined their Christianity to Confucian bottles, they also showed the degree to which the new wine of Christianity and the values Janes associated with it could burst through the bottles of the past. It was precisely in their response to the persecution, in their fearless self confidence, their reasoned arguments, their internalized sense of rightness, and their willingness to challenge traditional authority, that they demonstrated the degree to which the external revolution that Janes had initially engineered through the school had become an internal revolution which, while seen as a fulfillment of the tradition, could also be used to transform that tradition to new ends.

Nor were the students alone in their altered perceptions. Caught up in the emotional exhilaration of one of his strange joys and surrounded by the revival in the school, Janes came to emphasize more heavily the need for a spiritual revolution in Japan. If he had once seen his objectives in Higo as the development of Christian miners and mechanics who could lift up the Japanese people by improving their physical conditions and had called for a material revolution in which his boys were to play a leading part, he now shifted his focus to the spiritual side. "They blame me here, by implication, for educating preachers," he wrote to Davis, "I say nothing. But I have come to see that they need preachers and teachers of the 'true Light' more than any other educated workmen. The sham civilization they would build of a film of Western materialism dignified by the name of science and civilization, leaving the soul and all its needs unprovided for, is a hollow bubble that will burst one of these days." What Japan now needed, Janes emphasized, was a spiritual transformation "around the central principles of truth, justice, and liberty, and a wisdom large enough to satisfy the soul."[121] And it was to such a transformation that he hoped his students would address their future careers.

While Janes' correspondence for the summer of 1876 shows that he burned with a new evangelical zeal, which he shared with his Christian boys, it would be a mistake to see him, as some of the missionaries did, as an essentially conservative believer. Kozaki later insisted correctly that Janes was at heart a maverick Christian: staunchly antisectarian, an opponent of the organized church, and, even in his most evangelical phase, a firm believer in the Higher Criticism and a warm supporter of Henry Ward Beecher and Horace Bushnell.[122] Convinced that Christianity consisted primarily of "love to God, and love to man," as he wrote to Davis, he was not much taken with the Church's rituals.[123] Such attitudes expressed themselves quite clearly in his approach to the issues of baptism and the sacraments.

The question of baptism was raised by the arrival in Kumamoto of two Anglican clergymen, the Rev. Mr. Maundrel of Nagasaki and Bishop Burdon of the North China Mission. Both men had heard in Nagasaki of Janes' work, and despite the Captain's warnings to Stout not to ignite the locally volatile situation by an "intrusion from without," they had made their way to Higo, where they arrived on June 15.[124]

Maundrel and Burdon were concerned that Janes' converts receive proper Christian baptism, a rite which in their eyes could be administered only by a duly ordained representative of the Church. Hearing of Maundrel's plans, Janes had written to Stout that if the Reverend did not desire, or intend, to "neutralize, pervert, or destroy such work as I have been able under God to accomplish here . . . let him stay away." "I trust the day is coming," he added, "when we, and the heathen, are to have less of the Apostles and more of Christ; less of tradition and more Gospel; less theology and more God; less nonsense and more truth, in a word!"[125] As Janes saw it the Christian students had received the baptism of the Holy Spirit and that was good enough for him.

The students, moreover, seem to have shared these views, for when Maundrel and Burdon arranged a meeting with the boys to explain to them the importance of baptism and the exclusive right of the clergy to perform this ritual, they revealed a marked indifference. "You do not despise the ceremony of baptism, do you?" the Bishop asked. "No! We certainly do not despise a command of Christ," Miyagawa answered for the group, "but if it is made to precede a genuine baptism of the Spirit, we do." Maundrel, in turn, tried to explain to the group that just as one could not be received before the Japanese Emperor without formal dress, so one could not be allowed to stand before God without the raiment of baptism. Unbaptized, he observed, they would remain "naked before God." Miyagawa, now truly offended, snapped back the verse from the Letter to the Hebrews: "All are naked before God." With this the meeting broke up. Writing to Davis, Janes noted that Fuwa had come to see him afterwards stating that the impression Maundrel and Burdon had left "by their words and looks and manner, was, that they thought we were not Christians at all." Janes closed his letter to Davis with the line: "In the hope that Jesus thinks otherwise."[126]

In the weeks that followed the students appear to have made up their minds that if they were to be baptized it should be at the hands of the Captain, their spiritual father. The first to make such a request was Ōya Takeo, a member of the fourth class who was seriously ill, and who

Janes baptized "Frederick Ooya, in the name of the Father, and the Son, and the Holy Ghost," in a brief and simple ceremony on July 3. On July 10 the rite was repeated for Akamine Seichirō ("Frances"), the brilliant leader of the third class, who, like Ōya, had to be sent home for reasons of health. Writing to Davis on the thirteenth the Captain noted: "I determined to disregard your counsel as to the baptism of my boys," explaining that both had been seriously ill, and adding that "circumstances and God's leading will have to guide me for the rest."[127] Such "guidance" seems to have culminated in the baptism of the remaining Christian boys on July 30, a ceremony which Kozaki recalled was followed by a communion service at which all partook together and Janes officiated.[128]

The baptism of the Christian students corresponded in a broader sense with the graduation ceremonies of the school, which took place ten days later and brought to a close the secular aspects of Janes' work in Kumamoto. With the closure of the school, a task which occupied much of August, the exhilaration of the winter and spring, the excitement of conversion and persecution, gave way to a more melancholy mood. "It saddens me," he wrote, "to see the structure I have labored on, melting away, so, like a snowball."[129] Physically, too, the strain of the previous months had told seriously on his health. In addition to his persistent headaches and nervous prostration he now complained of increasing trouble with his eyes.[130] Writing to Davis he reiterated the need for a "complete change."[131] The effects of five years of isolation and seclusion, he underscored, had come to effect the health and well being of the family as a whole. August and September were therefore welcomed in that they provided a modicum of rest. Janes used the time to settle his affairs, patch up his relationship with Takezaki and Nonoguchi, and consider several employment opportunities, which included the choice of two professorships at the Kaisei Gakkō in Tokyo.[132]

In the meantime there were constant goodbyes as his students left Kumamoto in groups of twos and threes and made their way on foot to Kyoto and the American Board's "training school."[133] In a number of cases, which included Yokoi Tokio and Tokutomi, the destination was the Kaisei Gakkō in Tokyo, where Yamazaki and Yokoi Tokiyoshi had already established themselves among the best students and had drawn considerable attention to the Kumamoto school. As might be expected the farewell calls were emotional and often filled with tears. Janes urged the students, as he wrote in a book he presented to Tokutomi, to "Look Aloft!"[134] Sympathizing with those who were leaving "mother and father, brother and sister" for the first time, he told them that as Christians neither they, nor he, had reason to feel alone, because they were all now members of a larger family. "Find your mother and your brothers and your sisters in the one great family around you, as Christ found his," he told them in parting, "then you can never be alone or lonely."[135]

On October 7, with the family's preparations completed, Janes notes that "the four children and their mother were conducted, as often times before on picnics, to the houseboat by the bridge on the little river." Every effort had been made to give the appearance of a normal outing for fear that the revelation of other intentions might serve as a catalyst for violence. "But," as Janes emphasized, "this was to be the last descent of the four miles to the river's mouth." The Captain himself lingered behind. Wandering through the deserted rooms of the school and gazing out over the city from the porch of the family's former home, he briefly relived the "five year's drama" of "exile and effort" he had experienced in Higo.[136] Not long before he had written to Davis in a nostalgic mood that "there is manifestly a great softening of the ill feelings and prejudices generated during the difficulties and persecutions." These had virtually ceased. And the troubles, as he now looked back on them, he added, "have been worth all they have cost of suffering and anxiety in the wonderful lessons and powerful influence for good they have afforded these poor benighted people." Someday, he felt, he would "look back with wonder over the changes, the progress, the transformations I have witnessed here."[137] And yet, if such thoughts passed through his mind, they lasted for only a brief moment. With his last farewell calls completed, he wrote, "he also took to the river and sped swiftly away from what was soon to become an ineffaceable memory."[138]

At the mouth of the river the Captain and his family awaited the "wheezy little tub," the *Nomo*, which had brought them to Kumamoto five years earlier. Before boarding, Janes said goodbye to Nonoguchi, taking him firmly by the hand and telling him with tears in his eyes that "worthless" and "prone to anger" and "impatient" though he was by nature, the fact that he had been able to accomplish something in Kumamoto was entirely due to the old man's help.[139] At ten o'clock that night, with the tide in, the *Nomo* chugged its way out into Shimabara Bay, shot the dangerous passage between the island of Amakusa and the Hizen mainland, and sailed on for Nagasaki. Safely underway, neither Janes nor Harriet was conscious of the fortunate timing of their departure. Just two weeks later the Shimpūren—Janes' "malcontents"—was to perpetrate one of Meiji Japan's bloodiest incidents.[140] Had the Captain and his wife extended their departure by a fortnight, the "happy" *Nomo* might well have been faced with the more somber task of conveying to Nagasaki the coffins of Higo's only white family.

CHAPTER X

THE YEARS OF CONTROVERSY

I N NOVEMBER 1876, shortly after his initial interview with Janes, J. D. Davis wrote to Dr. Clark at the American Board in Boston: "I am astonished at the man after meeting him. I expected a great deal. I found a great deal more than I expected. His simple, yet Herculian faith, surprises and rebukes me. His power over men is wonderful. I have never seen his equal nor half his equal before in all my intercourse with men."[1] Seventeen years later Clark was to write to Davis: "He has shown himself at once in his true character, as an enemy of the gospel, and as an enemy of our work . . . let him show himself in his real character and all true, earnest, devout men will gradually withdraw from him."[2]

As the foregoing letters indicate, Janes' life, even after his accomplishments in Kumamoto, was to be filled with controversy and with changing images. One man's hero could easily become another's villain. Fame in one context could lead to notoriety in another. Indeed in the decade following his departure from Japan in 1877 Janes' reputation was to be much maligned, serious charges were lodged against him, and he was to undergo a further emotional and religious transformation that set the stage for his final years in both Japan and the United States.

None of this was yet apparent when the Janes family arrived in Kobe on October 17, 1876. Quite the opposite. Word of the Captain's accomplishments had preceded him and the family was warmly welcomed by the missionaries of the American Board. A few weeks later an even warmer welcome awaited Janes in Kyoto, where he was briefly reunited with his Kumamoto students and had the opportunity to meet Davis, Niijima, and the other members of the Kyoto station. Davis and Niijima were particularly delighted to see him. Both had been working assiduously to get the Prudential Committee of the Board to offer Janes an appointment in the mission. The arrival of the Captain's students reconfirmed Davis and Niijima's vision of establishing a nonsectarian Christian college, a dream which Niijima, in particular, had long harbored since his days at Amherst. Both men had been thoroughly impressed by the quality of the Kumamoto boys. "Intercourse with the graduates of Captain Janes' school in the classroom and elsewhere," Davis wrote to Clark, "has given me a new vision of the capabilities of this people." Even Edward Doane, who some students thought treated them as if they were natives of the

South Pacific, declared the Kumamoto students to be "heads and shoulders above anything else we have around us."[3]

Founded on November 29, 1875, with six students and two small buildings, the American Board's Kyoto Training School, or the Dōshisha as it later came to be known, left much to be desired as an educational institution. As Janes' students soon discovered, the rest of the student body, which had grown to around fifty by the summer of 1876, was an undisciplined and unruly lot which included several masseurs, a judo expert, and a former policeman. Most were older, and barring one or two exceptions none had received a preparatory education. "With no fixed rules or regulations, without a fixed course of study and with little order or discipline," Kozaki wrote, "the school was in a condition exactly similar to the old time private schools for the study of Chinese."[4] Students came and went as they pleased, paid little attention to their studies, and seem to have been much more interested in patronizing the local vendors who surrounded the school to hawk sweets than in pursuing a serious intellectual life. At night sweetmeat stands were transformed into bars and the students were liberally supplied with *sake*, which they consumed at drinking parties in the dormitories. Academically things were little better. Davis and his fellow missionaries, in contrast to Janes, insisted on teaching in the Japanese language, a language in which they could hardly communicate on even an elementary level. For the young men from Kumamoto the whole environment was appalling. Sorely disappointed, they complained among themselves and proposed an early departure for Tokyo.[5]

Hearing of the students' discontent from a deputation sent to him in Osaka, where he had taken a position in one of the government's English schools, Janes advised his boys to make an effort to reform the Kyoto school rather than run off to Tokyo. Urging them to regard themselves as founders of the school, he insisted that if they were dissatisfied with the way it was run, it was their duty to draft a new curriculum, draw up their own dormitory regulations, and establish a student code of conduct. Only if their reform proposals were rejected, he advised, should they consider going up to Tokyo.

The students took Janes' advice, drew up a list of grievances, and presented these to Niijima and Davis in the form of a memorial. To their surprise Niijima heartily approved their recommendations (later he told Janes that he had "saved Dōshisha")[6] and immediately set out to implement them. Within a matter of weeks the Kumamoto students had successfully transformed the school and had reestablished much of the order and discipline that prevailed at the Yōgakkō. Dōshisha, in effect, became a virtual replica of the Kumamoto School for Western Learning. The majority of the earlier students, who did not care for the new system, simply withdrew. By the time Dōshisha's first class was ready to graduate, the Kumamoto dominance of the school was only too obvious, as every member of the graduating class was one of Janes' students.

Janes' efforts on behalf of the school were greatly appreciated by Davis, who saw in the Captain the ideal figure to head the college that he and Niijima were hoping to establish. The more he heard about Janes from his students the more certain he became that Janes was the man to trust with the endowment drive for the school in the United States. "All we have heard of him, and all we see of the students who have been under him, and all we heard of him through these students," Davis wrote to Clark a day before the Captain's arrival in Kobe, "only confirms our impressions that he is just the man to be at the head of the proposed college here. You may look America through and not find ten men so well fitted for the position, and of those ten men if you find them he is probably the only available man among them." "Captain Janes can be secured for this work *now*," Davis added, "but *delay will be dangerous*."[7] After meeting Janes, Davis was even more enthusiastic. "You see the man," he wrote, "and you cease to wonder at his success . . . take Mr. Moody give him another foot of stature, a university education, and God's spirit in proportion and you have the man whom God has raised up and who is waiting to take hold of this institution which we have been asking for two years to have started in Japan."[8]

Moreover, as Davis' contacts with Janes became more intimate he gained access to information that explained certain peculiarities in the Captain's attitude toward the Mission and the Board. When the Mission's committee of three (Davis, Gulick, and Gordon) had initially proposed to Janes that he join the Board and continue his work in Kyoto, Janes had declined with regret, stating that he had committed himself to the Kaisei Gakkō in Tokyo just a few days earlier, but that this was for a limited period and that he would be favorably disposed to joining the Mission at its termination. It was therefore something of a surprise to Davis that with the cancellation of the Kaisei Gakkō offer, Janes chose to accept another secular position in Osaka rather than the standing offer from the Mission. All this became clear when the Captain informed him that the committee had not been alone in its communications with him in Kumamoto and that, already troubled by the issue of sectarian division, he had no intention of serving as a focal point for internal dissensions in an organization he would be joining as an outsider.

Davis explained the situation to Clark. "There is one man in this mission," he wrote, "who is opposed to the college. He worked against it during the year and a half while he was at home, and was greatly surprised to learn after his return here through your letter received by the mission during its last annual meeting that you had not given up the idea at Boston." "This anti-college brother," Davis continued, "without the knowledge of any of the committee (who did not learn of it till Captain Janes told them of it himself) sent the Captain a letter, which led him to give up going home and the service of the Board for the present." "With one man working in this way secretly against the twice unanimously expressed policy of the Mission," Davis wrote in exasperation, "we must expect delays, but we will wait as a mission until these facts are known and until we can again send an appeal for a College which will have no uncertain sound."[9]

The man opposed to Janes and the college was H. H. Leavitt, a member of the Mission's Osaka station and a firm advocate of indigenous support. Leavitt resisted any plan that called for the use of foreign funds for Japanese Christian enterprises, be they churches or schools. The vision of the college held by Niijima and Davis, which combined a religious and scientific education supported by an American endowment, was anathema to Leavitt, who regarded even a training school as premature. Although he was convinced of "the remarkable powers of the man and the work he has done," he questioned whether the Captain could work with a mission. Leavitt insisted that the very qualities of independence that had marked Janes' success in Kumamoto could work to his detriment in a mission school. "He who thinks he can do more by doing his own work in his own way and not as part of a great plan of laying siege to a country," he wrote to Clark, "fails to see one of the essential things in his work." Grudgingly accepting the idea of a college under the pressures of his colleagues, he insisted that the school should remain strictly a mission institution. "That College as a mission institution, for the church, by the church, of the church, is, to my mind, a very different institution, from a college, ever so successful, which stands alone and has no direct bearing upon and aim at the Christian efforts of evangelization of the country." Finally, Leavitt continued to insist that "Captain Janes chafes under criticism; he will hardly brook it. So he says he will be unwilling to have a school which shall be subject to mission criticism and control. I do not believe in any college which we have anything to do with which shall not be subject to mission criticism and control."[10]

While Leavitt's objections resulted in unexpected hurdles, Davis remained undaunted in his efforts to get the Captain to accept an appointment with the Mission. Meanwhile Janes' physical condition seems to have taken a turn for the worse. Davis, who was concerned that the Captain might have to leave Japan before a renewed effort could be made by the Mission, this time with "no uncertain sound," reported to Clark:

Captain Janes ought to have gone home and rested six months or a year instead of going into the Osaka school at all. The labor in that interior country six or eight hours a day for five years in that Kumamoto School with the terrible persecution that burst upon his beloved Christian boys a year ago—the *disappointment* in regard to taking hold of our school at once—and last but not least the terrible, as he expresses it indescribably rotten conditions of the Osaka School, where there are four or five other teachers who are not only im-moral—lost to all decency—living in open concubinage, but who have been for years teaching immorality and cupidity to the pupils— all this has brought on symptoms of nervous prostration which are too serious not to be heeded at once. These symptoms are appearing in his eyes and with the examples of Dr. Gordon and Dr. Berry before us [both were fellow missionaries who had come down with serious eye problems] every member of the mission feels that he ought to stop work at once and rest.[11]

Janes was also convinced that the only solution to his nervous ex-haustion and eye trouble was an extended rest in the United States. He told Davis that he was seriously considering a position he had been offered at Cornell University. Under the circumstances Davis became more than ever concerned with the need for clearcut action and decided to bring the matter before the Mission's winter meeting in December.

This time he came well prepared. Leavitt's complaint that Janes was set on teaching only in English was countered by a statement that the Captain did not oppose the use of the vernacular language in the school. To deal with the more important contention that Janes was predomi-nantly interested in a secular college whose aims were not directly linked to the goals of the Mission, that is, the direct propagation of Christianity in Japan, Davis presented those assembled with the goals Janes had set before his Kumamoto boys, i.e., that when they had thoroughly prepared themselves mentally and spiritually for their life work they were to strike out to as widely separated regions of the country as possible, choose a center for their work and stay there for the remainder of their lives forming a Christian company which should keep adding to itself and in the process become a missionary society to evangelize all that region. Ultimately the goal should be "to keep every one of these churches in close sympathy with every other one and with our Mission and with the Board, and make each one of these centers a feeder for our school here which should prepare the young men and women who come to us from every direction to be fitted to carry on the work."[12]

Next Davis rebutted Leavitt's arguments on the nature of the school itself. He stated that in his discussions with the Captain, Janes had always spoken of the school "not as a University, but simply and nobly as a school to fit out young men to enter the Theological Seminary or to become Christian teachers, or physicians, or to enter any other professional school." Janes, he reported, did not favor a large corps of foreign teachers and preferred an institution that stressed indigenous support and self-sufficiency. On this issue Davis noted: "He would prefer to use for the rest [of his teachers] some of the natives whom he has trained and make from the first the foreign element in it [the school] simply a help to place it ultimately upon an entirely Japanese basis, and so he would have the endowments of the Professorships, not in perpetuity, but to revert to the American Board whenever the Japanese were able to assume the whole burden; then about the young men when they go out to find their centers and begin their work he would not give a salary—not at all—they must have help but they are never to expect anything but souls for their hire, and they are to go out believing that Christ will take care of them."[13]

Davis had done his work so well that on December 28 the Mission unanimously and enthusiastically adopted a resolution for which H. H. Leavitt himself composed the first draft. "Whereas it is evident that the relations of Captain Janes with the Government School of Osaka must soon terminate," the resolution stated, "[it is] resolved that the Mission ask the Board to appoint Captain Janes at the earliest moment, to take charge of the Scientific Department of the Training School and to raise an endowment for himself and one or two other persons to be associated with him as missionary leaders in said school, for the purpose of building up as it may be needed in Japan, and with Japanese materials, a Christian college, such endowment to revert to the American Board at such times as in the judgement of the Mission and of the Board the native churches are ready to assume the whole burden."[14]

"The feeling of the Mission," Davis wrote to Clark, "is that if this request is acted upon promptly the appointment will reach him by the time he will feel it wise to start for America, and that he will gladly accept it." "The feeling was also very decidedly expressed," Davis continued, "that Captain Janes has done a missionary work here in Japan which was second to no other which has been done, that he had placed the results of that work both present and prospective in connection with the American Board, and that it is due him to appoint him here on the ground where he has labored so faithfully and with such glorious results for five years that the Board should be willing to take him here and offer to pay his expenses home if the Captain is willing that it should, which is doubtful."[15]

Davis concluded on the basis of these feelings that it was "the best meeting we ever had!" Janes, too, seems to have been enthusiastic. He attended the final session on December 29 and closed it with "prayer" and "praise."[16]

Davis' feelings were echoed by those of Dwight Learned, who wrote to Clark on December 30: "The request to the Board to appoint Captain Janes to a connection with the training school seems to me the most important action of the meeting, and I was very glad to see the hearty unanimity with which it was done. We shall be very glad to turn the scientific part of the school over to Captain Janes and his associates, and devote ourselves to the theological part and to the missionary work in the city. The more I see of the spirit and devotion of the young men who have been under Captain Janes' influence, the more I feel that it will be a great misfortune if he is lost to Japan."[17] These sentiments were shared by J. H. DeForest, who wrote to Clark: "The action we have just taken to send Captain Janes home to meet you and to represent us, will need no explanations: and we hope that in meeting with this royal man who has worked for 5 years at his own charges, turning the fruits of his work to the credit of the Board, and giving us more young men for the ministry than all the rest of us have, you will meet him in such a cordial way that his rest may speedily fit him to come back to us."[18]

By the early months of 1877, as these letters suggest, it was widely hoped by the missionaries that the Captain's appointment as a member of the Board was simply a matter of time.

Meanwhile the Mission became involved in a curious maneuver designed, as one missionary observed, "as a means of expressing to Captain Janes our appreciation of him," and of "constituting an influence which will contribute in securing his cooperation with us here in the future."[19] The plan was to make a grant of $1,500 to Janes to pay for his return passage to the United States. The idea had originated with Davis at the December meeting, and by mid-February had become incorporated into a circular letter that was passed among the missionaries for their individual approval.

The reason for the circular letter was that many of the missionaries were increasingly concerned about the Board's slow response to the Mission's request to offer Janes a position while he was still in Japan. A major cause of delay was, of course, the problem of transcontinental and trans-Pacific communications, which required almost six weeks in either direction. This meant that the Board's official reply to the Mission's December decision would not reach Japan until early April. Unfortunately this was also the approximate date for the Captain's planned departure for the United States. Most missionaries had come to realize that if Janes were to be secured for the Kyoto school some dramatic move recognizing his achievements and inviting him to join the Mission would be necessary.

The situation had been complicated by the fact that the Board, unaware of the Mission's December decision, had sent a letter indicating that Janes should make a formal application to the Board for service in Japan, and that the Prudential Committee would then follow up this application with an official appointment.

Even Leavitt, who was opposed to the idea of travel funds, but who had gained considerable insight into Janes' personality, thought the Board would have to treat him as a special case. "I would in this connection proffer my own request," he wrote to Clark, "that the Prudential Committee take some positive action respecting Captain Janes. The action of the Board thus far (though doubtless from no fault on their part) has been such as to exceedingly embarrass us as a Mission. Captain Janes' work in this country and independent profession—as well as his own natural feelings towards us as a Mission, are such as to make it most unnatural that he should apply to the Board to become a member of its mission company. The invitation must come from the other side or he will consider that he is not wanted. He has a profession by which he is able and desirous of carrying on his own work in this country and planting Christianity in the very citadel of thought and education. He has nothing to ask of the Board . . . if he comes in at all it must be by invitation of the Board . . . if it is a rule of the Board that all must apply, why, they cannot have this man, it is evident."[20]

Leavitt and the others thought this absurd. "Every mail for the last six months," he wrote, "we have expected would bring a warm, cordial invitation from the Prudential Committee to Captain Janes to become a member of the Mission. We have waited and held embarrassed relations with Captain Janes because we spoke so warmly of our desire that he be one of us and yet did nothing by which he really could be assured of that desire. When finally the letter came it was almost enough to make Captain Janes believe he either was not wanted or else he was to be impressed with the exceeding dignity of the Board that no account was to be made of his circumstances or the natural source of the invitation, but he must 'apply for appointment,' as a member of the Mission. Of course (we say here) he will not do that. He meets us, after receiving that letter, with the strangest feelings, as much as to say, 'what have you been writing about me?' "[21] DeForest added that "the slow, uncertain way in which we have acted has at last given rise to such remarks as these from Captain Janes, 'there are too many men to please in connection with a Board!' and 'it is getting to be a matter of conscience with me whether I can ever work under a Board!' "[22] On March 5 Davis wrote to Clark,

"I fear that we have lost him." At the same time he still hoped that the Board might have "taken such actions in response to the unanimous request of our Mission last December, or that it may take such action even now, as will save him."[23]

By April 5 the long-awaited letter allowing the Mission to make an appointment in the field had at last arrived. Its message was soon conveyed to Janes, but as Davis and Leavitt feared, the months of confusion and inaction had not endeared the Board to the Captain. On April 16 Janes sent his reply to the Mission, stating that he fully appreciated and gratefully valued the "testimony of your Christian esteem and confidence" that was reflected in the invitation to "connect myself with the Mission before leaving Japan, to the end that I might represent the Mission to the Churches at home." And yet, he regretted that he could not bring himself to accept the Mission's offer at this time. He hoped he would not be regarded as ungracious by elaborating on his reasons.[24]

To start with there was the question of his health and whether it would ever permit his return to Japan. "There is no certainty, whatever," he wrote, "that I shall ever return to Japan in any capacity, or for any purpose." Secondly there was the matter of control and authority about which Leavitt had expressed earlier reservations. "It is my present determination," Janes emphasized, "never formally to join any Mission, nor any organization of men especially for Christian work, in which my liberty of action is put into the hands of others or in which my methods are to be prescribed to me by an indefinite number of men. 'Teaching A.B.C.,' as it has been expressed by one member of the Mission, organizing and conducting the Department of Elementary Science in a Mission Training School, prosecuting the endeavor to inspire young men here with the love of Jesus, to the end that they may love their own poor people more, and more wisely, is a work all difficult enough in itself according to my experience for five or six years, without the added burden of divided responsibility and conflicting plans. Observation teaches me that it is so much easier to sit and speculate and theorize over this and other phases of Christian effort, than it is to go and do the work that the temptation to one class of minds may become the most serious obstacle to the hands of others." Finally he felt it somewhat presumptuous for one who knew almost nothing about the Mission and its work in Japan to represent the Mission to the churches of America. "Having hitherto no formal connection with the Mission," and being hardly "sufficiently well acquainted with its work," he wrote, he did not feel himself fairly or adequately qualified to "represent it to the churches interested in its work at home."

In conclusion Janes wrote: "I shall represent you at home dear Brethren, if spared to be there, but it will be in no formal capacity. And I shall carry you individually and all your work for men in Christ, so far as it is my privilege to know of it, in grateful remembrance and a prayerful heart."

Janes' open rejection of the Board's proposal was a serious disappointment to many of the members of the Japan Mission. On the other hand, most missionaries attributed it to the slowness with which the Prudential Committee had acted, to the Mission's lack of clarity on what kind of a school it wanted, and to the fact that the Captain's family had become seriously ill in the spring of 1877, placing his own already precarious health and nervous condition under even greater strains. John DeForest summed up their views when he wrote to Clark a few days after the Captain's departure: "He saw things here at a disadvantage, while sick himself, and while seeing one and another of his family attacked by Typhoid fever; and I for one feel quite sure that so much of his heart and longings are in Japan that you can hope to return to us a man truly great in the work he has already done."[25]

As DeForest indicated the winter and spring of 1876–77 had been particularly difficult for Janes and his family. Not only did the Osaka School prove to be a disappointment, but the family's health, which had been remarkably good in Kumamoto, now came to trouble him. Early in 1877 Henry came down with typhoid fever. Not long thereafter Harriet, who was again pregnant, was struck down as well. Janes and the other children seem to have exhibited symptoms of the same disease. Dr. Adams, the Mission's doctor, found the source of the problem in a polluted well that was contaminated by an overlooked drain. He insisted that the whole family be moved to the home of Justina Wheeler, one of the ladies of the Mission, where they could be properly attended to and treated under his supervision. For most of March Harriet and Henry remained in extreme danger, but under the kind care of the doctor and Miss Wheeler both were gradually nursed back to health.[26] By late April, Dr. Adams considered Harriet sufficiently well recovered to brave the journey across the Pacific. On May 6, 1877, the Captain and his wife joined Dr. Berry, another of the Board's doctors, for the sea voyage home. Stopping briefly at Yokohama, where Janes was able to say goodbye to Yamazaki and Yokoi, they arrived in San Francisco on May 28 after a rough three weeks at sea. Leaving the Berrys in San Francisco to recover from "sea sickness," Janes, Harriet, and the children started almost immediately for New York.

When Janes left Japan most of the missionaries thought that a few months of rest in the United States and the chance to communicate directly with the Board would overcome the Captain's reservations and return him to Japan to take up the challenges of the Kyoto school. They had been heartened in this opinion by the fact that he had agreed to accept the "loan" of $1,500 pressed on him by the Mission to pay for his return to America.[27] There seems to have been an understanding between Janes and the missionaries in Japan that this "loan" constituted a symbolic tie between the Mission and the Captain. He later wrote to Clark that the implied meaning of the grant was that "when you [the missionaries in Japan] hear of the refunding of this testimony of your love and confidence, you may know of our decision not to return to Japan to work with you, and that will be the signal of the severance of all connections between us as co-workers in the Master's field in Japan."[28]

Davis was more confident than the others that Janes would soon be back in Japan. From personal discussions with the Captain he was convinced that Janes did not commit himself to the Mission for two fundamental reasons, both of which Davis saw as having positive implications for the proposed college in Kyoto. To begin with, Janes told him that he thought he would have more influence with those from whom he sought to raise money for the school in America as an "independent man." And secondly, Davis wrote to Clark, "because he feels very decidedly that it will be better for the College to be constituted as was first proposed by the Mission three years ago, rather as an adjunct of the Mission than as a part of it." Davis added that most of the members of the Mission regarded Janes "wise" in this. The Captain's proposal, according to Davis, was for a school whose property would be held by a self-perpetuating corporation composed of the best members of the Japanese churches. Initially endowment funds were to be raised in the United States. These were to be held under the control of a Board of Trustees appointed by the Board. The school itself was to be under the general control of a committee appointed by the Board, the Mission, and the Japanese churches. At the head of the school there should be a forceful leader who had proven himself. This was the place for Captain Janes. Moreover, Davis wrote to Clark, he "wants to do just that thing," and "his whole soul is bound up in that thought." "I think that after you have a full correspondence with him," he concluded, "you and he will heartily agree upon a plan which will be satisfactory to all, and for the furtherance of the Kingdom here in Japan."[29]

As the foregoing indicates, in the spring of 1877 the majority of the missionaries, like Davis, were optimistic about the future relationship of the Captain and the Board. Almost everyone in the Mission regarded Janes as an outstanding Christian worker. Most were convinced that although the Captain had been reluctant to commit himself openly to the Mission while still in Japan, he did so for good reasons, and that these would be overcome after he had the chance to communicate directly with the Prudential Committee in Boston. Certainly no one in the Mission had the slightest inkling of the peculiar events that were to follow.

Janes' return to the United States took him to Saint Denis, Maryland, and the farm he had left six years earlier to come to Japan. Harriet and the children spent the summer of 1877 at Shelter Island, New York, where her father had a summer place, and where she gave birth to Elisha Paul, their fifth child. In the autumn she joined her husband at Elk Ridge. Meanwhile, in keeping with missionary expectations, Janes spent most of the remainder of 1877 recuperating amidst the comparative leisure of farming. Having regained much of his health by the spring of 1878, he began to correspond with the Board about his return to Japan.[30] On February 14 he sent to Clark an extensive outline for the proposed college.[31] Janes' proposal was discussed and debated by the Prudential Committee.[32] There is even some evidence that it was on the basis of this proposal that the basic plan for Dōshisha College was drawn up. What is clear is that by April 27 the Board's commitment to the college had been forwarded to an overjoyed Davis in Kyoto. Davis was ecstatic not only because of the "decision reached in regard to the school," but also because the letter contained further news that "Captain Janes will come" and our "brightest hopes will be realized."[33]

Unfortunately Davis's brightest hopes were not to be realized. In the autumn of 1878, when seven other missionaries arrived to support the work in Kyoto, Captain Janes and his family were not among them. Soon there were rumors that the Captain was postponing his intended return to Japan until the following spring. Janes' reasons for deferring were not precisely stated, but in his final letter to the Board, written on September 17, he noted that "domestic reasons" prompted such a course. "I will add," he wrote, "that a paragraph in the manual referring to health certificates; and especially my anxiety to avoid as far as human foresight might enable me, the possible necessity of putting upon the Board the burden of needless travelling expenses after our contemplated settlement in Japan, have been considerations forced upon me in this interval." "We are all well, *physically*," he insisted, "but the strain of our entire isolation for five years, and of the terrible sickness of Mrs. Janes and our little boy in the sixth year of Typhoid fever, and of my wife's confinement immediately after, at the close of the long journey, was very great."[34]

What Janes was referring to were certain domestic difficulties that had arisen involving Harriet and her father, Henry Martyn Scudder.

Upon her return from Japan, and at the time of the birth of Elisha Paul, Harriet appears to have experienced another of her deep depressions which had concerned Janes prior to their departure for Japan. As he later showed in the proceedings that led to their divorce in 1884, Harriet had a well-known history of hallucinating on the subject of his sexual relationships. Even before his departure for Japan she had accused him of affairs with other women.[35] Moreover, he pointed out that both families were aware of these problems and had learned to accept them as part of her "illness."

Back in the United States and in the final months of her pregnancy, Harriet announced to her parents that the Captain had been guilty of "conjugal infidelity," had regularly consorted with "a Japanese woman, or women," and had, in fact, contracted "syphilis, a loathsome disease," from which she had been able to protect herself only by sequestering herself and the children in a separate part of the house and avoiding him as much as possible.[36] She furthermore added that upon their arrival in Kumamoto, "according to the Japanese custom . . . an offer was officially made from the Prince or Daimio of Higo to Capt. Janes, in my presence, of handsome young women for his use, which offer he in no wise refused or resented."[37]

Similar accusations were also voiced by Harriet to Janes' father and mother on a visit to New Philadelphia, and at his sister's home in Toledo.[38] Janes' family, which by now was aware of her problems, tried to deal with the situation sympathetically but cautioned her not to air such accusations in public. The Scudders' response was another matter.

Janes never forgave his father-in-law for siding with the delusions of his ill daughter, and in the process "wrecking a family of infinite possibilities."[39] But Henry Martyn's decision to believe her accusations, despite her medical history, was influenced, in part, by a "confession" made to him in the summer of 1875 by his other daughter, Katie, that in 1869, while she was living with Harriet and Janes in Maryland (she was then nineteen), the Captain had made advances toward her, and, to put it in the language of the divorce suit, "had made to her the infamous proposal."[40] Janes later vehemently denied the latter accusation, although in court he admitted to having been guilty on one occasion of "too familiar deportment" with Katie that resulted in "undue and unbecoming liberties" being taken between them, but that these were the results of "momentary excitement, brought about not altogether by his own conduct." Moreover, he insisted that the whole scene had become "hateful to him," that he had apologized profusely for it, and that it had been "as fully repented of by the said sister . . . as by himself . . . and had been fully forgiven and condoned by his said wife and her father."[41]

By the summer of 1877 Scudder's attitude toward Janes, which had been complicated by the circumstances of the original marriage, hardened into a direct confrontation. Henry Martyn accepted his daughter's assertion that Janes had contracted syphilis, and he insisted on escorting him to a physician for confirmation of this allegation. When the doctor in question, an authority in the field, announced that "there is no ground whatever for a suspicion of a taint in this gentleman's blood," (a fact which all of Janes' previous and subsequent Army and Pension Office physical examinations were to confirm), Scudder, as Janes later reminded him, suddenly remembered that he had another appointment and stalked out of the room. "Have you had a conference with Dr. Webster since that day?" Janes later wrote to Scudder, "if so, he may have told you his first remark to me, when you had rid the room, of your presence, 'If you have a wife whose mind is possessed of such hallucinations—leave her! Put the continent between you, and take your name from her!' 'Doctor,' I replied, 'we have four children and I expect another in a fortnight or more. That man is my wife's father!' "[42]

What Janes found overwhelming was Scudder's vindictiveness and intolerance. Despite the medical evidence he persisted in supporting Harriet's delusions.

In the days preceding her delivery, Harriet became more and more obsessed with the idea that her newborn child would be covered with syphilitic sores. Janes tried to calm her fears and anxieties. As he later wrote to Scudder, how could he ever forget her "sallow, fever-bloated countenance and the unhallowed, sinister light that broke over it when I exclaimed in desperate, despairing anxiety, and *anguish*, over my child whose motions I felt responding to the unnatural mother's agitations— 'believe what you please of me, *say* what you choose about me, but for its sake, for your own, spare your child.' " Thereafter, he observed, Harriet was suddenly calm, and went to her father stating that he had "confessed" to his evil ways.[43]

Scudder later used this incident to maintain that Janes had confessed to his indiscretions at his home.[44] But the Captain insisted that this was the beginning of an atrocious and infamously unjust course of treatment for both himself and Harriet. As he later wrote to Scudder, he had no intention of "forgetting" what the Reverend Doctor had done. Janes did not blame Harriet, whom he assured he still loved, but also saw as seriously ill. "Your daughter, Sir., the mother of my children," he wrote, "knew not then, what she did. She was irresponsible. Her consciousness of her falsehoods, took no note of their moral turpitude. It was the consciousness of the agonizing, the drowning, which clutches the dearest and the best, indiscriminately in the fatal descent." "And you, Sir." Janes wrote in extreme bitterness, "who had no apology, no retraction; no qualification, but that of the speed of those who 'flee when no man pursueth'—for me. What did you do for your daughter? Did you go home, and from that hour devote yourself to the undoing of your wrong, and to the liberation of your daughter's mind from it's ghastly enthralments, the composing of troubled waters, to that peace making which is blessed? Not you Sir!"[45]

By the spring of 1878, as Janes was making preparations to return to Japan with the American Board, Scudder continued to persist in an affirmation of Harriet's delusions about his conduct in Kumamoto. On April 1 Scudder wrote the Captain a letter in which he threatened to expose him to the American Board. Scudder's letter was blunt and to the point.

> If you appeared to be truly penitent for your past life, I should not say anything about you to the Secretaries of the Board; for out of genuine repentance springs a good life, and much possible service for the Master . . . [but] to our great and ever present sorrow we have no such evidence concerning you, but the contrary. You, at my house, confessed to Hattie, in general terms, the adulteries you committed in Japan. Out of delicacy you were not pressed to particulars. Subsequently, to the unutterable amazement of us all, you retracted your confession, affirmed your innocence, and have ever since maintained the moral position which you then assumed. I will not speak of how much is involved in continuing in such a position . . . [but] knowing what I do, it would be wrong in me to allow the Board to send you out, in ignorance of the facts in your case.[46]

Janes regarded his father-in-law's position as pious hypocrisy. As Scudder had written him, if he would acknowledge his "sin," he would be prepared to forgive him and make no effort to expose him to the Board, but if he insisted on his innocence, Scudder would have no choice but to write Dr. Clark. Why Scudder maintained such a position given the medical clearance that Janes had received in July 1877, and Harriet's previous history of hallucinations, is difficult to understand. Janes, for his part, had no intention of "confessing" to unfounded accusations and imagined sins.

In his reply to Scudder he observed that he was currently too preoccupied with the planting season to take time to send a more detailed reply.[47] And although Scudder later wrote that the Captain "instantly dropped the project of going to Japan"[48] after receiving his letter, the records do not confirm such an assertion. Janes' letter to the Board in which he stated that they were all well *physically* was not written until September 1878, nearly six months after Scudder's threat.[49]

In the meantime Janes was prepared to start afresh with Harriet in Maryland. Dr. Webster had advised him that hallucinations of pregnancy sometimes pass afterward, and while the Captain had his doubts on the basis of their previous experiences, he was prepared to try once more. As he told Webster, there must be a "better way." "I will never abandon my children," he insisted. "I am weary with a long stretch of work. I have a little farm in Maryland. I will go there. I will rest and wait; and I will treat that woman with such affection and kindness that her morbid jealousies will die of atrophy; and the way of redress for these other outrages will come of itself—unless I have been dealing in fables in Japan."[50]

To Harriet he wrote almost immediately thereafter:

> I desire to do only what will please you, minister to your comfort, and bye and bye draw your love, afresh, to me; so that I may again be dear to you and capable of making you happy . . . I shall live and *love* and strive for your happiness Hattie, as I have never done; as my obtuse, stony, dull nature never hitherto knew how to do. I beg you to believe this deary. Not in words, not in professions like these with which I would fill these letters. But in the gentleness of a chastened, enlightened, affection. Two things I have learned darling: the great duty and beauty of self-restraint . . . and second, dear Hattie your own worth, and deserts, and great goodness. These two revelations have come to me with great power. They will ever remain with me to influence all my words and acts towards yourself darling and towards our dear little ones. . . .[51]

But as Janes soon discovered, his own idealistic solutions were easier to express on paper than to carry out in reality. Although he fixed up the farm to make it comfortable for Harriet and the children, and his earnings in Japan now provided a modicum of financial security, life at Elk Ridge became increasingly difficult in the years that followed. A part of the problem clearly stemmed from the Scudders' failure to support his efforts to deal with Harriet in a humane and realistic manner. As the divorce proceedings were to show, vindictiveness now began to appear on both sides. Frustrated by a deteriorating situation at home, and by worsening relations with his father-in-law, Janes was not above venting his anger on Harriet. By the early 1880s it was obvious that life at Elk Ridge Farm was filled with domestic discord and marital incompatibility.[52]

In March 1882, hearing from Harriet that her father had taken the liberty of discussing their relationship with the Warners, Janes wrote to Susan and Anna that he was no longer "bound to silence." He noted that his visit to Constitution Island, immediately after his return from Japan, had led to an expansion of Hattie's "insane jealousy" and had contributed to the "inhuman outrage" from which he was forced to suffer "immediately after his return to Brooklyn." Janes now spoke of Harriet's problem as an "unspeakably cruel mania of jealousy" and a "vindictive, merciless infirmity" that had come to be extended to his oldest daughter as well as to himself.[53]

The confrontation between Janes and the Scudders reached the point of no return later in the same year when Henry Martyn initiated a suit of divorce to dissolve the marriage of his daughter to the Captain. Harriet's "Bill of Complaint," which was submitted to the Circuit Court of Howard County on September 1, 1882, included all the previous allegations of Janes' "immoralities" and "conjugal infidelity" in Japan. In addition there were numerous allegations of cruelty, which ran the gamut from the Captain's refusal to provide her with adequate funds for clothing, to his use of physical force to eject her from their home at Elk Ridge.[54] On September 25 Scudder forwarded to Clark at the American Board a letter that included a statement by Harriet enumerating the many wrongs she had suffered at Janes' hands in Japan and once more outlined his "immoralities" and "syphilitic" condition.[55] "It has, for some time, been my belief," Scudder added, "that Captain Janes is insane." Finally, he advised Clark to show the whole correspondence to Davis. "He already knows the main facts in the case," he added, "and I am very desirous that he should see what I have written to you as soon as you meet him."[56]

The *Janes vs. Janes* Divorce Case dragged on for the next two years. Finally, on November 10, 1884, the court announced its decision.[57] Stating that the case had been well argued on both sides (Henry Martyn had hired the "best lawyer in Maryland"),[58] the judge agreed to a legal separation. But the conditions of the divorce granted by the court were not what Scudder had anticipated. In the original suit the Reverend Doctor had sued for court costs and legal fees, child support and alimony for Harriet, and the custody of all the children. Throwing out the hearsay testimony regarding Janes' "immoralities in Japan" (Scudder had made a concerted effort to get medical evidence from the Mission's doctors, from individuals in Kumamoto, and from others who had known Janes— but all to no avail),[59] he concluded there was no evidence that Janes was an unfit father. He found, indeed, that all the children were fondly attached to him, were "bright, interesting, and intelligent." The older two in particular had taken the father's side, and the judge concluded that it would be best to separate the family, giving custody of the three younger children, Hattie Lois, Annie Eunice and Elisha Paul, to the mother, and the older two, Fanny Elizabeth and Henry Martin, to the father. Instead of alimony and child support each parent was to be responsible financially for the children placed in their custody.[60]

While the Scudders saw the outcome as a "victory" for which they "thanked God,"[61] what the case showed quite clearly was that Harriet and Henry Martyn's allegations in reference to Janes' immoralities could not stand the test of a careful legal review. Indeed, the tragedy of the whole case seems to have found much of its roots in Janes' bitterness over the Scudders' allegations, and the effect that these had on his conduct toward the Reverend Doctor and his daughter. Given what now seems to be the complete overview of the case, Janes had much to be bitter about. And yet, it was precisely the deep anger of his response, especially as he expressed it toward Harriet in numerous petty incidents between 1877 and 1882, that provided the court with ample evidence of "cruelty" and resulted in the dissolution of his marriage.

Although the divorce proceedings actually vindicated the Captain in reference to the most serious charges lodged against him, his reputation never recovered from the damages inflicted upon him by the Scudders. As one of America's leading clergymen Henry Martyn was listened to with respect and deference. That the accusations brought against Janes were the products of a mentally unstable individual meant little as long as they were endorsed by a figure of Scudder's standing.

This could be seen only too clearly in Clark's response to the Reverend Doctor's letter. Clark wrote to Scudder on September 27, 1882:

> It is a very, very sad case, and you and your family and that dear daughter of yours have our tenderest sympathy in this time of trial. It seems almost inexplicable—impossible to believe—such baseness and weakness on the part of one so much trusted, and who has had so large a place in the thoughts and regards of friends of missions in connection with the work in Japan. I cannot get it out of my mind—the suffering of that poor child of yours! It is enough to stir the hardest heart. I think you have borne and borne and forborne almost too long. There is no alternative. The man should be cast out from all respectable society and from all possible relations to you. I hope that your dear daughter will secure care of her children and find comfort in returning to her father's home and to the sweet religious associations that belong to it.

"The more I think of it—recalling the strange ways when here and the whole stay—," Clark added in a postscript, "I am convinced that Captain Janes is insane, or at least think his mind has lost its balance. His moral fall has wrenched his mind out of focus."[62]

With the airing of such views in the highest echelons of the American church and missionary community the Captain was quickly transformed into a persona non grata in Christian circles. For those who had heard rumors of the case, the court's decision to grant a legal separation instantly confirmed the Captain's guilt. In the face of such developments the American Board and the missionaries' response to Janes became one of total silence. It became a matter of policy to drop all reference to him in connection with the Kumamoto work and the Dōshisha. Not only was the Captain never spoken of in the *Missionary Herald*, the Board's major publication, but occasionally efforts were made to deny him his proper place in the history of the Japan work.

In the wake of the divorce, Harriet moved to Chicago with the three younger children and lived with her mother and father, who had taken a new pastorate at the influential Plymouth Church. But then, on December 30, 1885, Harriet suddenly died.[63] The *Missionary Herald* carried her obituary. "Mrs. Janes' special Christian service," its author noted, "was rendered while residing in Kumamoto Japan. At that place she was able to reach a large company of Japanese young men, and largely through her influence they were brought into the Christian life. Fifteen of these young men afterward removed from Kumamoto, forming the nucleus of the Training School at Kioto, and they are now occupying the foremost places as pastors and instructors in Japan. Not until the day when all things shall be revealed will be known the far-reaching influence of the work done by Mrs. Janes in Japan."[64] One cannot help but add with a sense of irony that this was the same woman who had announced in Kumamoto that she "did not feel called upon to teach these people."

By the late 1880s it was obvious that as far as the American Board was concerned Janes might as well have been dead. Missionaries who had spoken in glowing terms of his character and achievements in almost every mail that left Kobe and Yokohama in the 1870s no longer mentioned his name in public. If Janes was discussed at all, it was in whispered tones hinting at his "moral fall," or staunch new "anti-Church" stand. In fact, if it had not been for his students the Captain would never again have come up to trouble the missionaries and the Board.

Janes' relationship with his students had also been shrouded in silence. At the time of his departure from Japan in 1877 he had told them that they were no longer to rely on him but on God, and that he entrusted them to the care of Niijima and Davis. To have them establish their independence he indicated that there should be no correspondence between them for several years.[65] Under the circumstances the students were little concerned with the Captain's silence. Moreover, when they heard rumors of Harriet's accusations, which seem to have reached them through the missionaries, on the one hand, and through Scudder's efforts to get information in Kumamoto, on the other, they thought these charges absurd and completely without foundation.[66]

The Captain, the students insisted, had been under close daily surveillance by both friends and enemies in Kumamoto, and while an assignation between him and a Japanese woman would not have been startling by Japanese standards, it certainly would have been known. And yet, as they underscored, not even his enemies had heard of any such conduct. Had it been known, it surely would have been used against him in the spring of 1876 when the persecutions erupted. Indeed, it must be added on the Captain's behalf that Harriet's statement, that he had "been offered women by the Daimyo" at the time of their arrival in Kumamoto, clearly contradicts the logic of Kumamoto's original request for "a married man," which was specifically designed to avoid such complications. The medical evidence before and after his arrival in Kumamoto, the far from credible aspects of Harriet's story, and the inability to find a single shred of evidence to incriminate him in Japan tend to confirm what became the students' explanation, i.e., that the danger, isolation, and loneliness of five years in Kumamoto had come to tell on Mrs. Janes, and that the family disputes, which had been known in Kumamoto, had erupted once more in Maryland, leading to further imagined wrongs and farfetched accusations.[67]

By the late 1880s and the early 1890s Janes' Kumamoto boys had gone on to become the leaders not only at Dōshisha, but also in one of the major streams of the Japanese Christian movement. In the process many of them travelled regularly to the United States. Unlike the missionaries, who avoided the Captain while home on furlough, the members of the Kumamoto Band made a point of stopping off to see him in Ann Arbor, Michigan, where he had settled after selling his Elk Ridge farm in 1885 and had taken up a life of "literary work."[68] Meanwhile Fanny (now Bertie) and Henry (renamed Leroy) attended the University of Michigan. As a result of these visits the members of the band came to feel that their "father" had been seriously wronged by the Scudder family. Moreover, the missionaries, they maintained, had indirectly contributed to this injustice by failing to stand up for him.

Such feelings were clearly expressed by Ukita Kazutami, who wrote to Clark from New Haven on September 30, 1892, shortly after visiting Janes in Michigan:

> Another important matter I think came also to your notice together with this case . . . I mean the life and work of Capt. L. L. Janes in Kumamoto, Japan. After his return home to America he was charged with immorality in Japan, credit of his work taken off in the interest of another family and his character discredited. The basis of the success of Mr. Niishima's work and the work of the American Board

in Japan was really laid by Capt. Janes who sent up all his pupils
to Kyoto. . . . While we his pupils are respected and loved by the
missionaries, Capt. Janes has been quietly buried, as it were out of
sight, simply by the interference of the jealous old Dr. Scudder. In
our eyes it amounted almost equal to the recent Chicago Case—a
spiritual robbery and a spiritual murder. We have been trying to
vindicate him privately, but hitherto we are unable to receive any
response.[69]

What the band wanted, Ukita continued, was the "opportunity to do
justice publicly to Capt. Janes." "Sooner or later," he added, "we think
we must publish this case to the whole world, if there is any justice and
righteousness yet to be extracted from this world."[70] Two months later
he wrote, "it is not an encomium of Capt. Janes that we want. It is simple
justice . . . and that publicly, because he was publicly impeached by Dr.
Scudder."[71]

The Chicago Case to which Ukita alluded was, in fact, the final act in
a series of tragic events that befell the Scudders in the wake of the Janes
divorce. Within a year of their "victory" Harriet died of a cerebral hem-
orrhage. In 1890 Katie died of tuberculosis. And on March 4, 1892,
Henry Martin Jr., Harriet's brother who had once served as a missionary
in India, was arrested in Chicago on the charge of murdering his mother-
in-law, Mrs. F. H. Dunton.[72] The case against him included allegations
that he had forged Mrs. Dunton's will, leaving her fortune to his wife.
On June 22, while the family's lawyers were mounting an "insanity"
defense, Harry injected himself with an overdose of morphine and committed suicide in the Cook County Jail. Prison authorities concluded that
"the morphine or other poison which caused his death was given to him
by someone who visited him while in jail."[73] Since Henry Martyn as a
physician had ready access to morphine, there was suspicion that either
he, or Harry's brother Doremus, had provided the fatal dose to terminate
what had become an intolerable scandal for the family. The Reverend
Doctor himself passed away in 1895, still hailed as one of "the strong
men of our time" who left behind "a noble work" and "an honored
name."[74]

To members of the Kumamoto Band, who continued to be influenced
by the Japanese concept of a family's "blood line," the Chicago Case
confirmed the rottenness of the Scudder house and the injustice that had
been done their teacher. Ukita was not alone in his efforts to have Janes
vindicated. In Japan pressures were applied to the missionaries to have
them take a stand on the issue. As D. C. Greene wrote to Clark, "the

Japanese want the Mission to organize itself into a court and investigate his life in Kumamoto."[75] The members of the band, particularly Ichihara, Ebina, and Yokoi, were adamant that the Mission take up the question at its annual meeting in 1892. The Mission, unwilling to adopt a public stand on the problem, buried the question in an appointed committee from which it never emerged.[76] At the same time individual members of the Mission were more willing to declare themselves.

After ten years of silence Greene at last wrote to Clark stating that he thought Janes "innocent of conjugal infidelity," although he regarded his conduct toward the Scudder family as that of a "brute" and an "idiot." Greene stated the common missionary interpretation of Janes' silence. "If he had taken us into his confidence, or even asserted his innocence in such a way as to give us a chance to help him," he wrote, "we could have helped both him and the whole family." "There has not been a time during the last dozen years when we could not have established his innocence in the eyes of almost any disinterested man, had we not been staggered by his silence. We could not understand it as anything other than as admission of guilt."[77]

Greene's interpretation echoed closely what Janes' former students were publishing in the *Kyūshū bungaku* and later expanded into their book, *Nihon no okeru taii Jiensu shi* (Captain Janes and his Work in Japan) which was published in 1894. He wrote:

> Our reasons for believing Captain Janes innocent are that it would be practically impossible for any man to carry on such a continuous course of looseness as was charged by Mrs. Janes, or even to be guilty of a single act without it becoming known to the Japanese. If it had been known while the feeling against him as a teacher of Christianity was so strong, it would most certainly have been published to the world. It would be on the whole easier to conceal such a matter in New England than in Japan. It is, however, perfectly clear that not only his pupils knew nothing of any such conduct, but it is also known that men violently opposed to him were so situated that it is inconceivable that they should not know if he were guilty, and have declared solemnly that they knew nothing of any dereliction of his. Under such circumstances the easiest explanation is that Mrs. Janes became morbidly suspicious, became perhaps a monomaniac on this subject and stated as facts what were half the fancies of a diseased mind. As in other matters she probably showed no lack of mental balance her father naturally believed her statements.[78]

By the 1890s the missionaries and the American Board found themselves in an increasingly difficult situation in Japan. As the Meiji Constitution and the Imperial Rescript on Education made amply clear, these years represented a turning away from the all-out Westernization of the 1870s and early 1880s toward a greater emphasis on the tradition and native institutions. Japanese nationalism was beginning to expand and move in new directions. And as might have been expected, such a swing brought a decided cooling in Japanese attitudes toward Christianity. On the other hand this was also a period during which liberal theology from Europe and America began to make inroads in Japan. The members of the Kumamoto Band were not free from the pressures of these trends. By the spring of 1893 Davis wrote to Clark that even Kozaki, the most conservative member of the band, was greatly troubled by Clark's recent article, "Twenty Years in Japan," in which Kozaki felt too much emphasis had been placed on the missionaries, and too little on the "greatest reason of all" for the success of Christianity in Japan, namely, "the Kumamoto Band."[79] At the same time there was a good deal of discussion among the missionaries of the American Board about the theological "drifting" of Janes' former students, particularly that of Ebina and Yokoi.

Insufficiently conscious of the broader themes sweeping the Japanese political and intellectual world, most of the American Board's missionaries associated the reaction they were experiencing from the band with the Captain Janes "affair." Davis confirmed such a view to Clark, writing, "from talks had with the members of the Kumamoto Band, I and others find that the Captain Janes matter is largely at the bottom of the trouble all around."[80] Efforts such as Greene's and Davis' to restore the Captain's reputation must therefore be seen as part of an overall attempt to improve deteriorating relations between the missionaries and the members of the band.

In their endeavor to placate his former students most missionaries were willing to defend Janes in private, and yet few contemplated the possibility that he would return to Japan to take up a new work in Kyoto.

But this is precisely what happened. In the autumn of 1893, through the good offices of Kozaki Hiromichi, Janes was offered a professorship of English and English literature in Kyoto at the Daisan Kōtō-chū Gakkō, the Third College, which served as the preparatory department for Kyoto Imperial University.[81] Delighted by the invitation, Janes quickly closed up his Ann Arbor house, and in the company of his new wife, Flora Oakley, arrived in Kyoto in September.[82]

While the members of the Kumamoto Band were overjoyed to see their old teacher back in Japan, the missionaries were more apprehensive, and not without good reason. Since his departure from Japan much had changed. This was true of the missionaries and the Dōshisha, as well as of the Captain. For Janes, as we shall see, the years of controversy resulted in a further intellectual and religious transformation. And while it is fair to say that the missionaries had never fully understood his basic liberalism sixteen years earlier, they were to be even less amenable to the new brand of Christianity he now brought to Japan.

CHAPTER XI

JAPAN AGAIN: KYOTO AND
THE DŌSHISHA LECTURES

AT THE TIME of Janes' arrival in Kumamoto in 1871 Japan had confronted a period of rapid reform and Westernization. The themes of civilization and enlightenment, which he encountered everywhere in Kumamoto, echoed a broader national movement that constituted an essential feature of the Meiji Restoration. During these years Westerners and their ideas had been in high demand. As bearers of the secrets of Western wealth and power they had been accorded both status and emoluments that went beyond normal expectations. In some instances they were allowed a sphere of influence that left its distinct imprint on men and institutions.

But by the 1890s the initial crisis of the Meiji years had passed. Most Western advisers and teachers had been replaced by a corps of well-trained Japanese specialists. Many of these had studied abroad and were reluctant to accept everything Western as good and necessary, and everything domestic as backward and in need of enlightenment. While national confidence had not yet reached the peak it was to achieve in the period following the Russo-Japanese War of 1904–1905, it had certainly progressed beyond the self-doubts and sense of inferiority that Janes had encountered in Kumamoto.

Sixteen years had brought other changes as well. No longer "boys" in any sense of the term, the Captain's Kumamoto students had taken their places as important national figures. Tokutomi had become Japan's most popular journalist, the leader of a whole generation of young people who saw themselves as shouldered with the mission to carry on the revolution that had led to the original Restoration. Ebina had become central to Tokyo's intellectual life, using the pulpit of his Hongo Church to influence a wide cross section of Japan's creative writers. Kozaki's *Rikugō zasshi* or *Cosmos Magazine* was one of the most highly respected intellectual journals of the day. In fact, three of Meiji Japan's most prominent journals of opinion, *Kokumin no tomo*, *Rikugō zasshi*, and *Taiyō*, were under the editorship of Janes' former pupils.[1] Others had become prominent in agriculture, education, and the business world.

The Kyoto to which Janes introduced his new wife had itself been much transformed since he had last seen it in the 1870s. The construction of Dōshisha's red brick buildings marked a new phase in a city proud of its long associations with the traditional architecture of temples and shrines, but other parts of the city revealed that the Church had no monopoly on bricks and mortar and Western facades. Reflecting the successful efforts at industrialization that had become a national quest, Kyoto sported its share of belching chimneys and representative industrial structures that indicated that Japan had moved more rapidly in the direction of the "quick pulsing life" of Europe and America than either Janes or many of his Western counterparts anticipated.

Settling into one of the houses belonging to the compound of the Third College in the Higashiyama district of Kyoto a few blocks from Kyoto University, Janes took stock of his new environment. Gazing westward toward the Imperial Palace, he must have noticed that much had been altered in the city, and that Japan had been extensively transformed in his absence. But if Japan had changed, so had the Captain.

For Janes the difficult years in the United States had led to a further reevaluation of his Christian position. As was the case with his earlier conversion, this change in religious emphasis was closely linked with his efforts to come to grips with his personality. In the wake of the turbulent years leading to his divorce, Janes had reexamined his Christian experience. Much of what the missionaries in Japan interpreted as his "silence," and consequently as an admission of guilt, was in fact a part of this introspective process. While living in Ann Arbor the Captain once again wrestled with the basic cleavage of his heritage: the scientific rationalism of his father and the emotional revivalism of his mother.

Coming to grips with his "ill nature," and trying to put into perspective his experiences in Japan and Maryland prior to the divorce, he concluded that the "strange joys" of his life, the periods of highly emotional religious fervor which he had experienced in Oregon and in his last year in Kumamoto, were in essence the ultimate forms of "intoxication" that he would have to guard against in the future. While rejecting the evangelical and emotional components of his Christian experiences, which had played such an important role in the conversion of his students in Kumamoto, Janes continued to regard himself a Christian. The Christian as radical reformer, the concept he had first brought to Kumamoto, remained his ultimate ideal. And Christianity as a teaching in league with science, stripped of its sectarian identities, and ultimately preoccupied with this-worldly reform and the improvement of man's lot, the Christianity he had first taught at the Yōgakkō one must add, remained the dominant focus of his religious concerns.

What was new to Janes' Christianity was a heightened social criticism and a tone of moral outrage that the Church had failed to address itself to man's most important problems, which he saw as something other than a preoccupation with the afterlife. Janes regarded the social stance of the American Church as deplorable: "The churches (here) they say are theaters of fashion," he wrote to the band reporting on a Decoration Day Address he had delivered in Ann Arbor, "they cultivate the folly and stimulate the pride of life of the well-to-do and wealthy. When sickness and death come, the religion of these churches surrounds these heartless devotees with consolation and sanctions that are fallacious and deceptive. Meanwhile the poor have no spiritual home or resource in these pompous edifices. . . ."[2]

In reference to this point he made it quite clear what he meant. "My friends," he wrote,

> you little know the state of profound apathy, bordering on contempt which prevails *here* (in America I mean) for *much* that is called religion. The dissociation of theology and morality, the wide divergence of "religion" from the prevailing needs and present wants and sense of immediate and overwhelming evils *impels* men to say with a sneer "qui bono" (what good), what is the use of this eternal (or at least weekly) palaver about heaven with an occasional glance at hell, when men are agonizing and dying like flies, from purely *preventable evils*. These evils are in great part all "created" and in most part tolerated by the sloth, ignorance, and folly of men. Religion, these men say, or feel, remedies neither of these causes. It stimulates a supine and sensuous sloth and inaction, for it says "only believe." It does nothing to educate; on the contrary its habitual attitude has been that of antagonism to science. It imprisoned Galileo and Roger Bacon, burnt Bruno, banished Priestly.

The Church, Janes underscored, had played on the common man's instincts that there should be something of infallibility in faith. By keeping man bound to the belief in the mysterious it kept him from addressing himself to solving the problems with which he was (and remained) confronted. It was this same church that played on man's superstitions, that ended up on the "side of tyranny (by divine right); on the side of slavery as a 'divine' institution; on the side of intoxicants by actual use in its ceremonies, and interpretations it has put on the passages sanctioning, seemingly, their use; on the side of war, as half the wars of Europe have been purely *religious* wars; and on the side of pestilence (which men *know* to be the result of filth and wholly preventable sanitary conditions) because it resorts to prayer when men should be studying and applying chemistry and hygiene."

In what could hardly endear him to the missionaries Janes next pointed out that the Church had subtly perverted Christ's efforts to rid the world of race hatreds. Missionaries, by their very need to raise funds at home, he argued, tended to distort the information they dispensed about the people and cultures with which they worked in order to play on the sympathy of the home audience.

You know it was amongst the first of the influences Jesus shed about him in the hearts of those who felt his personal presence, or lived in his "day," that the distinctions between Greek and Hebrew, native and foreigner, "barbarian, Scythian, bond and free" melted away in the fervent heat of *Christian* love. Now those prejudices are strongest today in "Christian" countries. I believe they are so because of the false and pernicious education, chiefly by missionaries, of the young in Christian countries. They have a "plan of salvation" to recommend and require means—money—to carry out their scheme. Appealing to the *feelings* of children and their unthinking parents, they portray all the evils and miseries they see or hear of in "heathen" lands, attributing them to "idolatry." They declare that there is no "hope" for these multitudes but in the *particular* scheme or philosophy of salvation to which the particular audience is devoted.

This attitude toward the "heathen," Janes insisted, had resulted in the exploitation of the rest of the world by the West:

Now it would matter little how they individually looked upon the heathen or non-Christian peoples, but through the persistent and pernicious inculcation of their theory, and the false representation of such people as those of India, China, and Japan by them, through their false and senseless representations of religious growth like Brahmanism, Buddhism, Taoism, Mohammedanism, etc.,—even your Shintoism and the semi-religious Confucianism—Europe and America have been led to occupy political, military, diplomatic, social and religious relations toward the people of three fourths of the human race, that would disgrace heathens not only, but devils. Our African slavery and the trade that fed it; the extinction of the Red Race of American Indians by the bullet and the rum-bottle; the progress of the same curse of intoxication propagated by Germany and England over all Africa; the brutal and inhuman conquest and robbery of India by England; the unutterable, indescribable, wrong by the same power inflicted upon China, its three wars and unspeakable curse of opium: all this and more like it, I attribute in great measure to this false teaching of missionaries at home regarding the "heathen." The heart and conscience of professedly Christian people of the white race are *seared* toward those unfortunate victims of the power and greed of Europe and America, or they would never permit such continuous outrages.[3]

Having stated his position on the organized church and the missionary movement, the Captain added his views on theology: "A religion or theology called by whatever name that can thrive and be propagated in the midst of miseries like those I have indicated here on earth, without making their *first* aim to mitigate and remove them, but poorly recommends a hypothetical heaven to myself." Janes remained clear on what he regarded as the essence of Christianity.

> The essence of *Christ*-ianity is Love and Duty. These combined are Christ's Plan of Salvation: the Sun of the Christian life, Earth is their theater, Humanity is their object, *Health, Sanity*, happiness, holiness, purity, peace, wisdom, strength, and devotion (i.e. *self* sacrifice and *mutual service* in love), long life, and *joy* in it; conquest, not *of man* but of his enemies, disease, suffering, pestilence, want, ignorance, passion, evil inheritance, selfishness,—and for death Euthanasia. In short, the perfection of these powers and possibilities with which we have been endowed, *for that very purpose*, by the Author of our being, and the realization of a natural, reasonable, practical, and possible state of happiness here, [are] more worthy to be called *heaven* than the misty region of maudlin theological speculation.

The emphasis of Janes' Christianity by the 1890s was therefore a renewed call for change in *this* world. Christian love and duty implied social reform. To believe in heaven and rest while passing without notice over the festering heaps of our own filth, he observed, be it moral, spiritual, or physical, is to make a mockery of truth, Christ, and God.[4]

While Janes rejected his earlier evangelical enthusiasm as a form of intoxication, the rhetoric of his new Christian position suggests that the intensity with which he had once called for an educational revolution, and then a spiritual revolution, in Kumamoto could now be directed into an attack on the organized Church and its representatives. The position he had developed on missionaries and their work was hardly one that endeared him to members of the American Board.

As might be expected, the Captain's return to Kyoto was met with apprehension by most missionaries, particularly those at Dōshisha where the tensions of the nationalistic revival and the new liberal theology had already created more than usual concerns. No one knew precisely what Janes' course toward the school would be, but since the missionaries regarded him responsible for many of their difficulties they were clearly worried.[5] At the end of September Davis wrote to Clark that the Captain had arrived in Kyoto, but that he was taking an aloof stand toward members of the Mission. "He did not answer my letter," Davis complained, "nor has he mentioned the matter, although I have called on him twice, the first time alone, and with rather a cold reception, the last time with Mrs. Davis . . . and he was more cordial, although he declined an invitation to our house to supper." "He is evidently going to stand on his dignity," Davis added, "but politely so, at least externally."[6]

Among others at Dōshisha there was considerable excitement. The Lecture Association of the College, which consisted largely of students, thought it would be appropriate for the man about whom they had heard so much from their teachers, and whose work in Kumamoto had become a legend in the intervening years, to give a lecture in the college. Makino Toraji, the head of the association, visited Janes at his new home and asked him to speak at Dōshisha. The Captain, obviously pleased, assured Makino that "he could not refuse the request of the students and would be delighted to come." He further suggested that he give not one, but a series of at least three lectures. The subject they agreed upon was "The Greatest Thing in the World."[7]

The first lecture was scheduled for October 21, 1893, and was looked forward to with great anticipation. Posters announced that the "Father of the Kumamoto Band" would speak, and on Saturday evening the Dōshisha Chapel was packed to capacity with students, members of the band, and the missionaries.[8] What followed led Davis to write to Clark, "THE BATTLE IS ON HERE!"[9]

Regarding the Captain's lecture Davis wrote: The man who was used of God to lead the class of fifteen to Christ, and whom those men love as a father, and who they believe had been made to suffer awful hardship partly by the Mission's fault; this man . . . was invited by the Lecture Association of Dōshisha to give a course of three lectures, and he said at the beginning of the first one, his subject was given him, "The Greatest Thing in the World." Davis outlined what followed.

> He spent the first evening telling what the greatest thing is *not*. It is not bodily strength, not mental power, not knowledge, nor love, nor the imagination, and upon that head he spoke forty-five minutes, classing religions as they have existed, creations of the imagination, and all Bibles from the Vedas to the Book of Mormon, including the Old and New Testaments as creations of the imagination; that the Bible needed theologians to interpret it, or men could not know from it what their duty is, and the theologians all differ in their

interpretations, and then spending half an hour in the most vituperative language I ever heard in my life, in denouncing all theology and theologians and teachers of theology, the Bible, the Christian Church, and all ministers of the church. He raked up everything past and present that could be said bad about the Church of Christ, its beliefs and practices, as the enemy of science and of the anti-slavery movement, etc., etc.; and ending by the most scathing picture of how the Church has also been in league with intemperance and that Christ (which is a product of the imagination) by the miracle of Cana was made to be the very cornerstone and bulwark of intemperance; hence he scouted the possibility of the truth of miracles, or of the Bible, which contained them; and that Christianity and the church had done some good but their work was done; they are passing away, and ending by asking his hearers whether they believed that the best thing in the world was to be found in the imagination?

"He is a most eloquent and impressive speaker," Davis added, "one of the teachers gave an epitome of what had been said in Japanese, leaving out most of the offensive part." But, as Davis added with discouragement, "fully half of his audience understood the English." When Janes rose to speak he was loudly clapped by all present. When he sat down, Davis observed with some consolation, "he was not so loudly clapped," although "most of the class of fifteen," he lamented, "joined in the clapping at the close."

While it is clear that the missionaries looked upon Janes' lecture as a vicious attack upon them and their faith, which they would have to counter to preserve Dōshisha as a Christian institution, it is worth taking a closer look at the ideas that Janes actually espoused.[10]

What disturbed Davis and the other missionaries was the Captain's disdain for the cardinal tenets of Dōshisha's conservative Protestant position. Outspokenly critical of "Supernaturalism," in which a theology of faith, miracles, and the revealed truths of scripture dominated men's lives, and in which a fatalistic belief in divine will had inhibited action in a variety of this-worldly spheres—a theology he pictured as dying—Janes called for a rejection of the old order, of sectarian dogma, of quiescent belief in a world to come rather than positive action in an effort to transform the existing world in the name of higher ideals.

More than ever a convinced evolutionist, he argued that the rules of science, and the laws of differentiation, which he saw as continuing to serve as evidences of a higher truth and the ultimate confirmation of divinity, had shouldered man with the responsibility of working out his salvation in the world that God had provided him and not in some realm of the imagination. If evolution was the fundamental law of God's world, then it was man's responsibility to follow the essential rules of differentiation to their highest levels; that is, it was man's responsibility to use his intelligence for the furtherance of the human race, for the solution of the problems not only of individual societies, but of mankind as a whole, and for a rejection of all that stood in the way of human progress and development. For Janes, as for Seeley, the significance of Christ and *Christ*-ianity lay precisely in Christ's "enthusiasm for humanity," in his service to the community, and in his rejection of the established religious traditions of his day. Social reform, which emphasized service to one's fellow man, and which concentrated on doing rather than being, remained the essential Christian message, and the Christian's duty was to achieve the millennium not surrounded by the pearly gates of the world beyond, but in the only world that man could really know, and in which the divine had placed him for that very purpose.

Despite the response of Davis and the other missionaries, who saw the lecture as indicative of the total transformation of the man they had known earlier, it must be pointed out that Janes' message at Dōshisha in 1893 remained closely aligned to the Christian reformism he brought to Kumamoto in 1871. Having come to know the Captain during his revivalistic phase the missionaries had never fully understood the "Father of the Kumamoto Band," nor the Christian position he had initially adopted in Kumamoto. Janes' antisectarian stand, his questioning of scripture and the formally organized church, his belief in evolution, and his predominantly action-oriented, this-worldly concern for social reform as the essence of Christian duty and the meaning of Christ's life were nothing new to the members of the band. To the Captain's former students, one of whom was now president of the university, the lecture brought back memories of the man who had told them to "grab their swords" while he went "for his pistols." Moreover, for those who had studied with the Captain in Kumamoto the linking of Christianity and social reform was hardly a radical departure. Most of the members of the Kumamoto Band were consequently loud in their applause at the close of Janes' talk. But the same can hardly be said for the missionaries.

Davis, who tended to be more liberal than his colleagues, quickly realized that the Janes lectures would result in a major conflict. Only a miracle, he felt, could prevent it. Writing to Clark he explained: "Capt. Janes cannot be allowed to go on and finish his lectures in the school without bringing a crisis to the Mission, and he cannot be prevented without bringing a crisis and division among the Japanese." It therefore seemed to Davis to be the most cunningly and deliberately planned thing he had ever encountered. According to Davis, Janes' plan was to "cause the Japanese to break away from the foreigners, to break up the school," and "if possible to divide the Japanese churches and workers connected with our work." "I cannot see (perhaps the Master can)," he wrote, "how a very difficult conflict, perhaps a division can be avoided now." Davis thought the only hope lay in allowing "the better Japanese sentiment to crystallize a little" in order to "solidify the most spiritual elements of our pastors and churches" in preparation for a counterattack.[11]

George Albrecht was even more disturbed than Davis. He went directly to Ichihara, who served as acting president in Kozaki's absence, stating that the Captain's lecture had been extremely rude and had defiled the Church in its own house. Albrecht insisted that Ichihara go before the student body and repudiate Janes' views. Ichihara replied that while he did not agree with everything Janes said, he did not feel a repudiation necessary. Albrecht was so angry that he threatened to resign. A station meeting was held the following day, and while Albrecht was dissuaded from his ultimatum most of the missionaries agreed with him that this was "but the first gun of a long and bitter struggle."[12]

On October 25 Davis wrote to Clark saying that the situation was "mostly unchanged." He doubted that the missionaries' protest would prevent Janes from giving his second lecture. Openly to prevent him would only make him into a martyr, one made by the very foreigners and theologians he decried. This Davis felt was playing into Janes' hands, and so they would have to be careful.[13]

"If he were not so closely bound to the school and linked to the very men who are among the trustees and teachers in the school," Davis wrote, "I and others should feel that it was very clear that we should take a stand and demand that he be not allowed to go on." But Davis felt that this was a special case: ". . . when a viper of this kind is coiled around the very foundations, the men who would take the school with them, it may be best to wait a little and see if he will not sting himself to death. It is one of the hardest questions for me to decide I ever met, what stand to take, but I incline now to 'give him more rope' and see if he 'will not hang himself.' "[14]

While Janes was given time to hang himself, the missionaries, students, and faculty of Dōshisha found themselves plunged into a serious debate. Although the Kumamoto Band stood solidly behind its former teacher, and even took secret delight in the obvious discomfort (if not paranoia) of the missionaries, the student body was split. None of the students knew Janes personally and very few had clearly understood his lecture.[15] While some students were influenced by liberal ideas, which Davis and his fellow missionaries saw as "rationalistic and Unitarian views," there was also a group that, as the missionaries saw it, held to the "fundamentals." Several of the latter group, including Makino, had gone to Janes after the first lecture to have him clarify points and, as Albrecht was pleased to observe, had come away "disappointed," wondering if he "were a Christian at all."[16] Others took the opposite view and were convinced that Janes stood for the independence of the Japanese Church from missionary domination. Despite misgivings on the part of some, almost everyone agreed, however, that the Captain should be given another hearing.

Janes' second lecture was delivered on the evening of December 2. The location was once more the Dōshisha Chapel. The Captain announced his title as "The Greatest Thing In the World. What it Is."[17] Davis saw the lecture as one proposing "blank materialism." In it there was "no God only humanity," he wrote to Clark, "no future save the future of the race perpetuated in the world," and all this with "caricatures of supernatural Christianity interlarded."[18] But again it may be best to listen to Janes himself.

Opening his lecture he announced to the students: "It is understood all round that we are seeking the Best Thing in the whole world, in order that we may follow, serve, and have it inspire us. In a period of transition, of the breaking up of old systems, and of an unprecedented eclipse of faith in them and their agencies, we are all in a state of expectancy. You want, and I want, firmer foundations than any existing artificial systems of duty has under it, and a clearer and surer truth than any such system stands for. We have in our hearts a desire for the Best Thing within the possible range of human intelligence, and we will be satisfied with nothing less."[19]

Appealing to the nationalistic sympathies of his Japanese audience, he urged them to break with outworn ideas. "How will you ever fulfill that Declaration which Japan published to the world, when it announced that this era of Meiji ... should be *the* era of Enlightenment, if you give yourself over to the beggardly elements of superstitions, which Europe and America discard? Yet that is just what you will continue to do until you cast from you forever all the temptations presented to you through the imagination." Janes assured those before him that they would continue to "wander in a maze of doubt and anxieties" until they could locate deep down in their consciousness "the true and only Best Thing in the World," and could rekindle their "pure enthusiasm for *that* alone, and vow eternal fealty to it."

Once again sounding like the earlier Captain in Kumamoto, who had argued for the truths of Christianity through science, Janes noted: "Now while the race is yet in the very vestibule of scientific investigation, an all comprehensive *truth* reveals itself to the astonished thought of men.

It is this, there is no chance in the world of nature—without nor within us. Just as little is there of miracle."

Instead of the arbitrary and miraculous, Janes pictured the new world as being founded on an imposing prospect of *order*. "Law, benificent and inflexible; an endless sequence of cause and effect, inheritance, adaptation, and finally intelligent choice," he told the students, "establish the impossibility of irresponsible fate." Science had dealt a death blow, he insisted, to the "old doctrines of arbitrary and capricious *authority*." "Approached along the avenues of *all* the sciences *alike*," he declared, "the law of progress through differentiation is encountered and compels acknowledgement: an ever widening complexity of form, organ, function, leads up from the protoplasmic cell, to an organism which now heads the procession of all the living forms on earth. The evolution of life in this world culminates in a racial entity perfectly defined, and representative of all the energies of nature at work upon our planet."

"But the work of evolution," Janes explained to the students, "is endlessly incomplete. Always approximating perfection it is at the same time a performance and a promise. Accomplishment ever more vividly and surely suggests the Ideal, toward which attainment points, and for which realization only prepares. The cell has its ideal in the organ, the organ in a higher function, function in a more complex aggregate of being; being in society; social life in intelligence, love, duty." The Captain regarded it no more conceivable that this endless sequence of cause and effect should stop now than that it should have ended with the beginning of the paleozoic age.

"The human race then, comprehending the ideal which its present attainment indicates," Janes announced, "is the best thing in the whole world.

Despite Davis's views that the Captain preached "blank materialism," Janes continued to emphasize the importance of Christ. "The character, teachings, life and death of Christ convey to my mind its highest conceptions of what is deific, and divine," he told the students. "It makes the conception of a divine ideal possible to me," he added, "not because Christ was an effigy, a manikin representative of a preconceived aggregate inhabiting the infinities, but as divinely epitomizing the possibilities of any individual of the human race. We know force, intelligence, love, compassion, sympathy, holiness, joy, goodness, truth, evil, suffering, falsehood, sorrow, birth and death. But we know them as powers and attributes of *men*, *not* as the mechanical synthesis of an *imaginary* personality."

Janes argued that religion as a whole and Christianity in particular had to be brought not only into harmony with science, but that its teachings would have to be built on a sound scientific foundation. As Janes saw it, "when the telescope of Galileo dissolved the crystaline spheres and the Ptolemaic tangle of cycles, the Infinite became inscrutable, retiring beyond the veil of law." "That instant the whole domain of ethics became related to enlightenment and reason. So far as duty and the moral relations out of which its springs are concerned, the only revelation of the will of the omnipotent is to be found in the highest embodiment of creative purpose known to man, namely in mankind itself."

"As the law of evolution is perpetually operating," Janes explained, "that ideal is at any moment only approximate. Becoming ever more complex, moral relations, becoming ever more diversified and refined, and therefore more peaceful and perfect, the relativity of moral law is vindicated by its multiplying and beneficent fruits, and its majesty established by purely human sanctions."

Directly challenging the missionaries' conservative position, Janes observed, "they tell you 'unbelief is a sin.' I tell you that doubt, questioning, incredulity—is the soul of intellectual progress, and that Humanity is the proper object of all effort and duty, and the first condition of moral certitude. The law of human life as well as that of the universe, so far as we know it and see it in operation, is that of incessant, harmonious movement; ceaseless, majestic, sublime *action*. 'Belief' fetishism, is a ministry of laziness; and it is a school of sordid desire when it teaches the victims of its tempting wiles that: '*Doing* ends in death.' "

Of man's obligations to the Divine Janes noted: "Regarding the relations of mankind to the Unknowable Infinite, the evolutionary theory and method of creation is, as I have suggested, explicit and positive. The human race is an end of infinite processes and possible purpose, only to become a *means* for the accomplishment of further evolutionary ideals or ends. Our duty toward the Inscrutable Creative Infinite is to study and to facilitate the attainment of those ideals. At any moment the ideal humanity actually attained is the highest, greatest, best thing in the world. It is in the diligent use of every means, the heroic application of every faculty, and the incessant cultivation of intelligence in order to their higher use and application, that we 'honor' the creative power and purpose."

Man's prime responsibility, as Janes viewed it, was to his fellow man. "The human race is a Solidarity," he told the students, but more importantly, "it is a messenger of some Unknowable Omnipotence sent on a mission of self-development toward ever perfecting ideals. The Supernaturalist confounds the purport of Christ's parable. He would have you regard the human race as a fallen prodigal, feeding on the husks of creation and consorting with harlots and swine . . . I am here as a messenger to you from Jesus Christ and from the humanity for whom he sacrificed his life, to tell you that the human race is not a fallen creature to be mocked by pharisees. I am here to bid the individual enemies of the race *beware* how they trample into mud the means of human development as swine so waste good corn."

Challenging the conservative Church's lack of social concern Janes exploded: "How dare any man assume the name of Christ and belittle, belie, ignore, or offend Him, in the person of the humblest members of the race. How dare they build structures of brick and mortar and wood and glass gaudily colored—consecrate *them*—and look with pharisaic scorn upon the 'unbelieving' poor, who die like flies of poverty, injustice, and of preventable disease. Are not these the brotherhood of Christ, rather than your Levitical and priestly following of 'Believers'?"

Reiterating his earlier position on the Christian as radical reformer, Janes added a note of caution that reflected his own new self-analysis. "Men have been content to sit, satisfied by the contemplation of paradise and the New Jerusalem, in the midst of darkness, ignorance, disease, pestilence, famine, and a multitude of lesser evils, all of which a little exertion would have long since removed and rendered impossible. Intoxication is not nourishment. The intoxications of religion are as baneful in their effects upon the emotions, the will, and the mind, as are those of the alcoholic cup, and of alkaloidal drugs, upon both the faculties and fibers of the organism. Therefore no healthy desire for life can be fed or founded on the material of dreams."

The new order, as the Captain saw it, would have to be built on "reality" and not on "dreams." "The best, holiest, greatest thing in the world, is a palpable reality," he insisted, "not an impalpable nonentity. The new order postulates man, humanity, mankind, a reality—the highest conceivable. The old system of Supernaturalism is built upon a hypothesis, a conceit, to which it devotes all its energies."

The worst of these conceits, he felt, was an overbearing concern with the immortality of the soul. "The 'immortality of the soul' is the crowning conceit of the least efficient, most egotistic, most sordidly selfish of the membership of the race. It is those who are least heroic in developing and making perfect conditions of our natural life, here upon this planet, who scorn most heartily the 'humanitarian' sentiments; who sigh and whine most over the insufficiency of the actual creation, who demand of omnipotence an eternal life, and a heaven of imaginary delights." For all too many, Janes felt, "modern Christianity is a religion of selfish desire, of 'soul saving' and heaven craving." "The religion of Christ," he added, "I conceive to have been the very reverse of this. The nearer we come to his person the less of selfishness and the more of the atmosphere of sympathy, brotherhood, humanity, love—of the boundless compassion that made the character of Gautama the Buddha unique—do we feel."

Janes did not reject the immortality of the soul or other Church "mysteries" as false in an absolute sense, but as unknowable in the light of man's current understanding. Moreover, as he saw it such doctrine became unimportant when compared with that which was knowable. "The *ultimate* destiny, as well as the *ultimate* origin of creation, culminating on earth in the evolution of the human race, is hidden of necessity from human intelligence. Only the nature and method of approach toward the destiny of mankind are at present within our comprehension; as are only the nature and method of the development of mankind from lower and lower origins, until we arrive at the beginnings of life. Men will push forward and backward the limits of human knowledge, as the means of enlarging its sphere are attained and understood. This is inevitable with a being possessed of reason and reflection. And genius will accomplish wonders in leading the whole race nearer and nearer to the outer bounds of finite capacity."

"Let only a leading morety of the race," Janes added, "besides breaking from the thralldom of these idols of desire, as a great majority of thinking men and women have already done, let these in addition, but attune the enthusiasm of their ransomed natures to the harmonies of the evolutionary methods of creation, and they will speedily draw the whole race after them to higher places of development."

Finally Janes summed up his position: "This then is the answer which the new order of duty, righteousness, and love will continue to make to the yearnings and the fears of the individuals. Ye are the members of a comprehensive whole, from whose destiny it is treason to seek a selfish severance. The immortality of which you are assured has been prophesied at every step and stage of the progress of evolution—which does not stop now leaving humanity in its present stage. The higher destiny of the race is part of your own continued existence—its realization and fulfillment. You shall make or modify that destiny so making and modifying your own. If you aspire to partake of Christ's salvation—enter with Him the lists of love and duty. As Christ loved and did, so love and do thou likewise. So shall selfish desire die, and fear be consumed of love. For us, this passing generation, there is a special command: 'Beware of the leaven of pharisaism.' Beware of the sham immortality with which it bribes desire and fear!"

Janes' second discourse underscored his firm commitment to a scientific Christianity. Throughout the lecture he hammered home his basic theme: that theology should be replaced by science. "The theories of the theologians are passing away," he told the students. "Within a century or so science has done more for the happiness and upbuilding of the race than Christianity did in fifteen centuries."

Once again it is not difficult to detect traces of the early Yōgakkō teacher. On the other hand, the Dōshisha of the 1890s was no longer the Kumamoto School for Western Learning. While members of the Kumamoto Band, who had come to Christianity through science, had ample reason to be attracted to the ideas of their former mentor, the majority of the Dōshisha students did not share their experiences or background. Despite the early Kumamoto influence, Dōshisha had, in fact, become more of a mission training school than either Janes or the members of the band had initially anticipated. It must be added that very few of the generation of Dōshisha students who were in the college in the 1890s shared the Confucian background of the Kumamoto Band. As a result they did not feel the compulsion of their elders to take the private and moral dimension of Christianity and extend it to society at large. Nor did they share the need to do this in the arena of social reform that went beyond the sphere of the Church and closely paralleled the scientific Christian mission Janes was espousing. Thus, while the members of the Kumamoto Band continued to be loud in their applause of the Captain, many of the Dōshisha students were not.

And yet, although student apprehension and missionary opposition mounted, little was done to stop the lectures. The question of Janes' appearances had become an issue of "free speech," which not even the missionaries dared oppose. The third lecture was presented on Saturday evening, December 9. "It was the worst of them all," Davis wrote to Clark, "I never before in my life had so clear an illustration of what blasphemy is."[20] After the second lecture Davis had written to the Board that no more endowment money should be sent to Japan because he thought Janes and the "Unitarians" were in the process of "taking over the college ala Harvard."[21] Now he felt more confident. Even some of the students were convinced that Janes had gone too far. As Davis saw it, his strategy of giving the Captain more rope so that he might hang himself appeared to be working. In his letter to Clark he added, "this lecture will do the business, I think. It will finish his influence for evil here."[22]

On the other hand an additional lecture was now proposed by the Lecture Association and scheduled for December 16. With momentum moving in his direction, Davis decided to act. Preparing for a showdown he slept only an hour and a half on the night of the third lecture, "thinking and praying all night." The next morning he had a long talk with Morita Kumando to try to get him to see that the lectures must be stopped. Morita remained uncooperative, but Davis went to work on the committee of the Lecture Association. On Monday, December 11, the Lecture Association had a two-hour meeting at which it still could not make up its mind about the upcoming lecture. That evening Davis worked with the teachers and the students of the lecture committee and the next morning the Lecture Association decided by an "almost unanimous vote" to halt the lectures.[23]

In the eyes of Davis and the other missionaries the termination of the Janes lectures represented a victory for the truth and for Dōshisha. As far as the school was concerned it had survived its most serious crisis to date. At the same time the myth of its founding father had suddenly crashed to earth. In the wake of the lectures there were plenty of recriminations. Attitudes toward Janes seem to have shifted even among some of the members of the Kumamoto Band.[24] Nakaseko Rokurō, who had interpreted for Janes, publicly apologized for having done so and for having aided a person who was "trying to tear down what Dr. Neesima had built up."[25] Davis and Yoshida Sakuya, one of the members of the band, once more raised the question of Janes' sanity. Both thought the Captain suffered from a "monomaniacy" that took the form of "spite against the Mission."[26]

Davis saw the outcome of the lecture controversy as a victory for Dōshisha and the missionaries, but J. H. DeForest recalled that Niijima Jo had told him long ago that "the Japanese love heroes and obey them with their lives."[27] For members of the Kumamoto Band such as Yokoi Tokio, Ebina Danjō, and Ukita Kazutami, even for Kozaki Hiromichi who tended to be more conservative than the others, Janes remained a hero, whose ideas coincided with their own moves toward a more liberal and national Christianity.

In fact Janes' Dōshisha lectures clearly underscored one of the principal dilemmas of the Christian movement in Meiji Japan. Working in the hostile environment of the early Meiji period the pioneer missionaries such as Verbeck, Hepburn, and Davis had emphasized the social outreach of the Church, its role in education, medical work, prison reform, and a variety of socially conscious areas that blended well with the prevailing national preoccupation with civilization and enlightenment. Given the precarious legal position in which the Church found itself, and the general Japanese hostility toward Christianity as a religion, this strategy proved to be sound and effective.

A Christianity that stressed social action, as the Kumamoto Band illustrated, could allow for a smooth transition from the Confucianism in which most Japanese of samurai background had been raised, to a new religious consciousness that not only preserved certain values of the past but permitted these to be successfully used to new ends. And yet, between

Janes and the missionaries, and subsequently between the members of the band and the missionaries, there was a fundamental difference that involved the question of means and ends. For the Captain, the pick, cement, tile, and clean water were prayer, praise, and sermon. The ends of Christianity were this-worldly social reform; the Christian's mission was the improvement of man's lot on earth. For the missionaries, on the other hand, social reform—the early emphasis on education, medical work, and prison reform—was a means of "laying siege" to Japan for its ultimate Christianizing. Even Davis and Niijima, in their initial correspondence with the Board, had stressed the need for the Captain to head the college precisely because his coming would allow them (as missionaries) to devote their full attention to the theological training of pastors and to direct missionary work—that is, the task of saving souls.[28]

As the Janes lectures amply illustrated, by the 1890s most missionaries complained bitterly about the New Theology (German Liberalism and Unitarianism) and about the rise of Japanese nationalism, which they saw as antiforeign and consequently antimissionary. To these forces they attributed the decline in the growth and vigor of the Christian movement that had earlier exuded optimism and had attracted to the Church some of Japan's brightest young minds. Few missionaries seem to have realized that they, too, had subtly shifted their focus. No longer new arrivals, but now well established, the missionaries felt less compelled to focus their attention on social reform. Indeed, in keeping with the missionaries' natural inclinations, social action had given way to theological concerns and to the practical problems of proselytizing. Saving souls, as Janes insisted, was the dominant missionary occupation. Confronted by the New Theology, the missionaries, including those at Dōshisha, had become even more conservative. In such an environment the overzealous waving of the banner of social reform could easily lead to doubts about one's theological position and accusations that one had sold out to the enemy. As a result, a preoccupation with clear doctrinal positions replaced the more creative flux of the early Meiji years.[29]

The effects of these trends were to shape the Japanese Christian movement. Increased conservatism, and a failure to pursue boldly the path of social reform with which the Church had been identified in the early Meiji years, in essence divided what had been a united movement. As Janes' lectures at Dōshisha revealed, the missionaries were not alone in their conservative emphasis. There were plenty of Japanese students who shared their views. And yet there were also many Japanese Christians who came to Christianity through Confucianism and continued to see the outworking of their faith in social action. Certainly most of the central figures of the Kumamoto Band, Ebina, Kozaki, and Miyagawa, persisted in this view. But the tragedy remained that by the turn of the century, the Church as a unified movement had lost its consensus on social reform. Japanese young people, who like Janes' original pupils burned with youthful zeal to complete the revolution of their fathers, increasingly sensed this and now turned to secular programs, particularly to socialism, to accomplish their transformational ideals.

Despite the Dōshisha response, Janes' expectations for Japanese Christianity remained high. He persisted in a view he had expressed earlier. "You Japanese Christians," he had written to the band from Ann Arbor, "occupy a peculiar position, and in my judgement might do much for Christ and truth and man." "You are capable of saying to Europe and America that their Christianity must be radically revised, or you will have none of it. You are in a position to compel ministers, churches, and church organizations to study history, abandon the husks of theology, and either represent and teach and inspire the spirit of Jesus, whatever comes of philosophy and 'plans of salvation,' or retire to the position of worn out religions and priesthoods like those of India and China."[30] By the mid-1890s many of the members of the Kumamoto Band had come to share Janes' vision, and while they had developed their own positions independently of his, there were also numerous parallels that suggest common convictions.

Indeed, the victory that Albrecht and Davis celebrated at the close of 1893 was short-lived. The Janes lectures widened the rift between the foreign and Japanese teachers at Dōshisha, and they precipitated the severing of connections between the school and the American Board.[31] The actual split took place in April 1896, when Dōshisha under Kozaki's leadership parted company with the missionaries and declared its independence.[32] Two years later, under the presidency of Yokoi Tokio, the school stripped from its constitution the article that made "Christianity the basis of its moral education."[33] By the late 1890s it was therefore clear that Dōshisha and the Kumamoto Band were moving steadily in the direction that Janes had foreseen. Despite the missionaries' efforts Dōshisha was, "*a la* Harvard," turning into a scientific and secular institution. To credit Janes alone for this transformation would be an injustice to the Kumamoto Band. On the other hand one should not underestimate Janes' genius for leading his students to discovering for themselves conclusions that were basically his own.[34]

In the wake of the Dōshisha lectures, Janes occupied himself with his teaching responsibilities at the Third College, the preparatory department of Kyoto Imperial University where he served as professor of English and English literature until the summer of 1899.[35] At the same time he pursued his earlier literary work. Initially there appears to have been some discussion of publishing the Dōshisha discourses in Japanese with Yokoi as translator, but while a manuscript was prepared, it was never released. Instead, much of the lectures' content found its way into a series of manuscripts that were the product of his Kyoto years: *Kumamoto: an Episode in Japan's Break from Feudalism*, "KOSEKI, The Mind of Japan in Faith, Monument, and Art," "Hieizan Colloquies," "Christian Pilgrims to Japanese Shrines," and "Hearts and Swords." There were also shorter pieces in which he explored new areas: "Gautama Siddharta—The Founder of Buddhism," an essay in which he applied his humanistic criteria to the life of the Buddha, and an article that later became "The Yellow Man as Pioneer of Modern Civilization," in which he argued against the standard Western conceptions of Asia and their origins. As a whole these writings reflected an expansion of his religious and reformist interests and demonstrated a willingness to consider other "ways" as having relevance to his life and thought.[36]

With time the Captain's manuscripts filled a good-sized trunk. But few were of publishable quality. The trouble with them, as Kozaki was told by one of the Chicago publishing houses to which he took "The Sword and the Spirit" (the former "Hearts and Swords"?) a few years later, was their argumentative style, which was inappropriate for novels and did not cater to the tastes of the day. A hundred years of aging have done little to alter this criticism. In fact, the very act of writing seems to have reflected the degree to which Janes' iconoclastic campaigns and argumentative self had come to serve as a barrier between himself and the broader society. Convinced of his prophetic role, he saw the alienation of the Dōshisha audience as a natural consequence of the supernaturalism the missionaries had instilled in their young wards. And while the missionaries continued to see him as the cause of their difficulties in Kyoto, he persisted in seeing them as responsible for his. Increasingly isolated, shunned by the missionaries and even by some of the members of the band, the Captain found consolation in putting his thoughts to paper. Therapeutic as such writing may have been, the results were often a dreary polemic that clouded important insights with a veneer of diatribe and invective.

When Janes vented his anger on the missionaries in his Dōshisha lectures, at one point referring to the students as "my friends" and the missionaries as "my enemies," the missionaries also made a quick about-face in their estimation of him. Just a few years earlier they had privately defended his innocence on the charges brought against him by Harriet, but now there was further invective and a readiness to associate his rejection of the conservative Church with other crimes. Davis, who had been shown the full text of Harriet's disclosures at Henry Martyn Scudder's insistence, could not resist impeaching him once more on charges of "adultery," although these proved as far-fetched as Harriet's imaginings.[37] All this confirms that in the far from humanistic arena of human relations in which Janes and the missionaries found themselves, the Captain had become transformed into a viper whose religious fall implied an equivalent moral debasement.

To Janes such attitudes merely confirmed the missionary mentality. Moreover, while he was hardly welcome at Dōshisha, this did not mean that he had lost his ability to inspire and lead. His students at the Third College remembered him as an imposing and majestic figure who overwhelmed the neighborhood. "Our teacher," one of them wrote, "was an admirer of Abraham Lincoln, and if the conversation turned to the problems of mankind, or if the lesson suggested such a direction, he would present a magnificent lecture and the hour would be over in an instant." Whenever they came to class unprepared, he noted, the students would try to draw the Captain to this topic. In addition to praising the humanism of Lincoln, he recalled, Janes also lectured them on the irrationality of Christian teachings, "shouting that missionaries were devils."[38]

While the Captain's growing introspection reflected his alienation from the traditional Church and its representatives, and was heavily rooted in his self-imposed role as prophet, there were other causes that undermined the high hopes with which he had returned to Japan in 1893. Kyoto in the 1890s represented a totally different environment from Kumamoto in the 1870s. Westernization, the dominant theme of the earlier decade, had given way to reaction. No foreigner in the 1890s would be entrusted with the role he had played in Higo. For Janes, whose this-worldly Christian reformism had found an ideal environment in Kumamoto, Kyoto proved frustrating. Except for his skills as an English teacher, the local community neither wanted nor needed him. Life in Japan had come to resemble his original experiences in Maryland, where his Christian reformism had been stymied by the local environment. Kumamoto suddenly seemed a long way off in both distance and time.

In the wake of the Sino-Japanese War (1894–95), Janes was confronted by the shift in national policy that overwhelmed even Tokutomi and transformed what had been a belief in evolutionary improvement, a confidence in natural law, and a general faith in the people—the themes he identified with the Restoration and his work in Kumamoto—into a predominant concern for national survival through a powerful state and military, often at the expense of the common man. Given the new environment, Janes' attitude toward Japan began to change.

The Captain's writings for the 1890s are filled with a growing note of estrangement. Just as the Kumamoto school had melted away like a snowball in the sun, so the ideals he had hoped to implement through it seemed to be rapidly fading. Confronted by the emergence of an absolute imperial state, Janes began to reevaluate the Restoration and its historical significance. Looking back on the early Meiji years he now complained that "the movement in search of this new order had very little in it of the spirit and essence of true reform." "Neither the Revolution of 1868–69, nor the upheaval of new forces" that followed, he insisted, "were spontaneous, originating in the necessities of an expanding intellectual life, and the maturing moral conditions of a higher order." Had the Restoration taken place on the heels of Nobunaga, Hideyoshi, and Ieyasu's efforts two and a half centuries earlier, events which he saw as "clearly evolutionary and unfolding," the "continuity of progress would have been consistent and apparent." But the movement "over which the Western world, especially America went into ecstasies of bright anticipation [and into which he had plunged with equal enthusiasm], was," he now argued, "compulsory, not spontaneous."[39]

The miracle of Japan's "awakening," Janes insisted, was all a myth. "She was never asleep," he noted, "but always stolid, stubborn, dotish in her selfishness and arrogance, and has been justly and righteously whipped into her place in the column of progress by the might and onward march of true civilization." "Not that our civilization is perfect by any means," he added, "but that it is true in character to the laws of development and progress. Not that it is free from past stains and present evils; but that it recognizes them and seeks to remedy and remove them. Not that its methods are faultless, but that its energies have procured for mankind the conditions that insure for humanity an endless unfolding of the best elements of human nature and the ultimate realization of the highest ideals."[40]

Japan, by contrast, he insisted, had brought nothing to the common stock of mankind, no scientific discoveries, no unique inventions, no original ideas. Instead, what had once again come to the fore, particularly after the Sino-Japanese War, were her "ingrained pride," her "hostile cynicism," and her "race hatreds." Given the nationalistic environment in which he found himself, it seemed to the Captain that Japan had "taken without gratitude or due appreciation" the Westernization which he and other foreign employees had brought in the early Meiji years, and that "except for a pretence," at change and a new international spirit, "as sturdily ignores and sneers at the claims of our common humanity as when she slammed the doors of her hospitality in the face of the world, and caged shipwrecked sailors of the white race as if they were beasts."[41]

Rather than culminating in a social revolution, which he pictured as the ultimate goal of the Restoration and had worked hard to instill in the consciousness of his students in Kumamoto, the Meiji era, as he saw it from the perspective of the 1890s, confirmed not a social revolution and the triumph of a new order, but the triumph of the old. What happened, Janes wrote, "is not difficult now to explain. Pride, humbled with more or less content, stooped low to conquer. The old military spirit took to the new channels with the alacrity which is characteristic of the genuine spirit of conquest or revenge." And for such a military spirit, the Captain insisted, "the mere pomp and glory of war, the indulgence of a fanatic loyalty and above all the sweets of retaliation and revenge, are the only counterpose to the chagrin of defeat, the only salve capable of healing the smart of insult, or of hiding the consciousness and shame of inferiority."[42]

But Janes' disappointments with the Meiji Restoration indicated above all the degree to which Japan had succeeded in the modernization efforts that had brought him to Kumamoto in the first place, and toward which he had made his own particular contribution. Victory in the Sino-Japanese War confirmed not only that Japan had absorbed the lessons of its foreign mentors more successfully than its continental neighbor, but that the majority of Westerners, unlike the Captain, approved of its military and colonial expansion. The defeat of China brought Japan instant recognition. Nowhere was this more apparent than in the area of the unequal treaties, against which the Tokyo government had struggled with difficulty for three decades using the tools of diplomacy, but which now disappeared almost overnight.

The Captain had introduced his students in Kumamoto to the theories of evolution in the 1870s. By the 1890s there were plenty of Japanese who had followed the evolutionary path from Darwin to Spencer, and from Spencer to the aggressive "dog-eat-dog" world of late-nineteenth-century imperialism. In this world the arguments Janes had used to kill his cow, that "the fit survive, and are served to that end by the faulty" applied no longer to animals but to nations. Hardly responsible for the creation of this international environment, the Japanese nevertheless had no intention of taking their place on the platter with the faulty.

By the turn of the century it was clear that the age that had brought the Captain to Japan in 1871 had come to a close. The all-out Westernization of the early Meiji years, which had placed such demands on him in Kumamoto, had run its course. What followed in its wake was a reassertion of more traditional values, and from Janes' perspective these could not help but be excessively conservative. And yet, what these years revealed most dramatically was the fact that history had passed him by. Japan no longer needed foreign advisers of his type, and while the good will of his former students made it possible for him to return once more,

Kyoto, as Otis Cary warned, could not replace Kumamoto. For Janes, who tended to be totalistic in his loves and hatreds, and who needed to be needed, the ambivalence of his position in Kyoto led to bitterness. Feeling superfluous and unwanted, he countered such feelings by becoming increasingly critical of Japan and the Japanese.

Janes' view of an aborted revolution that abandoned the cause of social justice in the name of military expansion has been echoed by twentieth-century historians critical of the Meiji Restoration. But it must also be added that his bitterness seems to have blinded him to other parts of the Meiji reality. The 1890s stood not only for the growth of Japan's military identity, but for the establishment of a constitution, a parliament, a systematic legal structure, and an effective system of public education. It is, in fact, to these that other historians have pointed as the sources of a gradually expanding and opening society, which, despite the setbacks to which militarism subjected it, was to move ever-forward on its course to becoming a modern democracy.

Had the Captain's personal blinders not inhibited his vision, he might well have seen that the legacy he had instilled in Kumamoto and among his students was destined to make its own contributions toward the achievement of such democratic ends.

CHAPTER XII

THE FINAL YEARS

ONE OF THE INTRIGUING FEATURES of Janes' life was the curious way in which cross-cultural perceptions of personality allowed an individual who was notably a failure in one cultural context to become a success in another. As we have seen, many of the Captain's accomplishments of lasting importance in Japan were the result of this unusual blending of personality and environment. Janes' years in Kumamoto demonstrated the degree to which behavior that verged on deviance in one society could be regarded as heroism in another. While the Kyoto years reduced the Captain to more human proportions, and subjected him to criticism from even some of his former Japanese admirers, his final years restored him to the position he had attained earlier. Indeed, it might be argued that Janes' last years, difficult though they became, served as the ultimate confirmation of the Japanese image of the hero that lay at the core of his earlier achievements in Japan.

The Captain's decision to return to the United States in 1899 was the result of a combination of circumstances. Six years of sustained activity as a teacher in Kyoto and Kagoshima had once again strained his precarious emotional and physical balance. Having fought his battles against the organized church and the vagaries of Japanese conservatism he was emotionally tired and physically exhausted. As he later wrote to Ebina he returned from Japan sick.[1]

Yet "sickness," as we have seen previously, often involved more than mere physical distress. In its broadest sense, life in Kyoto had been comfortable and well regulated by the normal academic routine of classes and lectures at the Third College. Kyoto, itself, provided a multiplicity of cultural diversions, and as Janes' writings reflect, he and Flora took advantage of what the environment offered. But if the charm of the city, its living history, and the beauty of its seasons provided pleasant diversions, there were also anxious moments and painful experiences. Some of these involved his relationship to the missionaries and the disappointment he felt with the course of Japanese development. Others were more personal.

Janes remained deeply troubled by death, particularly the deaths of loved ones. On December 14, 1893, three days after the termination of his Dōshisha lectures, his mother died of a stroke in Ohio.[2] The death of the "saintly woman of the bright intelligence," the only human being who, he felt, had really understood him, was a severe personal blow. Word of his mother's death was soon followed by the even more distressing news that his daughter Lois had committed suicide at the University of Michigan on April 11, 1894.[3] Lois, the first of his "Japanese" children, the dimple of a baby born in Kumamoto, had matured into the brightest and most precocious of his daughters. Always a favorite, she had followed her father's idealism and pursued his interests in philosophy at the university. Now, suddenly, she was dead. Just a few years earlier Yamazaki, whom he loved like a son and on whom the highest hopes of the Kumamoto school had rested, was snatched away in the prime of youth. Janes had not sufficiently recovered from his earlier bereavements, yet death had once again struck, plucking from him his beloved daughter.

Word of Lois's suicide was almost immediately paired with anxiety for Flora, who was in the last stages of pregnancy. Close to all the children, who had warmly supported her marriage to their father, she was greatly troubled by the news. Already thirty-five, and about to bear her first child, there were reasons for anxiety. But on May 16, to the relief of the Japanese doctor and the Captain, she safely gave birth to a son whom the couple named Phil.[4] Four years later, on January 28, 1898, she bore him a daughter, Iris.[5] Thus at the age of sixty-one, with a young wife and two infant children, the Captain was suddenly faced with the challenges of raising a new family.

Janes' return to the United States was accompanied by another period of "silence." Arriving in San Francisco he took Flora and the children to Palo Alto where they settled close to Stanford University.[6] Like other sufferers from rheumatic disorders and chronic bronchitis he hoped that the California sunshine would help to restore his physical condition. Renewed physical health would allow him to regain his sense of emotional wholeness, which lay at the core of his life-long struggle.

In its restorative powers Stanford proved to be a disappointment. Writing to Ebina and other members of the Band after finally breaking his "silence" in 1903, Janes explained that he had not written in several years because he suffered from a constitutional disability of imposing his cares, anxieties, troubles, or sufferings on others.[7] "And I have had some of each of these," he added.[8] Shortly after arriving in California, he explained, he had suffered from a "painful experience of exposure," which "lasted on and on several months until after we got settled at Stanford." As on earlier occasions, a severe physical illness seems to have accompanied the process of emotional restoration. "I believe it was a cleansing process from which my whole system has been greatly benefited," he wrote, adding that his illness had been "of a malarial rheumatic nature, at times very painful and continuing practically the whole time

—nearly quite a year—that I remained at Stanford." Settling in Palo Alto, he concluded, had been a mistake. "It was California," he wrote, "but one of the least healthy places . . . in America . . . a recent epidemic of typhoid fever has carried off nearly a dozen students of Stanford and the conditions are such that little improvement is possible."

Faced with such an environment, the Captain moved his family to Los Gatos, a small town about twenty-five miles up the bay from Stanford that lay halfway between San Jose and Santa Cruz.[9] Here he reported his "trouble entirely ceased." "I have improved in health," he wrote, "until I am in better condition than I have been for 10 or 12 years." In fact, "for a year or eighteen months," he added, "I have enjoyed almost uninterrupted health and improved spirits." "My bronchial trouble is practically a thing of the past." Feeling better, he explained, he had built two houses in Los Gatos. These construction projects had taken much of his time and had contributed to his silence. But unfortunately they had not reaped the anticipated financial rewards. "Pecuniary matters at one time gave me great anxiety," he wrote to Ebina, "until I got rid of one of the houses I had built. I am about to dispose of the other, suffering a loss on both."

But all these explanations were simply introductory to the real reason for his letter to the band. Life in America had become increasingly trying. Not only were there financial setbacks, but the Captain and his wife felt themselves unaccepted by the local community. "We are all very well," he noted, "but lonely. We are strangers in California, and all of us would be far more at home in dear old Japan." Now he addressed the issue directly: "I long earnestly to see you and to return to work in Japan. If I can do so it is our final determination to make your country our permanent home; to settle and remain to the end of life in Japan."

"My parents are gone," Janes wrote, "my former children are scattered and settled independently. Our two little ones, born there, can be fully educated by their mother. I have no ties here any longer. More than half my children were born in Japan. I have expended over twelve years of effort there. It seems more like home than America—at least than California. I feel sure of ten or twelve years more of hard and useful work with faculties riper and stronger than ever in my life—a wider, more useful range of experiences."

"I would delight to return to my old position in Kyoto—the one I vacated to return sick to America," he elaborated. "If you approve, dear Ebina, I beseech your assistance in this. I shall write, of course to Mr. Orita and to Pres. Kinoshita, but as now neither may be engaged as formerly, I shall make this a kind of general letter, with Mrs. Janes' assistance, to save time and enlist such interest as you and others of my boys may be kind enough to bestow."

"I speak of my former position," he added, "but I do not limit my application to that. I would like to work in the English Literature department of the Kyoto University or any similar position. If that is not feasible, then in the Koto Chiu [Third College]—or either of them— preferably in Kyoto or south rather than north of Tokyo." "I should be happiest in my old place in Kyoto." "I cannot for some years make a home and settle in some choice place in Japan," he emphasized, "without employment."

"I write somewhat hastily," he elaborated, "in view of the distance and my desire to be ready to work in September. I can pay my own passage. If a place is open and I am desired it may be well to cable . . . to save time to me to make my preparations here and sail a month before school opens." "Regarding the cablegram," he added, "should you conclude to cable from Yokohama I will leave my address, one word, 'Leroy' at the San Francisco Office. No signature being used and a single word 'Yes' or 'Come' for substance, the expense would be reduced to a trifle compared with the convenience it would be to me to have even 10 or 12 days additional time." His wife, he wrote, sends her "kindest rememberances" and agreed with him in these plans. "Phil and 'Ayami-san' [little Iris]" were both doing well. "I cannot remain inactive long," he added in conclusion. "I trust a new sphere of active usefulness may be opening to me in Japan. I am more full of drive, energy, and earnestness than when I went to Japan last time, and feel a far riper intellectual power than when I went first of all in 1871."

Janes' 1903 letter to the band was filled with the pathos of his final years. Increasingly alienated from the American environment, indeed incapable of making a living in California, he had come to look upon his Japanese experiences as the high point of his life. Hoping that the loyalty relationship he had developed in Kumamoto thirty years earlier could be called upon once more, he had issued what has to be seen as a final plea for help. But there are hints that even he was no longer confident of the outcome. "The least that this letter can do," he had written, "will be to convey our united and sincere gratitude to you all for the kindness shown and the beautiful and utterly unmerited present bestowed upon me just before our leaving at Yokohama. Whether we meet again or not, these testimonials of your regard will ever remain among the choicest treasures of my memory and life."[10]

But the cable "Leroy Come" was never sent. And the question why it was not sent remains difficult to answer. In fact, hidden below the surface of this decision there remains one of the intriguing mysteries involving the band and the Captain. By the first decade of the twentieth century there was certainly no lack of influence on the part of his former students, whose positions of prominence had risen, not declined, during the intervening years. In its broadest sense therefore the decision not to invite Janes back appears to have involved the band's own ambivalence regarding the Captain that stemmed from his Dōshisha lectures and the Kyoto years. And yet, given the nature of the plea, and more importantly given the principle of loyalty that tied Japanese students into a life-long obligatory relationship to their teachers, it is clear that this decision was not made lightly and without due consideration by the band.[11]

Still it is worth noting that the writings of the members of the band make no reference to Janes' 1903 request, and that unlike the Captain's other letters extant in Japan it has never been published. Kozaki's last account of the Captain is a case in point. In August 1905, Kozaki visited the West Coast at the request of the American Missionary Association to preach to the Japanese residing in Washington, Oregon, and California. During this trip he visited Janes. Kozaki's description of this visit, which retains a prominent place in his autobiography *Reminiscences of Seventy Years*, is often presented as the final and rather tragic portrait of the Captain.[12]

"Since his return to America," Kozaki writes, "we had had absolutely no tidings of Captain Janes, but we now learned that he was living on a hill at Wrights, California, and one day paid him a visit." One need hardly emphasize that the man writing this was a Christian minister fully aware of the ninth commandment. Wrights, Kozaki explained, was a village halfway between San Jose and Santa Cruz.[13] "As his residence was on a hilltop two or three miles from the station," Kozaki continued, "we took a carriage. His house was in such despair as to remind one of a hermit's cell in ruins, innocent of articles of furniture—a most pitiful makeshift for a human dwelling." "I afterward learned," Kozaki continued, "that after his return to America he had been for some time without occupation when one day he hit upon the plan of retiring among the hills at Wrights and keeping poultry. But his lack of experience had caused the enterprise to end in complete failure, his house and land were mortgaged, and about a month before we visited him his creditors had come and carried off all the furniture of any value." Kozaki found Janes living alone with his "twelve or thirteen year old son." His wife was teaching school in "Stockton" [actually San Jose]; "his two grown sons were now engaged in business, and the two grown daughters were married," Kozaki noted, "they were all living independently of him and none of them would see to the relieving of their aged father." All this Janes deplored to Kozaki "as one of the evils consequent to the materialistic civilization of America."

Kozaki's description of his encounter with the elderly Janes continued: "Our visit delighted him beyond measure," he wrote, "and he entertained us in every possible way. As Wrights is a famous grape producing place the table was loaded with the finest specimens of the fruit; as he was a poultry raiser there was an abundance of chickens and eggs; and he had bread and cakes specially baked for us by a neighbor's wife. The whole dinner was eloquent of his kindly feeling for us. At his invitation we spent the night with him; but we later heard that he gave us his own bed, slept himself in his son's bed and put his son on the floor."

"He spoke of his career since we had last seen him," Kozaki wrote, "and asked after the Kumamoto boys in detail inquiring what each one had been doing since and was doing now; and then he unreservedly told us his own ideas and views. According to him Western civilization has now reached an impasse and we are about to see a great change. It was extremely pleasing to us to hear him find fault with the materialism of the West for its evil consequences, and to have him say that hereafter the East should be the leader of the world in cultural advance, with Japan in particular at the head; and that even in religion that of the West was decadent and it should be the part of the Japanese Christians to reclaim the world to true life and to be the leader in this also. Thus did he urge us on."

Commenting on the Captain's loneliness and isolation, Kozaki observed that, "as it was his way to cite the evils of his own country and criticise it adversely, his neighbors treated him as an eccentric. He was living a lonely life with no friends at all with the exception of a Chinese and a Japanese both employed in a vineyard near by and the pastor of the village church."

About to leave the following morning, Kozaki asked Janes if there was anything he could do for him. The Captain mentioned that he had a financial obligation of seven hundred dollars that he had to meet immediately and asked him if there was any way of helping him with it. Kozaki agreed to try. Returning to San Francisco he went to the Golden Gate Bank, took out a loan for seven hundred dollars, and remitted the sum to Janes at Wrights.[14] Upon his return to Japan he contacted the former students of the Yōgakkō and raised over fourteen hundred yen to repay the loan.

Despite its obvious lack of accuracy in reference to what the band knew, and the failure or neglect that could have been charged to it as well as to the Captain's children, it must be added that the portrait of Janes that Kozaki created was one that resonated with deep emotion for many Japanese. The failed hero, or to be more precise the heroic figure whose uncompromising commitment to an ideal refuses to bend even at the cost of personal destruction, constituted the ultimate Japanese heroic type.[15] The Captain as a "noble failure," deserted by friends and family, even by his wife, living in abject poverty, ill, lonely, and frail, but unceasingly committed to his ideals and his vision, confirmed to Kozaki and the other members of the band that they had not erred in following him with their lives.

Kozaki's description of the late Janes is for the most part accurate. Having failed in his construction efforts in Los Gatos in 1903, he had no choice but to move. Wrights, or to be more exact Wrights Station, was located at the eastern end of a railroad tunnel that ran through the coastal mountains as part of a rail network connecting San Jose with the seaside resort of Santa Cruz.[16] Little more than a village, the setting was extremely rustic, and Janes had quite literally become a mountain hermit living in the most austere circumstances. But he was not quite as deserted and friendless as Kozaki suggested, nor had his wife left him.[17] A fully qualified school teacher with a degree from the University of Michigan, Flora decided to supplement the family's meager income, which stemmed largely from the Captain's Civil War pension, with a teaching position in San Jose.[18]

Living in the hills west of Los Gatos Janes continued to occupy himself with his writing. But if Kozaki pictured him as highly critical of the West and hopeful for Japan, as in a religious sense he was, his writings for these years also suggest that he had been deeply disappointed by the band's failure to invite him back to Japan. Feeling rejected by the country to which he had devoted so much of his life, and the young men for whom he had held such high hopes, Janes gave in to his natural inclination to counter rejection with rejection. This mood expressed itself in the increasingly harsh tones with which he painted aspects of the Japanese tradition he had earlier treated with generosity and praise. As revisions of his "Kumamoto" manuscript reveal only too clearly, the positive attraction to Japan and the Japanese people that had been so much a part of his Higo experiences and that permeated his letters from Kumamoto now became clouded with partially veiled invectives directed against Japanese pride, arrogance, race hatred, and a failure to live up to his expectations.[19] What in the 1890s had been disappointment with the course of the Meiji Restoration now became far more personalized. In fact, as his daughter Iris has suggested, Janes' final years involved a good deal of ambivalence toward Japan, an attitude which shaped her own perceptions of Japan and the Japanese.[20] While his conversations with Kozaki, and later with Ebina, tended to restore his positive mood and his high expectations for Japan as a leader of "world civilization," there were also darker moments that found their way into his writings.

This is not to say that the Captain became preoccupied with the personal dimension to a degree that precluded all objectivity. There were still lucid moments, and occasionally brilliant insights. In his article "The Yellow Man as a Pioneer of Modern Civilization," Janes not only praised the accomplishments of Asia, particularly Chinese inventiveness and the pace of Japanese modernization, but raised the issue of future American relations with the Far East.

As he pictured it, the ultimate question facing America and Americans in the twentieth century was what attitude to adopt toward the people of Asia: "Is it to be one of peace and the promotion of good-will and progress? Or is it to be patterned on the policies of European states—policies inaugurated under far less happy auspices and at a far lower stage of civilization?"[21]

"Personally, after four crossings of the Pacific and residence in Asia for over a dozen years," he wrote, "the present writer has no fears or doubts of the outcome. Spite of all opposition, spite of European jealousies and intrigue, spite of temporary misunderstandings and momentary lapses from the high plane of mutual respect and forbearance, the relations of America with Mongolian regions and peoples of Asia are destined to maintain a uniform course of peaceful and equitable intercourse. If these relations develop eventually into those of mutual defense and an attitude of positive and forceful resistance to the greed and aggressions of Powers that are in no position to render either a material or moral equivalent for the treasures of Eastern Asia, so much the better." As Janes saw it, "that would only be the transfer of America's Trans-Atlantic policies of principle and of armed resistance, and their application to the same Powers approaching us from the West."[22]

"Happy will it be for us," he wrote, "if, in the course of such coming struggles, we gain and maintain forever the respect, the confidence, and the heroic championship of our friends of the Yellow Race. The sky is relatively clear now. But when the storm of the coming conflict bursts upon us, the inevitable conflict between the grinding, petty States-system of Europe with its inky record of repression, human slaughter and suffering on the one side, and the growing forces of liberty, enlightenment, and justice on the other, America ought to find the millions of Mongolian Asia most effective and powerful allies."[23]

As the foregoing suggests, Janes could still champion the cause of Japan and Asia. And from our present perspective in the latter decades of the twentieth century, at least half of his prophecy has become a reality. Moreover, it can be argued that it was the Captain and others like him, who as carriers of the American ethos of "liberty, enlightenment, and justice"—the nineteenth-century messianic vision of American teachers and missionaries of Janes' type—who in their unsung, and sometimes unappreciated, ways were to lay the groundwork for the later relationship.

Indeed Janes could, and did, remain critical of both sides. Nor did age make him any less peppery. Trying to find a publisher for his main manuscripts on Japan, "Kumamoto," "Koseki," and "Hearts and Swords," he corresponded with various publishers. In response to a refusal notice from the United Literary Press, he fired off the following barb to its editor questioning the ability of his readers: "A long-eared 'Reader' whose brain would be blighted, crushed, by a really new thought if it ever found its way there, doesn't know what to make of a manuscript in which from the beginning to end there is neither a grammatical error for him to chuckle over nor a mispelled word. It takes a fool publisher to *expect* such a donkey to rise to the height of a work that has held a capable and well informed brain a year, two years, or longer, to elaborate upon a main central line of original research and thought."[24]

The Captain added that he regarded the prevalent American work published on Japan as superficial; that it emphasized "prettiness, courtesies, and toys," or "the need to mystify in order to be interesting."[25] Later he told Ebina that reading Lafcadio Hearn was like seeing Japan through "a veiled mist."[26] He argued that most Japanese had become offended by such interpretations of their country and culture. Moreover, this kind of misunderstanding could lead to miscalculations on the part of other nations who had to deal with expanding Japanese military power in a realistic manner. Such misunderstandings, he insisted, had decidedly worked to Japan's advantage in the Russo-Japanese War. The United States should not make the same mistake, he warned. "America, miseducated, will wake up one of these fine days and have on her hands the conflict of her existence, by reason of this very misleading twaddle *about* Japan." "I am telling you only what I know. The patronizing condescension on the one hand, and the vindictive attitude of exclusionists of this coast on the other," he added, ". . . are fast changing the feelings of millions across the Pacific towards us as a nation." A misunderstood Japan, he cautioned, could readily be transformed into an enemy on both sides of the Pacific. "As a patriot," he finished, "I wish 'Hearts and Swords' could be published in America and soon. If I were not reduced to my last cent, it would be. When I am dead it will be, and 'Koseki' the first manuscript I sent you, and 'Kumamoto' also."[27]

While the Captain had not abandoned his interest in Japan or the Japanese, many of his late writings were more privately oriented. Like those of any individual sensing his mortality, these writings were primarily concerned with his personal and spiritual odyssey. The upper

layers of his trunk became filled with thinly veiled and partially fictionalized accounts of his early years.[28] While useful in dealing with his youth
and childhood development, most are hopelessly marred by lengthy didactic sections. If anything, these works suggest, as Kozaki observed,
that he now possessed few friends willing to listen to his discourses and
consoled himself by putting his ideas on paper. Running through much
of this work is a deep sense of loneliness and isolation. Sometimes, as in
the case of "Out of Stony Lonesome," the Captain's mood even found
expression in his titles.

With the shadow of loneliness never far from his door, by 1907 and
1908 the Captain's major struggles no longer involved the Church, the
Japanese, or prospective publishers, but his rapidly deteriorating health.
In 1906 Janes' physician, F. W. Knowles, had observed: "Captain Janes
is aging very rapidly, which is very apparent to those who knew him
even four years ago." Continuing to suffer from his life-long headaches,
neuralgia, and bronchitis, he was now troubled by dizzy spells and a
serious heart condition.[29] By 1908 his deteriorating health forced him to
move from Wrights to San Jose, where he lived in a small house with
Flora and the children.

About the Captain's last years in San Jose we know relatively little,
other than the fact that his declining health and continuing poverty were
causes of constant concern and anxiety for the entire family. Visits by
his former students provided a few final insights. In June 1908 Ebina
Danjō, who was on his way to the World Congress of Congregationalists
in Edinburgh, stopped off in San Jose. Not having seen the Captain since
his departure from Japan in 1899, he looked forward to meeting him
again and spending an afternoon chatting with his former teacher. Kozaki's 1905 visit had alerted the band to Janes physical and financial
plight. In fact, Ebina and others had heard further rumors regarding the
Captain's declining health and poverty and had determined to do what
they could to help. Once again raising a subscription on behalf of their
former teacher, Ebina brought with him a substantial monetary gift that
had been donated by Kozaki, Miyagawa, Tokutomi, Ukita, Harada, and
several of the other Yōgakkō graduates.[30]

Increasingly excited by the prospects of seeing the Captain, he had
trouble sleeping the night before, and he could not bring himself to
concentrate on the English lecture he was preparing for the following
day.[31]

Chiba Toyoji, a Japanese newspaperman who accompanied Ebina to
the Captain's home on the afternoon of June 8, wrote of the experience
as follows:

It was after five in the afternoon when we reached San Jose that day. Mr. Hayashi, the head of the branch office of the Nichibei Newspaper, and the local secretary of the Japanese Association came to meet us at the station and provided us with a horsedrawn carriage in which we passed through the heavily shaded suburbs of the city. Leaving the city streets behind we drove eastward through open fields until we finally reached a clump of small houses. Captain Janes' house stood at the northwest corner of this group. While a solid structure, it was basically utilitarian and devoid of all ornamentation, with a low roof and an unraised floor. Only the windmill behind the house provided a slight artistic accent.

Taking in the scene, Ebina's only comment was "So this is the place."[32]

Approaching the house, Chiba tells us, "Hayashi knocked on the door, and after a while the portly figure of the Captain appeared. Seeing Ebina, he exclaimed 'Oh! Ebina it's you!' and rushed out of the house, firmly took him by the hand, and repeated several times 'How do you do! How do you do!' Ebina stood there for a while in silence stating only that he was 'Fine!' Firmly grasping each other's hand," Chiba observed, "the two said little in words, but much was communicated by their eyes."[33]

Ebina later recorded his own feelings. The house in which he found Janes, he noted was "extremely wretched and shabby," as were the Captain's clothes, which were those of "a common workman." Physically he had seriously aged, and "his health troubled him in various ways," he wrote, "he had difficulty even in walking," and the "whole scene made one want to weep."[34]

But as Ebina observed, no sooner had Janes shaken hands with his former student, than his appearance became animated and his face beamed with enthusiasm. He stood up and started to speak with full vigor like the Captain of old. Telling Ebina of his experiences since returning to the United States, he spoke of his sad and lonely life, and the joy he had experienced in meeting Kozaki in 1905. Then changing the topic he inquired after each of the "boys." "What is Tokutomi doing? What is Ukita up to? How about Miyagawa? Harada? And the others?"[35] Ebina, who found it difficult to break his own melancholy mood, thought of the strange irony that he was in the presence of a man who should have returned to his homeland a "victorious general," but who instead found himself in the lower depths of poverty, broken in health, devoid of friends, and deserted even by members of his own family.[36]

To shift the conversation in a happier direction Ebina told Janes that he had started preaching in English. "Oh my Boy Ebina, You have done well!," the Captain replied. Once more enthusiastic he reiterated the arguments he had presented to Kozaki in 1905, that American culture and civilization like that of the West as a whole was on the decline, that the cultural leadership of the world was shifting and that hereafter the Japanese should play a central role in the spiritual development of the world. Finally he told Ebina that he felt eternally grateful to Japan for allowing his "boyhood dream" to become a "manhood reality" during his years of service in Kumamoto.[37]

In the autumn of 1908, returning from Edinburgh, Ebina visited the Captain once more. This time he brought with him a photographer to make a commemorative photograph for the band. The portrait that resulted shows the seventy-one year old Janes, dressed in a pair of overalls sitting in a heavy wooden chair in the center of his living room. To his left we find the bearded Ebina wearing his overcoat, and on his right his ten-year-old daughter, Iris, to whom he later entrusted his manuscripts. Standing behind him is his wife Flora. Captured on film with his ever-piercing eyes and pursed lips, the Captain looks surprisingly vigorous. Indeed, Ebina recalled that the day ended with the Captain more concerned about the health of his foreign guest than with his own condition: warning him at the time of his departure to be sure to bundle up in his overcoat, as the California night could be deceptively cold and inimical to health.[38]

And yet, whatever signs of well being Janes' portrait may have conveyed, it indicated once more that surface appearances were largely deceptive. By the end of 1908 the Captain's physical condition took a decided turn for the worse. And on March 12, 1909, Janes' heart disease and chronic bronchitis necessitated his hospitalization at the Garden City Sanitarium in San Jose. Two weeks later, on March 27, on his seventy-second birthday, the Captain passed away of heart failure and old age.[39] Shortly afterward, in keeping with his final wishes, Flora and the children scattered his ashes among the trees at Wrights.[40]

Word of Janes' death seems to have been slow in reaching Japan. As a result the final scene involving the band and the Captain occurred in the summer of 1909. In July Miyagawa Tsuneteru, who had not seen Janes in a decade, was dispatched to the West Coast to preach to the Japanese communities of Washington, Oregon, and California, as Ebina had done the previous year. Looking forward to a reunion with the Captain he had set aside August 11 for a visit to his house. Arriving as the others had with a strong sense of nostalgia as well as a genuine concern, he knocked at the door of the Janes home only to be told by Flora that the Captain had died five months earlier. The fact that such a long period of time had passed without any of the members of the band knowing of their old teacher's death struck Miyagawa with overwhelming feelings of sadness and tragedy. Returning to his hotel he could not stop his tears. Faced with supper he could not eat. And finally, incapable of controlling his emotions, he was forced to cancel the lecture he was scheduled to give in San Jose that night.[41]

To Miyagawa, Ebina, and many of the Captain's former Yōgakkō students Janes' death, deserted and alone, unheralded and unmourned, buried in an unmarked grave, represented the final tragic end of a man who had once brilliantly "out samurai'd the samurai" and played such an important role in their personal growth and national development. But the very tragedy of his final years also allowed the Captain, this "American samurai," to transcend Japanese-American cultural barriers and permitted a very ordinary man to enter the sacred realm of Japan's tragic heroes, whose noble struggles against the world around them and against themselves contained not only the seeds of their inevitable demise, but the sources of their veneration.

IN LOOKING BACK over Janes' life and his involvement with Japan one is struck by the way in which an important historic era suited the personality of a particular individual. Moreover, it seems remarkable that the same personality operating in one cultural context could be doomed so distinctly to failure, only to arise phoenix-like in another to greatness.

Many of Janes' accomplishments in Kumamoto in the 1870s were the result of his domineering, demanding, and aggressive personality, which combined the polarities of the extreme disciplinarian with those of the religious enthusiast. Much of Janes' life, as we have seen, involved an on-going inner struggle between the cool rationalism of his father and the emotionalism of his mother, the twin legacies which he felt he had inherited, and which he desperately sought to integrate to constructive ends.

If Oregon illustrated the self-destructive potential of his dual self, Kumamoto revealed its latent dynamic for greatness. As Janes later noted, Japan in the 1870s provided what much of his early life had lacked—a sphere of joyous usefulness in which his talents were exploited to the fullest, and in which the obvious needs of those around him elicited an enthusiastic desire to serve. In a religious sense Kumamoto was part of a redemptive process that allowed him to transcend his earlier failures, his personality problems, and what he saw as his wasted youth. Consequently, as he told Ebina, his "childhood dream" had indeed become a "manhood reality."

For Janes, Kumamoto confirmed what he wrote in one of his fictionalized autobiographical accounts: that "simple goodness often displaces the reproach of intellectual, physical and even of formally moral—inferiority." While Janes' personality played a dominant role in his accomplishments in Japan, the environment was equally responsible for his achievements. Kumamoto, and Japan as a whole, were unusually receptive to foreign stimuli in the 1870s. As the voice of the West and the embodiment of what was regarded a superior civilization Janes was expected to innovate, to lead, and to transform. As the region's main Western representative he was expected to transmit the secrets of Western wealth and power to his young proteges. That he did so in a manner which not only opened their eyes to the importance of the West, but at the same time broadened their belief in the value and significance of their own cultural tradition, has to be underscored as one of the marks of his unusual ability to lead and teach in the Japanese setting.

Although environment and personality suited each other, it is equally important to point out that timing was also crucial to the Captain's success in Japan. The Christian as radical reformer, the theory of action which he exploited so successfully in Kumamoto, had been far less effective in Maryland a few years earlier, nor was it to retain the same appeal two decades later in Kyoto. The unleashing of the Captain's peculiar dynamism in the 1870s was therefore not merely the result of his personality, and his Christian convictions, but a fortuitous stroke of timing that combined an unusual release of pent-up energies in the private sphere with a marked public receptivity.

Given such circumstances it may be best to attribute Janes' accomplishments in Kumamoto to an auspicious blending of personality, environment, and timing. Moreover the manner in which these elements were blended argues for uniqueness, and does not readily allow us to extend his experiences to others. The Captain's colorful personality and experiences set him off from a majority of his fellow foreign employees—after all how many American samurai were there in Meiji Japan complete with their own retainer bands? Yet it must also be emphasized that Janes shared a great deal with other American teachers and missionaries who went to the Far East in the late nineteenth century.

As his work in Kumamoto underscored, he was filled with the revolutionary fervor of post–Civil War American Protestantism. Propelled by the ideas of America's "manifest destiny," proponents of this brand of Christianity hoped to export not only the Gospel but the political and social ideals of the American Revolution to the farthest reaches of the globe. Janes was fully convinced that his task in Japan was not only to transform men in the classical Christian sense, but to transform the society around him. The Meiji Restoration, as he directed it in Kumamoto—and he quite literally saw himself in this role—was designed to lead to the achievement of these ideals. Social and political equality, an educated and enlightened citizenry, a government for and by the people, and a general lifting up of the common man's lot through the economic transformation of the country were the dominant ideals he tried to instill in his students at the Yōgakkō and in the broader Kumamoto community.

In this he was hardly alone. Many of his fellow American teachers and missionaries shared similar ideals. But here it may be important to add that one reason for Janes' success—a reason he may well have shared with other Americans of his generation—was that he could serve as a direct link between the American transformation of the 1820s and 1830s in which his father and grandfather had participated, and the economic transformation the Japanese hoped to achieve in the 1870s. In short, idealism was backed with practical experience. For Janes, Christian reform called for the pick, tile, cement, and clean water; it moreover implied these not in some abstract Sunday sense that enjoined others to do the work, but in a manner that required daily personal implementation.

While there were high hopes in the 1870s, these were matched by serious dissatisfactions in the 1890s. Somehow, as he scratched out in his revised copy of *Kumamoto*, Japan no longer seemed interested in following "America's liberal spirit," and like the good ship *America* that had brought him to Japan in 1871, the revolutionary ideals he had tried to instill and implement were little more than a beached wreck, burned out and gutted to the waterline.

And yet, if Janes was disappointed that the Revolution had not come to Japan as he had intended it, and that disappointment resulted in notes of bitterness, his disappointment and bitterness were those of the totalist who had dared to imagine that one man, a foreigner and outsider, could play a significant role in the transformation of another society. In this dream he had much in common with the missionaries he despised, and like them he saw change in "all-or-nothing" terms. In this dream, it must be added, he was a carrier of the American messianic vision that played such an important role in sending American missionaries and teachers around the world in the nineteenth and twentieth centuries, and which all too often has remained equally totalistic in its views and goals.

But change in any society is rarely totalistic. While Janes saw himself displaced, his ideas discarded, and his vision for Japan abandoned, much of the Captain's influence lived on. It lived on in the lives and thought of the men he had taught in Kumamoto. It did so, moreover, not always in its purely American, or Janesian, form, but blended with elements of the Japanese tradition. What Janes left behind was not the obvious and external, the categories by which he judged his own failure, but the more subtle processes and methods he had worked so hard to instill in his young wards: a fearless quest for truth, a belief in the scientific method, a sense of self-respect and independence, a belief in the worth of the common man, and above all the conviction that service to the community was man's highest calling. Judged from such a perspective the years confirmed his accomplishments, not his failures. Though the Captain himself suffered at times under the critical evaluation of the boys who had turned into men, the fact that they had grown strong enough to see him realistically and were prepared to subject even their teacher and "father" to critical analysis served as the ultimate confirmation that the revolution he had initiated in Kumamoto had not been wasted but had borne its own fruit in due season.

As the founder of one of the major streams of modern Japanese Christianity, Janes holds an important place in the intellectual and religious history of the Meiji period. But the significance of his years in Japan transcended his intellectual and religious contributions.

Janes demonstrated the degree to which the American teacher and Christian reformer served as a carrier of American culture. Moreover, that culture, propelled by its Christian claims to universal validity, constantly rubbed at the Kumamoto environment, hoping to transform it in the American image.

But this rubbing process could not have taken place in a vacuum. Without the Practical Learning tradition as an intellectual bridge across which the members of the Kumamoto Band could move to a new conception of the world and their society, the Captain's efforts would have ended in failure. On the other hand, without Janes' Christian reformism, Kumamoto's Practical Learning tradition might well have died on the streets of Kyoto with its leading spokesman. For Japanese who have seen in Yokoi Shōnan and his ideas a native tradition with democratic potential, the melding of Janes' reform ideals with those of the Higo sage were to give Kumamoto Christianity a significance that went far beyond the confines of the church.

· NOTES ·

INTRODUCTION

1. Sidney L. Gulick, *Evolution of the Japanese* (New York: Fleming H. Revell, 1903), p. 91.

CHAPTER I
BOYHOOD IN THE OHIO HILLS

1. For a discussion of the *Morrison* expedition see Harry Emerson Wildes, *Aliens in the East* (Philadelphia: University of Pennsylvania Press, 1937), pp. 197–210.
2. Frederic Janes, *The Janes Family* (New York: John H. Dingman, 1868), p. 32.
3. Elisha Janes' birth date is from ibid., p. 185. The biographical details are from *The History of Tuscarawas County, Ohio* (Chicago: Warner, Beers, 1884), p. 707. Also *Combination Atlas Map of Tuscarawas County, Ohio* (Philadelphia: L. H. Everts, 1875), entry under "Colonel Elisha Janes," unpaginated.
4. *History of Tuscarawas County, Ohio*, p. 370, gives the following population statistics for New Philadelphia: 1820, 236; 1840, 531; 1850, 1,414; 1860, 2,360; 1870, 3,142; 1880, 3,070.
5. *History of Tuscarawas County, Ohio*, p. 467. New Philadelphia was originally settled by pioneers from the Susquehanna valley in Pennsylvania. Chief among these was John Knisely. Knisely came to New Philadelphia in 1804, the year after Ohio's admission to the Union. Gabriel Cryder arrived in 1808. A brief history of New Philadelphia is also included in *Guide to Tuscarawas County* (New Philadelphia, Ohio: New Philadelphia Chamber of Commerce, 1939), pp. 57ff.
6. Princeton University Library, Janes Papers, no. 405, "Ruth," unnumbered mss. Hereafter these papers will be cited as Janes Papers.
7. Ibid.
8. *History of Tuscarawas County, Ohio*, p. 707.
9. A description of Cryder's arrival is contained in ibid., p. 468. He is listed as county commissioner (p. 365) and county treasurer (p. 366).
10. Information on the grist mill is contained in ibid., p. 346. Cryder's pioneering role in "still house" construction is discussed in C. H. Mitchner, ed., *Historic Events in the Tuscarawas and Muskingum Valleys* (Dayton: Thomas W. Odell, 1876), p. 303.
11. Janes Papers, no. 405, "Ruth," unnumbered mss.
12. Ibid.
13. The history of agriculture in Tuscarawas County is discussed in *Guide to Tuscarawas County*, pp. 17ff.
14. Janes Papers, no. 405, "Ruth," unnumbered mss.
15. *History of Tuscarawas County, Ohio*, p. 707.

16. Ibid.

17. Janes' father owned not only farm land, but a portion of New Philadelphia itself. In 1857 the "Elisha Janes Addition" was made to the town consisting of "three out lots and sixteen lots, twelve on East Front and four on an extension of High Street, now East Avenue." Ibid., p. 473. The Janes property can also be located on the map of New Philadelphia contained in *Combination Atlas Map of Tuscarawas County, Ohio*, p. 51. To the present day, Janes Hill remains one of the topographical landmarks of the town.

18. The rank of colonel came from Elisha Janes' service in the Ohio state militia. See biographical account of "Colonel Elisha Janes" in *Combination Atlas Map of Tuscarawas County, Ohio*.

19. *History of Tuscarawas County, Ohio*, p. 366.

20. Ibid., pp. 477–78.

21. Ibid., p. 403.

22. Ibid., p. 395.

23. "Colonel Elisha Janes," in *Combination Atlas Map of Tuscarawas County, Ohio*.

24. The description of the Janes home is a composite of features described in his autobiographical notes "Boyhood of an Ohio Boy," "Boyhood in Ohio," and "Boyhood in the Ohio Hills," Janes Papers, nos. 307–8; and "Ruth," Janes Papers, no. 405.

25. Janes Papers, no. 307, "Boyhood in Ohio," unnumbered mss.

26. Janes Papers, no. 405, "Ruth," unnumbered mss.

27. Janes Papers, no. 306, "Kumamoto, An Episode in Japan's Break from Feudalism," ch. 1, p. 8. The manuscript bears the opening note: "This may be useful in writing up the Ohio Boy." This chapter contains a good deal of autobiographical material that does not appear in later drafts of the Kumamoto manuscript. Hereafter cited as "Kumamoto."

28. Ibid., p. 9.

29. Ibid., p. 8.

30. Ibid., p. 13.

31. Ibid., pp. 13–14.

32. The dates of births and deaths are taken from a list dated July 24, 1854. The list was apparently written by one of Leroy's sisters at the time of Martha's death. A copy of this list is in the possession of the author. See also Frederic Janes, *The Janes Family*, p. 305.

33. Janes Papers, no. 306, "Kumamoto," ch. 1, p. 9.

34. Ibid., p. 10.

35. Ibid., p. 9.

36. Capt. L. L. Janes, *Kumamoto: An Episode in Japan's Break from Feudalism* (Kyoto: Dōshisha University Shashi Shiryō Henshū Sho, 1970), part 2, p. 56. This book was published in a limited edition of 100 copies. Originally appearing in three parts in the Shashi Shiryō Henshū Sho's periodical, *Shiryō ihō*, and later bound into a single volume, its pagination is inconsistent. Parts 1 and 2 are numbered consecutively pp. 1–130; part 3 is numbered pp. 1–110. I have

divided the book into two parts according to its pagination—part 1, pp. 1–130; part 2, pp. 1–110. Hereafer cited as Janes, *Kumamoto*. Janes' mother's rejection of a theology that could allow her dead child to be eternally lost is also discussed in "A Story of the Ohio Hills," Janes Papers, no. 308; "Notes for Boyhood in Ohio," Janes Papers, no. 307; and in several letters, including two to his mother dated June 2 and June 13, 1876, Janes Papers, nos. 102 and 103.

37. Letter from Janes to the "Members of the Kumamoto Band," New Philadelphia, Ohio, July 13, 1885. Published in Dōshisha University's Shashi Shiryō Henshū Sho, *Shiryō ihō* 1 (March 1968), pp. 98–103.

38. Janes Papers, no. 406, "Out of Stony Lonesome," unnumbered mss.

39. Ibid.

40. Ibid.

41. Janes Papers, no. 307, "Boyhood of an Ohio Boy," p. 30. Also "Notes for Boyhood in Ohio," same item no., unnumbered mss.

42. Janes Papers, no. 306, "Kumamoto," ch. 1, p. 14.

43. Janes, *Kumamoto*, part 2, pp. 57–58.

44. Ibid. Janes' description of a "camp meeting" is echoed in *Guide to Tuscarawas County*, p. 41.

45. Letter from Janes to the "Members of the Kumamoto Band," New Philadelphia, Ohio, July 13, 1885. On this occasion Janes wrote his former students: "A strange joy seizes me! A sense of companionship I have felt before—in Oregon, in California, in Eastern America, in Japan—you know it." A further exploration of what these "joys" meant to him will have to be deferred to a later chapter. George E. Moore, in his article, "Samurai Conversions: The Case of Kumamoto," *Asian Studies* (University of the Philippines) 4, 1 (April 1966), pp. 40–48, pointed out some time ago that Janes' environment in New Philadelphia combined the "rational puritanism of Presbyterians" with the "anti-intellectual" and "highly emotional" revivalism of "frontier religion." Moore's observation is certainly correct, and the availability of the Janes papers now allows us to trace the effects of both forces on his development with greater accuracy and detail.

46. Janes, *Kumamoto*, part 2, p. 57. As we shall see, Janes' youth was not as closely identified with the temperance movement as he would like to have us believe.

47. *Guide to Tuscarawas County*, p. 35.

48. Janes Papers, no. 307, "Boyhood of an Ohio Boy," p. 30.

49. Ibid.

50. Fukunaga Bunnosuke, comp., *Nihon ni okeru taii Jiensu shi* [Captain Janes and his work in Japan] (Tokyo, 1894), p. 76. This book contains a number of articles about Janes written by his Japanese students which were first published in the journal *Kyūshū bungaku* in 1893.

51. Janes Papers, no. 307, "Boyhood of an Ohio Boy," p. 30.

52. Ibid.

53. Janes Papers, no. 307, "Notes for Boyhood in Ohio," unnumbered mss.

54. For a brief account of the career of the Rev. Joseph Gordon see Andrew E. Murray, *Presbyterians and the Negro—A History* (Philadelphia: Presbyterian Historial Society, 1966), pp. 121ff. A more complete review of his life and writings is contained in *The Life and Writings of the Rev. Joseph Gordon, Compiled by a Committee of the Free Presbyterian Synod* (Cincinnati, Ohio: Published for the Free Presbyterian Synod, 1860). One of the members of the committee designated to compose the biography was Thomas M. Finney. Finney and Gordon had been classmates at Washington College in Washington, Pennsylvania. Both men had become abolitionists while studying at the college. Upon graduation from seminary, Finney came to New Philadelphia in 1844 to serve as the first pastor by ordination of the new Presbyterian Church, which Janes' father and several other laymen had established. Later the same year he invited the twenty-four-year-old Gordon to join him in New Philadelphia. Finney and Gordon teamed up to run the New Philadelphia Male Academy. After a year Gordon left to take a pastorate elsewhere. Finney remained in New Philadelphia until 1849. In 1847 Gordon was called to the pastorate of the New Athens Presbyterian Church. From 1850 to 1857 he published the *Free Presbyterian*, the chief voice of the abolitionist group that split from the Old School after 1847. Elisha Janes, Thomas M. Finney, and Joseph Gordon were close associates not only in the abolitionist movement but in the church schism. Gordon died in 1858 at the age of thirty-eight. Finney died in 1859.

55. The position of Free Presbyterians such as Finney, Gordon, and Janes' father is discussed in Murray, *Presbyterians and the Negro*, pp. 120–21; that of Elisha Janes in Janes Papers, no. 306, "Kumamoto," ch. 1, pp. 14–18.

56. Murray, *Presbyterians and the Negro*, p. 120. Also Janes Papers, no. 306, "Kumamoto," ch. 1, p. 16.

57. The above and following portions are quoted from Janes Papers, no. 306, "Kumamoto," ch. 1, pp. 14–18.

58. Erik H. Erikson, *Childhood and Society* (New York: W. W. Norton, 1963).

59. Janes Papers, no. 306, "Kumamoto," ch. 1, p. 14.

60. Janes Papers, no. 307, "Boyhood of an Ohio Boy," p. 30.

61. Ibid., pp. 30–31.

62. Janes Papers, no. 307, "Notes for Boyhood in Ohio," unnumbered mss.

63. Ibid.

64. Ibid.

65. *History of Tuscarawas County, Ohio*, p. 370.

66. John Armor Bingham moved to New Philadelphia in 1840 and became a leading member of the Tuscarawas Bar. After serving as district attorney of Tuscarawas County from 1846 to 1849, he returned to practice law in Cadiz, Ohio, and became active as a stump speaker in the Harrison "log cabin, hard cider" campaign. In 1854 he was elected as a Republican to Congress, where he served, with one brief interruption, until 1873. A prominent orator, Bingham played a leading role in several important events of the period, including the trial of Lincoln's assassins and the impeachment of Andrew Johnson, at which he served as one of the managers. As a legislator he was responsible for drafting

a portion of the Fourteenth Amendment. In 1873 Bingham was appointed minister to Japan, and he served in that position until 1885. His early years in Japan were to overlap with those Janes spent in Kumamoto. For biographical details see the *Dictionary of American Biography* (New York: Charles Scribner's Sons, 1964), vol. I, pp. 277–78. Also *Biographical Directory of the American Congress, 1774–1971* (Washington, D.C.: G.P.O., 1971), p. 593.

67. For details regarding William Robinson Sapp see *Biographical Directory of the American Congress, 1774–1971*, p. 1655. Sapp, like Janes' father, was a member of the Whig Party. He was elected to Congress from Ohio's 15th Congressional District in 1852 and served until March 1857.

68. *History of Tuscarawas County, Ohio*, p. 475.

69. Janes Papers, no. 307, "Notes for Boyhood in Ohio," unnumbered mss. Also *History of Tuscarawas County, Ohio*, p. 475.

70. Janes Papers, no. 307, "A Boy's Life in the Ohio Hills 60 Years Ago," unnumbered mss.

71. His mother's attraction to Wordsworth's "Ode" ("Intimations of Immortality from Recollections of Early Childhood") is discussed at some length in Janes Papers, no. 308, "A Story of the Ohio Hills," pp. 28f. In this somewhat fictionalized version of his early years Janes has his hero, who is no mere captain but a General Wade, state: "My mother declared to me many a time, but more as if speaking to her own mind and heart, that Wordsworth had put more of the truth of human origin and destiny in that one poem, than St. Paul ever dreamed of. . . ."

72. Janes Papers, no. 307, "Notes for Boyhood in Ohio," unnumbered mss.

73. Information on the Albany Manual Labor Academy is taken from *The Life and Writings of the Rev. Joseph Gordon*, p. 40.

74. "Mission of the Free Presbyterian Church," in ibid., p. 56. The following quotations are from "Religion and Reform," in ibid., p. 51.

75. Wilbur H. Siebert, "The Underground Railroad in Ohio," in the *Ohio Archeological and Historical Society Publications* (Ohio, 1895), vol. 4, p. 61.

76. Janes Papers, no. 307, "Notes for Boyhood in Ohio," unnumbered mss.

77. *The Life and Writings of the Rev. Joseph Gordon*, p. 14. Gordon was appointed professor of mathematics at Franklin College in 1845.

78. Quotes from "War," in ibid., p. 137.

79. Ibid., p. 138.

80. Janes Papers, no. 307, "Notes for Boyhood in Ohio," unnumbered mss. In a letter from Janes to Dr. N. G. Clark, Saint Denis, Maryland, January 7, 1878, Janes describes Bingham as "the American Minister, a former townsman of mine, the friend of my father, and partner of my instructor in law." See ABCFM, Mission to Japan, vol. 4.

81. Janes Papers, no. 307, "Notes for Boyhood in Ohio," unnumbered mss.

82. Ibid.

83. Letter from William R. Sapp to Col. Joseph G. Totten, February 13, 1856, in the United States Military Academy Archives, West Point, New York.

84. Letter of acceptance from Janes to The Hon. Jefferson Davis, Secretary of War, April 3, 1856, United States Military Academy Archives.

CHAPTER II
LIFE AT WEST POINT

1. Leroy Lansing Janes, "Alphabetic Card," United States Military Academy Archives, West Point, New York.
2. For my discussion of West Point I have relied heavily on Stephen E. Ambrose, *Duty, Honor, Country, A History of West Point* (Baltimore: The John Hopkins Press, 1966); Joseph Pearson Farley, *West Point in the Early Sixties* (Troy, N.Y.: Pafraets Book Company, 1902); Morris Schaff, *The Spirit of Old West Point, 1858–1862* (Boston and New York: Houghton Mifflin, 1908); and the *Report of the Commission to Examine Into the Organization, System of Discipline, and Course of Instruction of the United States Military Academy at West Point, 1860* (Washington, D.C.: G.P.O., 1881). Ambrose uses the term the "Golden Age" to describe West Point between 1840 and 1860. The quality of West Point's curriculum in science, mathematics, and engineering is discussed by Ambrose, *Duty, Honor, Country*, p. 91.
3. Charles Dickens, *American Notes*, quoted in Ambrose, *Duty, Honor, Country*, unnumbered frontispiece.
4. Ibid., p. 89.
5. The following description of Janes' early cadet experiences is based on his own writings as well as those of Morris Schaff, Joseph Farley, George A. Custer, and Emory Upton. Schaff and Farley are cited above. For Custer I have relied on *The Custer Story, the Life and Intimate Letters of General George A. Custer and His Wife Elizabeth* (New York: Devin-Adair, 1950); Frederick Whittaker, *A Complete Life of General George A. Custer* (New York: Sheldon, 1876); Jay Monaghan, *Custer, the Life of General George Armstrong Custer* (Boston: Little Brown, 1959); and Frazier Hunt, *Custer, the Last of the Cavaliers* (New York: Cosmopolitan Book Corp., 1928). For Upton see Peter S. Michie, *The Life and Letters of Emory Upton* (New York: D. Appleton, 1885).
6. Thayer's role in the establishment of West Point as a major educational institution is discussed in Ambrose, *Duty, Honor, Country*, pp. 62–105.
7. The physical description is from Janes' original application for an "Invalid's Pension" and other affidavits filed in his Veterans Administration Claims File: Janes, Leroy L. XC 2 682 526. Hereafter cited as Veterans Administration Claims File. I am indebted to Mr. Roland A. Martone, Los Angeles District Counsel for the Veterans Administration, for making this file available to me. I first heard of the Janes "Pension File" from Prof. George E. Moore, who kindly provided me with the materials he had received from the National Archives.
8. Morris Schaff, *The Spirit of Old West Point*, p. 68.
9. Jay Monaghan, *Custer*, p. 21.
10. Robert H. Hall, comp., *List of Cadets Admitted Into the United States*

Military Academy, West Point, N.Y., from its Establishment till September 30, 1876, with Tables Exhibiting the Results of the Examinations for Admission, and the Corps to which the Graduates Have Been Promoted (Washington, D.C.: G.P.O., 1876), p. 8.

11. Leroy Lansing Janes, "Alphabetic Card," U.S. Military Academy Archives.

12. Ambrose, *Duty, Honor, Country*, p. 148.

13. Henry A. du Pont to mother, July 14, 1856, quoted in ibid., p. 148.

14. Cullen Bryant to father, June 17, 1860, quoted in ibid., p. 148.

15. The poem entitled "West Point Life" was presented at a meeting of the Dialectical Society in 1859. It was read by Cadet "Jack" Garnett, who was acknowledged to be the best reader in the corps, and was written anonymously by a cadet belonging to the class of 1860. The entire poem, which provides useful insights into cadet life, is included in Farley, *West Point in the Early Sixties*, pp. 181–94.

16. Bryant to father, August 30, 1860, quoted in Ambrose, *Duty, Honor, Country*, p. 159.

17. Ibid., p. 148.

18. Ibid., p. 90.

19. Ibid., p. 131.

20. Bryant to Sweete, May 2, 1860, quoted in ibid., p. 131.

21. Du Pont to mother, October 17, 1857, quoted in ibid., p. 132.

22. Edward Hartz to sister, July 30, 1852, quoted in ibid., p. 131.

23. George Cushing to father, November 28, 1854, quoted in ibid., p. 133.

24. Sidney Forman, *West Point: A History of the United States Military Academy* (New York: Columbia University Press, 1950), p. 86; Ambrose, *Duty, Honor, Country*, p. 133.

25. Jay Monaghan, *Custer*, p. 28.

26. Custer and Janes possessed a certain propensity for dramatic exaggeration. For Custer's account see ibid., p. 29.

27. These are the words of cadet George Cushing to his parents. Ambrose, *Duty, Honor, Country*, p. 133.

28. United States Military Academy, *Official Register of the Officers and Cadets of the U.S. Military Academy* (West Point, N.Y., 1857), p. 13.

29. Janes Papers, no. 307, "Notes for Boyhood in Ohio," unnumbered mss.

30. Leroy Lansing Janes, "Alphabetic Card," U.S. Military Academy Archives.

31. Ambrose, *Duty, Honor, Country*, pp. 156–57.

32. Ibid., p. 156.

33. Ibid., p. 150.

34. United States Military Academy, *Regulations of the U.S. Military Academy at West Point* (New York: J. & J. Harper, 1832), p. 38. Hereafter cited as *Regulations*.

35. United States Military Academy, *Official Register of the Officers and Cadets of the U.S. Military Academy*, p. 13.

36. *Regulations*, p. 21.

37. Emory Upton, in a letter to his sister September 7, 1857, noted: "In your

letter you allude to my demerit . . . you use the term 'bad marks.' *Bad* signifies to you, evil, wrong, immoral, and wicked, which placed before *marks* signifies that I have been doing something wrong or immoral—something which conscience disapproves. That is wrong, not only in the sight of a military man, but of God. Now, what moral wrong is there in 'laughing in ranks,' in being 'late at roll-call,' 'not stepping out at command,' 'not having coat buttoned throughout,' and kindred reports? Now, is that wrong in the sight of God? I say not! But it is wrong only in the sight of a military man, and it is from such reports that I get my demerits or 'bad marks.' " Michie, *Emory Upton*, pp. 13–14.

38. Ambrose, *Duty, Honor, Country*, p. 158.

39. United States Military Academy Archives, "Delinquency Record of Leroy Lansing Janes USMA Class of May 1861." Hereafter cited as "Delinquency Record."

40. United States Military Academy, *Official Register of the Officers and Cadets of the U.S. Military Academy* (West Point, N.Y., 1857, 1858, 1859, 1860, 1861), 1857, p. 13; 1858, p. 11; 1859, p. 11; 1860, p. 10; 1861, p. 10.

41. "Delinquency Record."

42. Ibid.

43. Janes was reported on ten occasions for "tobacco smoke in quarters" or "smoking in camp ground." For these reports he received 40 demerits. "Delinquency Record."

44. *Regulations*, p. 27.

45. Benny Havens' career is discussed in Ambrose, *Duty, Honor, Country*, pp. 163–64. Benny attracted many famous West Pointers, including Jefferson Davis, under whose signature Janes had been appointed to the Academy. Davis was, in fact, among the first group of cadets to be court-martialed for drinking at Benny's. He was found guilty, dismissed, and then, like many others after him, reinstated.

46. Ibid., p. 163.

47. A complete version of "Benny Havens, Oh!" including thirty-seven verses can be found in Farley, *West Point in the Early Sixties*, pp. 195–201.

48. Janes Papers, no. 602, W. H. C. Bartlett, *Elements of Analytical Mechanics* (New York, 1857). Poem inscribed on end pages.

49. Ambrose, *Duty, Honor, Country*, p. 166.

50. Janes' demerits show that he was caught "out of camp without authority" and "south of Fort Putnam" on at least three occasions. "Delinquency Record." His mother declared in a General Affidavit to the U.S. Pension Office in 1887: "My son is absolutely free from common evil habits, has used no tobacco nor any intoxicants, whatever, for twenty-five years." Veterans Administration Claims File. His sister, Ellen Anderman, noted, "I know that ever since the date of his resignation he has been entirely free from the use of any intoxicants, whatever, and extremely careful in every way of his health from necessity." Ibid. The limitation of dates to "twenty-five years" and "after his resignation"

tends to suggest that neither his mother nor sister was prepared to make such a claim for an earlier period.

51. United States Military Academy, *Official Register of the Officers and Cadets* (West Point, 1861), p. 10.

52. "Delinquency Record."

53. Janes Papers, no. 602, W. H. C. Bartlett, *Elements of Analytical Mechanics*, book marginalia.

54. Ibid.

55. Ibid.

56. United States Military Academy, *Official Register of the Officers and Cadets* (West Point, 1861), p. 10.

57. Daved Holland in "Ruth," Mr. Potter in "Pearl," and Mr. Hardruff in "Out of Stony Lonesome" all reflect the same pattern of a young man who is immersed in a family conflict, experiences loss in the form of the death of a loved one, and then, breaking with the father, leaves home and sinks into a life of dissipation from which he is eventually saved by illness and a conversion experience. See Janes Papers, nos. 403, 405, 406.

58. Janes Papers, no. 401, "Christian Pilgrims to Japanese Shrines," pp. 89–90.

59. Janes Papers, no. 103, Letter to mother, Kumamoto, Japan, June 13, 1876.

60. Ibid.

61. Ambrose, *Duty, Honor, Country*, p. 160.

62. Schaff, *The Spirit of Old West Point*, p. 144. "It was the most thrilling event of my life as a cadet," Schaff wrote, "and, in my judgement, it was the most significant in that of West Point itself. For it was really national and prophetic, in this respect, that this battle between two of her spirited cadets, one from the South, the other from the North, duly represented the issue between the States, and duly the courage and bitterness with which it was fought out to the end."

63. Ibid., pp. 145–48.

64. Ambrose, *Duty, Honor, Country*, p. 169.

65. Ibid.

66. Ibid.

67. Ibid., p. 172.

68. Schaff, *The Spirit of Old West Point*, p. 196.

69. Ambrose, *Duty, Honor, Country*, p. 171.

70. Frazer Hunt, *Custer*, p. 32.

71. Ibid.

72. Ambrose, *Duty, Honor, Country*, p. 171.

73. Schaff, *The Spirit of Old West Point*, p. 220.

74. Ambrose, *Duty, Honor, Country*, p. 172.

75. Ibid., p. 176.

76. Janes to Earl Townsend, August 11, 1865. Letter is contained in the Records of the Office of the Adjutant General, Record Group 94: Appointment, Commission, and Personal File Regarding Leroy L. Janes. National Archives, Washington, D.C.

77. For Janes' final standing and appointment see United States Military Academy, *Official Register of the Officers and Cadets* (West Point, 1861), p. 10. Appointments and official history of Janes and his class can be found in George W. Cullum, *Biographical Register of the Officers and Graduates of the United States Military Academy at West Point* (New York: D. Van Nostrand, 1868), vol. 2, pp. 520–48. Janes' biography is on p. 544.

CHAPTER III

WAR, LOVE, AND CONVERSION

1. General Affidavit, dated August 25, 1887, Veterans Administration Claims File.
2. Records of the Office of the Adjutant General, Record Group 94, Appointment, Commission, and Personal File Regarding Leroy L. Janes (RG 94 ACP file J 301 CB 1867—Leroy L. Janes). National Archives of the United States, Washington, D.C. Hereafter cited as "Appointment, Commission, and Personal File."
3. The photograph is contained in Frederick H. Dyer, *A Compendium of the War of the Rebellion*, vol. 2 (New York: Thomas Yoseloff, 1959), p. 696–16.
4. Appointment, Commission, and Personal File.
5. Ibid. See also George W. Cullum, *Biographical Register of the Officers of the United States Military Academy*, vol. 2 (Boston: Houghton, Mifflin, 1891), p. 806.
6. Janes Papers, no. 104, "Letter to Anna," Kumamoto, Japan, October 7, 1874.
7. For biographical details on Susan Bogert and Anna Bartlett Warner I have relied on Olivia E. P. Stokes, *Letters and Memories of Susan and Anna Bartlett Warner* (New York: G. P. Putnam, 1909); Anna B. Warner, *Susan Warner ("Elizabeth Wetherell")* (New York: Putnam, 1909); Mabel Baker, *Light in the Morning: Memories of Susan and Anna Warner* (West Point: Constitution Island Association, 1978); Stanley J. Kunitz and Howard Haycraft, *American Authors, 1600–1900* (New York: H. W. Wilson, 1955); and Dorothy Hurlbut Sanderson, *They Wrote for a Living, A Bibliography of the Works of Susan Bogert Warner and Anna Bartlett Warner* (West Point: Constitution Island Association, 1976). Susan Warner (1819–1885) was a precocious child who loved to read from an early age. Overly sensitive, she was often given to periods of melancholy and tears. Her heroines demonstrated similar dispositions. Anna, who was born in 1824, according to Mabel Baker's recent findings (her tombstone says 1827), was of a more even temperament. She died in 1915. While Susan possessed greater literary skills, Anna was very fond of children's stories and possessed a particular talent in this direction. She was also an able writer of hymns, writing the well-known "Jesus Loves Me" in 1860. Both Susan and Anna regularly held Bible Classes for West Point cadets. It was their joint wish that Constitution Island be made part of the Military Academy, and in 1908 Anna was able to achieve this goal with the financial assistance of Mrs. Russell Sage. As writers both sisters tended toward the sentimental and pious. Their

novels are largely devoid of action and are filled with heavy doses of introspection. While their realistic descriptions of nineteenth-century social customs
have aroused some recent interest in their work, most readers will find themselves in agreement with the French critic Taine who expressed considerable
astonishment that in America a "three-volume novel" could be devoted to "the
history of the moral progress of a girl of thirteen." Kunitz and Haycraft,
American Authors, p. 787.

8. Mabel Baker, *Light in the Morning*, p. vi. Quoted in the foreword by William
A. McIntosh.

9. Thomas Warner's career is discussed by Mabel Baker in ibid., pp. 21–25.

10. For the Warner genealogy see Olivia E. P. Stokes, *Letters and Memories of
Susan and Anna Bartlett Warner*, p. 216.

11. Janes Papers, no. 106, "Letter to Anna," Kumamoto, Japan, April 21, 1875.

12. See affidavits of Mrs. Ellen Anderman, April 23, 1910, and E. Paul Janes,
May 23, 1910, Veterans Administration Claims File. Both marriage and death
dates are confirmed in *The Genius of Liberty*, the Uniontown, Pennsylvania,
newspaper for this period. See *The Genius of Liberty*, December 18, 1862, p.
5, and December 22, 1864, p. 3. Franklin Ellis, *History of Fayette County
Pennsylvania with Biographical Sketches* (Philadelphia: L. H. Everts, 1882)
describes Eleazer Robinson, Nellie's father, as having brought the "Yankee
spirit" to Fayette County. Robinson was born in Vermont of Quaker stock in
1804 and emigrated to western Pennsylvania in 1837. He established an iron
foundry in Uniontown and produced the very popular Hathaway Stove on
which he made a small fortune. Later he sold the foundry and went into city
utilities, owning the Gas Company of Uniontown and several other Pennsylvania communities. In his biographical sketch Robinson is described as a man
who "took no extreme partisan cause . . . either in politics or religion," but
who enjoyed the "esteem of his neighbors and the business public as a man
of sterling integrity as well as clear judgement, genial sociability, and humane
sentiments" (pp. 361–62).

13. Veterans Administration Claims File.

14. Janes Papers, no. 106, "Letter to Anna," Kumamoto, Japan, April 21, 1875.

15. Ibid.

16. Janes' Pension File contains an 1893 questionnaire sent him by the commissioner of pensions which asks him to list all previous marriages and offspring.
Janes makes no mention of his marriage to Helen Robinson in his reply and
lists only his marriage to Harriet Scudder. See Veterans Administration Claims
File.

17. Frederick Janes, *The Janes Family*, p. 305.

18. See *The History of Tuscarawas County, Ohio*, p. 707; *Combination Atlas
Map of Tuscarawas County, Ohio*, unnumbered page entry under "Colonel
Elisha Janes." In all instances his father lists him as either "married to the
daughter of Dr. Scudder" or "married in San Francisco." There is no mention
of an earlier marriage.

19. Dorothy Hurlbut Sanderson in her bibliography of the Warners' writings,

They Wrote for a Living, lists *Daisy* (1868) and *Daisy in the Field* (1869) as part of a "trilogy" that began with *Melbourne House* (1864). While Daisy Randolph appears in *Melbourne House*, the latter two novels are clearly separate units and cannot in fact be seen as part of a genuine trilogy. The reason for this is precisely the fact that Susan was now writing about an entirely different topic and different characters. Most publishers later saw the 1868 and 1869 volumes as part of a whole and published them together. I have used the 1878 Lippincott edition, which includes both under the single title, *Daisy*.

20. Susan Warner, *Daisy* II, p. 81. The designations I and II indicate the 1868 and 1869 divisions in the original novel.
21. Anna B. Warner, *Susan Warner*, p. 490.
22. Mabel Baker, *Light in the Morning*, p. 84.
23. It is worth noting that in Anna's biography of Susan there is a curious absence of diaries for the years in which Warner-Janes contacts were at their peak. When Janes returned to West Point in 1863 and obviously spent a good deal of time at the island, as his letters from Japan indicated, Anna tells us in *Susan Warner*, p. 449, "the journals cease—and for the next half dozen years either none were written, or they were afterwards destroyed." When Janes arrived at the Warners with Harriet Scudder, his new wife, in January 1868 and boarded with them for nine months, we find Susan's last extant diary entry to have been written on December 31, 1867. Anna writes, "the journal ends abruptly at this point. If later ones were written, they must have been destroyed" (p. 485). Anna knew, of course, that they had been destroyed, but she fails to tell us why. Since Janes and the Warners were corresponding again in the 1870s while he was in Japan, the final break between them does not seem to have taken place until the 1880s. It was at this time that Janes was divorced from Harriet Scudder, and the controversy stemming from the divorce may well have been been the final straw in what, as we shall see, was to be a complex and stormy relationship.
24. *Daisy* I, p. 351; II, p. 254.
25. *Daisy* I, p. 292.
26. Ibid., p. 329.
27. Ibid., p. 358.
28. Ibid., p. 338.
29. For a description of Preston Gary see ibid., pp. 327–28.
30. Ibid., p. 314.
31. Ibid., p. 321.
32. *Daisy* II, p. 18.
33. Ibid., p. 69.
34. Ibid., p. 70.
35. Ibid.
36. Ibid., pp. 72–73.
37. Ibid., p. 81.
38. Janes' biographical statement before the United States Army Retiring Board, San Francisco, California, April 23, 1867. In Records of the Adjutant General's

Office, Record Group 94, National Archives. Hereafter cited as "Retiring Board File."

39. For a balanced assessment of Patterson's role see Allan Nevins, *The War for the Union* (New York: Charles Scribner's Sons, 1959), vol. 1, pp. 216–17. For an earlier view see James Ford Rhodes, *History of the Civil War* (New York: Macmillan, 1917), pp. 37–39. The interpretation of Patterson's failure was also adopted by Susan Warner in *Daisy*. At one point she has Major Fairbairn tell Daisy, "It is certain there is a battle going on, Miss Randolph, and a battle along the whole line. And it is certain that Patterson has orders to follow up Johnston and keep him from troubling us. And I am afraid it is also certain that he has not done it—confound him!" (*Daisy* II, p. 90). In a conversation with Mrs. Sanford, Fairbairn adds a comment on the exceedingly hot weather—to which Janes subsequently attributed his "sun stroke"—and suggests with a smile that it is best to "keep cool." Asked what Patterson was doing, the smile died out on his face. " '*He* has kept cool,' he said. 'Easy—when a man never was warm' " (*Daisy* II, p. 93). Janes did not personally blame Patterson. In his application for a pension in 1887 he accepted Patterson's argument of facing superior forces, writing that his battery had been retreating out the Shenandoah Valley with Patterson and Banks' army in the face of Joe Johnston's superior forces. Veterans Administration Claims File. It is, of course, true that by the time of Patterson's retreat across the Potomac, which Janes covered, Johnston's army was augmented by southern forces fresh from Bull Run.

40. Janes Papers, no. 406, "Out of Stony Lonesome."

41. Ibid., pp. 110–11.

42. Ibid., p. 111.

43. Ibid.

44. Ibid., pp. 117–19.

45. It does seem strange that both Susan Warner and Janes give Nellie southern roots when the record indicates that Helen Robinson was raised in Pennsylvania.

46. Robinson was married three times. His first wife was Cornelia Wells of York, New York, whom he married in 1837. She died in 1845, after bearing him four children of whom Nellie was the oldest. His second wife, Mary Ann McClelland, died childless in 1850. At the time that Janes married Nellie, Eleazer was married to Mrs. Elizabeth J. Porter, a widow, who bore him two more children. See Franklin Ellis, *History of Fayette County Pennsylvania*, p. 362.

47. Janes Papers, no. 106, "Letter to Anna," Kumamoto, Japan, April 21, 1875.

48. Janes was notoriously inaccurate at remembering dates, and the historical documents he left behind are full of errors. One of the most embarrassing mistakes occurred at the time of his pension application. In the document on which he was asked to list his previous marriages, mentioned above, he listed his marriage to Harriet Waterbury Scudder as having taken place on January 2, 1869. Further down the same form he listed the birth-date of his first daughter by Harriet, Frances Elizabeth, as having been December 27, 1868.

The Pension Office therefore concluded that "Bertie" must have been born "before wedlock." His marriage to Harriet had actually taken place on January 2, 1868, and his daughter was legitimately born later in the same year. But it took the Pension Office a while to clear up this mess. See Veterans Administration Claims File.

49. Letter from W. E. Bigglestone, Oberlin College Archivist, to author, March 19, 1979.

50. That Janes and John I. Rodgers were friends can be seen in the letters contained in the Veterans Administration Claims File. Susan Warner in her novel hints at a fight between Janes and southern cadets. She has Christian state, "It was on that ground that Gary and I split." When Daisy asks him what he means by "split," he is reluctant to answer. "I began to put things together though," Daisy observes, "I saw from Christian's eyes that he had nothing to be ashamed of, in looking back, I remembered Preston's virulence, and his sudden flush when somebody had repeated the word 'coward,' which he had applied to Thorold. I felt certain that more had been between them than mere words, and that Preston found the recollection not flattering, whatever it was. . . ." (*Daisy* I, p. 429).

51. Janes Papers, no. 106, "Letter to Anna," Kumamoto, Japan, April 21, 1875.

52. These are the words of George A. Custer. Jay Monaghan, *Custer*, p. 42.

53. Alan Nevins, *The War for the Union*, vol. 1, p. 217.

54. Leroy L. Janes, General Affidavit, August 25, 1887, Veterans Administration Claims File.

55. Ibid.

56. In a letter to the "Hon. Commissioner of Pensions," written from Ann Arbor, Michigan, February 7, 1888, Janes speaks of "the time I fell insensible from my horse at Harper's Ferry." All references dealing with this incident refer to him as "insensible." Veterans Administration Claims File.

57. Letter from John I. Rodgers to Mr. and Mrs. Janes from "Camp in Pleasant Valley Near Harper's Ferry, Md.," August 2, 1861. Copy in Veterans Administration Claims File. In this letter Rodgers identifies himself as "Leroy's classmate and friend."

58. General Affidavit of Elizabeth Janes, August 16, 1887, Veterans Administration Claims File.

59. General Affidavit of Dr. Edward S. Dunster, April 21, 1887, Veterans Administration Claims File.

60. General Affidavit of Elizabeth Janes, August 16, 1887, Veterans Administration Claims File.

61. General Affidavit of Mrs. Dr. Curry, February 3, 1888, Veterans Administration Claims File.

62. General Affidavit of Elizabeth Janes, August 16, 1887, Veterans Administration Claims File.

63. Statement by John I. Rodgers, Alcatraz Island, San Francisco, California, April 26, 1887, Veterans Administration Claims File.

64. General Affidavit of Leroy L. Janes, August 25, 1887, Veterans Administration Claims File.

65. General Affidavit of Emma R. King, May 17, 1887, Veterans Administration Claims File.

66. General Affidavit of Elizabeth Janes, August 16, 1887, Veterans Administration Claims File.

67. General Affidavit of Leroy L. Janes, undated but stamped "received 1887" by Pension Office, Veterans Administration Claims File.

68. Medical Certificate submitted by Surgeon F. C. Robinson, Uniontown, Pennsylvania, June 27, 1863, Appointment, Commission, and Personal File.

69. Letter from A. William to L. Thomas, June 1, 1864, in Records of the Adjutant General's Office, Record Group 94, Letters Received, 1166 M AGO 1864. National Archives. The date of Janes' appointment to West Point is found in Appointment, Commission, and Personal File. It was common practice to assign disabled officers to teach at West Point.

70. General Affidavit of Edward S. Dunster, April 21, 1887, Veterans Administration Claims File.

71. General Affidavit for Anne Beatty, February 6, 1888, Veterans Administration Claims File.

72. Janes' psychological state in the autumn of 1861 is difficult to evaluate. There are, however, numerous indications that he was under severe stress. The subject of war neurosis, was, in keeping with the development of psychoanalytical theory and research, largely a topic explored within the context of twentieth-century wars. It was in reading Eric J. Leed's provocative study of World War I combatants, *No Man's Land: Combat and Identity in World War I* (Cambridge: Cambridge University Press, 1979), in the context of another research project that I was struck by various parallels between Janes' experiences and those of later combatants who sought to escape from intolerable battlefield situations into illness. Leed quotes Ernst Simmel, one of the pioneers of war neurosis research, in reference to the personality of the typical war neurotic. Leed explained that "the neurosis was not the result of a conscious decision made by the patient. On the contrary, the neurotic soldier was one who could make no decision, who could repudiate neither his desire for survival nor the ideals and moral imperatives that kept him at the front. According to Simmel, both the 'hero' and the 'slacker' 'are sound . . . unified personalities generated by war. Between them stands the victim of war neurosis. He has the egocentric valuation of his own existence of the malingerer and the altruistic sense of duty of the hero. Incapable of taking the consequences of drawing to one side or the other he "flees" into his illness.' [Simmel, *Kriegsneurosen und psychisches Trauma* (Munich, 1918), p. 33.] The neurotic was the man in the middle," Leed concluded (p. 176). Janes' personality, possessing as it did elements of both the "hero" and the "malingerer," may have sought a similar avenue of escape. In "Out of Stony Lonesome" Janes speaks of the Great War and his "vicissitudes" in relation to it in terms of "wounds" that required the "cooling waters of *mental* refreshment" (p. 45, italics in original). On other occasions

he spoke quite freely of his "ill nature." While there is no indication that he was able to come to grips with his problem in other than a religious sense at this time, later years provided a broader perspective and self-analysis.

73. Janes Papers, no. 406, "Out of Stony Lonesome," pp. 108–10.

74. Ibid., p. 107.

75. Ibid., p. 41.

76. Letter from Janes to the "Members of the Kumamoto Band," New Philadelphia, Ohio, July 13, 1885. Published in *Shiryō ihō* (Dōshisha Daigaku Shashi Shiryō Henshū Sho) 1 (March 1968), 98–103.

77. Janes Papers, no. 406, "Out of Stony Lonesome," p. 43.

78. General Affidavit of E. Paul Janes, May 23, 1910, Veterans Administration Claims File.

79. Janes Papers. Unnumbered note in one of Janes' textbooks.

80. General Affidavit of E. Paul Janes, May 23, 1910, Veterans Administration Claims File.

CHAPTER IV
OREGON AND CALIFORNIA

1. Janes' animosity toward doctors is clearly apparent in his military record. One of the Army's complaints against him in Oregon was that he "ran off" the fort's contract surgeon, and later insulted his replacement. Appointment, Commission, and Personal file. His attitude toward the medical profession was also extremely negative in "Out of Stony Lonesome," in which he particularly denigrated American medical practices dealing with childbirth. Janes Papers, no. 406, "Out of Stony Lonesome," pp. 149ff.

2. Appointment, Commission, and Personal File.

3. The description of Fort Stevens is by Lieutenant John E. Wilson and is contained in "Outline Description of Military Posts in the Military Division of the Pacific, 1872," unpaginated, copy in the Oregon Historical Society Library.

4. Janes to Brig. General Earl Townsend, August 11, 1865, Appointment, Commission, and Personal File.

5. See memorandum dated August 15, 1865, Appointment, Commission, and Personal File.

6. Janes Papers, no. 104, "Letter to Anna," Kumamoto, Japan, October 7, 1874.

7. Letter from Iris Janes to Marius B. Jansen, San Jose, California, May 22, 1978. Iris writes: "Susan and Ann (sic) Warner were sisters and cousins of my father's. I know many stories and something, but not all, about that friendship. There was certainly some trouble—broken promises or a broken engagement with Ann—and bitterness and heart burnings on the Warner side." Janes Papers, no number, copy of letter in the possession of the author.

8. Elizabeth Dejeans (Frances Elizabeth Janes, or "Bertie"), *Nobody's Child* (Indianapolis: Bobbs-Merrill, 1918), p. 144.

9. See Janes Papers, no. 106, "Letter to Anna," Kumamoto, Japan, April 21, 1875, in which he contrasts his feelings for Nellie with those for Hattie. Another

indication of this can be found in a letter from Janes to Hattie, Saint Denis, Maryland, July 14, 1877, which can be found in *Janes vs. Janes* Divorce Proceedings Records.

10. Elizabeth Dejeans, *Nobody's Child*, p. 144.

11. Cable from Janes to Adjutant General's Office, Baltimore, August 17, 1865, Appointment, Commission, and Personal File.

12. Appointment, Commission, and Personal File.

13. Cable to Col. R. Williams, West Point, August 23, 1865, Appointment, Commission and Personal File.

14. Ibid.

15. Fukunaga Bunnosuke, comp., *Nihon ni okeru taii jiensu shi*, p. 104.

16. General Affidavit of Dr. Asahel K. Bush, March 9, 1888, Veterans Administration Claims File.

17. Quoted in a general memorandum of the Adjutant General's Office, Washington, D.C., December 13, 1866, which summarizes earlier correspondence, Appointment, Commission, and Personal File.

18. Ibid.

19. Years later he wrote in "Pearl," Janes Papers, no. 403: "There is a species of mental intoxication, an inebriation of the subjective emotions of fear, of craving desire, of illusive exaltation and of hopeless despair, which we believe to be as inimical to all the healthier vitalities of individual life—and sometimes, as in well-attested historical instances, of the life of entire communities, as opium or alcohol is injurious to the physical organism. As these agents emasculate their victims, and lower their vitalities, and cut short their career, so may the victims of habitual, hereditary spiritual intoxication be unfitted to survive the shocks and strains inevitable to the struggle for physical existence."

20. Records of the Adjutant General's Office, Record Group 94, Janes, Retiring Board File. Hereafter cited as Retiring Board File. See testimony of Surgeon Alden H. Steele.

21. Retiring Board File.

22. Ibid.

23. See memorandum of Adjutant General's Office, Washington, December 13, 1866, Appointment, Commission, and Personal File.

24. Retiring Board File.

25. Ibid.

26. Ibid.

27. Ibid. A similar comment on Janes' condition was rendered by then Captain, later Colonel, J. C. Tidball, who was initially assigned to the Retiring Board, but was later replaced. Tidball, writing to the commissioner of pensions in reference to Janes' physical condition at the time of his resignation from the Army, wrote: "At that time his general physical condition appeared to me— an unprofessional—sufficiently good, with exception of a nervous, restless and discontented disposition, the result, probably, of infirmities not apparent to me." Veterans Administration Claims file.

28. Retiring Board File.
29. Letter from Janes to the Honorable Commissioner of Pensions, Ann Arbor, Michigan, February 7, 1888, Veterans Administration Claims File.
30. Ibid.
31. Appointment, Commission, and Personal File.
32. Edward Arthur Wicher, *The Presbyterian Church in California, 1849–1927* (New York: Frederick H. Hitchcock, The Grafton Press, 1927), p. 159. Henry Martyn Scudder was born in Ceylon in 1822. His father, John Scudder, was one of the pioneering American missionaries in India. The family stemmed from Thomas Scudder, who settled in Salem, Massachusetts, in 1635. John Scudder had graduated from the College of Physicians and Surgeons, New York, in 1813 and seemed to be on his way to an extensive and lucrative medical practice when he chanced to read a tract that convinced him to devote his life to missionary work, and he sailed to India with his wife, Harriet Waterbury Scudder, in 1819. Henry Martyn came to the United States in 1832. After a year at Williams College, he entered the University of the City of New York in 1837 and received his B.A. degree from there in 1840. He graduated from Union Theological Seminary in 1843 and in the same year was ordained in the Presbytery of New York. In 1844 he married Fannie Lewis, and with his new bride he returned to India as a missionary of the American Board. Serving first at Madura, he later founded the Arcot mission in 1850. In 1863 he returned to the United States and served as pastor of the Reformed Dutch Church at Jersey City from 1864 to 1865. In 1865 he took the pastorate of the Howard Presbyterian Church in San Francisco, where he served until 1871. Thereafter he was pastor of the Central Congregational Church of Brooklyn (1871–80); the Plymouth Congregational Church of Chicago (1883–87); and served as an independent missionary to Japan with his son Doremus and his daughter Catherine from 1887 to 1889. He died in Winchester, Massachusetts, in 1895. According to the *Missionary Herald* Scudder's return to India in 1844 was the "first instance in which the son of a missionary has been sent forth as a preacher to the heathen" (vol. 41, 1845, p. 7). In Scudder's obituary notice in *The Outlook*, vol. 51 (June 22, 1895), p. 102, the writer observed: "In San Francisco, Brooklyn and Chicago he was one of the strongest, most brilliant, and most faithful Christian ministers . . . as a preacher he was peculiarly vivid, picturesque, and spiritual."
33. Henry Martyn Scudder, *A Discourse Delivered in the Howard Presbyterian Church, San Francisco, Thanksgiving Day, November 29th, 1866* (San Francisco: Edward Bosqui, 1866), p. 36.
34. Ibid., p. 16.
35. Edward A. Wicher, *The Presbyterian Church in California, 1849–1927*, p. 159.
36. Ibid., p. 160.
37. Ibid., p. 159.
38. "Advice to Preachers," *Howard Quarterly* (January 1868), p. 102.

39. Anna B. Warner, *Susan Warner*, p. 384. Anna quotes Susan's diary entry for January 30, 1859.

40. "Editor's Department," *Howard Quarterly* (January 1868), p. 105.

41. Edward A. Wicher, *The Presbyterian Church in California, 1849–1927*, p. 161.

42. Ibid.

43. Minutes of the Session of the Howard Presbyterian Church, June 10, 1865. These include Scudder's appointment letter. In it the church agrees to pay him "six thousand dollars per annum, payable in U.S. gold coin." One may presume his salary was even higher a few years later. I want to thank Mr. David Horosz, archivist of the San Francisco Theological Seminary Library, for making available to me the records of the Howard Presbyterian Church.

44. Susan Warner, *Daisy* I, pp. 218ff, gives the description of Faustina St. Claire. Cadet Thorold's first meeting with Faustina is described on p. 367.

45. Janes Papers, no. 104, "Letter to Anna," Kumamoto, Japan, October 7, 1874.

46. Photograph of Harriet W. Scudder in Janes' family album, contained in Janes Papers.

47. Susan Warner, *Daisy* II, p. 276.

48. Janes Papers, no. 306, "Kumamoto," ch. 1, p. 1.

49. In his letter to Anna written on October 7, 1874, Janes wrote, "In your letters, long ago, you asked for 'details' of it all. And if I can only get time and manage my thoughts a little, I will try to give them to you. And I will try to tell you something about the place and country. But in the light of a three year's delay, and of a corresponding fault as old as my stay in Oregon, it would be safer to restrain promises." Janes Papers, no. 104, "Letter to Anna."

50. The most dramatic examples of such themes were in *Dianna* and *Daisy Plains*. In *Dianna* (1877) we are presented with another young Army officer, who leaves the heroine for the West—this time for Fort Vancouver. The heroine, who is in love with the Army officer, does not know how to reach him at this frontier location and waits in vain for letters from him. Eventually despairing over his failure to write, she ends in marrying a minister who has settled in her village. *Daisy Plains* (1885) was the novel on which Susan was working at the time of her death. The book was finished by Anna. The plot is described by Dorothy Hurlbut Sanderson in *They Wrote for a Living*, p. 6, as follows: "Entrusted to a friend a letter from Bentley in China is forgotten and delivered years later to Helen at the old farm in Daisy Plains, presenting the question then of whose lives might have been changed if the letter had arrived on schedule." The theme of a missent letter was, of course, also important in the second volume of *Daisy*.

51. Letter of Resignation, November 23, 1867, Appointment, Commission, and Personal File.

52. See telegram from Janes to Adjutant General's Office, December 4, 1867, Appointment, Commission, and Personal File.

53. Ibid.

54. "Editor's Department: Editorial Correspondence, Pescadero, December 12th, 1867," *Howard Quarterly* (January 1868), p. 103.

55. Letter from Henry Martyn Scudder to Harriet Scudder Janes, San Francisco, California, February 1, 1870. This letter reveals considerable tension between Henry Martyn and his daughter. Scudder expressed "amazement" at some of the things she had written him in a recent letter. "I find such expressions as these," Scudder wrote, " 'Humble yourself I beseech you my dear father, for I am afraid you are great in your own eyes ... do not allow your heart to exalt itself, I pray you, Papa, for just as surely as you do, I fear there will fall on you some judgement from the Lord.' Then you compare me to Nebuchadnessar and to Herod. Surely this is not the way for a child to write to her father, so long as the divine command stands unrepealed 'Honor thy Father.' " Later he added, "how could a child of mine associated with me for 21 years, fall into a mental condition in which her father stands before her in the monstrous moral attitude which is portrayed in your letter? I remember once you fell into a melancholy condition and believed that you had committed the unpardonable sin, and it took me long to free you from that morbid state. For a long time, all proofs to the contrary which I could adduce, you perverted into self condemnating testimonies. I fear you have fallen into a similar morbid condition of mind. I am glad for your sake, that I instead of yourself am the victim of the groundless and distressing thoughts in which you now indulge." Scudder's letter is contained in the evidence submitted in the *Janes vs. Janes* Divorce Proceedings Records.

56. *Howard Quarterly* (January 1868), p. 103.

57. Letter from Janes to Hattie, Saint Denis, Maryland, July 14, 1877, *Janes vs. Janes* Divorce Proceedings Records.

58. See *Howard Quarterly* (January 1868), pp. 103ff.

59. *San Francisco Evening Bulletin*, January 2, 1868.

60. Letter from Henry Martyn Scudder to Harriet Scudder Janes, San Francisco, California, February 1, 1870, *Janes vs. Janes* Divorce Proceedings Records.

61. Letter from Janes to Henry Martyn Scudder, Saint Denis, Maryland, February 15, 1882, *Janes vs. Janes* Divorce Proceedings Records. In this letter Janes alludes several times to problems involving Harriet's truthfulness. Janes referred to a "long cherished spirit of evil thinking, and bearing of conscious false witness."

62. Statement made to the commissioner of pensions listing his marriage to Harriet W. Scudder and the dates of the birth of his children. This statement is dated November 10, 1892, Veterans Administration Claims File.

63. This is the indication in his letter to Hattie, Saint Denis, Maryland, July 14, 1877, *Janes vs. Janes* Divorce Proceedings Records.

64. The plot of *Nobody's Child* revolves around the marriage of the protagonist to a young lady he is in love with, but who is bearing the child of another man. Incorporating much of the setting of Elk Ridge, near Saint Denis, Maryland, where the Janes family resided in the early 1880s, the story is clearly close to Bertie's teenage environment. In the novel she seems to have combined portions

of her father's relationship with Nellie—the sudden death, need to go West, and mental turmoil and trouble—with strange discoveries, namely, that the father of the child was not the husband but someone else. These discoveries may well have been based on her own experiences and on "revelations" she became privy to during the bitter feuding that preceded the divorce. It is quite possible that hearing rumors about Nellie and her child, Bertie came to question her own origins.

65. Janes Papers, no. 406, "Out of Stony Lonesome," p. 107.

66. In Janes' letter to Anna Warner from Kumamoto there is a clear comparison between Harriet and Nellie, which shows that his family life with Harriet was becoming increasingly difficult. Something of Harriet's moods can be detected in her father's letter quoted above. But it should be added that Janes was often willing to be generous toward her. And even after their divorce he never blamed Harriet. What angered Janes the most about his father-in-law was that Henry Martyn, who knew of Harriet's emotional problems, encouraged her to pursue some of her worst illusions in reference to him—illusions, Janes insisted, which Scudder knew to be false but exploited to his own ends. This is a problem that will be dealt with in greater detail in reference to the divorce in 1885.

67. Janes Papers, no. 104, "Letter to Anna," Kumamoto, Japan, October 7, 1874.

68. Anna Warner, "Two Picnics," *Harper's* 47, 277 (June 1873), 900–907.

69. Ibid., p. 907.

70. Ibid.

71. *Daily Alta California*, January 3, 1868. "In this city, January 2nd, by Rev. Dr. Scudder, Captain Leroy Lansing James (sic) to Harriet Waterbury Scudder."

72. This is reflected in Janes' letter to Anna from Kumamoto. Janes Papers, no. 104, "Letter to Anna," Kumamoto, Japan, October 7, 1874.

73. The Janes Papers at Princeton University contain a number of "stories" (some quite lengthy) that were written by his children, Bertie (Elizabeth Dejeans), Henry, and Lois, at the time of the divorce proceedings in the early 1880s. These stories appear, in part, to have been inspired by tales that Janes told the children upon which they elaborated. In almost all cases there are young children who are orphaned, but more importantly there are several cases of children who die of lingering illnesses and who are placed in settings that bear a striking resemblance to Constitution Island. While the fear of becoming orphaned may well have expressed the children's genuine concern for their future, it is possible that their other concerns were attributable to their father's experiences.

74. Letter from Janes to Hattie, Saint Denis, Maryland, July 14, 1877, *Janes vs. Janes* Divorce Proceedings Records.

75. Janes Papers, no. 104, "Letter to Anna," Kumamoto, Japan, October 7, 1874.

76. Susan Warner, *Daisy* II, p. 379.

CHAPTER V
INVITATION TO JAPAN

1. Leroy L. Janes, "Answer to the Bill of Complaint of his Wife," in *Janes vs. Janes* Divorce Proceedings Records. Birthdate of Frances Elizabeth is from Veterans Administration Claims File.
2. *History of Tuscarawas County, Ohio*, p. 707.
3. In *Janes vs. Janes* Divorce Proceedings Records Harriet describes Janes as "not succeeding well with his farming operation and becoming reduced in circumstances." This was the reason, she insisted, that he accepted the invitation to go to Japan. Janes himself wrote in a letter in the Divorce Proceedings that he was convinced that "our farm here . . . can never be a source of *profit* upon any amount of toil I may expand on it."
4. For a description of Elk Ridge I have relied on Charles Francis Stein, Jr., *Origin and History of Howard County Maryland* (Baltimore: Howard County Historical Society, 1972), pp. 132ff. Also J. D. Warfield, *The Founders of Anne Arundel and Howard Counties, Maryland* (Baltimore: Regional Publishing Co., 1967), pp. 338ff. For his daughter's description see Elizabeth Dejeans, *Nobody's Child.*
5. Janes Papers, no. 603, "Kumamoto," ch. 1, p. 3.
6. Ibid., p. 2.
7. Ibid., pp. 1–2.
8. Ibid., p. 2.
9. Susan and Anna Warner's contacts with the American Protestant Church interested in missions were quite extensive. In a diary entry dated January 1859 Susan records a party she and Anna attended that included not only Bishop Boone of the China Mission, but Dr. and Mrs. Adams and Mr. Brown and his wife, who were missionaries to Japan. Samuel Robbins Brown, like Guido Verbeck, was one of the pioneer missionaries of the Reformed Church in America (Dutch Reformed) who reached Japan in November 1859. Dr. and Mrs. Adams also later went to Japan with the American Board. Henry Martyn Scudder was another of the guests. Anna B. Warner, *Susan Warner*, p. 384.
10. Minutes of the Annual Meetings (1870–77) of the Howard Presbyterian Church, Report of the Superintendent [of the Sunday School], February 12, 1871. Records of the Howard Presbyterian Church, San Francisco Theological Seminary Library, San Anselmo, California.
11. *San Francisco Evening Bulletin*, January 2, 1868, p. 1.
12. For a complete translation of the Charter Oath, which was issued in April 1868, see Ryusaku Tsunoda, Wm. Theodore DeBary, and Donald Keene, *Sources of Japanese Tradition* (New York: Columbia University Press, 1958), pp. 643–44.
13. Higo, officially ranked at 540,000 *koku* (bales of rice), but with an actual income of 720,000 *koku* by the end of the Tokugawa period, was one of the largest *tozama*, or outside, domains in the Tokugawa system. For details on the domain I have relied on Kumamoto Ken, *Kumamoto kenshi* (Kumamoto,

1961), vol. 1, pp. 14ff. Also Morita Seiichi, "Kumamoto han," in Kodama Kōta and Kitashima Masamoto, eds., *Monogatari han shi*, vol. 8 (Tokyo, 1965), pp. 389–525.

14. The role of the Jishūkan and the School Party (Gakkō-tō) is discussed in Kumamoto ken kyōikukai, eds., *Kumamoto ken kyōiku shi* (Kumamoto, 1931), vol. 1, pp. 90–106. Fukuda Reiju (Yoshinobu), *Gojūnen kinen Kumamoto Bando tsuikai roku* (pamphlet, n.d.), pp. 1–38, argues that Kumamoto was divided into three parties: the School Party organized around the Jishūkan, the Loyalist Group (*Kinnō-tō*) later identified with the Shimpūren, and the Practical Learning Party identified with Yokoi Shōnan and his followers.

15. The reform problem in Kumamoto was complicated by local conditions. While suffering from the general economic malaise that beset most feudal domains in nineteenth-century Japan, Kumamoto was less seriously affected by the crisis years of the Tempō period (1830–1843) than were other leading domains that later played a major part in the Restoration. The famine conditions of the 1830s, which led to extensive rioting in both urban and rural centers of north and central Japan, left Kumamoto largely untouched. In fact, as rice prices skyrocketed, Kumamoto's ample supply of rice permitted the domain to replenish its financially depleted treasury. It was not until the price of rice once again fell after 1840 that the need for reform became an overwhelming concern in the domain, and Yokoi and the Practical Learning Party began to air their own reform program. It should be added that even the Practical Learning Party's reform ideas were basically conservative and called for retrenchment in the form of reduced spending on the part of the domain and reduced consumption on the part of the samurai class. In his essay "Jimusaku" (1843), Yokoi suggested three concrete policies: the elimination of extravagance among upper samurai and assistance to lower class warriors; the return to the land of those who had left farming and the villages; and the elimination of costly and extravagant domain projects and the severance of domain ties to a select group of approved merchants. Little of this was new or radical. It was only in the late 1860s that the Practical Learning Party moved to more drastic solutions. Morita Seiichi, "Kumamoto han," in Kodama and Kitashima, *Monogatari han shi*, vol. 8, pp. 499–501.

16. See John D. Pierson, *Tokutomi Sohō, 1863–1957: A Journalist for Modern Japan* (Princeton: Princeton University Press, 1980), p. 14. Sohō's father, Ikkei, is often given as an example of the wealthy farmer (*gōnō*) type. Sohō's younger brother, Kenjirō (Roka), presents us with a remarkably dynamic portrait of such a figure in "Uncle Kengo," who plays an important part in his autobiographical novel, *Omoide no ki* (1901). This novel has been translated by Kenneth Strong as *Footprints in the Snow* (Tokyo: Charles E. Tuttle, 1971).

17. A brief discussion of the ideas of Yokoi Shōnan (1809–1869) can be found in G. B. Sansom, *The Western World and Japan* (New York: Alfred E. Knopf, 1962), pp. 266–69. Also Kosaka Masaaki, ed., *Japanese Thought in the Meiji Era*, trans. David Abosh (Tokyo: Pan Pacific Press, 1958), pp. 27–36. Yokoi is discussed in greater depth in H. D. Harootunian, *Towards Restoration: The*

Growth of Political Consciousness in Tokugawa Japan (Berkeley: University of California Press, 1970), pp. 321ff. The standard Japanese biography of Yokoi is Yamazaki Masatada, *Yokoi Shōnan*, 2 vols. (Tokyo, 1938). A briefer, more recent study is Tamamuro Taijō's *Yokoi Shōnan* (Tokyo, 1966). For an English account of Yokoi's life and career see Dixon Yoshihide Miyauchi, "Yokoi Shōnan: A Pre-Meiji Reformist," Ph.D. dissertation, Harvard University, 1957.

18. Yokoi was assassinated by a group of loyalist *rōnin* led by Tsuge Shirōzaemon on Teramachi street in Kyoto on February 15, 1869, as he was returning from his official duties as adviser to the Emperor. Although sixty-one years of age and armed only with a short sword, he ably defended himself against his assailants until he was mortally wounded. Mori Ōgai, the Meiji novelist, later wrote an account of the assassination in his historically accurate short story, "Tsuge Shirōzaemon." For a translation see David Dilworth and J. Thomas Rimer, eds., *Saiki Kōi and Other Stories, Volume 2 of the Historical Literature of Mori Ōgai* (Honolulu: University Press of Hawaii, 1977), pp. 61–89.

19. The pupil was Yuri Kimimasa, and the influence of Yokoi's ideas on the Charter Oath is discussed in Tamamuro Taijō, *Yokoi Shōnan*, pp. 270–71; Johei Asahara, comp., *Blessed Takezeki Junko* (Tokyo, 1954), pp. 12–13; Harootunian, *Towards Restoration*, p. 326.

20. Yokoi's reform ideas were not accepted in Kumamoto until after his death. As adviser to the powerful daimyo, Matsudaira Shungaku, in the late 1850s and early 1860s, his ideas were implemented with positive results in Fukui. But from 1863 to 1868 Yokoi was under house arrest in Nuyamazu outside of Kumamoto, stripped of his stipend, and removed from all official posts. Yokoi's temporary disgrace was largely the result of the powerful and conservative School Party that dominated domain politics and objected to his desire to open the country to foreign influences.

21. Yokoi and Sakuma Shōzan, another scholar who called for the end of seclusion, were known as the "two eyes" of Japan's open-door policy. See Johei Asahara, *Blessed Takezaki Junko*, p. 9.

22. The plans for the School For Western Learning drawn up by the Higo domain made this distinction clear. Science and English were to be entrusted to the care and supervision of the Western teacher, but ethics was to remain under the control of a native instructor, Takezaki Sadō, one of Shōnan's disciples. The Office of Western Learning stated Kumamoto's fears: "If only Western learning is taught, students will lose the concept of filial piety and loyalty." Consequently, "students will study Chinese texts every Sunday." *Kaitei Higo han kokuji shiryō*, vol. 10, pp. 692–93.

23. For a discussion of Yokoi's interest in Christianity see Imanaka Kanshi, "Higo jitsugakutō no shisō," in *Kumamoto Bando kenkyū*, pp. 35–46. Also Tamamuro Taijō, *Yokoi Shōnan*, pp. 124–25. Yokoi's involvement with Christianity is usually given as one of the reasons for his assassination. Yokoi saw Christianity as a unifying spiritual force in the West. He deplored the fact that Japan's religious tradition, split among Shinto, Buddhism, and Confucianism,

failed to perform a similar central role in the life of the Japanese. Tamamuro quotes Yokoi's poem: "The West says it has the true Teaching. This Teaching is centered around a Supreme Being. It guides people by means of commandments. It encourages good and castigates vice. Both high and low believe this Teaching. They establish their laws by it. Government and Teaching are one. In this way the people are inspired to action." I have used the translation of this poem found in David Dilworth and J. Thomas Rimer, eds., *Saiki Kōi and Other Stories*, p. 69.

24. Harootunian, *Towards Restoration*, p. 328. Harootunian quotes Yokoi's statement: "The Way is found through heaven and earth. It is not something possessed either by us or by foreigners. Wherever the Way is possessed, there you will find the central kingdom even among barbarians; where there is an absence of the Way, there you will find barbarians, even though they are the Chinese or the Japanese."

25. Ibid., p. 359. Also Marius B. Jansen, *Changing Japanese Attitudes Toward Modernization* (Princeton: Princeton University Press, 1965), p. 61.

26. Shōnan's interest in the United States is discussed in Tamamuro Taijō, *Yokoi Shōnan*, pp. 119–20. Yokoi Saheida (Ise Satarō) (1845–1875) and Yokoi Daihei (Numagawa Saburō) (1850–1871), Yokoi Shōnan's nephews, were among the first Japanese students to come to the United States. Arriving in New York in 1866 with a letter of introduction from Verbeck to Ferris, they were enrolled in the Rutgers Grammar School. While at Rutgers they were tutored by William Elliot Griffis. Griffis himself went to Japan in 1870 to teach in Fukui, the castle town where Yokoi had served as adviser to Matsudaira Shungaku and had carried out extensive reforms, including a revamping of the educational system. After completing their preparatory work at Rutgers Saheida and Daihei studied at the United States Naval Academy. Seriously ill with tuberculosis, Daihei was forced to return to Japan in 1869. In the two years before his death in 1871 he was a major force behind the establishment of the Kumamoto School For Western Learning. See Sugii Mutsurō, "Yokoi Saheida to Yokoi Daihei no Amerika ryūgaku," in Dōshisha Daigaku Jimbun Kagaku Kenkyūsho, eds., *Shakai kagaku 11* 3, 4 (1970–71), 457–565. Griffis's relationship to the Yokois is discussed in Edward R. Beauchamp, *An American Teacher in Early Meiji Japan* (Honolulu: University Press of Hawaii, 1976), pp. 15ff.

27. Pierson, *Tokutomi Sohō*, p. 24.

28. Tokutomi and Takezaki's plan is discussed in ibid., pp. 25–26. Tokutomi Kenjirō describes the preparations for the reform in his *Takezaki Junko*, in *Roka zenshū*, vol. 15, pp. 118–20. Ōe Shinobu argues that the 1870 reform in Kumamoto was basically a coup d'etat engineered by Restoration leaders such as Ōkubo Toshimichi, who worked in league with the local Practical Learning Party against the conservatives—the Shimpūren and School Party. Once in power, the Practical Learning group was willing to go much further than the central government wanted, and the reforms eventually became embarrassing to Ōkubo and his colleagues, who sent Yasuoka Ryōsuke as governor to Kumamoto in 1873 to keep the situation under control. Yasuoka

carried out his own "reforms," which included removing most of the Practical Learning men from power. As we shall see, the Yōgakkō (School for Western Learning) managed to ride out this storm, although it, too, was temporarily threatened with closure. Ōe Shinobu, *Meiji kokka no seiritsu*, pp. 83–91.

29. The complete text of the proposed reform can be found in Tokutomi Kenjirō, *Takezaki Junko*, in *Roka zenshū*, vol. 15, pp. 121–25. See also Pierson, *Tokutomi Sohō*, pp. 25–26. The proposal to raze the castle was not accepted. The castle, which Janes was to describe in detail in his writings, and which he saw as a monument to Japan's feudal past, was subsequently destroyed in the Satsuma Rebellion. The term "white heron" was applied to one of Japan's most impressive castles located at Himeji in Harima. It remains the best example of the massive fortresses constructed in the late sixteenth century.

30. *Kaitei Higo han kokuji shiryō* (Tokyo, 1964), vol. 10, p. 49. Sugii, "Kumamoto yōgakkō," in *Kumamoto Bando kenkyū*, p. 69.

31. The local situation is described in Tokutomi Kenjirō, *Takezaki Junko*, in *Roka zenshū*, vol. 15, pp. 120ff. See also *Omoide no ki*.

32. Janes, *Kumamoto*, part I, p. 23.

33. Kumamoto had an earlier Office of Western Learning, which sent students to Nagasaki. But at the time of the 1869–1870 reforms all the traditional offices, including this one, were disbanded. A new Office of Western Learning, out of which the Yōgakkō emerged, was established late in the summer of 1870. *Kaitei Higo han kokuji shiryō*, vol. 10, pp. 674–75.

34. The medical school was opened on October 30, 1870. At the same time a Western hospital was established. Kumamoto invited the Dutch physician C. G. Van Mansvelt to take charge of both. One of the first steps was to move the critically ill Yokoi Daihei to the hospital. Mansvelt arrived too late to prevent Yokoi's death from tuberculosis on May 20, 1871, but the school and hospital he developed were to become an important part of the Restoration in Higo. By a curious twist of fate, Mansvelt's most brilliant pupil at the medical school was Kitasato Shibasaburō, who later became one of Meiji Japan's best-known doctors. Kitasato, an outstanding bacteriologist, worked with Robert Koch in Berlin to isolate the tuberculosis bacillus, a feat which Koch accomplished in 1882. Kitasato later isolated the germ that caused bubonic plague. The history of the medical school is discussed in *Kumamoto ken kyōiku shi* (Kumamoto, 1931), vol. 1, pp. 312–14; 505–20. Mansvelt stayed in Kumamoto until June 1874, at which time he completed his three-year contract. For a biography of Kitasato see Miyajima Mikinosuke, ed., *Kitasato Shibasaburō den* (Tokyo, 1932). Also James Bartholomew, "Japanese Culture and the Problem of Modern Science," in Arnold Thackray and Everett Mendelsohn, eds., *Science and Values* (New York: Humanities Press, 1974), pp. 116f.

35. The plan for the Yōgakkō has often been attributed to Yokoi Daihei, who encouraged Hosokawa Morihisa and Nagaoka Moriyoshi to establish such a school. For details see *Kaitei Higo han kokuji shiryō*, vol. 10, pp. 674–77.

36. Ibid. Also *Kumamoto ken kyōiku shi*, vol. 1, p. 522. Sugii, "Kumamoto

Yōgakkō," *Kumamoto Bando kenkyū*, p. 68. Fukuda Reiju, *Gojūnen kinen Kumamoto Bando tsuikai roku*, p. 4.

37. One clause of the contract Janes signed with the Kumamoto domain in 1871 clearly spelled out what was to occur in case of civil war (*kokuran*). Sugii, "Kumamoto yōgakkō," *Kumamoto Bando kenkyū*, p. 103.

38. The Shimpūren, or Keishintō, was an outgrowth of the Loyalist Party (*kin-nōtō*) headed by the Kumamoto scholar of "national studies" (*kokugaku*), Hayashi Ōen (1797–1870). Lacking the power and contacts to influence domain politics directly, Kumamoto's loyalism failed to develop the political realism that allowed loyalists in other domains to make the crucial transition from pro-Emperor antiforeignism (*sonnō-jōi*) to the new view that the best way to protect the imperial state was to open the country to the West and to modernize as quickly as possible (*kaikoku*). Wedded to its Shinto ideology, the Keishintō formally established itself as the voice of loyalist ultraconservatism in 1872. Rigidly opposed to the government's efforts to bring an end to feudalism and the samurai class, members of the Keishintō prided themselves in outspoken opposition to anything Western, and in the maintenance of the symbols of the old order: the traditional samurai dress, top knot, and long and short sword. On the local scene Keishintō hatred focused on the Practical Learning Party and its reforms, including the proposed school for Western studies. Given the loyalists' violent inclinations, it was only logical to fear for the life of any Western teacher who dared to come to Kumamoto. In 1876 the latent violence of the Keishintō exploded in an open rebellion against the Meiji authorities and an attack on the Kumamoto prefectural offices and garrison, resulting in the death of the garrison commander and governor. The uprising was quickly suppressed by the government's forces, but it demonstrated that caution was not unwarranted in dealing with this group. For a discussion of the Keishintō see Ōkubo Toshiaki, "Meiji shinseiken ka no kyūshū," in Fukuoka UNESCO Kyōkai, eds., *Meiji isshin to kyūshū*, vol. 2 of *Kyūshū bunka ronshū* (Tokyo, 1973), pp. 483–88.

39. The debate over the safety of a Western teacher can be found in *Kaitei Higo han kokuji shiryō*, vol. 10, p. 676.

40. The Kagoshima bombardment stemmed from the Namamugi Incident, or the Richardson Affair, which occurred in September 1862. An Englishman named Richardson and three friends, one a woman, were riding on the Tōkaidō between Yokohama and Kawasaki when they encountered the procession of the daimyo of Satsuma, Shimazu Hisamitsu, near the village of Namamugi. Richardson's unfamiliarity with Japanese etiquette led to an unfortunate decision to ride his horse between the daimyo's palanquin and the main group of his bodyguards. Several of Shimazu's retainers regarded this as an unpardonable insult to their lord and went for their swords. In the fray that followed Richardson was mortally wounded and his two male companions were also seriously injured. In the wake of the incident the British government demanded redress. A British naval expedition was dispatched from China to Japan and an indemnity of 100,000 pounds was exacted from the Tokugawa government.

Seeking the execution of Richardson's assailants, the British decided to pursue matters directly with the Shimazu house in Kagoshima. An expedition of seven warships was sent to Satsuma in August 1863, and when Satsuma shore batteries opened fire on the British squadron during the negotiations, the British retaliated by destroying the domain's shore fortifications and in the process burned down a good portion of the city of Kagoshima. John R. Black, *Young Japan* (London: Oxford University Press, 1968), vol. 1, pp. 124–44.

41. *Kaitei Higo han kokuji shiryō*, vol. 10, p. 676.

42. Fukuda Reiju, *Gojūnen kinen Kumamoto Bando tsuikai roku*, p. 6.

43. *Kaitei Higo han kokuji shiryō*, vol. 10, p. 648. Nonoguchi contracted to have Nagasaki builders come to Kumamoto on November 17, 1870.

44. Fukuda Reiju, *Gojūnen kinen Kumamoto Bando tsuikai roku*, p. 6. Sugii, "Kumamoto yōgakkō," in *Kumamoto Bando kenkyū*, pp. 79–80, tells us that the school was built within the castle compound on a site that was previously used for the residences of the domain's upper class retainers. It would therefore appear that while the Practical Learning Party's plan for razing the castle was rejected, portions of the inner complex were cleared to allow for new construction.

45. *Kumamoto ken kyōiku shi*, vol. 1, p. 522.

46. The desired qualifications for the proposed teacher are outlined in *Kaitei Higo han kokuji shiryō*, vol. 10, p. 692. The request for a person of "samurai rank" is stated in Kozaki Hiromichi, "The Kumamoto Band in Retrospect" (Tokyo, February 28, and March 7, 1913. Free English rendering by H. Pedley. Typescript in the ABCFM documents, Houghton Library, Harvard University), p. 2. Verbeck, in his letter of reply to the domain request, "regretted that there was no samurai class in the United States, but recommended a military man as a substitute." Ibid. Given Daihei's familiarity with the United States the request for a samurai sounds rather naive and is probably a subsequent embellishment designed to underscore Kumamoto's backwardness in the early Meiji years.

47. Fukuda, *Gojūnen kinen Kumamoto Bando tsuikai roku*, p. 6.

48. Ibid. Also *Kumamoto ken kyōiku shi*, vol. 1, p. 522.

49. For Yokoi's arguments see *Kaitei Higo han kokuji shiryō*, vol. 10, p. 676.

50. Ibid., pp. 674–75, 692–93.

51. *Kumamoto ken kyōiku shi*, vol. 1, p. 522. The following biographical details are from William Elliot Griffis, *Verbeck of Japan* (New York: Fleming H. Revell, 1900).

52. Griffis, *Verbeck*, p. 125. Iwakura later headed the most important Meiji mission to the West (1871–73), which took many of Japan's new leaders to America and Europe. Soejima and Ōkuma became important political figures in the Meiji government.

53. Ibid., p. 117.

54. Yamazaki Masatada, *Yokoi Shōnan ikō*, pp. 453ff. Yamazaki includes Yokoi's correspondence with Iwao and Nonoguchi, who joined Yokoi's nephews Saheida and Daihei studying English with Verbeck in Nagasaki in 1865.

55. Sugii, "Yokoi Saheida to Yokoi Daihei no Amerika ryūgaku," *Shakai kagaku 11* (January 1970), p. 499.

56. Letter from Guido Verbeck to Rev. John M. Ferris, D.D., Yedo, August 20, 1870. [Dutch] Reformed Church in America Papers, Japan Mission, Gardener A. Sage Library, New Brunswick Theological Seminary. Hereafter cited as Dutch Reformed Papers.

57. Ibid. Also Griffis, *Verbeck*, p. 212. In 1868 Verbeck wrote to Ferris indicating the need for Christian laymen: "The prince of Hizen wishes to explore and open his mines. . . . I was desired to inquire for a suitable man to undertake this job." "If we could succeed in placing one such person satisfactorily, there would probably be a demand for more in time, and it would be well worth some trouble to supply the country with active Christian men in the various pursuits of life. You have no idea how the name of Christian is disgraced by most foreigners in Japan, and it would almost pay just to hire good Christian families and to make them live in various parts of the country to exemplify and adorn the doctrine. This too would put a stop to much of the open wickedness and immorality now prevalent among foreign residents of all nationalities and ranks." Griffis, *Verbeck*, pp. 152–53.

58. Letter from Verbeck to Ferris, Yedo, November 23, 1870, Dutch Reformed Papers.

59. Letter from Verbeck to Ferris, Yedo, August 20, 1870, Dutch Reformed Papers. The request for a married man seems to have been in keeping with Verbeck's concerns about the persistent temptations that corrupted single men in Japan. It is quite likely that Yokoi Daihei shared Verbeck's feelings in reference to this problem and for this reason recommended to the domain that Kumamoto invite a married teacher. On the other hand, the idea of bringing a family to Kumamoto involved further security risks for the Kumamoto reformers.

60. Ibid.

61. Letter from Verbeck to Ferris, Yedo, September 22, 1870, Dutch Reformed Papers.

62. Letter from Verbeck to Ferris, Yedo, March 22, 1871, Dutch Reformed Papers.

63. Letter from Verbeck to Ferris, Yedo, May 20, 1871, Dutch Reformed Papers.

64. Letter from Verbeck to Ferris, Yedo, July 20, 1871, Dutch Reformed Papers.

65. In his August 20, 1870, letter to Ferris, Verbeck wrote: "Numagawa [Yokoi Daihei] is to write to his brother about it too . . . ." Dutch Reformed Papers.

66. Janes Papers, no. 603, "Kumamoto," ch. 1, p. 1.

67. Janes, *Kumamoto*, part 1, p. 7.

68. Janes Papers, no. 603, "Kumamoto," ch. 1, pp. 4–5. That the Kumamoto offer came through President Grant seems highly unlikely, although Saheida's connections at Annapolis, and with the former consular official Robert Walsh, no doubt led to inquiries in official circles.

69. Ibid., p. 5.

70. *Janes vs. Janes* Divorce Proceedings Records.

71. Janes Papers, no. 603, "Kumamoto," ch. 1, p. 1. Janes wrote that he was reluctant to take his wife and two young children "eight or ten thousand miles away to a country, still cast in the throes of revolution, which seemed to have no valid claims upon my services."

72. Ibid., p. 8.

73. Griffis, *Verbeck*, p. 217.

74. Ibid., pp. 217–18.

75. *Janes vs. Janes* Divorce Proceedings Records.

76. Janes Papers, no. 603, "Kumamoto," ch. 2, p. 22. Harriet suffered from a prolapsed uterus, see *Janes vs. Janes* Divorce Proceedings Records.

77. Janes wrote that the "state of the mother's health necessitated immediate medical treatment and for that reason the long journey [to Japan] was arranged to begin from New York where the wife and mother was for a fortnight or more in the hands of the noted specialist Dr. Marion Sims." Ibid., p. 21. James Marion Sims (1813–1883) was one of America's leading gynecological surgeons. *Dictionary of American Biography*, vol. 9, pp. 186–88.

78. *Janes vs. Janes* Divorce Proceedings Records.

79. Letter from Janes to Mr. Ise [Yokoi Tokio], Ann Arbor, Michigan, May 1, 1888. Unpublished letter. Copy in the possession of the author. I am indebted to Prof. Sugii Mutsurō of Dōshisha University, Kyoto, for making this letter available to me.

80. Ibid.

81. Janes Papers, no. 603, "Kumamoto," ch. 2, p. 23.

82. Ibid., p. 24. Horace Capron (1804–1895) served as United States Commissioner of Agriculture from 1867 to 1871, when he resigned his post to accept an appointment from the Japanese government as commissioner and chief adviser to the Kaitakushi Department in the settlement and development of Hokkaido, Japan's northernmost island. Capron worked in Japan until 1875. Janes remembered him as "white haired and fine natured," who was particularly fond of "our little tot of the fairy foot and azure eye [Fanny]." Theodor Edward Hoffman and Leopold Müller were both German physicians hired by the Japanese government to establish a medical school as part of the Kaisei Gakkō, which eventually became the Medical Faculty of Tokyo University. Janes wrote that Müller helped save the life of his infant son, Henry, while aboard the *America*. For Capron see *Dictionary of American Biography*, vol. 2, pp. 484–85. Also Harada Kazufumi, *Oyatoi gaikokujin, vol. 13 Kaitaku* (Tokyo, 1975), p. 49. For Hoffman and Müller see UNESCO to Ajia Bunka Kenkyū Senta, eds., *Shiryō ōyatoi gaikokujin* (Tokyo, 1975), pp. 414–15, 434–35. For Janes' views see Janes Papers, no. 603, "Kumamoto," ch. 2, pp. 25–26.

83. Janes Papers, no. 603, "Kumamoto," ch. 2, p. 25.

84. In his much quoted poem, written for his nephews at the time of their departure for the United States in 1866, Yokoi had written: "In clarifying the Way of Yao, Shun, and Confucius we must exhaust the skills of Western technology. Why stop with enriching the nation? Why stop with strengthening

the army? Our task will be in spreading the great principles of the sages to the four seas." While clearly a nationalist, Yokoi visualized Japanese expansion, much as Janes did—that is, in cultural not military terms. Yamazaki Masatada, *Yokoi Shōnan ikō* (Tokyo, 1942), p. 728. I have used the translation in Harootunian, *Towards Restoration*, p. 397, with a minor modification.

CHAPTER VI
YOKOHAMA, EDO, AND KUMAMOTO

1. Janes, *Kumamoto*, part 1, p. 6. The Pacific Mail Line Steamer *America* burned in Yokohama harbor on August 24, 1872. Janes writes that "no one perished with the 'America.' Only a million or more of property was destroyed." Ibid. John R. Black, in *Young Japan: Yokohama and Edo 1858–79* (London: Oxford University Press, 1968), vol. 2, p. 381, records the burning of the ship as a "great catastrophe" and adds that the ship was destroyed "with a loss of 60 human beings."

2. For a description of Yokohama and the treaty-port community I have relied on Black, *Young Japan*; Harold S. Williams, *Tales of the Foreign Settlements in Japan* (Rutland, Vt.: Charles E. Tuttle, 1958) and his *Foreigners in Mikadoland* (Rutland, Vt.: Charles E. Tuttle, 1963); Pat Barr, *The Coming of the Barbarians: A Story of Western Settlements in Japan 1853–1870* (London: Macmillan, 1967) and her *The Deer Cry Pavilion: A Story of Westerners in Japan 1868–1905* (London: Macmillan, 1968). The subject of foreign employees in Meiji Japan is discussed in H. J. Jones, *Live Machines: Hired Foreigners and Meiji Japan* (Vancouver: University of British Columbia Press, 1980); the standard Japanese sources on foreign employees in Meiji Japan are the seventeen-volume *Oyatoi gaikokujin* (Tokyo: Kashima Shuppan, 1970s) and UNESCO Higashi Ajia Bunka Kenkyū Sentā, eds., *Shiryō oyatoi gaikokujin* (Tokyo, 1975). Excellent descriptions of the treaty ports can also be found in Sir Rutherford Alcock, *The Capital of the Tycoon: A Narrative of a Three Year's Residence in Japan* (London: Longman, Green, Longman Roberts, and Green, 1863); William Elliot Griffis, *The Mikado's Empire* (New York: Harper & Bros., 1876); and contemporary newspapers such as the *Far East* and the *Japan Weekly Mail*.

3. Williams, *Tales of the Foreign Settlements in Japan*, p. 43.

4. Williams, *Foreigners in Mikadoland*, p. 85. The term is used as Williams' chapter heading.

5. Ibid., pp. 291f. Williams' appendix includes the "Rules and Regulations for the Peace, Order, and Good Government of British Subjects Within the Dominions of the Tycoon of Japan," which were issued by the British consul, Rutherford Alcock, in 1860.

6. Arthur Collins Maclay, *A Budget of Letters from Japan* (New York: A. C. Armstrong & Son, 1889), p. 25. Maclay was one of a handful of Americans who taught in the interior, serving as teacher in the Tōō Gijuku in Hirosaki at the northern end of Honshu from May to November 1874. Maclay had few

good words for Yokohama. "As to the social features," he wrote, "the Japanese regard it as the wickedest place in the Empire. Not but what many good people live there, but it possesses a vast capacity for working iniquity. In this respect it is like all oriental settlements where the lower forms of our civilization come into contact with a degraded Eastern society. The most iniquitous people are generally to be found in the immediate vicinity of the civilization of the nineteenth century" (p. 24).

7. William Elliot Griffis, *A Maker of the New Orient: Samuel Robbins Brown* (New York: Fleming H. Revell, 1902), p. 188.

8. Griffis, *Verbeck*, p. 209.

9. Williams, *Foreigners in Mikadoland*, p. 87. The description is from George Smith, Bishop of Hong Kong and is taken from Smith's book, *Ten Weeks in Japan* (London: Longman Green, 1861).

10. Griffis, *Verbeck*, p. 237. Griffis added: "Mine was a Smith and Wesson's revolver, bought, just before I left New Brunswick, by the advice of my Japanese friends. It was snugly kept in a special pocket made inside the left lapel of my walking coat, whence it could be drawn quickly, as it seemed indeed more than once necessary. I am not certain but that the mere gesture of putting my hand into my bosom was more than once a means of impressing upon some scowling patriot that he had better not draw."

11. Griffis described the incident in *The Mikado's Empire*, pp. 374–77.

12. Griffis, writing to his sister from Fukui, noted: "In my own household, I have made another change. The young girl . . . whom I took for a servant to wait specifically on me proved to be very faithful, diligent and pleasant in every way, anticipated my every want, and made my house almost as comfortable as a home; I liked her very much. All of which to a sometimes weary and home-sick young man must necessarily be a strong temptation in his lonely hours. I found after a few weeks, that she made too much comfort for me, and was too attractive herself. After having her 11 days, I sent her away, before temptation turned into sin . . . and now, though with less comfort and a more lonely house, I can let all my inner life be known to you without shame." Quoted in Edward R. Beauchamp, *An American Teacher in Early Meiji Japan*, pp. 53–54.

13. F. V. Dickins in *The Life of Sir Harry Parkes* (1894) wrote: "It is an unalloyed truth to say that the majority of the 'Professors' in the schools of Tokei were graduates of the dry-goods counter, the forecastle, the camp, and the shambles, or belonged to that vast array of unclassified humanity that floats like waifs in every seaport. Coming directly from the bar-room, the brothel, the gambling saloon, or the resort of boon companions, they brought the graces, the language and the manners of those places into the school room. . . . Japanese pride revolted . . . after a report had been circulated that one of the professors was a butcher by trade." Quoted in Williams, *Foreigners in Mikadoland*, p. 84.

14. Hermann Maron, *Japan und China* (Berlin: Otto Janke, 1863), pp. 27–28. Maron wrote: "Es fehlt das rasch pulsierende Leben Europa's im Staat, in der Gemeinde, in der Familie; es fehlt überall."

15. The railway is discussed in Black, *Young Japan*, vol. 2, p. 332. The telegraph line between Tokyo and Yokohama was opened on January 26, 1870. Ibid., p. 281. For the role of Cobb & Co. see Williams, *Foreigners in Mikadoland*, pp. 122–31.

16. Beauchamp, *An American Teacher in Early Meiji Japan*, p. 78.

17. The Yedo Hotel is discussed in *The Far East*, vol. 1, no. 6 (August 16, 1870), p. 2. The same issue includes a photograph of the building.

18. Janes' stay at the Yedo Hotel is recorded in "Kumamoto yōgakkō," in *Kyūshū bungaku* 31 (January 30, 1893), p. 3.

19. Janes Papers, no. 603, "Kumamoto," ch. 2, p. 32.

20. Ibid., p. 33. Although the contract that Janes subsequently signed clearly indicated his position as "Professor of English Studies" in what was described as a "Grammar School," Sugii Mutsurō has noted that Kumamoto may well have originally aimed at a military academy. As indicated earlier, the domain's intention was certainly to use Janes' military expertise should civil war erupt. Sugii quotes Tokutomi Sohō's statement in his autobiography that the "original intent may well have been a military academy" (*Sohō jiden*, p. 53.). Harriet in the divorce suit stated that her husband had gone to Japan to "instruct the young men of one of the Provinces in military tactics, his appointment having been made for that purpose, however on his arrival the character of the school was changed." See Sugii Mutsurō, "Kumamoto yōgakkō," in *Kumamoto Bando kenkyū*, p. 104. Also *Janes vs. Janes* Divorce Proceedings Records.

21. The rebellions Janes referred to were the Saga uprising of 1874 headed by Etō Shimpei, the Kumamoto Shimpūren, Akizuki, and Yamaguchi (Maebara Issei) uprisings of 1876, and the full-fledged Satsuma Rebellion of 1877. Saigo Takamori, the leader of the Satsuma Rebellion, did make efforts to use his private school in Kagoshima to organize and educate the exsamurai of Satsuma.

22. Janes Papers, no. 603, "Kumamoto," ch. 2, pp. 32–33.

23. H. J. Jones, *Live Machines*, p. 51.

24. Janes Papers, no. 603, "Kumamoto," ch. 2, p. 34.

25. The contract Janes signed in Tokyo is not currently available, but on September 11, 1871, he signed a contract in Kumamoto that contained these conditions, and Sugii Mutsurō feels that this is the contract worked out in Tokyo. See his "Kumamoto Yōgakkō," in *Kumamoto Bando kenkyū*, pp. 102–104. Some sense of Janes' $400 monthly salary can be obtained from a letter Verbeck wrote to Ferris on June 19, 1871, in which he observed: "A man who wishes to get on economically here and who knows how to manage household affairs, can live comfortably for $50 a month, with a small family for $75 to $85 a month, so that out of $1,800 he could save annually from $700 to $1,000." At this rate Janes' annual savings could have run to $3,800 a year. The salary of a United States congressman in 1871 was $5,000 a year. Verbeck's comment on Janes' contract is from a letter to Ferris, August 22, 1871. Both can be found in the Dutch Reformed Papers.

26. Letter from Janes to Ferris, Yedo, Japan, September 11, 1871, Dutch Reformed Papers.

27. Letter from Verbeck to Ferris, August 22, 1871, Dutch Reformed Papers. Janes wrote: "I was tendered the choice of two positions out of several then vacant in the newly founded Imperial University." *Kumamoto*, part 1, p. 8.

28. See Edward R. Beauchamp, *An American Teacher in Early Meiji Japan*, pp. 62–64.

29. Janes Papers, no. 603, "Kumamoto," ch. 2, p. 34.

30. Ibid., p. 32.

31. Letter from Janes to Ferris, Yedo, Japan, September 11, 1871, Dutch Reformed Papers.

32. Janes Papers, no. 603, "Kumamoto," ch. 2, pp. 34–35.

33. Ibid., pp. 35–37.

34. Janes, *Kumamoto*, part 1, p. 19.

35. Letter from Janes to Ferris, "On Steamer at Kobe," September 15, 1871, Dutch Reformed Papers.

36. Janes Papers, no. 603, "Kumamoto," ch. 2, p. 37.

37. Janes, *Kumamoto*, part 1, p. 8.

38. Ibid.

39. Letter from Henry Stout to Ferris, Nagasaki, March 17, 1876.

40. Janes, *Kumamoto*, part 1, p. 9. The following account of the journey to Kumamoto is from pp. 9–10.

41. Ibid., p. 10.

42. Ibid., p. 11. Janes wrote "Serikawa" for the river Shirakawa. I have taken the liberty of correcting these minor errors on his part. Such mistakes were understandable given his unfamiliarity with Japanese.

43. Janes Papers, no. 603, "Kumamoto," ch. 3, pp. 50–51.

44. Janes, *Kumamoto*, part 1, p. 12.

45. Ibid.

46. Ibid., p. 13.

47. Ibid.

48. Ibid.

49. Ibid.

50. Janes Papers, no. 603, "Kumamoto," ch. 3, p. 56. In his later version of the manuscript, which was published long after his death as *Kumamoto: An Episode in Japan's Break From Feudalism*, Janes struck out the reference that the Kumamoto reformers were "striving to imitate our liberal spirit." Instead he continues to quote Harriet writing, " 'L' thinks they are on the right road. 'Nothing but enlightenment—education'—he says. But the sight of the hordes of two-sworded, dark-visaged men with their top-knotted bare heads and daredevil bearing all standing aloof from this movement which 'L' represents among them is not calculated to make one comfortable or confident. 'L' is determined to have the guards dismissed and has already sent one of his interpreters away. How is he ever to manage. . . ." Janes, *Kumamoto*, part 1, p. 14.

51. Ibid.

52. Ibid.

53. Janes Papers, no. 603, "Kumamoto," ch. 3, p. 59.

54. Janes, *Kumamoto*, part 1, p. 14.

55. It is interesting to note that Janes' description was not the only English-language account of what the castle looked like in 1871. On December 21 of that year Joseph Heco, one of the early Japanese castaways to be educated in the United States, visited Kumamoto castle and recorded some fascinating details in his diary. It is intriguing that Heco does not mention Janes, or vice versa. What Heco does mention is that the Practical Learning Party's proposal for the razing of the castle was taken seriously by the top administrators of the domain. Shown around the castle by the former *karō*, Hirano, Heco writes: "In the course of our walk the *Karō* informed us that it was intended to petition the Central Government to allow them to demolish the Castle. This for two reasons. The first that many of the *Samurai* were unwilling to see the fortress in the hands of the Central Government, and second that so long as the Castle was in their own hands, Kumamoto would be regarded as a possible center of disaffection and trouble by the Tōkiō authorities." "We deprecated this course," Heco continued, "pointing out the vandalism of destroying such a noble monument of antiquity, and pointing out that in the present civilized Japan, no Government would ever suspect them of disaffection merely because the Castle stood. Whether our representations had any effects or not, the Castle remained intact till the siege by the Satsuma troops in 1877." Joseph Heco, *The Narrative of a Japanese* (Tokyo: American-Japanese Publishing Association, n.d.), vol. 2, p. 159.

56. Janes, *Kumamoto*, part 1, p. 15. Katō Kiyomasa (1562–1611) was a leading daimyo in the late sixteenth and early seventeenth centuries. A trusted ally of Toyotomi Hideyoshi, he was placed in charge of Higo in 1588 and later led Hideyoshi's invasions of Korea in 1592 and 1597. Katō built Kumamoto Castle in 1601 and Nagoya Castle in 1610. In both cases he used new stone-wall construction techniques brought from Korea.

57. Ibid.

58. Janes Papers, no. 603, "Kumamoto," ch. 3, pp. 59–60.

59. Janes, *Kumamoto*, part 1, pp. 15–16.

60. Ibid., p. 17.

61. See Lafcadio Hearn, *Japan: An Attempt at Interpretation* (New York: Macmillan, 1904).

62. Janes, *Kumamoto*, part 1, p. 17.

63. Ibid., p. 20.

64. Ibid., p. 21.

65. Ibid., p. 23.

66. Ibid.

67. Ibid., p. 25.

68. Ibid.

69. Ibid., p. 22.

70. Ibid., p. 15.

71. Sidney L. Gulick, *Evolution of the Japanese People* (New York: Fleming Revell, 1903), p. 91.
72. Adachi Kinosuke, "Christian Missions in Japan," *Century Magazine* (September 1911), p. 82.
73. Janes, *Kumamoto*, part 1, p. 27.
74. It is also likely that the shift from domain to prefectural authority created a period of uncertainty on the part of the school administrators. Harriet's letters home suggest that there was clearly a lag in the implementation of the new structure. "You have heard of the marvelous changes the Government is undergoing," she wrote, "soon the provinces are to have governors appointed over them in place of the princes, whose doings shall be wholly subject to the general government. This latter change has been effected during the last two or three months, so that the one whom I have been calling the Prince, is now a common man like any other." Quoted in Janes Papers, no. 603, "Kumamoto," ch. 3, pp. 56–57. Kumamoto was divided into two prefectures: Shirakawa Ken and Yatsushiro Ken. The school was placed under the jurisdiction of Shirakawa Ken. No governor was initially appointed to this prefecture, but Yamada Buho, whom Janes described as "the truly noble, popular, and patriotic Mr. Yamada," was appointed *sanji*, or councillor. Tokutomi Iichirō, *Sohō jiden*, p. 57.
75. Janes, *Kumamoto*, part 1, p. 36.
76. Ibid., p. 35.
77. Ibid. These views seem somewhat exaggerated. The school buildings were very close to completion, and Janes' house was largely finished—although classes did begin in temporary quarters as he describes.
78. Ibid., p. 46.
79. Ibid., p. 37.
80. Ibid.
81. Ibid.

Chapter VII
The Kumamoto School for Western Learning

1. Fukunaga Bunnosuke, *Nihon ni okeru taii Jiensu shi*, pp. 131–32. The observation is that of Miyagawa Tsuneteru. Janes Papers, no. 613–02, consists of a partial translation into English of this volume, which seems to have been produced for the Captain by his students after the book appeared in Japanese. Where possible I have checked the translated materials against the original. Many of the articles in this book first appeared in *Kyūshū bungaku* 31 (January 1893), an edition of this journal that was devoted to the Kumamoto Yōgakkō. This edition was reprinted in *Kumamoto tenbō* 5 (Winter 1976), in a special edition devoted to the "Kumamoto Band." The standard Japanese studies on the Kumamoto School for Western Learning are Sugii Mutsurō, "Kumamoto yōgakkō: jitsugakutō no risō kyōiku kikan," in *Kumamoto Bando kenkyū*, and his "Kumamoto yōgakkō" in *Kirisutokyō shakai mondai kenkyū* 4 (March

1961) and 7 (April 1963). Various commemorative pamphlets have also appeared about the school. Of these I found the following useful: Fukuda Reiju (Yoshinobu), *Gojūnen kinen Kumamoto Bando tsuikai roku* (Tokyo, 1926); Fukuda Reiju (Yoshinobu) and Mitsui Hisashi, *Kumamoto Bando o omou* (Tokyo, 1965); Ebina Danjō, *Kumamoto yōgakkō to Kumamoto Bando* (a lecture delivered in Kumamoto at the Kaikosha, June 23, 1935); and *Hyaku nen kinen Kumamoto Bando: Kindai Nihon o hiraita seishun gunzō* (published for the 100th anniversary exhibition for the Kumamoto Band held at the Tsuruya Department Store, Kumamoto, January 30 to February 3, 1976). The Kumamoto school has been dealt with in other Western works. See Irwin Scheiner, *Christian Converts and Social Protest in Meiji Japan* (Berkeley: University of California Press, 1970); John D. Pierson, *Tokutomi Sohō* (Princeton: Princeton University Press, 1980); and George E. Moore, "Samurai Conversion: The Case of Kumamoto," *Asian Studies* (University of the Philippines) 4, 1 (April 1966). I have discussed the Yōgakkō previously in "Ebina Danjō: A Christian Samurai of the Meiji Period," *Papers on Japan* (Harvard East Asian Research Center), vol. 2 (August 1963).

2. Janes Papers, no. 104, "Letter to Anna," Kumamoto, Japan, October 7, 1874.
3. Janes Papers, no. 107, "Letter to Anna," Kumamoto, Japan, July 24, 1875. Janes wrote: "These dear people—so gentle—so kind—so *affectionate* my boys are to me—I love them."
4. Janes Papers, no. 306, "Kumamoto" (ch. not indicated), ms. p. 260.
5. Sugii Mutsurō, "Kumamoto yōgakkō," in *Kumamoto Bando kenkyū*, pp. 109–10. Janes' "plan" can be found in Fukunaga, *Nihon ni okeru taii Jiensu shi*, pp. 158–62. Kozaki Hiromichi wrote of the effects of Janes' plan: "Mr. Tameyoshi Nonoguchi, who had the general oversight of [the] Yogakko, entrusted Captain Janes with the whole task not only of the education of the scholars but also the management of the school. He therefore himself laid out the course of study, which comprised reading, mathematics, geography, history, physics, chemistry, geology and astronomy, to be completed in four years. He required that all the scholars should be lodged in the dormitory and be given special training. He undertook to do everything himself, from the instruction to the supervision of the scholars, so that all the teachers of mathematics, translation, and the like who had already been engaged were dismissed and he himself taught all the subjects." Kozaki Hiromichi, *Reminiscences of Seventy Years* (Tokyo, 1933), p. 12.
6. Janes, *Kumamoto*, part 1, p. 43.
7. Watase Tsuneyoshi, *Ebina Danjō sensei* (Tokyo, 1938), p. 78.
8. Janes, *Kumamoto*, part 1, p. 43.
9. Shimomura Kōtarō was typical of those who saw Janes as stern: "Being himself a soldier," he wrote, "Captain Janes naturally treated his pupils with extreme sternness." Fukunaga, *Nihon ni okeru taii Jiensu shi*, pp. 86–87. Ebina Danjō noted, "the way he taught his pupils was just like an officer drilling his men. He was very strict, and his censure and praise were taken to heart by the boys." Ibid., p. 101.

10. Ibid., p. 139.

11. Watase, *Ebina Danjō*, p. 78. As the daily routine suggests, the similarity between the Yōgakkō and West Point was obvious. Tanaka Keisuke has explored this topic at greater length in his "Uesuto Pointo rikugun shikan gakkō no Kumamoto yōgakkō e no eikyō," *Eigaku shi kenkyū* (Nihon Eigaku Shi Gakkai), no. 12 (September 1979).

12. Watase, *Ebina Danjō*, p. 79.

13. Fukunaga, *Nihon ni okeru taii Jiensu shi*, p. 9. For Janes, cleanliness clearly reflected godliness. Kozaki noted the effects of Janes' regulations on the school's sanitary facilities, which, as anyone who has taught or studied in Japanese institutions of higher learning, even in the second half of the twentieth century, is painfully aware, are hardly olfactory delights: "Every time they were used the user had to report his name to the Superintendent of the students: and if the next one found the place soiled he had to report to the Superintendent who then ordered the boy who had previously used it to clean it. Not excepting the Jishūkan [the former domain academy], all schools had this single place of their premises unspeakably unsanitary, but [the] Yogakko swept away this evil at a stroke." Kozaki, *Reminiscences*, p. 13.

14. Janes, *Kumamoto*, part 1, p. 37.

15. Janes Papers, no. 104, "Letter to Anna," Kumamoto, Japan, October 7, 1874.

16. Janes, *Kumamoto*, part 1, p. 40.

17. The student was Miyagawa Tsuneteru, who is quoted in Hisashi Mitsui, "Doshisha and the Kumamoto Band," *Japan Christian Quarterly* 25, 2 (April 1959), 115. It is worth noting that Miyagawa was the best speller in the class. See Shimomura Kōtarō, "Kyōiku no koto ni kanshite," *Kyūshū bungaku* 31 (January 1893), 36.

18. Ibid. Also Fukunaga, *Nihon ni okeru taii Jiensu shi*, p. 89. The impression that spelling lessons of this kind had on students was echoed by Kameyama Noboru at a reunion in the 1920s. Noting that fifty years had passed since he had been a student at the school, he recalled how hard they had all worked to master spelling—and then proceeded to amaze everyone by spelling "incomprehensibility" without the slightest hesitation. Mitsui, "Doshisha and the Kumamoto Band," *Japan Christian Quarterly* 25, 2 (April 1959), 115.

19. Fukunaga, *Nihon ni okeru taii Jiensu shi*, p. 89.

20. Watase, *Ebina Danjō*, p. 79.

21. Sugii, "Kumamoto yōgakkō," *Kumamoto Bando kenkyū*, p. 156. Sugii states the number of the entering class in 1871 was 45. The *Kumamoto ken kyōiku shi*, vol. 1, p. 533, gives the 1871 entering class as 46; that of 1872 as 80; and that of 1873 as 40. Sugii gives the number of graduates in the first class as 11. See Sugii, *Kumamoto Bando kenkyū*, p. 93.

22. Sugii, *Kumamoto Bando kenkyū*, p. 137.

23. Watase, *Ebina Danjō*, p. 80.

24. Ibid.

25. Janes Papers, no. 104, "Letter to Anna," Kumamoto, Japan, October 7,

1874. Janes outlined the curriculum to Anna. See also *Kumamoto ken kyōiku shi*, vol. 1, pp. 527–30.

26. Janes Papers, no. 104, "Letter to Anna," Kumamoto, Japan, October 7, 1874. Also Watase, *Ebina Danjō*, p. 84.

27. Ebina tells us that Janes taught that history began in the great river valleys of Egypt and Mesopotamia, and he traced its development from these to the modern world. Janes was also influenced by Buckle's efforts to link geography to history. Ebina further pointed out that Janes was basically an evolutionist. Ebina himself found Janes' explanation "that this world had come through various ages before man was finally born into it" as "truly fascinating." Watase, *Ebina Danjō*, p. 81.

28. Janes' approach to the problem of mathematics shows his unusual ability to understand and adjust to the environment in which he worked. Many samurai harbored an age-old disdain for mathematics, which stemmed from the Tokugawa division of society into four classes, and the association of counting, accounts, and mathematics with the lowest class, namely, the merchants. When he started his students on mathematics, Janes made the point that the purpose of this study was not to enable students to "keep money accounts," but to "help to improve their way of thinking." "One must think carefully about everything," he told the students, "and for this mathematics is the best tool." Ibid., p. 82.

29. Janes Papers, no. 104, "Letter to Anna," Kumamoto, Japan, October 7, 1874. Janes' growing enthusiasm was reflected not only in his correspondence with the Warners, but also by others who worked with him in the school. Fukunaga, *Nihon ni okeru taii Jiensu shi*, p. 11.

30. Kozaki Hiromichi, "The Kumamoto Band in Retrospect." Kozaki describes the entrance examination as unusual. "A good voice together with fluency in reading, was deemed essential for the study of English, so the teacher of Chinese was requested to test in regard to the quality of their voice. The announcement of these tests aroused no little indignation in the city and surroundings, for it was accompanied with a rumor that only good looking youths would be accepted—a proceeding regarded as utterly unfair where education is concerned. I took the examination but with little hope of passing, for in spite of a fair knowledge of the classics, I was halting in my speech, and my voice was far from good. With me in the examination was another boy who seemed to have just the proper requirements, for he read well, in clear and distinct tones. Judge of my surprise then, when it was made known that he had failed while I had passed. Afterwards I learned that I had had a friend at court—the teacher of Chinese [Kanezaka Junjirō]—who had put in a good word for me on the ground that although not gifted in speech I had other qualities that entitled me to admission." In his *Reminiscences* published twenty years later, Kozaki seems to have forgotten about the above "examination," writing, "I, however, was admitted without examination." Kozaki, *Reminiscences*, p. 14.

31. Sugii, "Kumamoto yōgakkō," *Kumamoto Bando kenkyū*, p. 79.

32. For a more complete account of Yamazaki see Sugii Mutsurō, "Yamazaki Tamenori," *Kumamoto Bando kenkyū*, pp. 346–61.

33. Mitsui Hisashi (Takenaka Masao, ed.), *Kindai Nihon seinen gunzō*, p. 117. The governor of Mizusawa prefecture, Yasuba Yasukazu, was a follower of Yokoi Shōnan. Yamazaki became Janes' favorite pupil. His standing at the school was almost always at the top of his class. After graduating from the Yōgakkō, Yamazaki went to Tokyo and entered the Kaisei Gakkō (which later became Tokyo University), where, Kozaki tells us, even Inoue Tetsujirō and Wadagaki Kenzō "were not his equal." Kozaki, *Reminiscences*, p. 26. On January 31, 1876, Janes wrote to Yamazaki in Tokyo, "I sincerely congratulate you on your fair success; and we are all greatly pleased at the unmixed honor its first graduate reflects on Kumamoto School." Janes Papers, no. 113. Yamazaki died of tuberculosis in 1881.

34. Jerome D. Davis, who taught theology at Dōshisha, later wrote that "they asked me questions, every day, which I had never thought of before, and the three years in which I had them as pupils were years of the most intense study for me." J. Merle Davis, *Davis-Soldier Missionary* (Chicago: Pilgrim Press, 1916), p. 170. The quotation is from Mitsui, "Doshisha and the Kumamoto Band," *Japan Christian Quarterly* 25, 2 (April 1959), 112. Mitsui tells us that while studying the atonement the class got involved in a massive argument with Davis which he could not handle and finally forced him to have a severe headache and fall ill. He tells us that the students referred to this as "Atonement Sickness." Commenting on the intellectual quality of the students, he added that students who had known no English at the outset were able to use the language to deal with difficult subjects such as Astronomy by the fourth year. The degree to which they mastered these subjects, he noted, could be seen in an astronomy text preserved in one of the Kumamoto churches (but unfortunately lost in World War II), which contained Kozaki's signature in the front and Miyagawa's in the back. Among the book's marginal notes, in a section dealing with calculations of the distance from the earth to the sun, one of the students had written, "in my plan," and then added the results of his own solution with appropriate figures that updated the text. Ibid., p. 115.

35. Fukunaga, *Nihon ni okeru taii Jiensu shi*, pp. 132–33.

36. Kozaki, *Reminiscences*, pp. 15–16.

37. Fukunaga, *Nihon ni okeru taii Jiensu shi*, p. 133.

38. Kozaki, *Reminiscences*, p. 16.

39. Watase, *Ebina Danjō*, p. 81.

40. Kozaki, *Reminiscences*, pp. 13–14.

41. Fukunaga, *Nihon ni okeru taii Jiensu shi*, p. 75. Arnold stated his preferences for a teacher as follows: "What I want is a man who is a Christian and a gentleman, an active man, and one who has common sense, and understands boys. I do not so much care about scholarship, as he will have immediately under him the lowest forms in the school; but yet, on second thoughts, I do care about it very much, because his pupils may be in the highest forms; and besides, I think that even the elements are best taught by a man who has a

thorough knowledge of the matter. However, if one must give way, I prefer activity of mind and an interest in his work to high scholarship: for the one may be acquired far more easily than the other." Quoted in J. J. Findlay, *Arnold of Rugby: His School Life and Contributions to Education* (Cambridge: Cambridge University Press, 1898), p. 52.

42. Fukunaga, *Nihon ni okeru taii Jiensu shi*, p. 75.

43. Ibid., p. 139.

44. Ibid., p. 140. There is no evidence indicating that any of Janes' relatives were hired to serve as physicians in Kumamoto. It is possible, however, that prefectural authorities temporarily considered hiring Harriet's brother, Henry Martin Jr., who was a missionary doctor in India.

45. Ibid., p. 99.

46. Ibid., p. 140.

47. Ibid., p. 87.

48. Ibid., p. 140.

49. "In the classroom," one of the students wrote, "his stern looks and dignified posture awed the students into obedience. When he was scolding them for idleness or dishonesty, it was like hearing a military officer shaming his soldiers into battle. But his kindness was unbounded. Whenever his pupils were taken ill, he would call on them and try to cheer and comfort them. He would often invite them to dinner and talk with them for hours, taking every opportunity to give them amusement or instruction. He would not let any virtuous act or any remarkable progress in learning pass without being noticed and praised. He would also not neglect dull boys, for whom he would try every means to push them on to progress. Between the teacher and the students, therefore, there existed a mutual affection not unlike that between parent and child." Ibid., p. 45.

50. The importance of Samuel Smiles is discussed by George Sansom in *The Western World and Japan*, pp. 396–97. More recently Earl H. Kinmonth has dealt with the role of Smiles and his translator Nakamura Masanao in his book, *The Self-Made Man in Meiji Japanese Thought* (Berkeley: University of California Press, 1981), pp. 9ff.

51. Samuel Smiles, *Self Help* (London: John Murray, 1873), p. 1. *Self Help* was first published in 1859. The first Japanese edition appeared in 1871.

52. Fukunaga, *Nihon ni okeru taii Jiensu shi*, p. 104.

53. Ibid., p. 105.

54. Ibid., p. 148.

55. Ebina Danjō, *Kirisutokyō gairon mikankō waga shinkyō no yurai to keika* (Tokyo, 1937), p. 53.

56. Janes Papers, no. 104, "Letter to Anna," Kumamoto, Japan, October 7, 1874.

57. Ibid.

58. Janes, *Kumamoto*, part 1, p. 116.

59. Ibid., p. 126. Tokutomi Hatsuko subsequently married Yuasa Jirō, and her

son Yuasa Hachirō became president of Dōshisha; later he served as the first president of International Christian University in Tokyo. Miya married Ebina.

60. Ibid., p. 127.

61. Kozaki, "The Kumamoto Band in Retrospect," unpaginated.

62. Ibid.

63. Mitsui, *Kindai Nihon no seinen gunzō*, p. 87.

64. Watase, *Ebina Danjō*, pp. 83–84.

65. Mitsui points out that there were only two schools in Japan that stressed public speaking at this time. One was Fukuzawa Yukichi's Keiō Gijuku, in which Fukuzawa experimented with students giving speeches in Japanese, and the other was the Kumamoto School for Western Learning, in which Janes had them presented in English. Mitsui, *Kindai Nihon no seinen gunzō*, p. 79. An early Meiji debate centered on whether Japanese could be used for "speech making." There were many who thought that Japanese was not suited for public speaking. But once Fukuzawa demonstrated the contrary, speeches and public lectures became something of a fad in the mid-Meiji years. See Miyatake Tobone (Gaikotsu), *Meiji enzetsu shi* (Tokyo, 1929), pp. 6ff.

66. Watase, *Ebina Danjō*, p. 83.

67. Ebina Danjō, "Jiensu shi ni tsuite no shokan," *Kyūshū bungaku* 31 (January 1893), 42. Yokoi Tokio noted, "He used to tell us that it was worse than useless for young boys to talk of the state and government and spend days without educating themselves. It would not only do them harm, but would also be injurious to the state." Fukunaga, *Nihon ni okeru taii Jiensu shi*, p. 148.

68. Kozaki, "The Kumamoto Band in Retrospect," unpaginated.

69. Fukunaga, *Nihon ni okeru taii Jiensu shi*, p. 148.

70. Ibid.

71. For a discussion of Tokutomi Iichirō (Sohō) see John D. Pierson, *Tokutomi Sohō*, ch. 5. which deals with the establishment of *Kokumin no tomo* and the Minyūsha.

72. Ibid., p. 153. Pierson describes Sohō's efforts to pursue his own course, first outlined in his book, *Youth and Their Education in 19th Century Japan* (Daijūkyū seiki Nihon no seinen oyobi sono kyōiku), as follows: "Whereas Niijima hoped to bring this spiritual essence of modern Western civilization to Japan through Christianity, Sohō wanted to do this by importing the secular ethics of individualism, the spirit of independence and autonomy, the self-assurance, self-reliance, and self-regulation, and the responsibility that, he believed, characterized the people of Western democracies, and that made these societies civilized and great" (p. 120). Pierson further tells us that "Sohō argued that the only way to achieve this goal was to give the younger generation a 'pure Western education.' Meiji youth must be taught that the 'natural law' (tennen no hō) of 'cause and effect'; applies to human affairs as well as to physics . . . young people must be taught 'self respect and self love' so that they can take upon themselves the responsibility for being the 'custodians' of their own 'human dignity,' and not allow this to be done for them by others. They must

be trained to be 'spontaneously self-regulating,' to be able to determine for themselves and by themselves what is 'useful and not useful, right and wrong.' They must also be educated in the spirit of altruism, to have understanding and compassion, 'sincerity and sympathy,' for their fellow men and in the way they relate to other men. Finally, they must be trained so as to have nurtured in them 'the spirit of patriotism, the firmness and courage of will and heart, and the industry and diligence' that are typical of 'citizens' in modern democratic nations" (p. 121). Tokutomi's program for educating nineteenth-century Japanese youth suggests distinct parallels with Janes' program in Kumamoto. Tokutomi's reasons for rejecting Christianity will be taken up in a subsequent chapter.

73. Janes Papers, no. 104, "Letter to Anna," Kumamoto, Japan, October 7, 1874.

74. Kozaki, *Reminiscences*, p. 28. Yokoi Tokio echoed the same theme. He remembered Janes telling them: "The greatest need at present is the improvement of agriculture and industry, and the general diffusion of education, through which he thought the nation's strength could be increased." Fukunaga, *Nihon ni okeru taii Jiensu shi*, p. 148.

75. Kozaki, *Reminiscences*, pp. 28–29.

76. Kozaki, "The Kumamoto Band in Retrospect," unpaginated. Also *Reminiscences*, p. 29.

77. For a description of Yokoi's career see Sakurai Takeo, "Yokoi Tokiyoshi hakushi," *Kyōiku* 2, 7 (July 1934), 86–101. For a discussion of Yokoi's role in the development of agrarian nationalism see Thomas R. H. Havens, *Farm and Nation in Modern Japan* (Princeton: Princeton University Press, 1974), pp. 98–111.

78. Fuwa Tadajirō wrote: "What we cannot help admiring even after such a lapse of time is the fact that in the classroom he said not a word about Christianity." Fukunaga, *Nihon ni okeru taii Jiensu shi*, p. 82. Ichihara noted: "It was his custom not to talk of religion in the classroom. So far as I remember, he only once explained to us the wonderful design in the work of nature, by pointing to the lilies blooming in the ditch surrounding the school house" (p. 141). Shimomura Kōtarō simply noted: "At the start Capt. Janes did not say anything about Christianity. It was supposed from his activity and frankness that he was no believer in such a gloomy thing as religion" (p. 90).

79. The issue of Christianity will be discussed in greater detail in chapter 9.

80. Fukunaga, *Nihon ni okeru taii Jiensu shi*, p. 12, gives the date of Janes' speech as October 4, 1874. "The continuation of the school was celebrated," it is stated, "with ken officials, Lord Hosokawa's representative, and several prominent persons of the district being invited to grace the ceremony with their presence." The full English text of Janes' address can be found in Janes Papers, no. 301. Janes dated this manuscript "December 1874." It would appear that this document is the revised version of his speech that was subsequently translated into Japanese by several of his students, and as Janes wrote, "widely circulated throughout the country." See *Kumamoto*, part 1, p.

129. The decision to continue the school for an additional two years involved some complex behind the scenes issues of which Janes was only partially aware. Writing to Anna Warner in 1874 he noted: "as to the continuance of the school in the future I cannot write so definitely. . . . Towards the close of last school year I thought it might end with the third year. As a consequence of the change through which the government was passing at the time I arrived in the country, it had assumed the expense and responsibility of engagements made under the Daimiates; and the Imperial Government long since withdrew from all responsibility for the school . . . but as the time of my engagement grew towards an end, local friends of the school were most anxious and earnest in their efforts to have it continue . . . but all efforts with the Imperial Government failed. At the last moment the late Prince, to whose notice it seems the matter was brought in Yedo . . . most generously came to their aid, and assured the continuance of the school for the fourth year." Janes Papers, no. 104.

Sugii Mutsurō has indicated that the school confronted a series of crises. The first came in 1871 when control was shifted from the domain to the central government. One reason the school was slow to get underway—although everyone had been waiting to get it started—was the general state of confusion that reigned at the end of 1871 with the shift from local to national authority. It appears to have taken time to confirm that the the central government had agreed to pick up Janes' salary.

Earlier it was noted that the Restoration in Higo proved too "liberal" for oligarchs such as Ōkubo, particularly in its proposed local political reforms and persistent rumors that spoke of a "republican" form of government. Consequently Yasuoka Ryōsuke was made governor of the prefecture to curb this trend. By the end of 1873 he had succeeded in removing virtually all the Practical Learning reformers from office. As the last outpost of the reform, the Yōgakkō also came under pressure. The central government's decision not to renew funding for Janes' contract was one way of attacking the Jitsugaku's final stronghold. On the other hand, Hosokawa Morihisa was not yet prepared to have Kumamoto fall to Ōkubo's forces. His decision to extend the life of the school, which Janes attributed to his educational interests, was most likely stimulated by his political concerns. See Sugii, *Kumamoto Bando kenkyū*, pp. 85–96; Ōe Shinobu, *Meiji kokka no seiritsu*, pp. 83–91; Tokutomi Iichirō, *Sohō jiden*, p. 59.

81. Janes Papers, no. 301, Kumamoto School Address, December 1874. The following quotations are all taken from the manuscript of this address.

82. Kozaki, "The Kumamoto Band in Retrospect," unpaginated.

83. Ibid.

84. Janes Papers, no. 104, "Letter to Anna," Kumamoto, Japan, October 7, 1874.

85. Fukunaga, *Nihon ni okeru taii Jiensu shi*, pp. 100–101.

86. As noted earlier, the separation of Western science and Eastern ethics was clearly spelled out in the initial regulations of the school. *Kumamoto ken kyōiku shi*, vol. 1, pp. 523–24. Fuwa Tadajirō wrote: "Among the subjects taught at

the school there was one on morality, in which the works of Confucius and Mencius were used as text books. Capt. Janes made a protest to this, alleging that he had no objection to teaching the boys those books as lessons on ethical science, but they were incompetent for the purpose of giving them practical lessons on morality; he would himself set them an example of sound morals. He carried his point, and the lesson was dropped ever since." Fukunaga, *Nihon ni okeru taii Jiensu shi*, pp. 80–81.

87. See note 78.

88. Janes Papers, no. 301, Kumamoto Address.

89. Of the eleven graduates of Janes' first class, six became university professors, two professors in technical schools (three of these subsequently became university presidents and two principals of technical schools), one a well-known doctor, another a member of parliament, and several were among the best known pastors and publicists of Meiji Japan.

90. The student was Morita Kumando. Fukunaga, *Nihon ni okeru taii Jiensu shi*, p. 76.

Chapter VIII
Yankee Ingenuity and Initiative

1. Portions of this chapter first appeared in my article "Leroy Lansing Janes; Out-of-Class Teacher and Agricultural Adviser in Kumamoto Japan, 1871–1876," in Sakata Yoshio and Yoshida Mitsukuni, eds., *Sekai shi no naka no Meiji isshin* (Kyoto, 1973), pp. 1–29.

2. William Elliot Griffis was in Fukui only ten months, from March 1871 to January 1872. Arthur Maclay spent eight months in Hirosaki in 1874. William S. Clark was in Sapporo for nine months in 1876–77. I have not been able to find another European or American teacher who can match the five years Janes spent in Higo.

3. Janes Papers, no. 306, "Kumamoto," ch. 3, p. 62.

4. Janes, *Kumamoto*, part 1, p. 12.

5. Ibid., p. 60. "The Japanese are religiously vegetarians," Janes wrote, "yet they have a list of vegetables too meanly primitive to mention, too gross in texture, too flavorless, and too inferior in nutritive quality to support healthy activities of the body and mind, even when eked out by a supplement of salt fish and a sauce of salt and fermented beans."

6. Ibid., pp. 59–60.

7. Ibid., pp. 61–62.

8. Ibid., p. 62.

9. Ibid.

10. Ibid., pp. 62–63.

11. Ibid., p. 69. Janes' use of foreign materials seems to have made its impression on Nagaoka Moriyoshi, the Prince, who Janes quotes as saying: "Ah! but your stoves; your baking ovens; your potatoes, your flour for bread; your milk, your, I don't know what, that makes your food so 'sweet' (a term for all things

savory and appetizing)—all these we must bring from foreign countries! But, you will help us, *Senshi*? Will you help us?"

12. Ibid.

13. For a discussion of *Seisan shoho* see Yamada Tatsuo, "L. L. Janes *Seisan shoho* ni tsuite," *Kyūdai nōgaku geishi* 26, 1–4 (1972), 445–54. Professor Yamada translates *Seisan shoho* as an "Introduction to Agricultural Production," a title I have also adopted, although a more literal translation would be "The ABC's of Production," or "A Primer on Production." The original volume lists "Beikoku Kabiten Zensu shi" as the author, and Yamazaki Tamenori, Matsumura Genji, and Ichihara Morihiro as the joint translators. The volume was published under the Yōgakkō's imprimature in Tokyo in the summer of 1873 (Meiji 6). *Seisan shoho* was reprinted in *Kumamoto tenbō* 5 (Winter 1976), 66–76. This special issue devoted to the Kumamoto Band also includes an article by Ueda Jōichi, " 'Seisan shoho' to Higo jitsugaku tō," tracing the relationship between Janes' study and the agricultural reforms of the Practical Learning reformers.

14. Kabiten Zensu, *Seisan shoho*, pp. 1–3.

15. Ibid., p. 8.

16. Ibid., pp. 5–6.

17. Ibid., pp. 10–14.

18. For the development of silk production in Kumamoto see Araki Seishi, ed., *Kumamoto no rekishi*, vol. 5 (Kindai), pp. 83–86. This history also states that Takezaki Sadō organized an agricultural association (*Kōunsha*) in 1873 that was initially to address itself to the raising of silkworms and the production of silk and tea, but that this association soon branched out and approached Janes to have him order seeds and tools for an experimental farm it wanted to run for the development of agriculture in Kumamoto. (p. 83) This sounds a good deal like Janes' "Horticultural Society." At the same time there seems to have been another Agricultural Association (usually identified with Nonoguchi) that was more officially connected with the prefectural authorities. It was this group that approached Janes on the importation of equipment and projects such as the madder experiment, which will be taken up later.

19. Tokutomi Kenjirō, *Takezaki Junko*, in *Roka zenshū*, vol. 15, p. 142.

20. Janes' close relationship with Takezaki is discussed in "Eru Eru Jiensu shi," *Kyūshū bungaku* 31 (January 30, 1893), 14. This article states not only that Janes worked closely with Takezaki Sadō on various projects, but that he "often put out his own money" for these projects. Kinoshita Junji, in his play, *Fūrō*, in which both Janes and Harriet appear, includes a lengthy scene in which Janes and Takezaki work together on various agricultural projects. Kinoshita Junji, *Fūrō* (Tokyo, 1955), pp. 38ff.

21. Tokutomi Kenjirō, *Takezaki Junko*, in *Roka zenshū*, vol. 15, p. 142.

22. Ibid. See also Ueda Jōichi, " 'Seisan shoho' to higo jitsugaku tō," *Kumamoto tenbō* 5 (Winter 1976), p. 57.

23. Tokutomi Kenjirō, *Takezaki Junko*, in *Roka zenshū*, vol. 15, p. 142.

24. Not only was Kumamoto producing over 10 percent of the nation's silk

output, but Kumamoto silk was fetching substantially higher prices than that of other prefectures. See Chihōshi Kenkyū Kyōgikai, eds., *Nihon sangyō shi taikei, vol. 8, Kyūshū hen,* p. 135. Percentage figures have been calculated on the basis of a 7.5-million-pound annual output between 1889 and 1893 that is given in William W. Lockwood, *The Economic Development of Japan* (Princeton: Princeton University Press, 1954), p. 27.

25. Johei Asahara, *Blessed Junko Takezaki,* p. 15.
26. Janes Papers, no. 104, "Letter to Anna," Kumamoto, Japan, October 7, 1874. For Roka's evaluation see Tokutomi Kenjirō, *Takezaki Junko,* in *Roka zenshū,* vol. 15, p. 143.
27. Janes, *Kumamoto,* part 1, pp. 58–59.
28. Ibid.
29. Quotations in the following section on madder are taken from ibid., pp. 85, 90–94.
30. Ibid., pp. 95–96. "Hyaku Man Ben" is the popular name of the Chionji Temple in Kyoto, not far from which Janes later resided in 1893–96. The temple is referred to as "Hyaku man ben" (one million invocations) because in 1331, when an epidemic was raging in Kyoto, the presiding abbot held a service at which the Buddhist prayer of "Namu-Amida-Butsu" was recited one million times.
31. Ibid., p. 95.
32. Ibid., p. 94.
33. Quotations on orange culture are taken from ibid., pp. 94–95.
34. Tokutomi Kenjirō, *Takezaki Junko,* in *Roka zenshū,* vol. 15, p. 143.
35. Janes, *Kumamoto,* part 1, p. 94.
36. Ibid., p. 70.
37. Quotations from the following section on bread are from ibid., pp. 68–72.
38. Tokutomi Kenjirō, *Takezaki Junko,* in *Roka zenshū,* vol. 15, p. 143.
39. Quotations in the following sections on wheat production and plowing are taken from Janes, *Kumamoto,* part 1, pp. 72–76.
40. Quotations in the following section on milk and meat are taken from ibid., pp. 102–14.
41. Tokutomi Kenjirō, *Takezaki Junko,* in *Roka zenshū,* vol. 15, p. 143. Ueda Jōichi tells us that one of Takezaki's sons, Takagi Daishirō, went into the dairy business, and that Takezaki taught others how to process milk and butter. See Ueda Jōichi, " 'Seisan shoho' to higo jitsugaku tō," *Kumamoto tenbō* 5 (Winter 1976), pp. 59–60.
42. Tokutomi Kenjirō, *Takezaki Junko,* in *Roka zenshū,* vol. 15, p. 143.
43. Ibid., p. 142.
44. Tokutomi Kenjirō, *Footprints in the Snow,* trans. by Kenneth Strong (Tokyo: Charles E. Tuttle, 1971), p. 101.
45. Janes, *Kumamoto,* part 1, p. 113.
46. Kumamoto-shi Kyōiku Iinkai, eds., *Kumamoto yōgakkō kyōshikan* (Kumamoto, 1979), unnumbered pamphlet.
47. "Eru Eru Jiensu shi," *Kyūshū bungaku* 31 (January 30, 1893), p. 13.

48. Janes, *Kumamoto*, part 1, pp. 47–48.

49. Ibid., p. 50.

50. Ibid., pp. 48–49.

51. Janes writes that Ebina got details of the plot from "the responsible authorities in Higo." He narrated the plan as follows: "Sometime in 1875 one of his chief lieutenants went to the leader of the Higo insurgents—Kaya [Harukata] by name, an elderly Shinto ecclesiastic—and begged his assent to the following plan for the assassination of the foreign teacher: to waylay the latter near a certain lonely Shinto Shrine north of the city while he was out for his daily exercise. There, wholly unobserved, the would-be assassin would kill him, cast his body into one of the old, abandoned wells of the vicinity, and fill it up. . . . but Kaya was not ready for this . . . the reasons he urged for his refusal were these: 'this foreigner came here into the heart of Kyushu with his family alone. The Prince assigned him quarters in the castle and appointed a guard of soldiers for his protection during his stay. This foreigner would not be so guarded—why we don't know. We only know that he, the foreigner, insisted upon the dismissal of the guard. After a few weeks he persuaded our Prince to remove, first half, then all the guard of twenty-four soldiers. He almost daily went through our streets alone, where, at first he had a troop of soldiers with him. He thus put himself into our power, and put us on our honor to spare if not to protect him. You don't know the true Japanese spirit. You must not kill that man now!' " (Ibid., part 2, p. 95).

52. Ibid., part 1, p. 49.

53. Janes Papers, no. 306, "Kumamoto," ch. 15, pp. 233–34.

54. Ibid., p. 234.

55. Janes Papers, no. 107, "Letter to Susan and Anna," Kumamoto, Japan, July 24, 1875.

56. Janes Papers, no. 306, "Kumamoto," ch. 15, p. 235.

57. Ibid., p. 236.

58. Tokutomi Kenjirō, *Takezaki Junko*, in *Roka zenshū*, vol. 15, p. 143.

59. Janes, *Kumamoto*, part 1, p. 50.

60. Tokutomi Kenjirō, *Takezaki Junko*, in *Roka zenshū* vol. 15, p. 143.

61. Janes Papers, no. 103, Letter to Mother, Kumamoto, Japan, June 2, 1876.

62. Lois was born on September 1, 1873, and Eunice Ann was born on August 31, 1875. In Fukunaga, *Nihon ni okeru taii Jiensu shi*, p. 48, his students noted: "Capt. Janes was not fond of amusements. It seemed to be his greatest delight to be with his child, for he was frequently seen in his garden carrying his son in his arms, and later on teaching him how to write or to sing, or making him learn to make a speech."

63. Janes Papers, no. 102, Letter to Mother, Kumamoto, Japan, July 2, 1876. Reference to "Fannie" seems to be to his daughter by Nellie who died in 1868.

64. Ibid.

65. Janes Papers, no. 104, "Letter to Anna," Kumamoto, Japan, October 7, 1874.

66. Janes Papers, no. 106, "Letter to Anna," Kumamoto, Japan, April 21, 1875.

67. Janes Papers, no. 104, "Letter to Anna," Kumamoto, Japan, October 7, 1874.
68. Fukunaga, *Nihon ni okeru taii Jiensu shi*, pp. 108–109.
69. Ibid., p. 47.
70. Janes' appearance in everyday dress is recorded in Tokutomi Kenjirō, *Takezaki Junko*, in *Roka zenshū*, vol. 15, p. 128. Harriet's description is from Kumamoto-shi Kyōiku Iinkai, eds., *Kumamoto yōgakkō kyōshi kan*, unnumbered pamphlet.
71. Janes Papers, no. 112, Letter to Mr. Carter, Kumamoto, Japan, August 24, 1875.
72. Janes Papers, no. 306, "Kumamoto," ch. 15, pp. 237–38.
73. The Saga Rebellion broke out on February 1, 1874, and represented the first attempt by disaffected samurai to overthrow the Tokyo government by force. The rebellion was led by Etō Shimpei, one of the Restoration leaders from Hizen who had been disturbed by the defeat of the proposed (and imperially sanctioned) Korean Expedition of 1873, which was rescinded with the return of Ōkubo and others who had gone abroad with the Iwakura Mission. Etō left the government and returned to Saga to organize dissatisfied samurai in northern Kyushu. He hoped that with the outbreak of a rebellion, Itagaki Taisuke of Tosa and Saigo Takamori of Satsuma, both of whom had left the government over the same issue, would join him in a general uprising against the Meiji administration. Unfortunately for Etō, neither chose to join him (although Saigo led the larger Satsuma Rebellion in 1877), and the government, using its new conscript army under Ōkubo's personal supervision, quelled the rebellion in quick order. Etō and eleven of the other leaders were executed. For a discussion of the Saga uprising see Chitoshi Yanaga, *Japan Since Perry*, p. 63. As Janes noted, samurai discontent, caused by a reduction in samurai stipends and the piece-by-piece dismantling of the feudal structure, was widespread in Higo as well. Roka wrote that in the wake of the rejected Korean Expedition, "Japan gave one the feeling of sitting on a land mine." Tokutomi Kenjirō, *Takezaki Junko*, in *Roka zenshū*, vol. 15, p. 162.
74. Janes Papers, no. 111, Letter to Mr. Carter, Kumamoto, Japan, May 23, 1874. Mishima Yukio, who has written one of the most detailed accounts of the Shimpūren in the second volume of his tetralogy, *The Sea of Fertility*, suggests that the League of the Divine Wind saw the Saga uprising as a perfect time to act in Kumamoto. With much of the Kumamoto garrison pressed into service to the north, Kumamoto was weakly defended and ripe for a local uprising. Mishima argues that the reason the Kumamoto rebellion did not break out at this time was due to the superstitious beliefs of its Shinto leaders who "consulted the will of the gods through the Ukei [a form of divining] rite," only to receive the reply that the time was "not propitious." Mishima Yukio, *Runaway Horses* (Tokyo: Charles E. Tuttle, 1973), pp. 71–72. Janes' account of the constant arson certainly does suggest the instability of the period.
75. Fukunaga, *Nihon ni okeru taii Jiensu shi*, p. 80.
76. In reference to the printing press Janes noted that he tried to convince the

reformers and the students of the school of the importance of "a free press and generally of free speech." Finally the local authorities agreed that a printing press would be useful, but "the government at Tokyo had to be consulted; and leave to import and set up a press was actually secured chiefly on the pretense of economy and necessity. Laws and edicts and regulations emanating from Tokyo as well as from the local Kencho, were at that time multiplying so fast as to be a serious charge upon the clerical force at the command of the Kencho officials." In the end a printing press was ordered from New York. At first there was a problem with type, "but this was solved by the substitution of blocks, which were soon reduced to sections and used until the large font of Japanese and necessary Chinese characters became available." Janes thought that the press he had ordered from New York was the only printing press outside of the treaty ports in 1873. This is difficult to substantiate, but the *Shirakawa Shimbun*, Kumamoto's newspaper, which began to be published in 1874, was the first newspaper in Kyushu. The publicly elected Prefectural Assembly, or Sei-in as Janes referred to it, was the third such body in the nation. See Morita Seiichi, "Kumamoto han," in *Monogatari hanshi*, vol. 8, p. 524. Janes' discussion of the press is from Janes Papers, no. 306, "Kumamoto," ch. 17, pp. 283ff. The ordering of stereoscopic pictures and apparatus is mentioned in Janes Papers, no. 106, "Letter to Anna," Kumamoto, Japan, April 21, 1875.

77. Fukunaga, *Nihon ni okeru taii Jiensu shi*, p. 80.
78. Janes Papers, no 104, "Letter to Anna," Kumamoto, Japan, October 7, 1874.
79. Janes Papers, no. 106, "Letter to Anna," Kumamoto, Japan, April 21, 1875.
80. Letter from Janes to the Honorable Commissioner of Pensions, Ann Arbor, Michigan, February 7, 1888, Veterans Administration Claims File. In his book *Kumamoto* Janes added that "his eyes had begun to suffer" and had almost "collapsed from incessant strain of day and night use." "He was, in short," he wrote, "almost blind." Janes, *Kumamoto*, part 2, p. 88.
81. Janes Papers, no. 306, "Kumamoto," no chapter indicated, ms. p. 248.
82. Ibid., ms. p. 245.
83. Janes, *Kumamoto*, part 2, p. 47.
84. Janes Papers, no. 306, "Kumamoto," no chapter indicated, ms. p. 248.
85. Ibid., ms. p. 246.
86. Janes, *Kumamoto*, part 2, p. 49.
87. Janes Papers, no. 306, "Kumamoto," no chapter indicated, ms. p. 248.
88. Ibid.
89. Ibid., ms. p. 253.
90. Janes, *Kumamoto*, part 2, pp. 51–52.
91. Ibid., p. 52.
92. Ibid.
93. Miyamoto Musashi (1584–1645) was not only a superb swordsman, who we are told never lost a duel, he was also a first-rate artist, whose paintings, including "Shrike on a Reed," remain among the classics of Japanese ink painting. Miyamoto retired to Iwado in 1643 and spent the last two years of

his life writing his treatise on swordsmanship, *Go rin no sho* (The Book of Five Rings), which, as a "guide for men who want to learn strategy," as he called it, was to become the classic text for Japan's two sworded class. See Miyamoto Musashi, *A Book of Five Rings*, trans. Victor Harris (Woodstock, New York: Overlook Press, 1974). For a romantic biography of Miyamoto see Walter Denning, *Japan in Days of Yore* (London: Griffith Farran, n.d.), also reprinted by Fine Books, 1976. The most popular current account is the massive novel by Eiji Yoshikawa, *Musashi: A Novel of the Samurai Era*, trans. from the Japanese by Charles S. Terry. (New York: Harper & Row, 1981).

CHAPTER IX
CHRISTIANITY

1. For a discussion of the Catholic Church in sixteenth- and seventeenth-century Japan see C. R. Boxer, *The Christian Century in Japan 1549–1650* (Berkeley: University of California Press, 1967); George Elison, *Deus Destroyed: The Image of Christianity in Early Modern Japan* (Cambridge: Harvard University Press, 1973); Masaharu Anesaki, *History of Japanese Religion* (London: Kegan Paul, Trench, Trubner, 1930); and Joseph M. Kitagawa, *Religion in Japanese History* (New York: Columbia University Press, 1966). For an account of the Shimabara Rebellion see "Amakusa Shirō: Japanese Messiah," in Ivan Morris, *The Nobility of Failure* (New York: New American Library, 1975), pp. 143–79. The role of Christianity in Meiji Japan is discussed in Otis Cary, *A History of Christianity in Japan: Roman Catholic, Greek Orthodox, and Protestant Missions* (Tokyo: Charles E. Tuttle, 1976); Charles W. Iglehart, *A Century of Protestant Christianity in Japan* (Tokyo: Charles E. Tuttle, 1959); and Irwin Scheiner, *Christian Converts and Social Protest in Meiji Japan* (Berkeley: University of California Press, 1970).

2. Kanamori Tsūrin, one of Janes' students, gives an interesting description of this ritual: "My grandfather was an officer of some position in our provincial government. At one time he was appointed chief officer over a large district. It was the duty of such officials to examine the religion of the people over whom they were placed. For this purpose he used to call all the people of his district once a year to his official residence. The day of such a gathering was counted among the great days of the year. It was called the 'Feast of Picture Trampling.' I remember my grandfather had a small iron crucifix, such as the Roman Catholic priests carry with them. This crucifix was put in a small box, which was covered with an iron grating, so that the figure within might be seen from the outside, and this box was placed in a small hole dug for the purpose, in the middle of a large courtyard, where usually the criminals were examined. Then the people were called in, one by one, by name, in the presence of the Government officer, all dressed in their official robes with swords and spears to guard against emergencies. The people of each township, headed by the mayor, were called in by themselves, and when they came to the place where the box was placed they trampled upon it and passed on. To this feast

all the people, men and women and even children, were ordered to come. When the women came into the yard after they themselves had stepped on the box, they put down their children and made their little feet touch the crucifix, thus testifying that they were not of this religion. If anyone refused to trample upon the cross he was arrested at once, and put into prison on the charge of being a Christian. My grandfather had a prison in which to put such men."

When Kanamori asked his grandfather, "what is that figure in the box on which these people are treading?" his grandfather replied, "Oh, that is an unclean worm! if it is not put in that box and trampled upon by the people, it will creep out and do immense mischief to the country." Paul M. Kanamori, *Kanamori's Life-Story* (Philadelphia: Sunday School Times, 1921), pp. 19–21.

3. Katō was a staunch supporter of Buddhism and was one of the first daimyo openly to persecute Christians. See C. R. Boxer, *The Christian Century in Japan*, pp. 182, 187.

4. Hosokawa Tadatoshi (1586–1640) had been baptized as a child. His mother was the famous Gracia Hosokawa, the beautiful daughter of Akechi Mitsuhide, the man who assassinated Oda Nobunaga in 1582. Gracia was much admired by the Jesuits. In 1600, when Ishida Mitsunari tried to take her hostage in order to prevent her husband, Hosokawa Tadaoki, from joining Tokugawa Ieyasu at Sekigahara, she took her own life to foil the plot. Gracia has long been admired as a paragon of feminine virtue in Japan. More recently she served as the model for James Clavell's Mariko in *Shogun*. Tadatoshi, despite his early Christian background, submitted to Tokugawa Ieyasu's orders to banish all Christians from his domain, and at the age of fifty-two became a leading general in the suppression of the Christians at Shimabara. See Ivan Morris, *The Nobility of Failure*, p. 399n7.7.

5. Janes Papers, no. 306, "Kumamoto," ch. 21, p. 388.

6. Joseph M. Kitagawa, *Religion in Japanese History*, pp. 238–39.

7. G. B. Sansom, *The Western World and Japan*, p. 469.

8. The man involved was Ishikawa Einosuke, who had served as a Japanese-language teacher for Rev. O. H. Gulick, one of the American missionaries in Kobe. Ishikawa was arrested in 1871 for possessing a part of the New Testament in Japanese. After eighteen months of imprisonment he died in jail. The case resulted in numerous Western protests. Otis Cary reports that missionaries who went to the governor of Kobe about the matter were told that if Ichikawa had been baptized "he would certainly be put to death." Otis Cary, *A History of Christianity in Japan*, vol. 2, p. 73. Sansom indicates that the American minister protested to Iwakura about the case, only to be told that the Japanese government need not answer to foreigners about the treatment of Japanese citizens at home. When the Iwakura Mission went abroad later in 1871 its members were disturbed to hear that the Ishikawa case was widely known in the West and was cited as an example of backwardness in matters of legal rights and religious freedoms. Shortly after the mission's return in 1873 the proscription boards against Christianity quietly came down, but the government made no open declaration that Christianity would now be tolerated. See Sansom, *The Western World and Japan*, pp. 468–69.

9. Verbeck is quoted in ibid., p. 468.

10. These statistics are from ibid., p. 470*n*10.

11. Kozaki, "The Kumamoto Band in Retrospect," unpaginated.

12. Kozaki, *Reminiscences*, p. 34.

13. Kozaki wrote: "It was generally believed that Europeans and Americans were highly advanced in material sciences, but as regards ethics and morality, they were by far our inferiors. It was a sign of their being superstitious that they believed in the existence of God. I pitied Captain Janes for his ignorance and with a view of enlightening him, I went to his house several times and preached *jingi* (humanity and justice) and *chūkō* (loyalty and filial piety). When I think about it today I blush and sweat all over." Fukunaga, *Nihon ni okeru taii Jiensu shi*, p. 69.

14. Janes Papers, no. 112, Letter to Mr. Carter, Kumamoto, Japan, August 25, 1875.

15. This is the view of Fuwa Tadajirō in Fukunaga, *Nihon ni okeru taii Jiensu shi*, p. 82.

16. Janes Papers, no. 107, "Letter to Anna and Susan," Kumamoto, Japan, July 24, 1875.

17. Ibid.

18. Janes Papers, no. 112, Letter to Mr. Carter, Kumamoto, Japan, August 24, 1875.

19. Janes Papers, no. 107, "Letter to Anna and Susan," Kumamoto, Japan, July 24, 1875.

20. Watase, *Ebina Danjō*, p. 92.

21. Ibid., p. 82.

22. "About that time, probably seeing the change in my mind," Miyagawa wrote, "Captain Janes would take me to his garden and showing some cucumbers growing there explained to me the wonderful design in the work of nature. . . ." Fukunaga, *Nihon ni okeru taii Jiensu shi*, p. 135.

23. Watase, *Ebina Danjō*, pp. 92–93.

24. Janes Papers, no. 106, "Letter to Anna and Susan," Kumamoto, Japan, July 24, 1875.

25. Janes Papers, no. 306, "Kumamoto," ch. 21, pp. 388–92.

26. Ibid., pp. 392–93.

27. Janes Papers, no. 107, "Letter to Anna and Susan," Kumamoto, Japan, July 24, 1875.

28. For a discussion of the separation of politics from ethics in late Tokugawa thought see Maruyama Masao, *Nihon seiji shisōshi kenkyū* (Tokyo, 1952), which has been translated by Mikiso Hane as *Studies in the Intellectual History of Tokugawa Japan* (Princeton: Princeton University Press, 1974). Maruyama argues cogently in this brilliant study of Tokugawa thought that starting with the Sorai School there was a clear separation of the political order from the natural (or ethical) order in Tokugawa thought. However, in the 1974 introduction to the English translation of this study he carefully qualifies how widely disseminated such a new perception of Confucianism had become. On this point he writes: "If one asks not just about scholarly Confucianism but about

the basic thought categories of Confucianism that constituted the *Aspekts-truktur* of Tokugawa society, then one can argue that they tenaciously retained a currency until the very last instant of the Tokugawa regime." Ibid., p. xxxv.

29. I have not been able to find a single case of a Yōgakkō student who followed Sorai's interpretation and argued that personal morality, or self-cultivation, was of no direct importance to a political career. Quite the opposite, whether a student came from Yanagawa like Ebina, or from Mizusawa like Yamazaki, or from the Confucian academies of Kumamoto like many of the others, all continued to emphasize the classical formula of "*shūshin seika chikoku hei-tenka*," which linked "self-cultivation" with "the governance of the realm." In my article on "Ebina Danjō: A Christian Samurai of the Meiji Period," *Papers on Japan* (Harvard East Asian Research Center), vol. 2 (1963), I tried to indicate why a concern for personal morality increased in the late Tokugawa and early Meiji years.

30. The foregoing biographical details are from Watase, *Ebina Danjō*, pp. 23ff.

31. Yanagawa Castle burned on January 18, 1872. Ibid., p. 49.

32. Ibid., p. 65.

33. Ebina wrote of his young lord's death: "The young lord was a person quite different from us. Having received friendship from him, I had firmly decided to 'offer up' my life for him. However, the Yanagawa *han* was lost, the castle burnt, and my young lord had been killed. I felt terribly lonely. Because the young lord was dead, there was no one to whom I could offer my life, and this was the essence of my loneliness. To whom could I offer my life after this?" Ibid. About his family he observed, ". . . due to this there existed, even in regard to my parents, painful situations, and I felt lonely." Ebina, *Kirisutokyō gairon mikankō*, p. 54.

34. Ibid., pp. 53–54.

35. One of the first to make this observation was Yamaji Aizan. See his *Kiri-sutokyō hyōron* (Tokyo, 1966), pp. 25ff. The same argument is made in Ma-saaki Kosaka, ed., *Japanese Thought in the Meiji Period* (Tokyo, 1958), p. 163. See also Irwin Scheiner, *Christian Converts and Social Protest in Meiji Japan*, p. 23.

36. This is the central argument of Irwin Scheiner's book, *Christian Converts and Social Protest in Meiji Japan*.

37. The shift of interest from Confucianism to Christianity was recorded by several of the students. Ebina recalled that Kanamori had decided to spend the summer of 1875 studying the Confucian classics with Naitō Taikichi, one of Shōnan's leading disciples, but that before long he lost interest in Naitō's lectures and found Janes' sermons much more to his liking. Watase, *Ebina Danjō*, p. 103. Kozaki wrote: "Soon it began to spread abroad that Christianity might be of little account, but Bible study was certainly interesting. A little later it was said that those not attending were missing a treat . . . then I began to hear from Miyagawa, Ichihara, Ebina and others that while the Chinese teacher's exposition of Confucianism was good, Janes' teaching of the Bible

was in a class by itself." Kozaki, "The Kumamoto Band in Retrospect," unpaginated.

38. Letter from Henry Stout to Ferris, Nagasaki, March 17, 1876, Dutch Reformed Papers.

39. Scheiner, *Christian Converts and Social Protest in Meiji Japan*, p. 90. Watase,
Ebina Danjō, p. 90. Takeda Kiyoko, as Scheiner notes, has made the additional
point that conversion to Christianity from Wang Yang-ming (Ōyōmei) was
made easier by the transposition of the concept of *tentei* or *jōtei* into God.
Takeda Kiyoko, *Ningen kan no sōkoku*, p. 71. Before this these concepts were
regarded as an "impersonal heaven," or as "reason." Yokoi's presentation of
Heaven incorporated the Wang Yang-ming approach.

40. Kozaki translated Yokoi Shōnan's poem as follows in his *Reminiscences* (p.
34):

> Make clear the Way of Gyo, Shun and Confucius.
> Master the secrets of the mechanical arts of the Western Ocean,
>> Not merely to enrich the country,
>> Not merely to strengthen the army,
> But all to let Great Righteousness prevail in the Four Seas.

41. Janes, *Kumamoto*, part 2, pp. 59–60.

42. Ibid., p. 59.

43. Ibid., p. 60. It should be pointed out that Yamazaki, who graduated from
the Yōgakkō in July 1875 and went directly to the Kaisei Gakkō in Tokyo,
did not experience the school's revivalistic phase. The following conversation,
which Janes recorded took place just before his departure for Tokyo, is therefore a good gauge of Janes' Christian emphasis in the period that preceded his
own transformation at the close of the year. Janes notes that Yamazaki came
to say goodbye and return a book the Captain had lent him. The book was
John Robert Seeley's *Ecce Homo: A Survey of the Life and Work of Jesus
Christ*: " 'Ecce Homo' had been published, and a copy of it came to my hands
from a friend in New York. It was the product of a mind in the maelstrom of
doubt, pursued by the nemesis of faith, yet clutching vainly to the straws of
tradition—one of the most pregnant, perplexing, and provoking books I ever
read. The phrase, 'the enthusiasm of humanity,' seemed to have struck to the
roots of Yamazaki's being. He was in no wise disconcerted by the tangle of
human love to Christ as a preliminary to the possibility of this enthusiasm's
assuming its perfect and saving efficacy. 'That,' said this youth of the fervent
soul and frail form, 'that is religion, inspiration enough for me. No one,' said
Yamazaki, his cheeks aglow and his eyes sparkling with the fervors of a fresh
and vital conviction, 'no one can better please the Father of a family than by
cultivating the peace, the welfare, and the happiness of the brotherhood. There
is no better way of showing love to a father than by loving and serving his
other children.' Simple, yet sublime reasoning!" Janes, *Kumamoto*, part 2, p.
69.

44. Fukunaga, *Nihon ni okeru taii Jiensu shi*, p. 142. Ichihara Morihiro wrote: "We had early been taught to believe in the teachings of Gyo, Shun, and Confucius, and to regard Christianity as a heresy. We could not, therefore, be easily prevailed on to come to his house. After much deliberation among ourselves and consultation with the members of the Practical Learning Party, we came at length to the conclusion that we should go, not for the purpose of studying the Bible in earnest, but for taking advantage of it for the better study of English, and for detecting any fallacy that might be found in the doctrines of this wretched religion."

45. Hisashi Mitsui, "Doshisha and the Kumamoto Band," *Japan Christian Quarterly* 25, 2 (April 1959), 116.

46. Watase, *Ebina Danjō*, p. 86.

47. Mitsui, "Doshisha and the Kumamoto Band," p. 116. Fukunaga, *Nihon ni okeru taii Jiensu shi*, p. 149. Kanamori writes: "Captain Janes had a very peculiar way of teaching the Bible. He did not explain much, nor argue much with his students. . . ." *Kanamori's Life-Story*, p. 12.

48. Fukunaga, *Nihon ni okeru taii Jiensu shi*, p. 149.

49. Kozaki, "The Kumamoto Band in Retrospect," unpaginated.

50. Janes Papers, no. 106, "Letter to Anna," Kumamoto, Japan, April 21, 1875. Parts of this letter were written under subsequent dates. The portion quoted is dated May 12, 1875. Janes' Sunday morning services seem to have begun with the arrival in Kumamoto of an army medical doctor named Sasaki who had studied medicine with James C. Hepburn in Yokohama and had become a Christian. Sasaki came to Janes and asked him if he would hold a Sunday worship service. Janes agreed to do so and invited Ebina to the first meeting. Ebina Danjō, *Kumamoto yōgakkō to Kumamoto Bando to*, printed pamphlet of a lecture Ebina delivered in Kumamoto on June 13, 1935, p. 14. Sasaki's identity remains something of a mystery. Mitsui Hisashi in *Kindai Nihon no seinen gunzō* speculates that Sasaki may have been Itō Tomoyoshi. According to the *Itō Tomoyoshi shoden*, Itō was born the fourth son to Sasaki Shōan of the Sendai domain. He was adopted into the Itō family, which served as domain physicians in Sendai, to marry the Itō's only daughter. Thereafter he was sent to Yokohama, where he studied medicine with Hepburn and received Christian baptism in the second group of converts baptized by James Ballah in 1872. In 1874 he accompanied the Taiwan Expedition. Thereafter he appears to have been attached to the Kumamoto garrison and participated in the quelling of the Satsuma Rebellion in 1877. Itō later divorced his wife and took back the Sasaki name. Mitsui notes that the divorce took place in 1880, that he later remarried, and that one of his daughters by the second marriage became the wife of the well-known Meiji novelist, Kunikida Doppō. While in Kumamoto (in 1875) he should have been using the name Itō, according to Mitsui, and because he is usually referred to as Sasaki, Mitsui remains unsure whether the two are in fact the same person. See *Kindai Nihon no seinen gunzō*, pp. 129–30. Writing to Anna Warner in his letter of April 21, 1875, Janes specifically mentions a Dr. Itō, "a native army physician or surgeon," with whom he had

sent a letter to her by way of Yokohama. There are other references to Dr. Itō in Janes' writings. Students such as Ebina who kept up their contacts with Itō over the years naturally referred to him as Sasaki after the divorce and used this name in their recollections of the school.

51. Paul M. Kanamori, *Kanamori's Life-Story*, p. 13. Kanamori writes: "Though he had no theological training he used to preach fine sermons, and very long ones, often two or three hours at a time. It may be that I learned my three hour sermon from him." Ichihara recalled that Janes preached with great zeal and that in the sermons the students "found out for the first time what kind of a man he was." Unlike most clergymen, Kanamori noted, "his sermons lacked that formality common to professional preachers." Ichihara thought them "all the better for it, for the listeners were thoroughly moved by the open and bold profession of his belief, so that during his sermons, which often went on for hours, no one yawned or showed any other sign of weariness. The subjects on which he liked to preach were 'The Love of God,' 'The character of Christ,' 'The power of Truth,' 'The meaning of life,' etc." Fukunaga, *Nihon ni okeru taii Jiensu shi*, pp. 142–43.

52. Janes' letter to Henry Stout, Kumamoto, January 3, 1876, quoted in Stout letter to Ferris, March 17, 1876, Dutch Reformed Papers.

53. Watase, *Ebina Danjō*, p. 90.

54. Janes, *Kumamoto*, part 2, p. 69.

55. Ebina Danjō, *Kirisutokyō gairon mihankō*, p. 56.

56. Ibid., p. 55.

57. This incident is explained in ibid., p. 57. Also Watase, *Ebina Danjō*, pp. 95–96. Ebina dates the event as the first Saturday in March, 1875.

58. Ibid., p. 96.

59. Ebina Danjō, *Kirisutokyō gairon mikankō*, p. 57.

60. Ibid.

61. I have explored this transition in greater detail in "Ebina Danjō: A Christian Samurai of the Meiji Period," *Papers on Japan*, vol. 2 (1963).

62. Janes, *Kumamoto*, part 2, p. 69.

63. Fukunaga, *Nihon ni okeru taii Jiensu shi*, p. 142.

64. Kozaki, "The Kumamoto Band in Retrospect," unpaginated.

65. Ibid. Horace Bushnell (1802–1876), *Nature and the Supernatural, as Together Constituting one System of God* (New York: C. Scribner, 1858).

66. Fukuda Reiju (Yoshinobu), *Gojūnen kinen Kumamoto Bando tsuikai roku*, p. 23–24. Also Mitsui, *Kindai Nihon no seinen gunzō*, p. 145.

67. Paul M. Kanamori, *Kanamori's Life-Story*, pp. 14–15.

68. Janes wrote to Stout: "The blessed, ever blessed Spirit has taken His own time to come. And I rejoice to feel that all this time He has been answering the fervent prayers, that I have depended on as my best wisdom, and strongest power." Quoted in Stout's letter to Ferris, March 17, 1876, Dutch Reformed Papers.

69. The term is Kanamori's used in a lecture on the Kumamoto Band delivered at Dōshisha in 1889; quoted in Mitsui, *Kindai Nihon no seinen gunzō*, p. 144.

Kozaki, "The Kumamoto Band in Retrospect," unpaginated. See also Kozaki, *Reminiscences*, p. 19.

70. Kozaki, "The Kumamoto Band in Retrospect," unpaginated.

71. M. L. Gordon, *An American Missionary in Japan* (Cambridge: Houghton Mifflin, 1892), p. 58. Janes wrote in a letter to Davis: "A Japanese gentleman who respects and loves me, came to consult with me about forbidding the boys to study the Bible in the school. I told him he should issue orders thereto if he wished for I had no objection to the authorities taking those steps which were in their power, nor should the boys disobey such orders." The "gentleman" was Nonoguchi. The letter to Davis is quoted in Fukunaga, *Nihon no okeru taii Jiensu shi*, p. 53.

72. Watase, *Ebina Danjō*, p. 110. Ebina tells us that if Kozaki had been a Christian at the time, he would have been asked to write the Hanaoka Declaration. Moreover, Ebina, Miyagawa, and Kanamori would have liked to have written it, but none of them had confidence in their written Japanese to draw up such a document. For this reason Furushō and Sakai were asked to draft the covenant.

73. Okada Matsuo noted that they sang "Jesus Loves Me." Mitsui, *Kindai Nihon no seinen gunzō*, p. 146. None of the students seems to have been aware of the fact that Anna Warner wrote this hymn and that she was a special friend of the Captain.

74. Watase, *Ebina Danjō*, p. 111.

75. The following students endorsed the Hanaoka Declaration (in the order of their signatures): Miyagawa Tsuneteru, Furushō Saburō, Okada Matsuo (Shōsei), Hayashi Harusada, Fuwa Tadajirō, Yufu Takesaburō, Ōshima Tokushirō, Kurahara Ikaku (Korehirō), Kanamori Michitomo (Tsūrin), Yoshida Mankuma, Tsuji Toyokichi, Kameyama Noboru, Ebina Kisaburō (Danjō), Uramoto Takeo, Ōya Takeo, Morozumi Masayuki, Noda Takeo, Shimomura Kotarō, Kitano Yoichirō, Katō Yujirō, Harai Junta, Shidō Akira, Matsuo Keigo, Kaneko Tomikichi, Koga Yoshiaki, Uehara Masatatsu (Horiyū), Tokutomi Iichirō (Sohō), Morita Kumando, Ise (Yokoi) Tokio, Ukita Kazutami (Wamin), Sakai Teiho, Ichihara Morihiro, Kawakami Torao, Suzuki Yorozu, and Imamura Shinshi. Watase, *Ebina Danjō*, pp. 111–12.

76. Ibid., p. 111.

77. Ibid., p. 112.

78. Tokutomi Kenjirō attributes this statement to Akamine Seichirō, one of the Christian students of the third class who was also the second of the boys to be baptized by Janes in the summer of 1876. See Tokutomi Kenjirō, *Takezaki Junko*, in *Roka zenshū*, vol. 15, p. 153. Akamine claimed the students often referred to the declaration as the beginning of the revolution in Japan.

79. Janes Papers, no. 110, Letter to Rev. Stout, Kumamoto, Japan, February 25, 1876. Ebina tells us that Janes' response to hearing of the declaration was very subdued. His main concern seems to have been whether age limitations had been placed on those who could sign, stating that this was a common practice

when churches were established in the United States. Watase, *Ebina Danjō*, p. 112.

80. Janes letter to Henry Stout, February 4, 1876, quoted in Stout letter to Ferris, March 17, 1876, Dutch Reformed Papers.

81. Ebina stated that the Practical Learning reformers were shocked by the transformation of their students in the school as if "chicken eggs placed under a hen had suddenly produced ducklings." Ebina Danjō, *Kumamoto yōgakkō to Kumamoto Bando to*, p. 15. M. L. Gordon in *An American Missionary in Japan*, p. 59, writes: "Those in charge of the school were particularly disturbed crying 'Alas!' the students have become Christian priests. Captain Janes has made Christians of them. If this is not stopped, our hopes for the school will be lost."

82. Janes Papers, no. 108, Letter to Jerome D. Davis, Kumamoto, Japan, February 7, 1876. This letter can also be found in the ABCFM documents.

83. Ibid.

84. Jerome D. Davis, *A Maker of New Japan, Rev. Joseph Hardy Neesima* (New York: F. H. Revell, 1894), p. 69. Hereafter cited as *Joseph Hardy Neesima*.

85. Janes letter to Henry Stout, written "a few days after February 4, 1876," quoted in Stout letter to Ferris, March 17, 1876, Dutch Reformed Papers.

86. Janes Papers, no. 110, Letter to Rev. Stout, Kumamoto, Japan, February 25, 1876.

87. The anti-Christian organization was generally known as the Suizenji Party or the Seigi-ha (Righteous Party). The photograph they posed for on January 30, 1876, has often been included in historical collections as showing the students of the Kumamoto School for Western Learning.

88. For the details of this debate see Watase, *Ebina Danjō*, pp. 116–17.

89. Ibid.

90. Mitsui, *Kindai Nihon no seinen gunzō*, p. 168.

91. Davis, *Joseph Hardy Neesima*, p. 76. Davis quotes Janes' letter of March 4, 1876.

92. Janes Papers, no. 108, Letter to the Rev. Davis, Kumamoto, Japan, February 7, 1876. Janes wrote: "There has been opposition to my Christian work, but I have made them like the school so much they are willing to bear with it."

93. Janes Papers, no. 110, Letter to Rev. Stout, Kumamoto, Japan, February 25, 1876. A portion of this letter was written under the date February 28, 1876.

94. Fukunaga, *Nihon ni okeru taii Jiensu shi*, p. 80.

95. This incident is related in John H. Deforest, *Sunrise in the Sunrise Kingdom* (New York: The Young People's Missionary Movement, 1904), p. 120. Janes' letter to Stout of February 28 indicates that this incident took place on the prior evening, i.e., February 27, 1876.

96. In his letter to Stout, February 25, 1876, Janes wrote: "I have been notified by Mr. Nonoguchi that they will have no further need of me after this year's agreement expires. Of course every effort is making to get me away at once. But I yield not to threats!" In a letter to his mother in June he wrote: "They

tried their best to drive me out. Their first disappointment came to them from that direction. The Japanese head of the school came to me, and tried to end matters by getting me off. He got a very calm answer that I should stay till the last hour of my engagement." See Janes Papers, no 103, Letter to Mother, Kumamoto, Japan, June 13, 1876.

97. Janes Papers, no. 110, Letter to Rev. Stout, Kumamoto, Japan, February 25, 1876.

98. For an account of Kanamori's experiences see Mitsui, *Kindai Nihon no seinen gunzō*, pp. 169–73. On one occasion Kanamori returned to the school feeling that his cross was too heavy to bear. His persistence, he felt, was causing great distress for his mother and ill older brother. Seeing him waver, Ebina encouraged him and told him to hold fast. As he was about to return home Ebina shouted after him, "Kanamori die! There is nothing to do but die. Die!" Wada, one of the other students, regarded Ebina's call for hardness "too cruel." Later Ebina and some of his friends went and stood outside the room in which Kanamori was being confined. On one occasion they threw in a rock with a message attached stating "we're with you." In the margin of Kanamori's Gospel of John, which he had been able to conceal on his person when all his other books were destroyed, the name of Ebina is written again and again, "Ebina, Ebina, Ebina. . . ." See Mitsui, "Doshisha and the Kumamoto Band," *Japan Christian Quarterly*, p. 118. In his autobiography Kanamori wrote only briefly: "I was one of the most bitterly persecuted. After receiving severe treatment at the hands of my relatives for many months, I was finally disowned and cast out of my father's house." Paul M. Kanamori, *Kanamori's Life-Story*, pp. 26–27.

99. For Yokoi Tokio's experiences during the persecution see Mitsui, *Kindai Nihon no seinen gunzō*, pp. 173–80.

100. Mitsui, "Doshisha and the Kumamoto Band," *Japan Christian Quarterly*, p. 118. Junko was the older sister of Yokoi Shōnan's wife, Tsuseko, and of Tokutomi Ikkei's wife, Hisako.

101. Watase, *Ebina Danjō*, p. 113; Mitsui, "Doshisha and the Kumamoto Band," *Japan Christian Quarterly*, p. 118.

102. Janes, *Kumamoto*, part 2, p. 73. Kozaki presents us with a slightly different version of the event: "She said [to Tokio] 'you are the only son of Shōnan Yokoi and the one born to succeed to his spirit as well as his name. For you to throw yourself away on this evil religion is inexcusable misbehavior. But I, your mother, am responsible to your father, my deceased husband, for having brought you to such folly, and I feel myself condemned. If you do not listen to your mother's words I have no recourse but suicide.' So saying she took her short sword in her hand and showed that she really intended to commit suicide, when suddenly the whole house was thrown into great confusion: for Juka, who had been a faithful housemaid from before the death of Shōnan, turning towards the Yōgakkō which was very near, shouted out: 'The old Madam is about to kill herself. Come quick and help!' At this manager Nonoguchi and several of the older students at once ran to the house, intervened

and prevented further trouble." Kozaki, *Reminiscences*, p. 22. Yokoi was kept in confinement until he was allowed to go to Tokyo to enter the Kaisei Gakkō in April.

103. Tokutomi Iichirō, *Sohō jiden*, pp. 61–67.

104. Kozaki, *Reminiscences*, p. 23. The quotations are from Kozaki, "The Kumamoto Band in Retrospect," unpaginated.

105. Janes Papers, no. 110, Letter to Rev. Stout, Kumamoto, Japan, February 25, 1876. The portion quoted is written under the date, February 26, 1876.

106. Janes' letter to Stout, March 3, 1876, quoted in Stout letter to Ferris, March 17, 1876, Dutch Reformed Papers.

107. There are one or two cases in which students got off lightly. When word of the conversions spread, Takezaki made the rounds of the Christian students' homes urging parents to deal firmly with their sons' heterodox views. When Takezaki approached Shimomura Kōtarō's father he was told by the elder Shimomura that "he had confided his son to the care of the school, and that he believed a teacher could not teach his pupils things that were wrong, and so he would not interfere, whatever Capt. Janes might teach his son." Fukunaga, *Nihon ni okeru taii Jiensu shi*, p. 93.

108. Watase, *Ebina Danjō*, p. 112. Shimomura recalled that "Mr. Takezaki was greatly offended at my professing Christianity, and he invited me to his house, and together with one Mr. Yamada, one of his pupils, pressed me to abandon the faith. But when he found he had been wasting his words, he told me that I should get no more pecuniary assistance. All this time some delicious cakes had been baking on his brazier which had been intended for me had I taken his advice." Fukunaga, *Nihon ni okeru taii Jiensu shi*, pp. 94–95.

109. Shimomura noted, "I was not the only one who had to suffer a loss of financial support. In order to live on as little money as possible, about a dozen of us were obliged to cook our own food at Capt. Janes' and did not stir out for a long time. He was greatly anxious for our sake, and great was the assistance and encouragement he rendered us on that occasion." Ibid., p. 95.

110. The behind-the-scenes negotiations on this issue are not well known. On February 26 Janes had written to Stout, "You have doubtless asked 'where is the government all this time?' Well it has not been my habit to trouble the government much . . . they have sought me much more than I have them . . . but if the question of legal toleration of Christianity might be hastened or helped to a settlement by an appeal to Caesar, from here, I might be led to send it up." But, he added, "in sober truth I doubt if the government is strong enough to make the attempt." Janes Papers, no. 110, Letter to Rev. Stout, Kumamoto, Japan, February 25, 1876. Section quoted is dated February 26, 1876. Later Janes wrote to Stout, "I think we have practically conquered in our difficulties here. We have the *unofficial* declaration of Government officers up to the Ken Rei (the Governor) himself, that 'religion is free' . . . The answer of the government, and a warning to the school officers I think it was, which sent the students back to their recitations. Sections have sprung up again, from four and three, to which they had been reduced by the action of the opposition,

to their normal numbers, sixteen and twelve." Letter to Stout, March 3, 1876, quoted in Stout letter to Ferris, March 17, 1876, Dutch Reformed Papers. In his letter to his mother in June Janes indicated that Nonoguchi went to the governor, Yasuoka Ryōsuke, to try to have him fired, but that Yasuoka gave him a "cold answer," indicating that he could not terminate Janes' contract. Yasuoka, no friend of the school and the Practical Learning Party, seems to have taken some personal pleasure in seeing the Practical Learning reformers' political plans for the school go awry. Having failed in his earlier efforts to close the school, he was now content to let it self destruct. Janes Papers, no. 103, Letter to Mother, Kumamoto, Japan, June 13, 1876.

111. Ibid.

112. Yoshida's experiences are discussed in Watase, *Ebina Danjō*, p. 121. See also Kozaki, *Reminiscences*, p. 23.

113. Fukunaga, *Nihon ni okeru taii Jiensu shi*, p. 92.

114. Kozaki, *Reminiscences*, pp. 36–37.

115. Watase, *Ebina Danjō*, p. 110.

116. Kozaki wrote that in the midst of the persecution he took up Kanamori's cause. "He had been a long time in confinement," he wrote, "had no books to read, in fact no resource but prayer, so I determined to rescue him. One night I secretly got him away from his house and took him to the bank of a small stream near by. It was pitch dark, a dreary rain was falling, and Kanamori had about reached the limits of endurance. He lamented his hard fortune, sighed over the bitterness of the prospects before him, and declared he was ready to die rather than live on as at present. I was astonished enough to hear him go on like this, and finally after repeated remonstrances, I succeeded in persuading him to give up that idea and to accompany me into the country. I tell you," Kozaki added, "I did not spare myself for those Christian boys, although as yet I had not become one of their number." Kozaki, "The Kumamoto Band in Retrospect," unpaginated.

117. Kozaki, *Reminiscences*, p. 38.

118. Ibid., p. 31.

119. Janes letter to Stout, dated "a few days after February 4," quoted in Stout letter to Ferris, March 17, 1876, Dutch Reformed Papers. Kozaki writes that this event took place "towards the end of February." Kozaki, *Reminiscences*, p. 37.

120. Ibid., p. 39.

121. Davis, *Joseph Hardy Neesima*, p. 76.

122. Kozaki observed that Janes "stood for the widest freedom in matters of faith, lectured his pupils on higher critical lines, when dealing with the Old Testament, and in general introduced us to the new thought of the West. He ridiculed scholasticism, was an ardent admirer of Henry Ward Beecher, took special delight in reading the "Christian Union" and Bushnell's works, and on the whole was looked upon as having heretical tendencies." Kozaki, "The Kumamoto Band in Retrospect," unpaginated.

123. Janes Papers, no. 109, Letter to Rev. Davis, Kumamoto, July 13, 1876.

Shimomura noted that Janes used to speak badly of "clergymen, baptism, and the Lord's Supper, and some other things. Not knowing what these were, we supposed they were merely things of form to be much abhorred." Shimomura saw Janes as contradicting himself on a number of these issues. "When, therefore, he said he would baptize us, I was very sorry," he wrote, "however I was at last prevailed on by my friends to be baptized. He held clergy in utter abhorrence, but when I asked him what profession I should choose, I was told to my great astonishment to turn a minister." Fukunaga, *Nihon ni okeru taii Jiensu shi*, pp. 95–96. What these contradictions really indicated is Janes' shift from his rational to his revivalistic phase. Some signs of the inner content of this shift can be seen in a letter to his mother written in June 1876: "Never has my faith in Him, and my love for Him been so powerful to overcome in me the selfishness and sinfulness of my soul, or so crystal clear and mirrorlike to show and expose to me these traits of the old Adam. But just as Christ becomes precious to me, just in proportion as I feel the debt of my own saving, and the joy of this love, I see more clearly and grieve at the state of these hundreds of millions." Janes Papers, no. 102, Letter to Mother, Kumamoto, Japan, July 2, 1876.

124. Janes Papers, no. 109, Letter to Rev. Davis, Kumamoto, July 13, 1876.

125. Janes Papers, no. 110, Letter to Rev. Stout, Kumamoto, February 25, 1876. Janes added: "If it is absolutely necessary for him to indulge the proselytizing spirit some of his denomination display, I recommend to him Madagascar as a suitable field, where he will already find companions of kindred spirit. Heathendom, in the interests of a purer Christianity than yet prevails after 1800 years of 'Apostolic Succession,' ought to be spared a repetition of such scenes; which the heathen rightly and justly and most effectively cast up as a reproach to Christianity."

126. Janes Papers, no. 109, Letter to Rev. Davis, Kumamoto, July 13, 1876.

127. Ibid.

128. Janes' letter to the Revds. Davis, Gulick, and Gordon, Kumamoto, August 1, 1876. ABCFM, Mission to Japan, vol. 4, no. 348. Janes writes: "Seventeen of the boys were baptized on Sunday, and after our earnest effort to set before them as the last impressions to be carried away from our parting services, the Cross of Christ, the mystery of Godliness, *Christ Crucified* . . . we partook of the Lord's Supper . . . I had no thought of either the baptism or the Lord's Supper till late Saturday evening and as I yielded only to the solicitations for the first presented by one of the Christian boys deputed to request it of me, I felt the latter to be appropriate." Dates previously given for the students' baptism have varied from April 4 (according to Kozaki) to June 5 (according to Ebina) and July 27 (according to Miyagawa). The July 30 date appears to have been the correct one as Janes wrote in the above letter that the students had been baptized on Sunday (the previous Sunday was July 30, 1876).

129. Janes Papers, no. 109, Letter to Rev. Davis, Kumamoto, July 13, 1876.

130. Janes, *Kumamoto*, part 2, p. 88. Janes later learned that overwork and

excessive use of his eyes had led to a serious inflamation of the conjunctiva and retina. *Janes vs. Janes* Divorce Proceedings Records.

131. Janes Papers, no. 109, Letter to Rev. Davis, Kumamoto, July 13, 1876.

132. Janes wrote to Davis on July 4, 1876: "Early in May I received instruction that one of two Professorships at the Kai Sei Gakko had been tendered to me and on the 1st of June . . . I received a communication from Yedo, from the Acting Superintendent of the Kai Sei Gakko through one of the graduates of my school stating that my appointment to one of two (and perhaps of three) Professorships, subject to my choice, depended only upon my notifying the Department of my willingness to accept . . . I sent a letter which left on the 3rd of June . . . accepting the appointment, expressing a willingness to work in any department in which I might be most useful." Letter to Revds. Davis, Gulick, and Gordon, Kumamoto, July 4, 1876. ABCFM, Mission to Japan, vol. 4, no. 345. On August 1 Janes wrote: "I will not be 'invited' to the Kai Sei Gakko by the Educational Department where appointments in that school must be made . . . this is not in the least unexpected to me. It was perhaps too much to expect that officials would put themselves out of the way to set the seal of approval on all that has caused trouble here, in the face of the opposition, or that they have backbone enough, Christians though some may be, so signally to express their satisfaction at a semi-official school, and the work in it, whose most marked result, so far as they see it, is to 'make' or 'educate' 'preachers.' " Janes letter to Revds. Davis, Gulick, and Gordon, Kumamoto, August 1, 1876, ABCFM, Mission to Japan, vol. 4, no. 348. The reasons for Janes' refusal at the Kaisei Gakkō remain unclear, but they may well have had their sources in his Christian activities, as he notes. The Ministry of Education did, however, offer him an appointment as professor at the Osaka Eigo Gakkō, which he held from November 1876 to May 1877.

133. By October Davis wrote to Dr. Clark of the American Board, "we now have 22 young men on the grounds from Kumamoto and expect 4 or 5 more in a few days." Letter from J. D. Davis to N. G. Clark, Kyoto, October 16, 1876. ABCFM, Mission to Japan, no item no. Some of the students reached the American Board's "training school" by devious routes. Kozaki writes about Kanamori: "The latter's entry into Doshisha was unique. His relative who kept him locked up was intensely interested in industrial pursuits, and when a friend cunningly suggested that Kanamori be sent to the Uji tea factories to study the process there, his guardian fell into the trap, said that was just the thing, and thus under the cover of going to study the tea industry Kanamori was started in the direction of Kyoto. . . ." Kozaki, "The Kumamoto Band in Retrospect," unpaginated.

134. John D. Pierson, *Tokutomi Sohō*, p. 53.

135. Janes, *Kumamoto*, part 2, p. 81.

136. Ibid., p. 89.

137. Letter to Revds. Davis, Gulick, and Gordon, Kumamoto, August 1, 1876, ABCFM, Mission to Japan, vol. 4, no. 348.

138. Janes, *Kumamoto*, part 2, p. 89.

139. Fukunaga, *Nihon ni okeru taii Jiensu shi*, pp. 27–28.

140. The Shimpūren (League of the Divine Wind) uprising began on October 24, 1876. For a discussion of the group behind it see chapter 5, fn. 38. In his book *Kumamoto*, Janes writes that the uprising took place the day after his departure from Kumamoto. He furthermore notes that once the bloody uprising was underway "a detail of six of the two sworded gentry, to whom had been assigned the work of exterminating the only foreign family within their reach, made a diligent search of the late home of the foreign teacher, ranging its rooms from attic to foundation." *Kumamoto*, part 2, p. 91. Kurahara, one of the students, writing in *Kyūshū bungaku*, vol. 31 (1893), p. 12, also notes that Janes left Kumamoto the day before the uprising and that this was a hairbreadth escape. But others writing at the time disagreed. Johei Asahara in *Blessed Takezaki Junko*, which incorporated the materials from Tokutomi Kenjirō's *Takezaki Junko*, writes: "A few weeks later [after Janes' departure] the riot of the Jimpuren, ultranationalist group, broke out, when Prefectural Governor Yasuoka, Commander of Garrison Major General Taneda and other officials were killed. If Janes' departure had been delayed only slightly, Japan might have been liable for the life of this American benefactor." *Blessed Takezaki Junko*, p. 20. Sugii Mutsurō in his article "Kumamoto Yōgakkō," in *Kumamoto Bando kenkyū*, p. 97, notes that the *Kumamoto Shimbun*, the newspaper whose presses Janes had ordered from the United States, ran a story on October 9, 1876, that the Captain had completed his contract and left Kumamoto on October 7. Sugii adds the ironic note that the civil trial of the staunchly anti-Western Shimpūren insurgents was to take place in the Yōgakkō buildings.

CHAPTER X
THE YEARS OF CONTROVERSY

1. Letter from J. D. Davis to N. G. Clark, Kyoto, November 3, 1876, ABCFM, Mission to Japan, vol. 4. Some of the American Board's Mission to Japan documents were read at the Houghton Library, Harvard University, others were read at Dōshisha University in Kyoto, where there is a fairly complete microfilm run of the Japan correspondence of the Board up to the mid-1890s in the Kirisutokyō Shakai Mondai Kenkyū Kai (abbreviated at Dōshisha as C.S.). Materials read at Dōshisha have been cited as "Microfilm, C.S. Dōshisha" plus the film roll number. Portions of this chapter originally appeared as "Leroy Lansing Janes and the American Board," in Dōshisha Daigaku Jimbun Kagaku Kenkyū Sho—Kirisuto Shakai Mondai Kenkyū Kai, eds., *Nihon kindaika to kirisuto kyō* (Tokyo: Shinkyō Shuppansha, 1973). I wish to thank the editors of this volume for permission to reprint passages from this article.

2. Letter from N. G. Clark to J. D. Davis, November 21, 1893, ABCFM, Correspondence from the Board to the Missionaries.

3. Letter from J. D. Davis to N. G. Clark, Kyoto, November 3, 1876, ABCFM, Mission to Japan, Microfilm, C.S. Dōshisha, Roll 2.

4. Kozaki, *Reminiscences*, p. 40.

5. Kozaki noted that the students had other complaints. They particularly disliked the food they were served under Dr. Taylor, the school's dietitian, who, Kozaki wrote, "had no understanding of the food of the Japanese," and who insisted on feeding the students oatmeal, or as Kozaki labeled it "mush," for breakfast, beef broth with barley or boiled beans for lunch, and allowed them to eat rice only once a day. Kozaki was more concerned, however, with the difference of educational approach than with the food. He saw the missionaries as far more rigid than Janes. He was particularly disturbed by the literal interpretations of Edward Doane, who expected the students to memorize scripture and accept it as written. "Captain Janes," Kozaki wrote, "had been sufficiently imbued with the scientific spirit to adopt the results of the higher criticism in the exposition of the Old Testament; he considered the Pentateuch not the work of Moses and regarded the creation of the world as having taken place millions of years ago. But Professor Doane spoke of the creation as an event which had taken place in 4004 B.C. As we could not accept such thinking he was greeted with outbursts of laughter and there was much complaint." Ibid., pp. 45–46.

6. Janes, *Kumamoto*, part 2, p. 103.

7. Letter from J. D. Davis to N. G. Clark, Kyoto, October 16, 1876, ABCFM, Mission to Japan, Microfilm, C.S. Dōshisha, Roll 2.

8. Letter from J. D. Davis to N. G. Clark, Kyoto, November 3, 1876, ABCFM, Mission to Japan, Microfilm, C.S. Dōshisha, Roll 2.

9. Ibid.

10. Letter from H. H. Leavitt to N. G. Clark, Arima, June 12, 1877, ABCFM, Mission to Japan, Microfilm, C.S. Dōshisha, Roll 5.

11. Letter from J. D. Davis to N. G. Clark, Kyoto, December 30, 1876, ABCFM, Mission to Japan, Microfilm, C.S. Dōshisha, Roll 2.

12. Ibid.

13. Ibid.

14. Ibid.

15. Ibid.

16. Ibid.

17. Letter from Dwight W. Learned to N. G. Clark, Kyoto, December 30, 1876, ABCFM, Mission to Japan, Microfilm, C.S. Dōshisha, Roll 5.

18. Letter from J. H. DeForest to N. G. Clark, Osaka, January 29, 1877, ABCFM, Mission to Japan, vol. 3, no item no.; Microfilm, C.S. Dōshisha, Roll 2.

19. Letter from J. C. Berry to N. G. Clark, Kobe, February 16, 1877, ABCFM, Mission to Japan, Microfilm, C.S. Dōshisha, Roll 1. Berry added, "we certainly ought to be able to assure him of our deep interest in him and appreciation of his noble work in a less expensive manner, and I am afraid that Captain Janes' present exalted opinion of the Mission would be lowered if he knew the latter thought found a place in the motives which actuate us in this action." In voting on Circular Letter No. 30 the Mission split eight to four, eight in favor and four opposed. However, even Berry, who was opposed to an outright grant, favored "loaning" Janes the money if he needed it.

20. Letter from H. H. Leavitt to N. G. Clark, Osaka, March 3, 1877, ABCFM, Mission to Japan, Microfilm, C.S. Dōshisha, Roll 2.
21. Ibid.
22. Letter from J. H. DeForest to N. G. Clark, Osaka, March 3, 1877, ABCFM, Mission to Japan, Microfilm, C.S. Dōshisha, Roll 2.
23. Letter from J. D. Davis to N. G. Clark, Kyoto, March 5, 1877, ABCFM, Mission to Japan, Microfilm, C.S. Dōshisha, Roll 2.
24. Quotations that follow are from Letter of Janes to "The Members of the American Board Mission in Japan," Osaka, April 16, 1877, ABCFM, Mission to Japan, vol. 4, item no. 350, Microfilm, C.S. Dōshisha, Roll 6.
25. Letter from J. H. DeForest to N. G. Clark, Osaka, May 18, 1877, ABCFM, Mission to Japan, Microfilm, C.S. Dōshisha, Roll 3.
26. The Janes' family's illness is discussed in a letter from Justina Wheeler to Miss Carruth (Woman's Board), Osaka, May 5, 1877, ABCFM, Mission to Japan, Microfilm, C.S. Dōshisha, Roll 32.
27. Two copies of receipts for $750 each dated Yokohama, May 9, 1877, are included in ABCFM, Mission to Japan, vol. 4, item no. 351; Microfilm, C.S. Dōshisha, Roll 6.
28. Letter from Janes to N. G. Clark, Saint Denis, Maryland, January 7, 1878, ABCFM, Mission to Japan, vol. 4, item no. 353; Microfilm, C.S. Dōshisha, Roll 6. According to this letter, which was a reply to an inquiry from the treasurer of the Mission, there was some misunderstanding over the return of the money Janes had borrowed. The Board in Boston felt that the money should have been returned immediately after his return to the United States. Janes seems to have thought of the arrangement, as did some on the field, as a kind of advance against his account with the Board when he joined it.
29. The quoted passages are from a letter from J. D. Davis to N. G. Clark, Kyoto, May 5, 1877, ABCFM, Mission to Japan, Microfilm, C.S. Dōshisha, Roll 2.
30. The minutes of the Prudential Committee recorded the following: January 8, 1878, "The case of Capt. Janes, who now proposes to return to Japan was considered." Also January 15, "a letter from Capt. Janes was read in relation to the circumstances of his return from Japan, his accepting a loan from the Mission and his readiness to return to labor in Japan." ABCFM, Minutes of the Prudential Committee.
31. I have not been able to locate the lengthy paper that Janes wrote for the Prudential Committee on the subject of education in Japan, but we do have his covering letter mailed with the proposal, February 14, 1878, and sent from his Elk Ridge farm. Janes wrote in this letter, "It has been difficult for me to forsee just the points to which it might have been most desirable to have me direct my attention. Hence the inordinate length of the paper, my desire to make it complete, so far as I was able, as a whole plan. I have written wholly from the head, scarcely having put pen to paper upon the subject before; though I have given the whole subject of Education in Japan a good deal of very careful thought and not least at this great distance from the scene." ABCFM, Mission to Japan, vol. 4, item no. 354; Microfilm, C.S. Dōshisha, Roll 6.

32. On February 19 the minutes of the Prudential Committee noted, "a paper from Capt. Janes in regard to education in Japan was presented and referred to the subcommittee of the Japan Mission, who were requested to circulate it among other members of the committee." ABCFM, Minutes of the Prudential Committee.

33. Letter from J. D. Davis to N. G. Clark, Kyoto, July 5, 1878, ABCFM, Mission to Japan, Microfilm, C.S. Dōshisha, Roll 2.

34. Letter from Janes to N. G. Clark, Saint Denis, Maryland, September 17, 1878, ABCFM, Mission to Japan, vol. 4, item no. 356; "Microfilm, C.S. Dōshisha, Roll 6.

35. *Janes vs. Janes* Divorce Proceedings Records, Circuit Court, Howard County, Ellicott City, Maryland. Hereafter cited as *Janes vs. Janes* Divorce Proceedings Records. In his answer to Harriet's "Bill of Complaint," Janes stated under oath that, "these charges [of adultery] have not startled this defendant, for during the greater portion of his married life, in the presence of his aged mother, and of his children, and of the domestics about his house, he has been charged with adultery not only while in the empire of Japan, but with illicit intercourse with the servants about his house, and often times with ladies in the neighborhood, but he has borne patiently with the same, attributing the conduct of his wife in this regard to mental and physical infirmities under which she has long and grievously suffered."

36. "Bill of Complaint of Hattie W. Janes," *Janes vs. Janes* Divorce Proceedings Records.

37. Memorandum, dated 1881, titled "A few facts which I, Mrs. Harriet Scudder Janes place in the hand of my father, Rev. Dr. Scudder to be used at his discretion in my defense," enclosed by Henry Martyn Scudder in a letter marked "Confidential" written to N. G. Clark, September 25, 1882, ABCFM, Mission to Japan, "Captain L. L. Janes File," Houghton Library, Harvard University. This file has been restricted for many years and I wish to thank Mary Walker, formerly the librarian of the United Church Board of World Ministries in Boston, for indicating to me the importance of its contents, and David M. Stowe, executive vice president of the United Church Board for World Ministries, for permission to have access to this file. In giving me permission to use these materials, Mr. Stowe wrote, "I do feel that it is wise to provide the maximum freedom for research in history, because this is an essential part of intellectual freedom and because only in this way can we learn as much as possible of what history has to teach us." I fully share these sentiments and appreciate all he has done on my behalf.

38. Letter from Janes to H. M. Scudder, Baltimore, February 8, 1882, *Janes vs. Janes* Divorce Proceedings Records.

39. Janes Papers, no. 603, "Kumamoto," ch. 2, pp. 21–22. Janes later wrote with bitterness that the failure of his marriage was largely due to Harriet's deteriorating condition "which was as directly due and traceable to the neglect and incompetency of her parents, and their preoccupation with the conceits and concerns of supernaturalism as the entire train of tragedies which even-

tually wrecked a family of infinite possibilities in a storm of pride and avarice, and crime and shame and death [was to show]."

40. "Bill of Complaint of Hattie W. Janes," *Janes vs. Janes* Divorce Proceedings Records.

41. "The Answer of Leroy L. Janes to the Bill of Complaint of his Wife, *Janes vs. Janes* Divorce Proceedings Records.

42. Letter from Janes to H. M. Scudder, Baltimore February 15, 1882, *Janes vs. Janes* Divorce Proceedings Records. Scudder took Janes to Dr. David Webster. Initially, Janes tells us, Henry Martyn wanted him to use an alias instead of his real name in the doctor's office for the official report of the examination. Janes insisted on announcing himself as "Capt. Janes late of the U.S.A. and recently from Japan." None of Janes' physical examinations, at the time of his Retiring Board case, or later when he was applying for a disability pension from the Army, shows any record of syphilis. In several instances such as the October 24, 1888, examination by Drs. Batroell, Breaky, and Kapp, "no evidence of syphilis" is clearly recorded.

43. Ibid.

44. In 1882 Scudder wrote to Clark: "On his return from Japan, I learned the fact of his adulteries, and of his having had syphilitic disease. At my house he confessed that he had been guilty of even more than was charged upon him. He subsequently retracted, and assumed a defiant position. . . ." Letter from H. M. Scudder to N. G. Clark, Brooklyn, New York, September 25, 1882, ABCFM, "Capt. L. L. Janes File."

45. Letter from Janes to H. M. Scudder, Baltimore, February 15, 1882, *Janes vs. Janes* Divorce Proceedings Records.

46. A copy of this letter was forwarded to Clark along with Janes' reply in 1882. See ABCFM, "Capt. L. L. Janes File." A second copy is included in the *Janes vs. Janes* Divorce Proceedings Records.

47. "Provision for my family for the current year depends too much upon my use of this busiest of the planting season, to allow of my hands being immediately withdrawn from the work in which I am at present engaged," Janes wrote to Scudder on April 8, indicating that he had no intention of making an immediate reply. Later he thought it best not to send a reply at all. For Janes' letter to Scudder see ABCFM, "Capt. L. L. Janes File."

48. Letter from H. M. Scudder to N. G. Clark, Brooklyn, New York, September 25, 1882, ABCFM, "Capt. L. L. Janes File."

49. See note 34 above.

50. Letter from Janes to H. M. Scudder, Baltimore February 15, 1882, *Janes vs. Janes* Divorce Proceedings Records.

51. Letter from Janes to Hattie Janes, Saint Denis, Maryland, July 14, 1877, *Janes vs. Janes* Divorce Proceedings Records.

52. In her "Bill of Complaint" Harriet listed under the "meanly, cruel treatment and excessively vicious conduct" of the Captain (these were the legal grounds upon which a divorce could be granted) the following: that he had 1) made every effort to alienate her from her children, 2) refused to supply her with

sufficient money for food and clothing, forcing her to get such funds from her parents, 3) refused to allow her the use of a horse or conveyance to attend Church, 4) impuned her chastity before the black servants and others, 5) on August 24, 1882, physically ejected her from their house and pushed her down the stairs outside, refusing to allow her to reenter, and finally 6) used foul language toward her in the presence of the children. Janes countered with his own complaints, stating that he had always supported his family financially, had made no effort to alienate Harriet from the children, but had put up with a good deal of unreliability on her part, forcing him to depend more and more on his oldest daughter Fanny for the management of the household. "In November 1881 his wife," he stated, "left his residence, taking with her their youngest child, and returned in March 1882, after her return she was absent three or four days in every week, and owing to her entire neglect of her household duties, and to the impossibility of the defendant retaining servants in his employment, the children were suffering from the want of proper and sufficient nutriment and this defendant was compelled to rely upon the exertions of his eldest daughter of the age of fourteen years." See *Janes vs. Janes* Divorce Proceedings Records.

53. Letter from Janes to Susan and Anna Warner, Saint Denis, Baltimore Co. Maryland, March 18, 1882, Warner Papers, The Constitution Island Association, West Point, New York.

54. See "The Bill of Complaint of Hattie W. Janes," *Janes vs. Janes* Divorce Proceedings Records.

55. See ABCFM, "Capt. L. L. Janes File."

56. Letter from H. M. Scudder to N. G. Clark, Brooklyn, New York, September 25, 1882, ABCFM, "Capt. L. L. Janes File."

57. See the "Decision of Judge Oliver Miller," *Janes vs. Janes* Divorce Proceedings Records.

58. "I have employed the best counsel in Maryland," Scudder wrote to Clark. The lawyer was William A. Hammond. Letter of H. M. Scudder to N. G. Clark, Brooklyn September 25, 1882; also *Janes vs. Janes* Divorce Proceedings Records.

59. On December 6, 1882, Scudder wrote to Clark, "The suit brought by my daughter Mrs. Janes is impending and I need *immediately* some evidence which I may be able to get from the following missionaries returned from Japan, now in this country: Rev. DeForest, Rev. and Mrs. Leavitt, Rev. Mr. Gulick, who was in Kobe in 1st part of 1877 living with his father and mother." ABCFM, Domestic Correspondence, vol. 79. Scudder also tried to contact the Mission doctors. In the document that Harriet composed for her father, which he sent to Clark, she specifically mentioned that Mr. Iwao had rebuked the Captain for his "immoralities," a conversation she overheard only in part from a room next door, and which most likely involved the matter of the Christian converts, about whom Iwao was angry. Scudder appears to have made an effort to get Iwao to provide "evidence" of Janes' "indiscretions" even before the divorce suit. Janes wrote to Scudder on February 15, 1882, that "even the persecutor

of my Christian boys in Japan, Mr. Iwao, refused to heed your appeal, or to aid you in your fiendish, malicious wickedness, by treating your letter to him with silent contempt!" *Janes vs. Janes* Divorce Proceedings Records.

60. "Decision of Judge Oliver Miller," *Janes vs. Janes* Divorce Proceedings Records.

61. Letter from Doremus Scudder to N. G. Clark, November 18, 1884. Doremus wrote: "we are all rejoicing in God's goodness in bringing the victory to her side and in giving her the three younger children. The two older must return of their own free will to her and this we trust will take place ere long. It has been a long sad night of weeping for her, but the morning of joy has begun now to dawn." It should be added that the Scudders' interpretation of the child custody settlement was not exactly in keeping with Judge Miller's decision.

62. Letter from N. G. Clark to H. M. Scudder, Boston, September 27, 1882, ABCFM, Domestic Correspondence, vol. 9.

63. Veterans Administration Claims File.

64. *The Missionary Herald* 82 (1886), 82.

65. Fukunaga, *Nihon ni okeru taii Jiensu shi*, p. 114.

66. Ukita Kazutami notes that the Band first heard of the allegations against Janes in 1882 when Davis returned to Japan having had access to Scudder's communications with Clark and the Board. Davis approached Ichihara with all the accusations that Harriet had made, including Scudder's interpretation that Janes had "confessed" to his crimes at his house. Ichihara told Davis that he had never heard of any such conduct in Kumamoto. When Ebina was told of the story he replied that he "could not believe it." Ukita added that inquiries in Kumamoto soon indicated that "Mr. Scudder tried to obtain proofs of Captain Janes' misconduct from members of the Practical Learning Party, but in vain. They replied that they had never heard anything against the Captain. Moreover, when the persecution had raged most fiercely there had been no censure uttered against Captain Janes' private conduct." Fukunaga, *Nihon ni okeru taii Jiensu shi*, pp. 114–18.

67. Ibid., p. 18.

68. In July 1885, after receiving a letter from the band with news of Yamazaki's death, Janes told the students that "the time for this long and cruel silence is now over." Writing from New Philadelphia he further added, "I am closing my business selling my farm in the old slave breeding state of Maryland . . . preparatory to settling elsewhere . . . I am engaged in literary work." Letter of Janes to the Kumamoto Band, New Philadelphia, Ohio, July 13, 1885. Published in *Shiryō ihō* (Dōshisha Daigaku Shashi Shiryō Henshū-sho) 1, (March 1968), 98–103. Janes settled at Ann Arbor, and some of his students claimed he had a job in one of the University of Michigan's laboratories. I have not been able to confirm this. It is clear that he spent most of his time writing while in Ann Arbor while the older children went to the university. It was also through the university that he met Flora Oakley, the woman he married in 1893.

69. Letter from K. Ukita to N. G. Clark, New Haven, September 30, 1892, ABCFM, Mission to Japan, vol. 25.
70. Ibid.
71. Letter from K. Ukita to N. G. Clark, New Haven November 21, 1892, ABCFM, Mission to Japan, vol. 20.
72. The alleged murder of Mary Dunton by Henry Martin Scudder Jr. received extensive publicity in the United States. The *New York Times* ran articles on the case on March 4, 5, 6, 8, 10, and 16. Harry, who had recently married Mrs. Dunton's daughter, was accused of bludgeoning her to death with a wooden club. The motive was the Dunton estate, and it was alleged that Harry had forged a will in Mrs. Dunton's name, leaving her fortune to his wife. Harry's record in India had also been less than satisfactory. On August 20, 1880, the field committee of the Arcot and Arnee Stations brought a formal complaint against Harry and urged the Board to call for his resignation. Among the charges listed by Jacob Chamberlain, J. H. Wycoff, and J. W. Scudder were the following: 1) That during famine conditions he took the Mission's imported relief food and speculated on it, making a profit of 600 rupees which he put in his personal account. 2) That he made money for his own private account by loaning sums of money to the natives at 24–percent interest. 3) That he had native officials imprison a number of men because they refused to sell him some building stone on terms he claimed they agreed to but which they denied, and he consented to have them released only when they gave the stone to him on his terms. 4) That he threatened to expose a native contractor to the British authorities unless he would supply him with bricks at a price far below the market price. When the Mission remonstrated with him regarding the last charge he is reported to have replied, "How could I build my churches so cheaply, if I did not use such expedients?" The Mission concluded that Harry's "influence over our Native Agents and Native Christians is exceedingly pernicious." The Board of Missions of the Reformed Church of America decided to take the field's advice and accepted Harry's resignation. See Letter from Jacob Chamberlain, J. H. Wycoff, and J. W. Scudder to The Board of Foreign Missions, R.C.A., Madanapalle, India, August 20, 1880, Dutch Reformed Papers.

A final curious touch connected Janes with the Chicago murder case. The Janes Papers include a letter from Francis Walker, the prosecutor in the Scudder trial, to Janes stating that he was greatly interested in "your important letter . . . to Mr. F. H. Dunton." "I deem it very important in the interest of a just administration of the law," Walker wrote Janes, "that you should come to Chicago at once in order that full knowledge may be obtained of all that information which was not disclosed in the letter." Walker offered to pay the Captain's way to Chicago so that he could present his information. It is not clear what kind of information Janes had that was of such interest to Walker.
73. *New York Times*, June 22, 1892, p. 8.
74. *The Outlook* 51 (June 22, 1895), 1102.

75. Letter from D. C. Greene to N. G. Clark, July 23, 1892, ABCFM, Mission to Japan, vol. 20.
76. Otis Cary in a letter to N. G. Clark explained the position of the Mission: "As you know, at our last annual meeting a letter was received from the Kumamoto Band asking us to aid them in vindicating Captain Janes before the world. The letter was referred to a special committee made up of persons who had known Captain Janes, and they met several of the young men to talk over the matter. . . . An attempt was made to show them that we were in no position to give any positive judgement about the charges; there was no way in which we could get the evidence even though we might believe in Captain Janes' innocence, any utterance by us would only do him harm, since comparatively few in America who had heard of Captain Janes knew the charges; to publish anything would bring the charges to the knowledge of the public, and with the sympathy of the Scudders it would be prejudicial to Captain Janes. All of this was not very convincing to the young men." ABCFM, Mission to Japan, Microfilm, C.S. Dōshisha, Roll 22.
77. Letter from D. C. Greene to N. G. Clark, July 23, 1892, ABCFM, Mission to Japan, vol. 20.
78. Ibid.
79. Letter from J. D. Davis to N. G. Clark, Kyoto, February 4, 1893, ABCFM, Mission to Japan, Microfilm, C.S. Dōshisha, Roll 23.
80. Letter from J. D. Davis to N. G. Clark, Tokyo, April 11, 1893, ABCFM, Mission to Japan, Microfilm, C.S. Dōshisha, Roll 23.
81. Shigehisa Tokutarō, *Oyatoi gaikokujin 14 chihō*, p. 120. Shigehisa tells us that Janes' salary at the new position was two hundred yen a month, fifty yen less than his salary had been in Osaka in 1876–77.
82. Janes married Flora Oakley on July 24, 1893. The marriage license gives Flora's age as twenty-five (she was actually thirty-five). It seems that Janes came to know her through the older children, who attended the university. Flora graduated from the Literary College of the University of Michigan in 1891.

CHAPTER XI
JAPAN AGAIN: KYOTO AND THE DŌSHISHA LECTURES

1. *Kokumin no tomo* [The Nation's Friend] was organized by Tokutomi Sohō in 1887. From 1887 to 1898 it was a severe critic of the Satsuma-Chōshū dominance of Japanese politics and opposed the emergence of the autocratic state. Chiefly a spokesman for the liberty and equality of the individual, the journal's position was identified with radical liberalism, and many regarded it as the "voice of democracy" in Meiji Japan. Its power and scope are said to have been so great that it was commonly remarked that among the first-rate minds of Meiji Japan only Fukuzawa Yukichi could not be found as a contributor to its columns. In the wake of the Sino-Japanese War (1894–95) Tokutomi shifted his position to greater support of Japanese nationalism, par-

ticularly in relations with the outside world. Many of the journal's younger readers regarded this as a "sell out" to the state and abandoned it, leading to its demise in 1898.

Rikugō zasshi [Cosmos Magazine] was founded by Kozaki Hiromichi in 1880. Kozaki hoped to establish a journal for the Christian position in Japan. As the voice of Christian reformism, and later Christian socialism, *Rikugō zasshi* was to have great influence in the intellectual world of Meiji Japan. A supporter of the arts, education, literature, and cultural interests that went far beyond any narrow Christian position, the magazine was widely read and highly respected. A pioneer in adopting social issues and social causes, it was at the heart of the Meiji Christian-Socialist movement. The first reference to the ideas of Karl Marx in Japan occurred in a *Rikugō zasshi* article written by Kozaki in 1881.

Taiyō [The Sun] was founded in 1895. By late Meiji-early Taisho times *Taiyō* became one of the most widely read general magazines in Japan. Ukita Kazutami became editor of *Taiyō* in 1909 and directed the magazine through its most important period. See *Nihon Kindai shi jiten* (Tokyo, 1958), pp. 191; 357; 622.

2. This and the following quotes are from Letter from Janes to Mr. Ise (Yokoi Tokio), Ann Arbor, Michigan, May 1, 1888. Unpublished letter, copy in the possession of the author. I am indebted to Prof. Sugii Mutsurō of Dōshisha for making this letter available to me.

3. Ibid. Writing in Ann Arbor in 1890 Janes added: "Breed up the youth of a prospective statesman in the belief that all who are not of his faith are heathen, incapable of civilization until they are 'Christianized,' and when he is a man he will not depart from that way of thinking. Feed his youthful imagination on the uncouth distortions, and lurid falsehoods to which begging missionaries resort in order to justify their equivocal vocation as peddlers of creeds, and he will never recover from the shock which his ardent sympathies have felt. And this has been done throughout the past century." Janes Papers, no. 202, "Religion and Morality."

4. Letter from Janes to Mr. Ise (Yokoi Tokio), Ann Arbor, Michigan, May 1, 1888.

5. Early in 1893 Otis Cary wrote to Clark noting that at a recent meeting of the churches the criticism of the missionaries, with one exception, was made by the "Kumamoto men." He felt that the recent uneasiness of the members of the band was directly related to the Janes matter. "Notwithstanding some things that have been unpleasant," he wrote, "we cannot but admire the loyalty of the young men towards one to whom they owe so much. There can be no doubt that they believe in his innocence. Capt. Janes has become their idol and they can brook nothing that seems to take from his glory.

"What would be the result of Capt. Janes' coming to Japan, it would be hard to prophesy. Japan has changed: Kyoto is not Kumamoto; few men could live up to the ideal that these young men hold in their hearts as they think of him; the requirements of government schools are growing higher, and in case the teacher should not meet the desires of the directors, the term of service might not be long. In the latter case some troublesome propositions might be made to the mission and the board. If he is alienated from the Churches by what his friends say is unjust treatment by a prominent minister; the results of such disaffection might appear in his influence upon his old pupils. There is, however, no advantage in borrowing trouble. If he comes our duty of being as friendly with him as possible is plain." Letter of Otis Cary to N. G. Clark, Kyoto, April 25, 1893, ABCFM, Mission to Japan, Microfilm, C.S. Dōshisha, Roll 22.

6. Letter from J. D. Davis to N. G. Clark, Kyoto, September 30, 1893, ABCFM, Mission to Japan, vol. 18.

7. Makino Toraji, *Hari no ana kara* (Kyoto, 1958), pp. 54–55.

8. Ibid., p. 55.

9. The following quotes are from Letter from J. D. Davis to N. G. Clark, Kyoto, October 23, 1893, ABCFM, Mission to Japan, vol. 18.

10. The Janes Papers, include manuscripts for four lectures, three of which were given at Dōshisha. The fourth, as we will see, was never delivered. These manuscripts conform quite closely to the outlines made by Davis and Albrecht. But the length of the first two (forty-one and sixty-six pages) suggests that what remains are the updated versions of the lectures that Janes hoped to publish in Japanese. However, in their content, the extant lectures seem to conform closely to what he delivered in the Dōshisha Chapel. See Janes Papers, no. 206, "Kioto Discourses."

11. Letter from J. D. Davis to N. G. Clark, Kyoto, October 23, 1893, ABCFM, Mission to Japan, vol. 18.

12. Letter from George E. Albrecht to Dr. Clark, Kyoto, October 24, 1893, ABCFM, Mission to Japan, Microfilm, C.S. Dōshisha, Roll 20.

13. Letter from J. D. Davis to N. G. Clark, Kyoto, October 25, 1893, ABCFM, Mission to Japan, vol. 18.

14. Ibid.

15. Makino Toraji and several of his friends went to Janes for explanations of portions of his lecture they had not understood. Makino, *Hari no ana kara*, p. 56. Makino adds that the students complained about Janes' invectives against the missionaries and requested him to tone down his next lecture. For his second lecture the Captain prepared an outline that was distributed among the students beforehand.

16. Letter from George Albrecht to Dr. Clark, Kyoto, November 16, 1893, ABCFM, Mission to Japan, Microfilm, C.S. Dōshisha, Roll 20.

17. Janes Papers, no. 206, "Kioto Discourses."

18. Letter from J. D. Davis to N. G. Clark, Kyoto, December 5, 1893, ABCFM, Mission to Japan, vol. 18.

19. The following quotations are from Janes' ms. of his "Kioto Discourses: The Greatest Thing in the World. What it Is." Janes Papers, no. 206, "Kioto Discourses," ms. pp. 1–66.

20. Letter from J. D. Davis to N. G. Clark, Kyoto, December 11, 1893. Unfor-

tunately the Janes Papers, do not include a complete manuscript copy of this lecture, although there seems to be a fifteen page fragment preserved, entitled, "The best and greatest thing in the World, What it Is," which would indicate that he wanted to continue the earlier theme. Davis described the content as being: "No soul; the soul is a fetish of the imagination. He criticized and caricatured the Church and supernatural Christianity, and missionaries, etc., etc., and said that he was the messenger of Jesus Christ to teach us that there is no God, no soul, no hereafter, etc., etc." Janes' manuscript indicates that he was primarily concerned with the issue of "divinity," on which he differed radically from the conservative Church. On the issue of God's existence, Janes did not argue what Davis represented him as saying. Janes' argument was that using the tools of modern science and philosophy God was not knowable as other things are knowable. "To my reverent search," he noted, "God is unattainable, unknowable: to the human he will forever remain super-human, Infinite, Universal, Creative Cause, to the creature he will remain forever inscrutable." At the same time Janes insisted that if modern science had altered man's perceptions of God, it was just as important for the modern Christian to "declare with equal firmness, 'God Is!' And he is not the monas monadum of the machinist; nor the intellectual fetich of the doctor of divinity; less still is he the even lower conceit of the sentimental anthropomorphist. 'God is,' not mere hypothesis, but the one incommensurable and to finite powers, unknowable, fact." Janes Papers, no. 206, "Kioto Discourses: The best and greatest thing in the World. What it is," ms. p. 15.

21. Quoted in a letter from Mrs. Carrie G. Atkinson to Dr. Clark, Kobe, December 6, 1893, ABCFM, Mission to Japan, vol. 15.

22. Letter from J. D. Davis to N. G. Clark, Kyoto, December 11, 1893, ABCFM, Mission to Japan, vol. 18.

23. Ibid.

24. While Ebina, Yokoi, Kozaki, and Ichihara remained firm in their support of their teacher, others like Shimomura and Yoshida were less supportive. Davis wrote: "the school is safe from his influence now; I think every one of the teachers except possibly the members of Capt. J's old band are opposed to his lecturing further, and I think at least Mr. Shimomura of the band is opposed." Ibid.

25. J. Merle Davis, *Davis-Soldier Missionary* (Boston: Pilgrim Press, 1916), p. 219.

26. Letter from J. D. Davis to N. G. Clark, Kyoto, December 11, 1893, ABCFM, Mission to Japan, vol. 18.

27. Letter from J. H. DeForest to N. G. Clark, Kyoto, January 1, 1894, ABCFM, Mission to Japan, Microfilm, C.S. Dōshisha, Roll 23.

28. In 1876 Davis had written to Clark: "What we hope may seem wise for you to do will be to secure as soon as possible, Capt. Janes to raise in America an Endowment for himself and for one or two others like minded with himself, and let them come right in here and take the collegial part of our training school off our hands and release two or three of our number for direct gospel

work. . . ." Letter from J. D. Davis to N. G. Clark, Kyoto, October 16, 1876, ABCFM, Mission to Japan, Microfilm, C.S. Dōshisha, Roll 2.

29. The problem of fixed doctrinal positions became particularly troubling at Dōshisha. Kozaki pointed out in his autobiography that even before Janes' return there had been serious disagreements between the missionaries and the members of the band about the principles of Christian education. "The missionaries emphasized the outward form and insisted on using the Bible as a text book," he wrote, "while the Japanese teachers thought more of the spirit and paid less attention to the outer form so that there was ceaseless conflict of opinion between them." The Janes lectures simply served as a catalyst to bring the problem to a head. The doctrinal position of the school was soon mixed together with the issue of property ownership, with the independently minded members of the band insisting—what was in fact legally correct—that the Dōshisha property belonged to the corporation, and not to the Mission. All this resulted in the dispatching by the American Board of a deputation of four representatives to deal with these problems. The deputation concluded, as Kozaki tells us, "that, although Dōshisha was a Christian institution it was not clear what the Christianity it professed was, and that therefore we should make a brief declaration of faith in regard to such points as God, Christ and immortality." Kozaki, while maintaining that "Dōshisha held as its fundamental principle . . . historical Christianity such as that professed by the majority of Christians in all lands," refused to commit the school to any more definite theological position. Writing to members of the Prudential Committee on April 30, 1896, Kozaki observed, "In one sense, there is no Christian in Japan who would deny the personality of God. But there are many whose views will differ widely from each other, if by personality of God is meant some anthropomorphic representation of God. There are some people here who regard as atheists our pastors who are very earnest and faithful, or denounce as pantheists those who proclaim God as the absolute reason of the Universe. Under such circumstances as this, it is extremely perilous to make such simple statement of these truths as was demanded by the Deputation. It is especially perilous for the institution of education to make such statement, and will produce more misunderstanding, where there are so much discordance of views between the missionaries and the Japanese on the Divinity of Christ, the Immortality of the Soul, and the Nature of the Supernatural Revelation." See Kozaki, *Reminiscences*, pp. 104–107. For Kozaki's reply to the Board see *Dōshisha hyakunen shi* (Kyoto, 1979), *Shiryō hen II*, pp. 345–46.

30. Letter from Janes to Mr. Ise (Yokoi Tokio), Ann Arbor, Michigan, May 1, 1888.

31. Kozaki, *Reminiscences*, p. 105.

32. Dōshisha's self-government and independence from the Mission were guaranteed in 1896 when the continuing disagreement over the school's Christian position resulted in the resignation of all the missionary teachers. The Kumiai Churches (the leading pastors of which were Janes' students) had declared their independence of the Mission in 1894. In both cases the American Board's

efforts to get the Japanese to commit themselves to clear-cut doctrinal positions, sufficiently conservative to meet with missionary approval, backfired to the Mission's disadvantage. See Kozaki, *Reminiscences*, pp. 98–100, 102–108.

33. This act led to renewed crisis and ushered in a protracted period of turmoil between not only the missionaries and the Dōshisha (Kozaki argued that the missionaries saw this act as a way of getting their influence back into the school) but between the Kumiai Churches and the school. In 1899 Yokoi resigned under pressure and an effort was made to return Dōshisha to its original constitution. But such efforts failed to turn the historic tide, which pushed Dōshisha in the direction of becoming a secular university. For details see *Dōshisha hyakunen shi, tsūshi hen I*, pp. 445ff.; Kozaki, *Reminiscences*, pp. 158ff.

34. Two items of evidence may be cited to confirm such an appraisal. In August 1894 Ukita Kazutami published an article in *Rikugō zasshi*, titled "Gaikoku senkyōshi ron" [On Foreign Missionaries], in which he argued that missionaries did not understand the true essence of Christianity, were generally inferior men (a favorite Janes argument), stood in the way of social progress, and ought not to be cooperated with in the evangelization and education of Japan. *Dōshisha hyakunen shi, Tsūshi hen I*, pp. 434–35. In December 1895 Davis reported on a speech Ebina had given at Dōshisha. Ebina started, "by giving the reasons for the rapid progress of Christianity in Japan during the first ten years after it began to be preached . . . Japan was all ready to adopt everything foreign, or western, and the missionaries came with Christianity and with crude science and philosophy, which were superior to anything which the Japanese then had, and the result was that they had great success. But about 1886, the Japanese had gotten hold of the theories of Darwin and Spencer, and the philosophies of Kant, Hegel, Fichte, etc., and they made a great impression upon the scholars, but unfortunately the missionaries opposed these theories and philosophies, especially fighting evolution. The result was that evolution gained the victory and the missionaries were worsted and Christianity put under a cloud. Just at this time came also the wave of reaction, nationalism and opposition to things foreign . . . [yet] the time is ripe for a wise propagation of Christianity again, but it all depends upon how it is attempted. Systematic Theology is dead. It will not do to preach Christianity as it was first taught here. We cannot go back to that. We must not teach theories about the Bible, about miracles about the supernatural birth of Christ, etc., etc., we shall only raise doubts by so doing . . . how many people were ever converted by the miracles? How many were ever converted by the story of Christ's supernatural birth? How many were ever converted by the story of Adam and Eve? Very few indeed. The only two principles of ethics we need to preach are, 'Be ye therefore perfect as your father in heaven is perfect' and 'the golden rule.' Christ said these are the two great commandments. Getting our feelings wrought up in a prayer meeting is all bosh. Revivals are a great damage. We want none of these things, but a mind and purpose fixed immovably upon the one God

and on love to our fellow men." Quoted in letter of J. D. Davis to Dr. Barton, Kyoto, December 24, 1895, ABCFM, Mission to Japan, Microfilm, C.S. Dōshisha, Roll 23.

35. Janes served as professor of English and English literature at the Daisan Kōtō Chū Gakkō (Third College) from 1893 to 1899 with one break, from June 1896 to August 1897, when he served at the Kagoshima Kōtō Chūgaku Zōshikan as professor of English. This move stemmed from the temporary closure of the preparatory section of the Third College, which resulted from the educational reforms of 1895. With the reinstatement of this division in 1897 he was invited back to Kyoto. Contrary to Otis Cary's feelings that Janes might fail to live up to Japanese scholarly expectations, the Captain appears to have done well in his secular work. Starting out at a salary of 200 yen a month, his salary was raised to 250 yen a month in 1898 to mark his distinguished service to the institution. Janes is reported to have resigned from the Third College in 1899 due to his "advanced age." He was then sixty-two.

36. The foregoing manuscripts are all included in the Janes Papers. The Kumamoto book was not published until many years after his death.

37. In 1896, as Janes was preparing to go to Kagoshima, Davis passed on what has to be seen as scurrilous gossip: "A report has appeared in one of the leading daily papers of Kyoto," Davis wrote, "describing Capt. Janes as definitely as possible without calling his name and saying that he had become enamored of a Japanese woman, and that she is about to give birth to a child and that her friends are coming to the father of the child for redress, but as he has no money, he is greatly troubled, etc. Whether this is true or not I do not know, but it will doubtless affect the questions which are upon us here. I should think this report would prevent the employment of Capt. J in the school next fall, but I do not know." Letter of J. D. Davis to Dr. Barton, Kyoto, May 10, 1896, ABCFM, Mission to Japan, vol. 18. As far as it can be determined today, Janes had no intention of joining Dōshisha as a teacher, although some of his former students may have wanted him to do so. A few weeks later Davis reported that the Janes' were not speaking to one another, or so the servants at the Kyoto Hotel reported, and that he feared that "history was repeating itself." This was particularly sad because the new Mrs. Janes was an orphan. Letter of J. D. Davis to Dr. Barton, Kyoto, June 18, 1896, ABCFM, Mission to Japan, vol. 18. All this simply confirms that if Janes was paranoid about Davis, sometimes referring to him as his "Great Enemy" (Dai Teki), Davis had become equally vindictive about the Captain.

38. The student was Azukisawa Hideo, whose recollections are included in Shigehisa Tokutarō, *Oyatoi gaikokujin 14—chihō bunka* (Tokyo, 1976), pp. 121–22.

39. Janes Papers, no. 306, "Kumamoto," ch. 3, pp. 63–64.

40. Ibid., pp. 65–66.

41. Ibid., p. 66.

42. Ibid., p. 67.

CHAPTER XII
THE FINAL YEARS

1. Letter from Janes to Rev. Danjō Ebina, Los Gatos, California, May 20, 1903. Copy of letter in the possession of the author. I wish to thank Prof. Sugii Mutsurō of Dōshisha University for making this letter available to me.

2. Death Certificate of Elizabeth Janes, Probate Court, Tuscarawas County, Ohio. Janes' mother lived to the ripe old age of eighty-eight. His father died in 1886.

3. When the Captain and Flora came to Japan in 1893, the four older children, Frances Elizabeth (Fanny), Leroy Lansing Jr. (the former Henry), Lois Harriet, and Eunice Anna were all enrolled at the University of Michigan. Lois was in her fourth year in 1894. The reasons for her death remain unclear, but she appears to have suffered most from the divorce of her parents in 1884. Following Lois's suicide all the other children left the University of Michigan. See *General Catalogue of the Officers and Students of the University of Michigan, 1837–1901* (Ann Arbor, Michigan, 1902), p. 493.

4. Affidavit of Fuwa Yu and Dr. Saeki Riichiro, Kyoto, Japan, September 15, 1909, Veterans Administration Claims File. Saeki noted that the delivery had been "a difficult case."

5. Affidavit of Orita Sato and Fujita Sumi, Kyoto, Japan, September 21, 1909, Veterans Administration Claims File. Mrs. Orita was the wife of the principal of the Third College and Fujita was the nurse who had attended Flora at the time of Iris's birth. Flora asked for these affidavits in 1909 after Janes' death because there were no birth certificates for her children born in Japan and she needed these to get a widow's pension and child support from the U.S. Pension Office. Orita and Fujita wrote that Iris was born on June 28, 1898. Flora, however, insisted to the Pension Office that this was a mistake and that Iris was born on January 28, not June 28, 1898.

6. Letter from Janes to Rev. Danjō Ebina, Los Gatos, California, May 20, 1903.

7. Ibid.

8. This and the following quotations, unless otherwise indicated, are from ibid.

9. In addition to its healthful climate Los Gatos may have appealed to Janes in other ways. Although little more than a village, it maintained an interesting connection with Japan in that the chief local attraction was an inn that carefully incorporated the principles of the classical Japanese farmhouse. The inn, built in 1901 and named the "Nippon Mura," was the product of a retired clipper ship captain, Theodore Morris, who had been on the Yokohama run and was particularly taken with Japan and Japanese architecture. Evidently Los Gatos attracted other former "Japan hands," and Janes, who already felt lonely and nostalgic for Japan, may have been drawn to the location for this reason.

10. At the time of his departure in 1899 members of the band had presented the Captain and his wife with several commemorative gifts including a beautiful album.

11. None of Janes' former students has chosen to clarify this problem. Most, in fact, have dealt very gingerly with the Captain's Kyoto years, indicating dif-

ferences of opinion on his role during his second stay in Japan. Without a consensus the band was not prepared to invite him back to Japan in 1903.

12. It may be that figures such as Kozaki and Ebina, who had been clearly influenced by the Captain during his Kyoto years, wanted to forget this phase of their own lives by the time they composed their memoirs. This was certainly the case with Kanamori, who later returned to the Church convinced that the New Theology had nearly ruined his life. Yet it does seem strange that none acknowledged receipt of the Captain's 1903 letter. Or, as we shall see in some instances, there was a clear distortion of fact, dealing with the matter. There is certainly no question of the letter's receipt as the extant copy includes its envelope and appropriate Japanese postal seals. Kozaki's visit to the Captain at Wrights is discussed in *Reminiscences*, pp. 195–98. The following quotations are from this source.

13. Kozaki refers to the "sea bathing resort of Santa Clara" rather than Santa Cruz, but he obviously meant the latter.

14. The person who appears to have vouched for the loan was Abiko Kyūtarō, the head of the Nichibei Newspaper who introduced Kozaki to the Golden Gate Bank.

15. The late Ivan Morris has written on the typology and appeal of the failed hero in Japan. In the introduction to his book, *The Nobility of Failure, Tragic Heroes in the History of Japan*, he notes that Japan has its share of successful heroes but, "there is another type of hero in the complex Japanese tradition, a man whose career usually belongs to a period of unrest and warfare and represents the very antithesis of an ethos of accomplishment. He is the man whose single-minded sincerity will not allow him to make the manoeuvres and compromises that are so often needed for mundane success. During the early years his courage and verve may propel him rapidly upwards, but he is wedded to the losing side and will ineluctably be cast down. Flinging himself after his painful destiny, he defies the dictates of convention and common sense, until eventually he is worsted by his enemy, the 'successful survivor,' who by his ruthlessly realistic politics manages to impose a new, more stable order on the world." Ivan Morris, *The Nobility of Failure* (New York: Holt, Rinehart, Winston, 1975), p. xiii.

16. Wrights Station no longer exists. With the demise of the railroad that connected San Jose with Santa Cruz the village disappeared. Its symbolic end came during World War II, when the railroad tunnel at whose entrance it was located was blown up in a demolition exercise.

17. In addition to his poultry raising the Captain also taught some of the local children. On his trip to the United States in 1978 Tanaka Keisuke found one of Janes' former students, Shelly Cothran, still living near Los Gatos. Cothran recalled that the Captain was an inspiring teacher and a hard taskmaster who had not given up on his use of "daily examinations." Cothran spent four years under the Captain's supervision, studying with him for three hours a day.

18. Janes repeatedly tried to get the U.S. Pension Office to raise his Civil War

disability pension during these years but to no avail. See Veterans Administration Claims File.

19. One reason that the "Kumamoto" manuscript was so slow to be published no doubt stemmed from such tones. A passage on Japanese literature may make the point: "As for the pretence of a literature to begin with," Janes wrote, "they have a language which ceased to grow the instant a foreigner taught them a way of writing it. Too weak to stand alone, it accepts and keeps fast hold of alien hieroglyphics. Not a page of its literature is learned, and everything that passes for learning in it is today as in all former times deliberately stolen without the grace of an acknowledgement or a thank you, but with a ridiculous parade of profound originality." *Kumamoto*, part 2, p. 14. These are rather strong words when we consider a literary tradition that produced *The Tale of Genji*, and they seem even less appropriate when we consider the fact that they were made by a man who could not read a sentence of Japanese.

20. In a letter to Professor Marius B. Jansen, dated San Jose, California, May 17, 1963, Iris Janes wrote: "His Kumamoto is excellently well written with no 'fine' writing in the rhetorical sense, and no obtrusive use of the first person singular. There is a lot of philosophy in it and all through he shows an acute understanding of the Japanese and *this* is what I want to keep from being edited and annotated out of existence. What no one understands, is that he was totally unaffected by that 'charm' so intoxicating to the average Occidental—he could admire the beauty of the art, give full credit to the intelligence and never for a moment loose sight of the basic character of that race. He was too original a genius to have his work and his account of that work altered to fit some preconceived idea. This is very true of the Japanese. They would not hesitate to cut and alter any one of my father's conclusions which did not please them or which did not fit into what I really believe is beginning to take the shape of a legend, with the legend's usual mixture of fact and fancy."

In an earlier letter she had written, "I have also the poignant memory of the last words that my father uttered in regard to the Japanese and his charge to me in regard to this manuscript. Even after these long, long years I cannot think of that day without tears." Letter from Iris Janes to Professor Marius B. Jansen, San Jose, California, April 25, 1963.

21. Janes Papers, no. 309, "The Yellow Man as a Pioneer of Modern Civilization," ms. frag. p. 3.

22. Ibid., p. 4.

23. Ibid., pp. 4–5.

24. Janes Papers, no. 117, Letter from Janes to D. M. Murphy, San Jose, California, November 2, 1906.

25. Ibid.

26. Watase, *Ebina Danjō*, p. 330.

27. Janes Papers, no. 117, Letter from Janes to D. M. Murphy, San Jose, California, November 2, 1906.

28. These included "Out of Stony Lonesome," "Ruth," and "Pearl," which are contained in the Janes Papers. None of these manuscripts seems to be complete,

and it is possible that the Janes hoped to integrate portions of all three into a final draft.

29. Surgeon's Certificate from F. W. Knowles, M.D., to U.S. Pension Office, San Jose, California, February 1, 1906, Veterans Administration Claims File.

30. Watase, *Ebina Danjō*, p. 329.

31. Ōshimo Aya, *Chichi Ebina Danjō* (Tokyo, 1975), p. 37. Ōshimo Aya is Ebina's daughter.

32. Ibid., p. 39.

33. Ibid.

34. Watase, *Ebina Danjō*, p. 329.

35. Ibid.

36. Ōshimo Aya, *Chichi Ebina Danjō*, p. 38.

37. Ibid., p. 40.

38. Watase, *Ebina Danjō*, p. 330. The photograph can be seen reproduced in Ōshimo Aya, *Chichi Ebina Danjō*, p. 2.

39. Medical Affidavit from Lewis J. Belknap, M.D., to United States Pension Office, stamped August 5, 1909, Veterans Administration Claims File.

40. The site of Janes' grave was debated for some years. Ebina indicated that he was buried in the Military Cemetery of the San Francisco Presidio. But a search of the records there showed no such burial. In 1966 Harada Mikio wrote in an article in the *Asahi* in Tokyo that the Captain was buried at the Cypress Lawn Cemetery in Colma just south of San Francisco. Following Harada's lead in 1978, Tanaka Keisuke confirmed that Janes was indeed cremated at the Cypress Lawn Cemetery and that there is a commemorative record of him there, but no grave or gravestone. On Tanaka's visit to Iris a few days later he was told that the family had taken the Captain's ashes to Wrights and had scattered them among the trees as Janes had requested in his will.

41. Miyagawa's visit is discussed in Takahashi Masashi, *Miyagawa Tsuneteru* (Tokyo, 1957), p. 324.

· BIBLIOGRAPHY ·

A NOTE ON ARCHIVAL SOURCES

As MANY of Janes' writings, and the materials surrounding his life and work in Japan, have not been published, an explanation of archival materials is in order. The major collection of materials on the Captain, including his manuscripts and remaining correspondence, can be found in the Janes Papers housed in the rare books and manuscript collection of Princeton University Library. The Janes Papers, consisting of fifteen manuscript boxes, have been catalogued by Professor Morimitsu Ushijima, and I have used the numbering of "The Catalog: Captain Janes's Materials," issued by Princeton University Library in 1978. For Janes' years at West Point and in the Army I have relied on the United States Military Academy Archives, and the National Archives in Washington, D.C. The latter included "Janes: Appointment, Commission, and Personal File" (RG94, Records of the AGO ACP File J 301 CB 1867—Leroy L. Janes) and "Janes: Retiring Board File" (Report of Retiring Board 281–R-AGO 1867). The U.S. Veterans Administration was consulted for the Captain's "Claims File" (Janes, Leroy L. XC 2 682 526). The *Janes vs. Janes* Divorce Proceedings Records are located in the Circuit Court, Howard County, Ellicott City, Maryland. For the Janes-Warner relationship I consulted the Warner Papers in the Constitution Island Association, West Point, New York. For the Captain's relations with the missionaries in Japan I have used the American Board of Commissioners for Foreign Missions (ABCFM), Mission to Japan, documents in the Houghton Library Archives, Harvard University, and portions of the Mission to Japan documents on microfilm at the Kirisuto Shakai Mondai Kenkyūkai at Dōshisha University, Kyoto, Japan. I have also relied on the [Dutch] Reformed Church in America Papers, Japan Mission, at the Gardner A. Sage Library, New Brunswick Theological Seminary. Various private letters and documents were consulted and have been acknowleged in the notes.

LIST OF WORKS CITED

Adachi, Kinnosuke. "Christian Missions in Japan," *Century Magazine* (September 1911).

Alcock, Sir Rutherford. *The Capital of the Tycoon: A Narrative of a Three Year's Residence in Japan.* London: Longman, Green, Longman Roberts, and Green, 1863.

Ambrose, Stephen E. *Duty, Honor, Country, A History of West Point.* Baltimore: John Hopkins Press, 1966.

Anesaki, Masaharu. *History of Japanese Religion.* London: Kegan Paul, Trench, Trubner, 1930.

Araki Seishi, ed. *Kumamoto no rekishi* [A History of Kumamoto]. vol. 5 *Kindai* [Modern]. Kummamoto: Kumamoto Nichi Nichi Shimbun Sha, 1962.

Asahara, Johei, comp. *Blessed Junko Takezaki*. Tokyo: Rokuroku-Kai, 1954.

Baker, Mabel. *Light in the Morning: Memories of Susan and Anna Warner*. West Point: Constitution Island Association, 1978.

Barr, Pat. *The Coming of the Barbarians: A Story of Western Settlements in Japan, 1853–1870*. London: Macmillan, 1967.

———. *The Deer Cry Pavilion: A Story of Westerners in Japan, 1868–1905*. London: Macmillan, 1968.

Bartholomew, James. "Japanese Culture and the Problem of Modern Science," in *Science and Values*, edited by Thackray Arnold and Everett Mendelsohn. New York: Humanities Press, 1974.

Bartlett, W.H.C. *Elements of Analytical Mechanics*. New York, 1858.

Beauchamp, Edward R. *An American Teacher in Early Meiji Japan*. Honolulu: University Press of Hawaii, 1976.

Beikoku Kabiten Zensu Shi [American Captain Janes]. *Seisan shoho* [Introduction to Agricultural Production], translated by Yamazaki Tamenori, Matsumura Genji, and Ichihara Morihiro. Tokyo: Yōgakkō, 1873.

Biographical Directory of the American Congress, 1774–1971. Washington, D.C.: G.P.O., 1971.

Black, John R. *Young Japan: Yokohama and Yedo 1858–79*. 2 vols. London: Oxford University Press, 1968.

Boxer, C. R. *The Christian Century in Japan 1549–1650*. Berkeley: University of California Press, 1967.

Bushnell, Horace. *Nature and the Supernatural, as Together Constituting one System of God*. New York: C. Scribner, 1858.

Cary, Otis. *A History of Christianity in Japan*. 2 vols. New York: Fleming H. Revell, 1909.

Chihōshi kenkyū kyōgikai, eds. *Nihon sangyō shi taikei* [An Outline of the History of Japanese Industry]. Vol. 8. *Kyūshū hen* [Kyushu Volume]. Tokyo: Tokyo Daigaku Shuppan Kai, 1970–71.

Combination Atlas Map of Tuscarawas County, Ohio. Philadelphia: L. H. Everts, 1875.

Cullum, George W. *Biographical Register of the Officers and Graduates of the United States Military Academy at West Point*. New York: D. Van Nostrand, 1868.

The Custer Story, the Life and Intimate Letters of General George A. Custer and His Wife Elizabeth. New York: Devin-Adair, 1950.

Daily Alta California (San Francisco).

Davis, Jerome D. *A Maker of New Japan, Rev. Joseph Hardy Neesima*. New York: Fleming H. Revell, 1894.

Davis, J. Merle. *Davis Soldier Missionary*. Chicago: Pilgrim Press, 1916.

DeForest, John H. *Sunrise in the Sunrise Kingdom*. New York: Young People's Missionary Movement, 1904.

Dejeans, Elizabeth (Frances Elizabeth Janes). *Nobody's Child*. Indianapolis: Bobb-Merrill, 1918.

Dening, Walter. *Japan in Days of Yore*. London: Griffith Farrau, n.d.

Dickens, Charles. *American Notes*. London: Chapman and Hall, 1842.

Dickins, F. V., and S. Lane-Poole. *The Life of Sir Harry Parkes*. 2 vols. London: Macmillan, 1894.

Dictionary of American Biography. New York: Charles Scribner's Sons, 1964.

Dilworth, David, and Thomas J. Rimer, eds. *Saiki Kōi and Other Stories, volume 2 of the Historical Literature of Mori Ōgai*. Honolulu: University Press of Hawaii, 1977.

Dōshisha Daigaku Jimbun Kagaku Kenkyū Sho, eds. *Kumamoto Bando kenkyū* [Research on the Kumamoto Band]. Tokyo: Misuzu Shobo, 1965.

———. *Nihon kindaika to kirisutō kyō* [Christianity and the Modernization of Japan]. Tokyo: Shinkyō Shuppan Sha, 1973.

Dōshisha hyakunen shi [The Centennial History of Dōshisha University]. 4 vols. Kyoto: Dōshisha Daigaku, 1979.

Dyer, Frederick H. *A Compendium of the War of the Rebellion*. Vol. 2. New York: Thomas Yoseloff, 1959.

Ebina Danjō. "Jiensu shi ni tsuite no shokan" [Correspondence Concerning Mr. Janes], *Kyūshū bungaku* [Kyushu Literature] 31, (January 1893).

———. *Kirisutokyō gairon (mikankō), waga shinkyō no yurai to keika* [An introduction to Christianity (unfinished), The origin and development of my religious faith]. Tokyo: Ebina Kazuo, 1937.

———. *Kumamoto yōgakkō to Kumamoto Bando* [The Kumamoto School for Western Learning and the Kumamoto band]. Pamphlet of a lecture delivered in Kumamoto at the Kaikosha, June 23, 1935.

Elison, George. *Deus Destroyed: The Image of Christianity in Early Modern Japan*. Cambridge: Harvard University Press, 1973.

Ellis, Franklin. *History of Fayette County Pennsylvania with Biographical Sketches*. Philadelphia: H. L. Everts, 1882.

"Eru eru Jiensu shi" [Mr. L. L. Janes]. *Kyūshū bungaku* [Kyūshū- Literature] 31, (January 1893).

Erikson, Erik H. *Childhood and Society*. New York: W. W. Norton, 1963.

The Far East (Yokohama).

Farley, Joseph Pearson. *West Point in the Early Sixties*. Troy, N.Y.: Pafraets Book Co., 1902.

Findlay, J. J. *Arnold of Rugby: His School Life and Contributions to Education*. Cambridge: Cambridge University Press, 1898.

Forman, Sidney. *West Point: A History of the United States Military Academy*. New York: Columbia University Press, 1950.

Fukuda Reiju (Yoshinobu). *Gojūnen kinen Kumamoto Bando tsuikai roku* [Reminiscences on the occasion of the fiftieth anniversary of the Kumamoto Band]. Pamphlet dated 1926.

Fukuda Reiju (Yoshinobu) and Mitsui Hisashi. *Kumamoto Bando o omou* [Remembering the Kumamoto Band]. Kyoto: Dōshisha Daigaku, 1965.

Fukunaga Bunnosuke, ed. *Nihon ni okeru taii Jiensu shi* [Captain Janes and his work in Japan]. Tokyo: Keiseisha Shoten, 1893.

General Catalogue of the Officers and Students of the University of Michigan, 1837–1901. Ann Arbor: University of Michigan, 1902.

The Genius of Liberty (Uniontown Pennsylvania).

Gordon, Rev. Joseph E. *The Free Presbyterian*. 1850–57.

Gordon, M. L. *An American Missionary in Japan*. Cambridge: Houghton Mifflin, 1892.

Griffis, William Elliot. *A Maker of the New Orient: Samuel Robbins Brown*. New York: Fleming H. Revell, 1902.

———. *Verbeck of Japan*. New York: Fleming H. Revell, 1900.

———. *The Mikado's Empire*. New York: Harper & Bros., 1876.

Guide to Tuscarawas County. New Philadelphia, Ohio: New Philadelphia Chamber of Commerce, 1939.

Gulick, Sidney L. *Evolution of the Japanese People*. New York: Fleming H. Revell, 1903.

Hall, Robert H. *Lists of Cadets Admitted into the United States Military Academy, West Point, N.Y., from its Establishment till September 30, 1876, With Tables Exhibiting the Results of the Examinations for Admission, and the Corps to which the Graduates Have been Promoted*. Washington, D.C.: G.P.O., 1876.

Harada Toshiaki, comp. *Kumamoto ken no rekishi* [History of Kumamoto prefecture]. Tokyo: Bungadō, 1957.

Harada Toshiaki, Tamamuro Taijō, Gotō Sezan, and Araki Seishi, compilers. *Kumamoto kenshi* [History of Kumamoto prefecture]. 8 vols. Kumamoto: Kumamoto Kenchō, 1961.

Harada Kazufumi. *Oyatoi gaikokujin* [Foreign employees of the Japanese government]. Vol. 13. *Kaitaku* [Colonization]. Tokyo: Kashima Shuppan, 1975.

Harootunian, H. D. *Toward Restoration: The Growth of Political Consciousness in Tokugawa Japan*. Berkeley: University of California Press, 1970.

Havens, Thomas R. H. *Farm and Nation in Modern Japan*. Princeton: Princeton University Press, 1974.

Hearn, Lafcadio. *Japan: An Attempt at Interpretation*. New York: Macmillan, 1904.

Heco, Joseph. *The Narrative of a Japanese*. Tokyo: American-Japanese Publishing Association, n.d.

The History of Tuscarawas County, Ohio. Chicago: Warner, Beers, 1884.

Hosokawa Ke Hensan Sho, eds. *Kaitei Higo han kokuji shiryō* [The revised compendium of Higo domain documents dealing with state affairs]. vol. 10. Tokyo: Kokusho Kankō Kai, 1974.

Howard Presbyterian Church. Minutes of the Annual Meetings, 1870–77. "Report of the Superintendent of the Sunday School." February 12, 1871.

Howard Quarterly (Howard Presbyterian Church, San Francisco). 1867–68.

Hunt, Frazier. *Custer, the Last of the Cavaliers*. New York: Cosmopolitan Book Co., 1928.

Hyakunen kinen Kumamoto Bando: Kindai Nihon o hiraita seishun gunzō [The hundredth anniversary of the Kumamoto Band: A group of young men who opened modern Japan]. Published for the 100 year anniversary exhibition for the Kumamoto Band held at the Tsuruya Department Store, Kumamoto, January 30 to February 3, 1976.

Iglehart, Charles W. *A Century of Protestant Christianity in Japan*. Tokyo: Charles E. Tuttle, 1959.

Imanaka Kanshi. "Higo jitsugakutō no shisō" [The Thought of the Higo Practical Learning Party]. In *Kumamoto Bando kenkyū* [Research on the Kumamoto Band]. Tokyo: Misuzu Shobo, 1965.

Janes: Appointment, Commissions, and Personal File (see Note on Archival Sources).

Janes, Capt. L. L. *Kumamoto: An Episode in Japan's Break from Feudalism*. Kyoto: Dōshisha University Shashi Shiryō Henshū Sho, 1970.

Janes, Frederic. *The Janes Family*. New York: John H. Dingman, 1868.

Janes Papers (see Note on Archival Sources).

Janes: Retiring Board File (see Note on Archival Sources).

Janes: Veterans Administration Claims File (see Note on Archival Sources).

Janes vs. Janes Divorce Proceedings Records (see Note on Archival Sources).

Jansen, Marius B. *Changing Japanese Attitudes Towards Modernization*. Princeton: Princeton University Press, 1965.

Japan Weekly Mail (Yokohama).

Jones, H. J. *Live Machines: Hired Foreigners and Meiji Japan*. Vancouver: University of British Columbia Press, 1980.

Kanamori, Paul. *Kanamori's Life-Story*. Philadelphia: Sunday School Times, 1921.

Kinmonth, Earl H. *The Self-Made Man in Meiji Thought: From Samurai to Salary Man*. Berkeley and Los Angeles: University of California Press, 1981.

Kinoshita Junji. *Fūrō* [Wind-whipped Waves]. Tokyo: Kadokawa Shoten, 1955.

Kitagawa, Joseph M. *Religion in Japanese History*. New York: Columbia University Press, 1966.

Kodama Kōta and Kitashima Masamoto, eds. *Monogatari han shi* [The narrated history of the domains]. Vol. 8. Tokyo: Jimbutsu Ōrai Sha, 1965.

Kosaka, Masaaki, ed. *Japanese Thought in the Meiji Era*, translated by David Abosh. Tokyo: Pan Pacific Press, 1958.

Kozaki, Hiromichi. "A Chapter in the History of Christianity in Japan: The Kumamoto Band in Retrospect." Tokyo, February 28 and March 7, 1913. Free English rendering by H. Pedley. Typescript in the ABCFM Documents, Houghton Library, Harvard University (see Note on Archival Sources).

————. *Reminiscences of Seventy Years*. Tokyo: Kyo Bun Kwan, 1933.

Kumamoto Joshidaigaku Kyōdōbunka Kenkyū Sho, eds. *Meiji no Kumamoto* [Kumamoto in the Meiji period]. Vol. 12 of *Kumamoto ken shiryō shūsei* [A collection of the historical records of Kumamoto prefecture]. Kumamoto: Nihon Dangi Sha, 1957.

Kumamoto Ken Kyōiku Kai, eds. *Kumamoto ken kyōiku shi* [A history of education in Kumamoto prefecture]. 3 vols. Kumamoto: Kumamoto Ken Kyōiku Kai, 1931.

Kumamoto Shi Kyōiku Iinkai, eds. *Kumamoto yōgakkō kyōshikan* [Guide to the Janes Mansion]. Pamphlet. Kumamoto: Kumamoto Shi Kyōiku Iinkai, 1979.

Kumamoto tenbō [Kumamoto Observer]. (Kumamoto)

Kunitz, Stanley J., and Howard Haycraft. *American Authors, 1600–1900*. New York: H. W. Wilson, 1955.

Kyūshū bungaku [Kyūshū Literature]. (Kumamoto)

Leed, Eric J. *No Man's Land: Combat and Identity in World War I*. Cambridge: Cambridge University Press, 1979.

The Life and Writings of the Rev. Joseph Gordon, Compiled by a Committee of the Free Presbyterian Synod. Cincinnati, Ohio: Published for the Free Presbyterian Synod, 1860.

Lockwood, William W. *The Economic Development of Japan*. Princeton: Princeton University Press, 1954.

Maclay, Arthur Collins. *A Budget of Letters from Japan*. New York: A. C. Armstrong and Son, 1889.

Makino Toraji. *Hari no ana kara* [Through the eye of a needle]. Kyoto: Makino Toraji Sensei Beiju Kinen Kai, 1958.

Merington, Marguerite, ed. *The Custer Story*. New York: Devin-Adair, 1950.

Maron, Hermann. *Japan und China*. Berlin: Otto Janke, 1863.

Maruyama Masao. *Nihon seiji shisōshi kenkyū*. Tokyo: Tokyo Daigaku Shuppan Kai, 1952. Translated by Mikiso Hane as *Studies in the Intellectual History of Tokugawa Japan*. Princeton: Princeton University Press, 1974.

Michie, Peter S. *The Life and Letters of Emory Upton*. New York: D. Appleton, 1885.

Mishima, Yukio. *Runaway Horses*. Tokyo: Charles E. Tuttle, 1973.

Missionary Herald.

Mitchner, C. H., ed. *Historic Events in the Tuscarawas and Muskingum Valleys*. Dayton: Thomas W. Odell, 1876.

Mitsui, Hisashi. "Doshisha and the Kumamoto Band." *The Japan Christian Quarterly*, 25, 2 (April 1959).

Mitsui Hisashi. *Kindai Nihon seinen gunzō: Kumamoto Bando monogatari* [A group of modern Japanese young men: The story of the Kumamoto Band], edited by Takenaka Masao. Tokyo: Nihon YMCA Dōmei Shuppanbu, 1980.

Miyajima Mikinosuke, ed. *Kitasato Shibasaburō den* [A biography of Kitasato Shibasaburō]. Tokyo: Iwanami Shoten, 1932.

Miyamoto, Musashi. *A Book of Five Rings*, translated by Victor Harris. Woodstock, N. Y.: Overlook Press, 1974.

Miyamoto Nakashi. *Sakuma Shōzan* [Biography of Sakuma Shōzan]. Tokyo: Iwanami Shoten, 1932.

Miyatake Tobone. *Meiji enzetsu shi* [A history of public speaking in the Meiji period]. Tokyo: Seikōkan Shuppan, 1929.

Miyauchi, Dixon Yoshihide. "Yokoi Shōnan: A Pre-Meiji Reformist." Ph.D. dissertation, Harvard University, 1957.

Moore, George E. "Samurai Conversion: The Case of Kumamoto." *Asian Studies* (University of the Philippines), 4, 1 (April 1966).

Monaghan, Jay. *Custer, the Life of General George Armstrong Custer*. Boston: Little, Brown, 1959.

Morris, Ivan. *The Nobility of Failure: Tragic Heroes in the History of Japan*. New York: Holt, Rinehart, and Winston, 1975.

Morita Seiichi. "Kumamoto han" [Kumamoto domain]. In *Monogatari han shi*, edited by Kodama Kōta and Kitashima Masamoto. Vol. 8. Tokyo: Jimbutsu Ōrai Sha, 1965.

Murray, Andrew E. *Presbyterians and the Negro—A History*. Philadelphia: Presbyterian Historical Society, 1966.

Nevins, Allan. *The War for the Union*. New York: Charles Scribner's Sons, 1959.

New York Times.

Nihon kindai shi jiten [A dictionary of modern Japanese history]. Tokyo: Tōyō Keizai Shimpō Sha, 1958.

Notehelfer, F. G. "Ebina Danjō: A Christian Samurai of the Meiji Period." *Papers on Japan*. Vol. 2. (Harvard University, East Asian Research Center), 1963.

―――. "Leroy Lansing Janes and the American Board." In *Nihon kindaika to kirisutō kyō* [Japanese modernization and Christianity], edited by Dōshisha Daigaku Jimbun Kagaku Kenkyū Sho—Kirisuto Shakai Mondai Kenkyū Kai. Tokyo: Shinkyō Shuppan Sha, 1973.

―――. "Leroy Lansing Janes: Out-of-Class Teacher and Agricultural Adviser in Kumamoto Japan, 1871–1876." In *Sekai shi no naka no Meiji isshin* [The Meiji Restoration in world history], edited by Sakata Yoshio and Yoshida Mitsukuni. Kyoto: Kyoto Daigaku Jimbun Kagaku Kenkyū Sho, 1973.

―――. "L. L. Janes in Japan: Carrier of American Culture and Christianity." *Journal of Presbyterian History* 53, 4 (Winter 1975).

Ōe Shinobu. *Meiji kokka no seiritsu* [The formation of the Meiji state]. Kyoto: Mineruba Shobo, 1959.

Ōhira Kimata. *Sakuma Shōzan* [Biography of Sakuma Shōzan]. Tokyo: Yoshikawa Kōbunkan, 1959.

Ōkubo Toshiaki. "Meiji shinseiken ka no kyūshū" [Kyūshū under the new Meiji administration]. In *Meiji isshin to Kyūshū* [The Meiji Restoration and Kyūshū], edited by Fukuoka UNESCO Kyōkai. Vol. 2 of *Kyūshū bunka ronshū* [Writings on Kyūshū culture]. Tokyo, 1973.

Ōshimo Aya. *Chichi Ebina Danjō* [My father, Ebina Danjō]. Tokyo: Shufu no Tomo Sha, 1975.

The Outlook.

Pierson, John D. *Tokutomi Sohō, 1863–1957: A Journalist for Modern Japan*. Princeton: Princeton University Press, 1980.

Records of the Office of the Adjutant General, Record Group 94 (see Note on Archival Sources).

Report of the Commission To Examine into the Organization, System of Discipline, and Course of Instruction of the United States Military Academy at West Point, 1860. Washington, D.C.: G.P.O., 1881.

Rhodes, James Ford. *History of the Civil War*. New York: Macmillan, 1917.

Sakurai Takeo. "Yokoi Tokiyoshi hakushi" [Dr. Yokoi Tokiyoshi]. *Kyōikū* 2, 7 (July 1934).

Sanderson, Dorothy Hurlbut. *They Wrote for a Living, A Bibliography of the Works of Susan Bogert Warner and Anna Bartlett Warner.* West Point: Constitution Island Association, 1976.

San Francisco Evening Bulletin.

Sansom, G. B. *The Western World and Japan.* New York: Alfred A. Knopf, 1962.

Schaff, Morris. *The Spirit of Old West Point, 1858–1862.* Boston and New York: Houghton Mifflin, 1908.

Scheiner, Irwin. *Christian Converts and Social Protest in Meiji Japan.* Berkeley: University of California Press, 1970.

Scudder, Henry Martyn. *A Discourse Delivered in the Howard Presbyterian Church, San Francisco, Thanksgiving Day, November 29, 1866.* San Francisco: Edward Bosqui, 1866.

Seeley, John Robert. *Ecce Homo: A Survey of the Life and Work of Jesus Christ.* Boston: Roberts Brothers, 1866.

Shigetsuma Tokutarō. *Oyatoi gaikokujin* [Foreign employees of the Japanese government]. Vol. 14. *chihō* [Local districts]. Tokyo: Kashima Shuppan Kai, 1976.

Shiryō ihō (Dōshisha Shashi Shiryō Henshū Sho).

Siebert, Wilbur H. "The Underground Railroad in Ohio." In the *Ohio Archeological and Historical Society Publications.* Vol. 4. Ohio, 1895.

Simmel, Ernst. *Kriegsneurosen und psychisches Trauma.* Munich, 1918.

Smiles, Samuel. *Self Help.* London: John Murray, 1873.

Smith, George, Bishop of Hong Kong. *Ten Weeks in Japan.* London: Longman Green, 1861.

Stanley, A. P. *The Life and Correspondence of Thomas Arnold D.D.* 2 vols. London: John Murray, 1844.

Stein, Charles Francis Jr. *Origin and History of Howard County, Maryland.* Baltimore: Howard County Historical Society, 1972.

Stokes, Olivia E. P. *Letters and Memories of Susan and Anna Bartlett Warner.* New York: G. P. Putnam's Sons, 1925.

Strong, Kenneth, trans. *Footprints in the Snow.* Tokyo: Charles E. Tuttle, 1971.

Sugii Mutsurō. "Eru Eru Zēnsu ni tsuite" [Concerning L. L. Janes]. In *Kobata Atsushi taikan kinen kokushi ronshū*, edited by Kobata Atsushi Kyōju Taikan Kinen Jigyōkai. Kyoto, 1970.

———. " 'Hōkyō shui-sho' seiritsu ni kansuru jakkan no kōsatsu" [A few observations regarding the emergence of the Hanaoka declaration]. *Kirisutokyō shakai mondai kenkyū* (Dōshisha Daigaku Jimbun Kagaku Kenkyū Sho) 16–17 (March 1970).

———."Kumamoto yōgakkō" [The Kumamoto School for Western Learning]. In *Kumamoto Bando kenkyū* [Research on the Kumamoto Band], edited by Dōshisha Daigaku Jimbun Kagaku Kenkyū Sho. Tokyo: Misuzu Shobo, 1965.

————. "Yamazaki Tamenori" [On Yamazaki Tamenori]. In *Kumamoto Bando kenkyū* [Research on the Kumamoto Band], edited by Dōshisha Daigaku Jimbun Kagaku Kenkyū Sho. Tokyo: Misuzu Shobo, 1965.

————. "Yokoi Saheida to Yokoi Daihei no Amerika ryūgaku" [Yokoi Saheida and Yokoi Daihei's studies in the United States]. *Shakai kagaku 11* (Dōshisha Daigaku Jimbun Kagaku Kenkyū Sho) 3, 4 (January 1970).

Sweet, William Warren. *Religion on the American Frontier*. Vol. 2. *The Presbyterians*. New York: Harper & Bros., 1936.

Takahashi Masashi. *Miyagawa Tsuneteru* [Biography of Miyagawa Tsuneteru]. Tokyo: Hiei Shobo, 1957.

Tanaka Keisuke, Ueda Jōichi, and Ushijima Morimitsu, eds. and trans. *Jiensu Kumamoto kaisō* [Janes' recollections of Kumamoto]. An edited translation of Capt. L. L. Janes, *Kumamoto: An Episode in Japan's Break from Feudalism*. Kumamoto: Kumamoto Nichi Nichi Shimbun Sha, 1978.

Tanaka Keisuke. "Uesto Pointo rikugun shikan gakkō no Kumamoto yōgakkō e no eikyō" [The influence of the United States Military Academy at West Point on the Kumamoto School for Western Learning]. *Eigaku shi kenkyū* (Nihon Eigaku Shi Gakkai) 12 (September 1979).

Tamamuro Taijō. *Yokoi Shōnan* [Biography of Yokoi Shōnan]. Tokyo: Yoshikawa Kōbunkan, 1966.

Tokutomi Iichirō. *Sohō jiden* [Autobiography of Tokutomi Sohō]. Tokyo: Chūō Kōron Sha, 1935.

Tokutomi Kenjirō (Roka). *Omoide no ki* [Memoirs]. Tokyo: Minyūsha, 1901. Translated as *Footprints in the Snow* by Kenneth Strong. Tokyo: Charles E. Tuttle, 1971.

————. *Takezaki Junko* [Takezaki Junko]. Vol. 15 of *Roka zenshū* [The collected works of Tokutomi Roka]. Tokyo: Shinchō Sha, 1929.

Tsunoda, Ryusaku, Wm. Theodore DeBary, and Donald Keene. *Sources of Japanese Tradition*. New York: Columbia University Press, 1958.

Ueda Jōichi. " 'Seisan shoho' to Higo jitsugaku tō" ["An Introduction to Agricultural Production" and the Higo Practical Learning Party]. *Kumamoto tenbō 5* (Winter 1976).

UNESCO Higashi Ajia Bunka Kenkyū Senta, eds. *Shiryō oyatoi gaikokujin* [Historical documents on foreign employees of the Japanese government]. Tokyo: Shōgakukan, 1975.

United States Military Academy. *Regulations of the U.S. Military Academy at West Point*. New York: J. & J. Harper, 1832.

————. *Register of the Officers and Cadets of the U.S. Military Academy*. West Point, N.Y.: 1857, 1858, 1859, 1860, 1861.

Warfield, J. D. *The Founders of Anne Arundel and Howard Counties, Maryland*. Baltimore: Regional Publishing Co., 1967.

Warner, Anna B. *Dollars and Cents*. 2 vols. New York: Putnam, 1852.

————. *Susan Warner ("Elizabeth Wetherell")*. New York: Putnam, 1909.

————. "Two Picnics." *Harpers* 47, 277 (June 1873).

Warner, Susan. *Daisy*. 2 vols. Philadelphia: Lippincott, 1878. Original edition published in 1868–69.

―――. *Daisy in the Field*. New York: Carter, 1869.

―――. *Daisy Plains*. New York: Carter, 1885.

―――. *Dianna*. New York: Putnam, 1877.

―――. *Melbourne House*. New York: Carter, 1864.

―――. *Queechy*. 2 vols. New York: Putnam, 1852.

―――. *The Wide Wide World*. New York: Putnam, 1851.

Watase Tsuneyoshi. *Ebina Danjō sensei* [The Reverend Ebina Danjō]. Tokyo: Ryūgin Sha, 1938.

Whittaker, Frederick. *A Complete Life of General George A. Custer*. New York: Sheldon, 1876.

Wicher, Edward Arthur. *The Presbyterian Church in California, 1849–1927*. New York: Frederick H. Hitchcock, Grafton Press, 1927.

Wildes, Harry Emerson. *Aliens in the East*. Philadelphia: University of Pennsylvania Press, 1937.

Williams, Harold A. *Foreigners in Mikadoland*. Rutland, Vt.: Charles E. Tuttle, 1963.

―――. *Shades of the Past Or Indiscreet Tales of Japan*. Rutland, Vt.: Charles E. Tuttle, 1960.

―――. *Tales of the Foreign Settlements in Japan*. Rutland, Vt.: Charles E. Tuttle, 1958.

Wilson, Lieutenant John E. "Outline Description of Military Posts in the Military Division of the Pacific." Typescript in Oregon Historical Society Library.

Yamada Tatsuo. "L. L. Janes *Seisan shoho* ni tsuite" [Concerning L. L. Janes' *Seisan shoho*]. *Kyūdai nōgaku geishi* 26, 1–4 (1972).

Yamaji Aizan. *Kirisutokyō hyōron* [A critical evaluation of Christianity]. Tokyo: Iwanami Shoten, 1966.

Yamazaki Masatada. *Yokoi Shōnan* [Biography of Yokoi Shōnan]. 2 vols. Tokyo: Nisshin Shoin, 1938.

―――. *Yokoi Shōnan ikō* [The posthumous works of Yokoi Shōnan]. Tokyo: Nisshin Shoin, 1942.

Yanaga, Chitoshi. *Japan Since Perry*. New York: McGraw-Hill, 1949.

Yoshikawa, Eiji. *Musashi: A Novel of The Samurai Era*. Translated from the Japanese by Charles S. Terry. New York: Harper & Row, 1981.

In this index, the name Leroy Lansing Janes is usually shortened to L. L. Janes.

Library of Congress Cataloging in Publication Data

Notehelfer, F. G.
   American samurai.

   Bibliography: p.
   Includes index.
   1. Janes, Leroy Lansing.   2. Christian biography—Japan.
   3. Kumamoto Band.   4. Christian biography—United States.
   5. Educators—Japan—Biography.
   I. Title.
   BR1317.J36N67   1985   266'.0092'4 [B]   84-42896
   ISBN 0-691-05443-6 (alk. paper)

F. G. Notehelfer is Professor of History at the University of
California—Los Angeles. He is the author of *Kōtoku Shūsui:
Portrait of a Japanese Radical* (Cambridge).